Praise for *Understanding Context*

"Engaging, never shying away from tackling and unraveling the complexity that lies behind the simplest turns of language, this book explains plainly and clearly why designers should pay attention to much-misused concepts such as sense and place, and simultaneously provides sound and elegant foundations for a new and embodied approach to the architectures of information spaces. A necessary read for both those who want to understand the interplay of language, place, information architecture, and design practice and for those who create products and services spanning the digital and the physical, where context is everything."

ANDREA RESMINI, PHD—AUTHOR, *PERVASIVE INFORMATION ARCHITECTURE*; SENIOR LECTURER IN INFORMATICS, JÖNKÖPING INTERNATIONAL BUSINESS SCHOOL

"For all those times when someone says something like, "this is not my beautiful life" when they're using your design, you've probably ignored their context. Andrew masterfully makes the case for meeting users where they are, and putting context in its proper place: at the center of making meaningful design."

DANA CHISNELL

"Andrew Hinton has created a rigorous and wide-ranging framework for thinking about how we perceive and interact with our linguistic and digital environments. This framework is based on cutting edge cognitive science, and the result is an invaluable guide and common language for all the different people who create and want to understand these relatively new human environments places."

ANDREW D. WILSON, PHD—SENIOR LECTURER IN PSYCHOLOGY, LEEDS BECKETT UNIVERSITY, LEEDS UK

"Understanding Context is a door to knowledge that will allow an entire generation of digital designers to more properly consider the context in which their work is used. This book is easy to read, but also full of important academic concepts more designers should be talking and thinking about in this messy cross-channel world. Hinton's writing is like attending a master's program in Gibsonian psychology while having the smartest kid in class sitting next to you explaining what the heck is going on in everyday language. I applaud O'Reilly in bringing this work to the world and Mr. Hinton for pouring his heart into writing it."

ABBY COVERT—AUTHOR, *HOW TO MAKE SENSE OF ANY MESS*

"Context is hard for humans. It's even harder for the machines that we oddly hope will guide us through the growing chaos and complexity of modern life. Andrew is a better guide; his book helps us perceive, make sense of, and engage with the contexts that surround us—from cities to kitchens to Minecraft."

LOUIS ROSENFELD—AUTHOR, *INFORMATION ARCHITECTURE FOR THE WORLD WIDE WEB*; FOUNDER OF ROSENFELD MEDIA

"Andrew Hinton's well-organized, useful, conversational approach makes this vast ontology of context not only accessible, but indeed like a long walk with J.J.Gibson himself. Come along for a day, come away better situated in a world remade (but not replaced) by technology, and get ready to give it better architecture."

MALCOLM MCCULLOUGH— PROFESSOR OF ARCHITECTURE, UNIVERSITY OF MICHIGAN; AUTHOR, *AMBIENT COMMONS* AND *DIGITAL GROUND*

"As computers become smaller they are becoming more ubiquitous. Computers and computing are not only in our mobile phones, but they are rapidly being embedded in everything. Cars, kitchens, street corners and shopping malls are becoming smart and connected. In this connected world, understanding context is more important than ever before. Andrew Hinton has written a thoughtful, well-researched and insightful book, full of key ideas to help you navigate the connected future. "

DAVE GRAY—AUTHOR, *THE CONNECTED COMPANY* AND *GAMESTORMING*; FOUND, XPLANE

Understanding Context

Environment, Language, and Information Architecture

Andrew Hinton

 Beijing · Cambridge · Farnham · Köln · Sebastopol · Tokyo

Understanding Context

by Andrew Hinton

Published by O'Reilly Media, Inc., 1005 Gravenstein Highway North, Sebastopol, CA 95472.

O'Reilly books may be purchased for educational, business, or sales promotional use. Online editions are also available for most titles (*http://safaribooksonline.com*). For more information, contact our corporate/institutional sales department: (800) 998-9938 or *corporate@oreilly.com*.

Editors: Mary Treseler and Simon St. Laurent	**Cover Designer:** Ellie Volkhausen
Production Editor: Melanie Yarbrough	**Interior Designers:** Ron Bilodeau and
Copyeditor: Octal Publishing Services	Monica Kamsvaag
Proofreader: Sharon Wilkey	**Illustrator:** Rebecca Demarest
Indexer: Bob Pfahler	**Compositor:** Melanie Yarbrough

December 2014: First Edition.

Revision History for the First Edition:

    2014-11-24   First release

See *http://oreilly.com/catalog/errata.csp?isbn=0636920024651* for release details.

978-1-449-32317-2

[LSI]

[Contents]

Foreword

IT'S IMPOSSIBLE TO UNDERSTAND context. There's always something we're missing. Not long ago, during a rim-to-rim hike of the Grand Canyon, I was thinking deep thoughts about two-billion-year-old rocks. They made me feel small. Although we're more stable than a tornado or a sandbar, we belong in the same category. We are delicate, imperfect patterns that come and go in the blink of an eye. Yet, we're also more ancient than rocks. We are made of stardust, indestructible matter as old as the universe.

That's when I heard the rattle.

Lost in thought, I nearly stepped on a snake. In unfamiliar territory, it's impossible to understand context, but it's still vital that we pay attention.

In the 1990s, I helped to grow a company called Argus. Over the course of seven years, we pioneered the practice of *information architecture* and bootstrapped our way from two to forty souls. Unfortunately, when the tech bubble burst at the end of the decade, we sunk the ship. We didn't see it coming. Later, while packing books into boxes, I suddenly realized what I'd lost. It wasn't just a company; Argus was a part of me. We'd built an organization of people, systems, and information that embodied and extended ourselves. That's the thing about context. It's impossible to see until it's gone.

A year after we closed Argus, I met Andrew Hinton. A group of us were gathered on the beautiful conference grounds of Asilomar to discuss how we might advance the practice of information architecture. At the time, our work was tied to websites, but Andrew told us to embrace "the structural design of information environments." So, we wrote those words into the bylaws of the *Information Architecture Institute* and into the new edition of the "polar bear book," and that became the definition of information architecture that's celebrated by thousands of people in dozens of countries each year on *World IA Day*. Our words and actions have unforeseeable consequences beyond our current context.

There's a new ship in town by the name of TUG. It's reframing information architecture. The Understanding Group was founded by Dan Klyn and Bob Royce, and I'm a strategic advisor. It's the perfect place for Andrew to be an information architect. He gets to tackle massive projects while surrounded by amazing people. And he's able to continue what he began in Asilomar: building out the "architecture school" of information architecture.

In articles and talks and in this book, Andrew is helping us all to realize that we're not designing software or websites. Because "language is infrastructure" and "the map is the territory," the things we build and inhabit are "places made of information." From the perspective of experience, these digital ecosystems are as real as the Grand Canyon. This unfamiliar territory can engage, inspire, or overwhelm. It's easy to become lost, and there are snakes. That's why this book is important. It's a map for mapmakers. It won't explain everything from here to there. That's impossible. Still, if you're brave enough to hike its crags and canyons, you will be better at making places and understanding contexts. This book is not a straightforward journey, nor is it short, but it's one I highly recommend.

—PETER MORVILLE

[*Preface*]

A PREFACE CAN BE MANY THINGS; this preface is *two* things. First, it gives a practical introduction to what this book is and what you can learn from it. Second, it tells a personal story about my reasons for writing the book and what I hope it will mean to you.

The Practical Bit

This book is about how information shapes and changes the way people experience context in the products and services we design and build. It's not only about how we design *for* a given context, but how design participates in *making* context. It begins with how people understand context in any environment. Then, it explores how language takes part in that understanding, and how information architecture helps to shape context, and to make it better. It's also an exploration, where "understanding" is more verb than noun; it's less about defining the right answers than discovering the right questions.

Context is an abstract idea, but it brings concrete challenges. What defines the "place" a customer is in, if he's shopping "online" and "in a store" at the same time? What determines the boundaries of a user's identity if her social network has multiple layers of privacy controls? How does a user know if something is a button and not just a label? What does it mean if you put something "in the cloud," but it's also "on your phone" and "in your laptop"? When we say we are "here" what does that actually mean now that we can be interacting and talking in many places at once? From accidentally hitting Reply All to an email, to discovering that Facebook shared embarrassing photos with your in-laws, we're facing the challenges of being immersed in contextually confusing environments.

Design needs handles we can grasp and manipulate to make context do what we intend: form understandable environments where users can meet their needs. To get there, we need to do some digging to understand what those handles are and what we're changing in the world when we use them. So, although the book does cover a lot of *theory*, there's nothing more *practical* than understanding the nature of our materials. If context is a material or medium that we can affect in user experiences, we should know what it's made of and how it works.

Who Should Read This Book?

If you design or make products or services that connect one part of our lives to another part, you will get value out of this book. In coming years, context is going to be an increasingly critical part of any design project. And yet, we don't have a mutual understanding of what context is, or what happens to context when we design something one way versus another. We talk a lot about "information" and "experiences" and "environments" and even "context," but they're amorphous, fuzzy concepts. We've reached a point in design practice at which we can't rely on such foggy notions anymore. This book provides a way to understand and work with context, using information as a medium for making.

That said, I did write this book with an assumption that you have some experience as a designer and are interested in exploring these strange, complex questions that underlie the surface of our work. If you're a beginner, you can get a lot out of it, but you won't get "the basics"— even though the concepts here are, in some ways, more foundational than what we usually think of as "basic" theory and practice.

So This Book Teaches Methods for Designing Context?

Not really. This is definitely an "understanding how it works" book more than a "how to make stuff" book. It touches on methods and materials and has a lot of concrete examples. But really it's meant to inform the methods we already use and to suggest some new ways of looking at them or doing them.

I also hope the book helps reframe some important aspects of what and how we design. For myself, the process of researching and writing this book has fundamentally rewired the way I see the world, especially when I plan and design environments for my clients. I've found this new perspective to be immensely valuable in my own work.

Why Information Architecture?

Although "information architecture" is in the title, this book isn't only for self-described "information architects." The structures we make and depend on for all sorts of design work involve information architecture. Architecture is the starting place for figuring out foundations, boundaries, and connections. Still, the book discusses areas of focus for other disciplines in some detail throughout, especially in the first half. If you're an interaction designer, content strategist, usability engineer, researcher or other such profession, you will find plenty here that relates directly to your main work. And in the second half, hopefully it becomes clearer how intermingled and interdependent these practices are with one another and with information architecture.

Additionally, the reason why I became interested in context to begin with was information architecture, which is also my "home" community of practice. As a community (and as a relatively young, forming discipline) we have a complicated history of figuring out what information architecture is, what it actually does in the world, and what all that means. Although context is a much bigger topic than information architecture, and information architecture is about more than context, I decided the concerns of information architecture were where I'd spend most of my time in this exploration.

What Will You Learn from This Book?

Here is a sampling of the sorts of things you should take away from reading this book:

- How people experience and comprehend context
- Principles for designing environments in which context is more understandable and trustworthy
- How *affordance* works, and how it informs everything users perceive and do

- What *placemaking* and *sensemaking* mean, and how digital information can both enhance and disrupt how they work

- How language, in all its forms, works as an important "raw material" for context design

- Also how language has *semantic function* similar to the way that physical things have affordance, and what that means for digital interfaces and other environments

- Models for understanding the personal context users bring to the environments we design—their situations, motivations, and narratives

These are just some highlights. Overall, the main take-away from this book will be a fresh perspective on what it means to design in a time when digital technology is saturating everything around us.

A Tour Through the Book's Six Parts

The book is made up of 6 parts, each a sort of small book in itself. The parts build on each other through 22 continuously numbered chapters.

Part I   The Context Problem: What It Is and How To Think About It
This first part explains what the book means by "context" and introduces some core ideas about context that will be explored throughout. Using an everyday travel scenario and a bit of historical background, it explains what the challenges are and how they came to be. It also sets up the three-part model we work with through the rest of the book.

Part II   Physical Information: The Roots of Context
This part provides a foundation for how users comprehend environments. It explains the theory of affordance, the essential dynamics of perception and embodied cognition, and a framework for describing the structural elements of environments, including the Principle of Nesting, and how Surfaces, Objects, and Events combine to make Places. Although this part is mainly about nontechnological topics, it includes examples to show how these concepts are relevant to designed products and services.

Part III   Semantic Information: Language as Environment

In this part, we investigate how language (speech, gestures, text, and pictures) works as an additional environmental layer of "semantic function," and how that affects context. This part touches on essential concepts about signs and symbols and how we use forms of semantic information for simulating physical environments in user interfaces. It also discusses placemaking and sensemaking and how language structures our contextual experience.

Part IV   Digital Information: The Pervasive Influence of Code

Part IV shows how digital information is, at its core, meaningful to computers more than humans. It also shows how that dynamic influences how we experience physical and semantic information. This part demonstrates how digital information makes it possible to create environments and places that don't behave like the physical world, and how that can be both good and bad.

Part V   The Maps We Live In: Information Architectures for Places and People

This part brings the ideas from the previous four parts together to show how information works as systems of meaning. The chapters within it explore examples from different kinds of placemaking, using "maps" as a framing device for how we change our territories, or make new ones. It explains how these environments affect our social relationships, conversations, and identities. This part focuses more on the architectural concerns of how *place* works and less on the object-level concerns of a particular interaction.

Part VI   Composing Context: Making Room for Making Meaning

The last part introduces *composition* as a useful way of looking at how we use information to shape context, including how the composed environment requires a stable ground to build and act upon. Part VI describes how we use materials of semantic function in the form of Labels, Relationships, and Rules—aligned with ontology, taxonomy, and "choreography." It explores how people construct their experience through narrative and story, and how they participate in creating those narratives. And finally, Part VI looks at some principles for accommodating meaning-making, and some techniques for understanding context and modeling new environments.

The Personal Bit

When I began this writing project, my aim was to make a slender, deft volume of focused essays. A "thoughts about context, for design" kind of book. Three years later, I'm putting the final touches on a tome collecting, in essence, six little books, trying to solve the mysteries of the universe.

Funny how things like this work out.

* * *

Here's what got me started:

For a long time—since before I worked with technology for a living—I've wondered about how it is that language makes experience. How is it that a novel can captivate us and make us feel as if we've lived through those events? How does a table-top game construct a shared place in which events occur that we might remember and talk about years later, even though nothing "real" happened? Why is it that a poet can break a line—in just such a way that it breaks the reader's heart?

When I eventually found myself in a software-related profession, my obsession only grew. When logging in to a system to move files around, what is it I'm affecting with commands such as "get" or "put." It's just bits, being rearranged on the same disc, but somehow those words make it relevant to my body. When exploring early social architectures such as UseNet, Internet Relay Chat, or later, LiveJournal, I noticed how deeply I sometimes felt about my conversations there, and how these places were meaningful *as places.* How is that possible? They're just virtual marks on virtual surfaces, which aren't even as real as the printed type in a paper book.

Soon, I found a community where many people were wondering similar things. They were talking to one another under a loosely shared label: *information architecture.* Something about that phrase clicked for me—yes, I thought, that's what's going on: information that somehow feels as if we live in it; structures, rooms, passageways. Not virtual reality, exactly. It's information that shares some of the qualities of space, whose places become as meaningful for us as any other places in our lives.

As someone who now identifies as an "information architect," I kept working at these questions, until it occurred to me that so much of what I was doing for a living was repairing problems with *context*. Software is doing something to the world that is detaching and rupturing context from whatever helped it make sense before we had computers, networks, and hyperlinks. Eventually, with encouragement, and after many conference talks and articles, I decided to write a book about that.

* * *

When you start writing a book about something, suddenly ideas that you thought you had all figured out seem flimsy and unformed. After finishing what I thought was the first third of the book, I grew worried—what if none of what I think about this is true? So, I did some further research to validate my hunches.

I discovered my hunches were sometimes on track, and often really wrong, and that this thing we call context is actually not well understood. Among academics, there is rigorous work being done, but it isn't exactly settled science. Yet, even the best of that work wasn't making it into the general conversation of design practitioners and in the popular "UX" literature.

I realized that if I were to take this book seriously, I couldn't just think aloud on the page about what the answers *might* be. So, six months into my work, I had to set aside the chapters I'd already drafted and take the time to really learn the subject as best I could, while writing about what I was discovering. A couple years and quite a few pages later, here I am revising the preface for publication.

Here's the thing: I'm not finished. The more I learned, the more I saw there would be to discover. Hence, as I mentioned at the beginning, "understanding" is something I hope we can do together, both in this book and beyond it. To that end, I invite you to visit this book's home site (*www.contextbook.com*), where additional content and links will accumulate, including a bibliography.

My wish for these ideas isn't that they be absolutely right (though some of that is nice), but that they help move along the work we do together toward making better places, good and human places, for the people who dwell in them.

So, now, let's dig in.

Acknowledgments

I WANT MOST OF ALL TO THANK MY WIFE, Erin, who has been a patient supporter through the long, often angst-ridden process of writing this book. She not only went without a husband for many weekends, evenings, and so-called vacation days; she then weathered my verbose ruminations and bouts of self-doubt when I was in her presence. She doesn't believe it, but it's true that I could not have done this without her.

Thanks also to Madeline, my daughter, who has also endured my authorial tribulations, and who has been such an inspiration to me as I've watched her grow up, tackle huge challenges, and already become so much more than I could've imagined.

Thanks to Peter Morville, who told me a long time ago, regarding a completely different subject, "you should write a book," and who then helped me find a path to get it done, with wise counsel along the way. Also thanks to Lou Rosenfeld, who has also given me such generous encouragement and advice over the years. And thanks to Christina Wodtke, especially for that email invitation circa 2001, and all the invaluable conversations since.

A special thanks to Dan Klyn and Bob Royce, who both have enriched and influenced my perspective on this book's subject, and who invited me along on their joint mission to bring "making things be good" to the world—something they called The Understanding Group. I can't imagine any other vocational home giving me the room to work out these ideas and be the self I needed to be while writing this book.

There are many other wonderful people who have contributed their energy and care in ways large and small toward making this book happen; some have been sources of conversations and knowledge that have become part of the book's fabric, and some have even taken time out of their lives to review drafts and help make the book better. I can't possibly list them all, but I should especially mention, Jorge Arango, Andrea Resmini, Abby Covert, Marsha Haverty, Andrew Wilson, Sabrina Golonka, Karl Fast, Dave Gray, Christian Crumlish, Richard Dalton, Lis Hubert, Malcolm McCullough, and Don Norman.

Thanks also to a mentor from what seems like a previous life, poet and teacher Jeffrey Skinner, for telling me I'm a writer and showing me what it means to be one. When I catch myself just talking about something I could make or do, I hear his rightfully impatient voice from decades ago, saying, "Stop talking about it and just do it!" He also taught me it's better to be done than perfect, advice without which I would still be researching, writing, and revising this tome.

Thanks to my publisher, meaning everyone there who played a part in making this book a reality. When I started working with O'Reilly, I wasn't sure how it would turn out. I knew I wasn't writing something that fit a standard "technology book" mold, but I also knew that O'Reilly was one of the first publishers that really mattered to me—starting with the copy of *The Whole Internet User's Guide and Catalog* I found in 1992—and that O'Reilly's deeply humanist vision would make a good home for my wandering, philosophical ideas about information technology. Sure enough, I found everyone involved to be thoughtful and welcoming, patient with my journey but responsible in prodding me along. So, in particular to Mary Treseler, Simon St. Laurent, Amy Jollymore, and Meghan Blanchette, I want to thank you all for your belief in this project, your encouragement when I struggled, and your kind guidance through the entire process.

Finally, to my mother, Mary; my dad, George; and (in memoriam) my stepfather, Paul: thank you for getting me to adulthood, showing me what was possible if I took the time to do something right, and teaching me that—with hard work—I could accomplish what I set out to do.

Part I

The Context Problem

What It Is and How to Think About It

PEOPLE HAVE BEEN TRYING TO FIGURE OUT HOW WE UNDERSTAND THE WORLD FOR A VERY LONG TIME; and from all evidence, there are no certain answers for many of the most important questions. So, it would seem that writing a book about "context" would be a fool's errand. Why try to tackle it to begin with? What do we mean by it when we say it? And after going to all this trouble, what real-world problems will it help us to solve?

FIGURE I-1
A seventeenth-century illustration by Robert Fludd, illustrating his somewhat occult, prescientific ideas on metaphysics, bodily senses, thought, and inspiration*

---

* Utriusque cosmi maioris scilicet et minoris [...] historia, tomus II (1619), tractatus I, sectio I, liber X, De triplici animae in corpore vision (from Wikimedia Commons)

Part I helps to answer these questions. It introduces the basic challenges of a growing "context problem" to establish reasons why we should bother with understanding context at all. It also presents common scenarios to help illustrate those challenges. Finally, it introduces a working definition of context, and some models we will use to explore how information works to create and shape context in the chapters to come.

[1]

Everything, Yet Something

All and everything is naturally related and interconnected.
    —ADA LOVELACE

Birds in Trees, Words in Books

IT WOULD BE GREAT to say there's a simple secret that lets us figure out
a subject such as context quickly and easily. But let's not kid ourselves;
context is a big, hairy, weird topic. By nature, it's about everything. And
if something is about everything, how can we even begin to understand it? When we think we've caught it and we try to crack it open to
see what's inside, all we seem to get is more context. It's the stuff of
late-night dorm conversations among philosophy students, or tedious
debates among philosophers and physicists. Context shifts and dances,
it slips and slides. It insists on its mystery, yet it demands we come to
terms with it every single day.

Still, in some ways, context actually isn't so mysterious, because from
one moment to the next we seem to know it when we see it. Whenever
we're trying to figure out *what one thing means in relation to something
else*, we say we're trying to understand its context.

It can be a bird in a tree, or a stone in a stream. It can be a single
word in a sentence. It can also be that sentence in a paragraph, that
paragraph in a book, and that book's context in a library or on a bedside table—all of which can influence how we interpret the single word
where we started.

It can be the context of a text message I receive on my phone, where a
":-)" emoticon can make the difference between an insult and a friendly
jest. It can be a *channel* as in "cross-channel" design, like mobile, desktop, telephone, or broadcast. Or, it can be all those channels, but from
the separate perspectives of a child and a senior citizen, or a user on
a bus versus a customer in a store. It can be also the context of one's

own identity, and how one behaves around family versus the workplace. The more closely we look, the more we see how many parts of our lives depend upon context for meaning anything at all.

Whatever context is in any given situation, though, one aspect remains consistent: we need context to *be clear* and to *make sense*. We know that when context is not clear or it doesn't make sense, it means we don't understand something. And misunderstandings are almost always *not good*.

How do we get beyond this general sense of "good" or "clear" or "understandable"? What makes anything more clear or not clear? These are philosophical questions with practical implications. So let's begin with a practical scenario involving an airport, a calendar, and getting from one place to another.

Scenario: Andrew Goes to the Airport

On the morning before a cross-country business flight, I was already getting packed. I knew a seven-day trip would mean extra effort compressing everything into my small carry-on bag, and an early departure meant no time to pack on the day of the trip. While rolling my shirts into tight bars of cloth to prevent wrinkles—wrinkles I knew would manifest anyway regardless of my efforts—my iPhone started trilling and buzzing. Two apps on my phone—one from Delta Airlines and the other from the TripIt travel service—were each reminding me I could check in and get my digital boarding pass.

I opened the Delta app and tapped my way through the check-in process. After a few steps, it offered me an "Economy Comfort" seat for just a few dollars more. Because I don't especially like folding myself into my laptop like human origami, I agreed to pay for the perk. I half wondered if now being "Economy Comfort" would give me any other privileges, but I was busy, so I decided to find out when I got to the airport.

To economize a bit and get a better fare, I'd decided to depart from an airport a bit further from home. On the day of the flight, when I arrived inside the terminal, I realized I wasn't used to this airport and found myself having to learn a new layout. I scanned the environment in front of me, thinking through the options. I didn't need to print a boarding pass, and I didn't need to check my luggage bin–sized bag, so I looked for the right queue for going through the TSA security check.

Similar to my usual airport, this one had queue lanes organized by various categories. I was so used to going to a particular lane at my home airport that I hadn't thought about how they were labeled in a long time.

One was for fast-track-security TSA Pre-Check passengers, which I was pretty sure I wasn't (though I also wasn't sure how I would know). One was for "SkyPriority" flyers, and that one made me wonder: I was a "Medallion" member of Delta's SkyMiles program, but I only had a "Silver" Medallion. I was also a holder of Delta's branded American Express Gold card, which provides some of the benefits of Medallion status, but not others. (Even though the card is "Gold," it has nothing to do with the "Gold Medallion" level in Delta's loyalty hierarchy.) In my hurried state, I couldn't remember if Silver Medallion qualified me as "SkyPriority" or if my Gold Card did, or if Economy Comfort got me in, or if none of these conditions applied.

I approached a Delta service representative and asked where I should go. She said, "Let me see your boarding pass; it will say if you're SkyPriority." I got out my iPhone and opened the Delta app to show her. But no dice—I couldn't get it to open the boarding pass. The app was having to recheck the network to update the boarding information, and couldn't reach the cloud for some reason, even though the phone's WiFi indicator had full bars. What was happening? Then, the phone popped up a screen about paying for airport WiFi access. Ah, so my phone was naively assuming it had Internet access because it was connecting to WiFi, but the Internet was not available without payment. How annoying.

I had no time to fuss with that in the moment. So, I fumbled until I turned WiFi off, allowing me to use my carrier's data network instead. But that didn't help either—I couldn't get a signal inside the building. I had to apologize and walk back outside for a cell connection to get my digital boarding pass to update.

I then saw a button on the boarding pass inviting me to "Add to Passbook." I had heard of Apple's Passbook app but just hadn't used it yet. Thinking maybe this would help me avoid the forced-data-refresh issue, I added the Delta pass to the Passbook app. I also noticed there was no mention of SkyPriority or any other special security line status, so I reentered the terminal and used the slower queue, with all the other standard travelers.

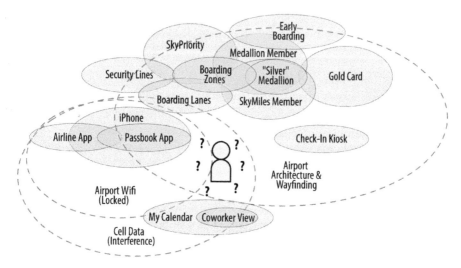

FIGURE 1-1

Some of the many contextual structures to keep track of, just to get to my plane on time

While waiting in line, I noticed that every time I tapped my phone's Home button to bring up the unlock screen, there was a notification about my flight. I hadn't seen this sort of alert before. I tried swiping it to either dismiss it or open the app that was generating it, but that only brought up a strange-looking version of my boarding pass. It was odd behavior because normally I can't interact with apps when the phone is in locked mode, other than a few things such as audio controls. I wondered if the notification engine on the phone was on the fritz, so I rebooted the phone—no change. By then it was time to go through security anyway, so I just showed my boarding pass and ID and then finished the tedium of the security screening.

After finishing the security ritual and getting my belt and shoes back onto my body, I received a text message from my employer's operations manager, asking about my travel schedule. I answered back that my itinerary should be on my calendar. I could see it on my iOS Calendar app; why couldn't he? I finally just told him the details and said I'd try to figure out the calendar problem later.

TripIt had just alerted me via text message which gate I should use for my flight, so I kept glancing at the message to remind myself where I should go in the airport. Eventually, I made it to the correct gate, following signs and pointers along the airport passageways.

At the gate, I heard the airline associate announce who could board and when, over the public address system. I waited until I heard the category I saw listed on my boarding pass—Zone 1—and boarded when it was called. Then, I had one more label to follow, my seat number. On this flight, I was known as the passenger in 24 C. I finally plopped into it, pondering all the confusing things I'd just encountered.

Breaking It Down

In scenarios like this, we find ourselves in a tangle of digital, semantic, and physical structures. We are *agents* trying to take *action* in our *environments*, and we have to *understand* those environments well enough to take the appropriate actions. For myself, even though I'm a frequent traveler, I was still running into issues that caused me to have to stop, think, and figure out my environment. When I'd try to act out of habit, it would either work or it wouldn't, depending on how the environment accommodated my action. Each element of the environment made a demand on my ability to understand what I was doing. These moving parts were all in play at a wide variety of environmental levels, from the broad level of a mobile phone network, to the level of a little virtual switch deep in the settings of my phone. Some required almost no effort, but many required a lot, to the point that I was reduced to talking to myself to figure them out.

For example, we don't normally have to wonder about *what* we are. But there were many labels for me in these overlapping systems that made me have to think hard about *what I was to the environment I was in* and what that meant about the actions I could take.

The categories for security and boarding and even my assigned seat presented many overlapping facets that defined what I was to the airport. In each instance, I had to determine the rules represented by the labels involved. Was I a Gold Card traveler? A Silver Medallion traveler? An Economy Comfort traveler? What Zone, what seat? Some labels still made no sense to me.

For example, what did any of these have to do with "SkyPriority"? After I was seated on the plane, waiting for others to board, I checked Delta's site on my phone. I discovered this answer among their Frequently Asked Questions: "SkyTeam Elite Plus members and customers with First and Business Class tickets are eligible for SkyPriority." This sounded nonsensical to me, because I had no idea what SkyTeam Elite Plus meant, or how a passenger who is already "Elite" might possibly benefit from an appendage of "Plus."

Then there was my phone. I tried dismissing that pesky flight notification from the phone's lock screen, but it wouldn't leave. It was only after I'd had a moment to breathe that I realized it was a feature, not a bug. Passbook was taking an action without my prior approval or awareness, trying to do me a favor by making it possible for me to open my boarding pass without having to unlock my phone. (I've since found this to be a useful feature!) But it was hard for me to learn as such, because the app took agency that broke the structural expectations that I'd learned to date by using iOS, and the alert gave no indication it was coming from Passbook.

Regarding my calendar, it occurred to me that I could see the TripIt itinerary information in my own calendar view because I had subscribed to it, but that subscription must be visible only to me, not those with whom I shared the calendar. I was thinking of "calendar" as the whole thing I was seeing, but in fact it contained a number of calendars, some of which were subscribed to rather than part of the specific calendar I had opened to coworkers. The meaning of "calendar" was disjointed, and the relationships between the various meanings resulted in confusion.

I also mused at the level to which airline travel is now depending on people to use networked devices, even though most airports have complicated network access. Think of the thousands of people who have the same problem with refreshing their boarding passes, not to mention getting gate updates and other information they've come to depend upon. (To Delta's credit, the app avoids this problem in its most recent updates.)

All of these complications were largely problems with context. I struggled to accurately perceive the *meaningful relationships between elements* in my environment. These problems caused extra work and stress for an activity that used to be much more straightforward. Yet, they all happened in an environment that people designed and built. Each encounter was part of a human-made place, composed of physical surfaces, language structures, and digital bits, woven together into a complex system—a system that should be much less confusing and ambiguous than it turned out to be.

Now, imagine this same journey only a few years from now, when sensors in the terminal will be able to pair with my smartphone, pumping updates to its screen, chatting with me about where I should go through a wearable device, buzzing about which vendors close by serve my favorite foods, and who in my social network might be coming through the same terminal. How will that ecosystem know how to be truly relevant? Will it be overburdened with the noise of advertisements or "pay for more" services? Will it even have the rules figured out any better than I do about what queue I should use or if I can check my luggage for free? Whom will it be alerting to actions that I assume are private, or at least confined to the walls of the airport? How many more "calendars" will be overlapping and intermingling with mine by then?

Humans are much better at sorting out the vagaries of cultural meaning than machines. Yet, if we trip over these contextual conundrums so frequently, how are digital systems going to understand them any better? Moreover, how are we to keep absorbing so much contextual ambiguity and complexity from the multiplying layers of information we're expected to comprehend just to finish basic tasks?

[2]

A Growing Challenge

Where is it, this present? It has melted in our grasp, fled ere we could touch it, gone in the instant of becoming.
—WILLIAM JAMES

Early Disruptions

THE AIRPORT SCENARIO PRESENTED IN CHAPTER 1 IS JUST A MUNDANE EXAMPLE OF A BIGGER ISSUE: context is a lot more complicated than it used to be, and it is only going to become more disrupted and detached from the physical clues we've relied on until now. For most of human existence, the context of people, places, and objects has been pretty straightforward. If you're in a field surrounded by trees, that's where you are. The field won't magically transform into a bustling village square in the blink of an eye. If you pick up a tool, a hammer perhaps, it does what its form suggests it will do. Physical laws dictate that the concrete world behaves in certain ways that we evolved to comprehend, usually with little or no explicit thought. So bodies and brains developed to prefer environments in which we don't have to think so hard about what we're doing.

But contemporary life is more complex. Now, we're surrounded by stuff that requires conscious thought for us to get what we need from it. For a long time, technology has been chipping away at the immediate clarity of context. The invention of writing meant that something said (written) in one place could be read—and therefore, "said" all over again—anywhere the document might go, separate from its original utterance. Writing thus set the stage for later technologies to disrupt the connection even further. The nineteenth and twentieth centuries transformed the way we communicate by "radically separating the contexts of message transmission and reception."* With the telegraph, tapping an apparatus in one place could send messages across continents and oceans. And, we still hear of celebrities and politicians being caught saying embarrassing things when they don't realize their clip-on microphones are still live.

In a sense, this is just the extension of all mechanical technology, which introduced contraptions that separate a specific action from its effect. Turning a crank can lift heavy objects via pulleys. Pulling a lever can cause a railroad track to change the course of massive locomotives. Eventually these interactions became so numerous and complicated that they required new fields of study and specialized training. Hidden complexities enter our environment, and the further the specific physical act is from its effect, the more the *context* of cause-and-effect requires explaining and learning.

Most of these changes happened slowly enough that we could keep up with them. Complex machines were mainly run by specialists, and major new communications devices emerged at a slow rate of only a few every generation. It helped that much of it was tied to geography, with all of the physical and cultural context that implies. However, digital networks quickly detached us even from physical location. As William J. Mitchell explains in *City of Bits: Space, Place, and the Infobahn* (MIT Press):

> Unlike telephone calls or fax transmissions, which [used to] link specific machines at identifiable locations (the telephone on your desk and the telephone on my desk, say), an exchange of electronic mail (e-mail) links people at indeterminate locations....You will not know whether I transmitted it from my office or typed it in at home while sipping a glass of wine or entered it into my laptop on a trans-Pacific flight and then sent it from a public telephone at Narita airport.†

The *.edu* domain of a university might imply that the addressee has some connection to that school's campus, but even early dial-up access broke that connection because it allowed access from anywhere there

---

* Mitchell, William J. *Placing Words: Symbols, Space, and the City*. Cambridge, MA: MIT Press, 2005: 13, Kindle edition.

† ———. *City of Bits: Space, Place, and the Infobahn (On Architecture)*. Cambridge, MA: MIT Press, 1995: 68–9, Kindle locations.

was a phone line. The "where" of an email address is just the text in the address itself, a string of characters with only the barest literal connection to the sort of physical "place" in which we evolved. Of course, nowadays, we appropriate domain extensions such as *.tv*—created for the country of Tuvalu—as meaning "television," instead. Geography and "place" have drifted into a strange, turbulent relationship. Back when we were online only part of the time (when dialing through a modem or sitting at a desk), that relationship seemed manageable. But now that we're personally connected to a global network 24 hours per day, we find ourselves both walking on the ground and living in a cloud, all the time, all at once.

The Role of the Web

A big reason why digital networks became so ubiquitous was the advent of the World Wide Web. The Web became the petri dish in which the culture of "being digital" explosively grew. The Web meant that we didn't have to worry about what server we were on or to which directories we had access. It meant that we could just make links and think about structure later.

The principle driving the original development of the Web was to add a protocol (HTTP) to the Internet that facilitated open sharing. In the phrasing of its creators—in the Web's founding document—its purpose was "to link and access information of various kinds as a web of nodes *in which the user can browse at will.*"* When you give people the capability to create environments with more ease and flexibility than before, they will use it, even beyond its intended boundaries.

The Web has now become something that has far outstripped what we see in dedicated "web browsers" alone. The characteristics of hyperlinks that once were only about linking one metaphorical "page" to another are now fueling all manner of APIs for easy, fluid syndication and mashing-up of information from many different sources. The spirit of the hyperlink means everything can be connected out of context to everything else. We can link enterprise resource management platforms with loading docks, map software with automobiles, and radio frequency ID (RFID) chips injected into pet dogs that include the

---

* *http://www.w3.org/Proposal.html* (emphasis mine)

dog's records in licensing databases. Even our sneakers can broadcast on a global network how far we run, for anyone to see. The Web is now more a property of human civilization than a platform. It is infrastructure that we treat as if it were nature, like "shipping" or "irrigation." HTTP could be retired as a network layer tomorrow, but from now on, people will always demand the ability to link to anything they please.

Additionally, these technologies have allowed us to create a sort of space that's made of bits, not atoms. This space is full of places that aren't just supplementary or analog versions of physical environments; they are a new species of place that we visit through the glowing screens of our devices. Writing about one of those places—YouTube—cultural anthropologist Michael Wesch describes how users sitting in front of a webcam struggle to fully comprehend the context of what they're doing when communicating on "the most public space in the world, entered from the privacy of our own homes":

> The problem is not lack of context. It is context collapse: an infinite number of contexts collapsing upon one another into that single moment of recording. The images, actions, and words captured by the lens at any moment can be transported to anywhere on the planet and preserved (the performer must assume) for all time. The little glass lens becomes the gateway to a black hole sucking all of time and space—virtually all possible contexts—in upon itself.*

The disorienting lack of pre-Web context one faces on YouTube is not confined to videos. We're spending more and more of our lives inhabiting these places, whether it's Facebook or a corporate intranet. If we measure reality by where meaningful human activity takes place, these places are not merely "virtual" anymore. They are now part of our public infrastructure.

The contextual untethering the Web brought to computer networks is now leaking out into our physical surroundings. Structures we assume have stable meanings from day to day are shot through with invisible connections and actions that change those meanings in ways we often don't understand. We live among active digital objects that adjust our

---

* *http://mediatedcultures.net/projects/youtube/context-collapse/*

room temperature, run our economies, decide on our financial fitness, route our trains and car traffic, and advise us where we should eat and sleep.

As Rob Kitchin and Martin Dodge explain in *Code/Space: Software and Everyday Life* (MIT Press), "Software is being embedded in material objects, imbuing them with an awareness of their environment, and the calculative capacities to conduct their own work in the world with only intermittent human oversight."* These digital agents introduce rules of cause-and-effect into our environment that happen beyond our immediate perception, like a lever that switches far-away railroad tracks. Or, even more puzzling, we might pull a lever that does something different each time, based on some algorithm; or we watch as the algorithm pulls the lever itself, based on its own mysterious motivations.

At the center of all this disruption is how we understand basic elements of our environment: What place am I in? What objects does it contain, and how do they work? Who am I, and who can see me, and what I am doing? What used to be clear is now less so.

Case Study: Facebook Beacon

Some of the infrastructure we take for granted now was almost unimaginable only a decade ago. And perhaps no digital "place" is more ubiquitous in more people's lives than Facebook. With billions of registered users, it's become the "telephone network" of social interaction online.

Back in 2007, Facebook launched a service it called *Beacon*, which tracked what users purchased on participating non-Facebook sites, and published that information to the recently introduced *News Feeds* seen by their Facebook "friends." It took many people by surprise, and sparked a major controversy regarding online privacy.

Facebook is an especially powerful example of context disruption, partly because of how it has shape-shifted the sort of place it is since it began as a closed network for Harvard students alone.

---

* Kitchin, Rob, and Martin Dodge. *Code/Space: Software and Everyday Life*. Cambridge, MA: MIT Press, 2011: 47.

In fact, much of Facebook's architectural foundation was structured based on the assumption that a user's network would be limited to people she had already met or could easily meet on her campus. The intrinsic cultural structures of one's college provided natural boundaries that Facebook re-created in code form.

Over time, Facebook grew rapidly to include other schools, then businesses, and then finally it was opened to the entire Web in 2006. Yet, it wasn't until much later that it introduced any way of structuring one's contacts into groups beyond the single bucket of "Friends," as if everyone you could connect to was the equivalent of someone you met during freshman orientation.

So, for users who had started their Facebook memberships back when their Friends included only their classmates, the sudden shift in context was often disorienting. With pictures of college parties still hanging in their galleries—meant for a social context of peers that would understand them—they were suddenly getting friend invitations from coworkers and family members. Facebook had obliterated the cultural boundaries that had normally kept these facets of one's personality and personal life comfortably separate.

Before Beacon, the introduction of the News Feed had already caused a lot of concern when users realized it was tracking what they did within Facebook itself and publishing an ongoing status report of those activities to their friends. Actions and changes that had once been quiet adjustments to their profile had been turned into News, published to everyone they knew.

Take, for instance, changes in relationship status. Breaking up with a partner is an intimate, personal event that one might prefer to treat with some subtlety and care. Facebook's structure made it seem users were changing relationship status within a particular place, separate from other places. Consequently, it was horrifying to discover that changing the setting in a drop-down list in one's personal profile was simultaneously announcing it to everyone he knew. Facebook broke the expectations of cause-and-effect that people bring to their environment.

Just as users were getting used to how the News Feed worked, Beacon launched, publishing information about actions users were taking *outside of Facebook*. Suddenly, Facebook was indiscriminately notifying people of purchases (books about personal matters, medicines for private maladies, or surprise gifts for significant others) and other actions (playing on a video game site during the workday; signing up for a dating site), with confusing contextual clues about what was going on. For example, Figure 2-1 shows a small opt-out pop-up window that the system used, which was easy to overlook. In addition, it quickly defaulted to "Yes" and disappeared if you didn't acknowledge it in time.[*]

FIGURE 2-1

The small Beacon opt-in message that would appear in the lower corner of the screen (from MoveOn.org)[†]

Unlike one's Facebook profile, this was not information that was already available to your friends; this was information that, in the physical dimension, has always been assumed to be at least implicitly contained within a "store" or "site."

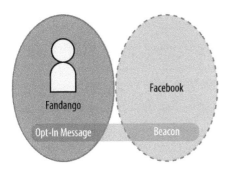

FIGURE 2-2

The user perceives the Fandango site as a separate environmental place and might not notice a small, ambient opt-in message

* Martin, Kirsten E. "Facebook (A): Beacon and Privacy," *Business Roundtable: Institute for Corporate Ethics. http://bit.ly/1nAWYkK*

† *http://civ.moveon.org/facebookprivacy/beacon_demo.html*

The result? User revolt, widespread controversy, and the eventual dismantling of the Beacon program. And to top it off, it prompted a $9.5 million class-action lawsuit that was finally settled in February 2013.[*]

Facebook has notoriously and publically struggled with these issues of place confusion since its founding. But what is true of Facebook is just as true of nearly every networked environment. Although Beacon was the metaphorical equivalent of having networked cameras and data feeds for your every action available for public consumption, that breakdown of context is no longer merely metaphorical. As our every action and purchase is increasingly picked up by sensors, cameras, brand-loyalty databases, and cloud-connected smartphones, Beacon's misstep seems almost primitive in comparison.

---

[*] Cohen, David. "Ninth U.S. Circuit Court Of Appeals Upholds Facebook Beacon Class-Action Settlement," February 27, 2013. *http://bit.ly/1nAX6Rh*

[3]

Environments, Elements, and Information

Context is worth 80 IQ points.
—ALAN KAY

A Wall and a Field

SOCIAL NETWORKS AND AIRPORTS don't exist in a vacuum. They're part of a wider world. And humans didn't evolve with mobile phones in hand. Our bodies and brains grew in predigital environments that shaped the way we understand our surroundings. If context in digital environments is so hard to get our heads around, maybe we need to begin by establishing up front what an environment actually is. Take a look Figure 3-1, an idyllic landscape in Derbyshire, England.

FIGURE 3-1
A bucolic Derbyshire landscape[*]

---

[*] Wikimedia Commons: *http://bit.ly/1uDL7m6*

We might look at this landscape and assume that there's not much information here, but there actually is. This is as much an "information environment" as any website or city intersection. That is, for us to just get around in a place like this, there has to be information about the structures in the environment that our bodies somehow understand well enough to take action. Where can we walk? What can we eat? What can we hold in our hands?

Most of this environment happened all on its own, growing naturally. But also note the stone wall in the field. Some of the earliest structures humans ever added to their environment were of this sort: stones stacked to create barriers and boundaries. Such structures have a physical effect of stopping or slowing terrestrial motion, but they also carry a cultural meaning, such as "this land belongs to someone" or "keep your sheep on the other side, away from my sheep." The wall changes the context of the field, transforming an open, undifferentiated vista into a specific human *place* with additional layers of significance.

Keep this field in mind as a starting point, because from here on out, we will be looking at everything we make—digital devices or websites, phone apps or cross-channel services—as structure we add to the environment around us, not unlike this wall, which is deceptively simple at first glance, but full of meaningful layers upon closer reflection.

A Conventional Definition of Context

One challenge we have when grappling with contextual issues comes from our conventional assumptions about what context is to begin with. Yes, we would all agree it has to do with relationships between things. But, we tend to focus on the things, not the context. I mean, we tend to want to understand what a thing is in relation to what contains it, as if that container is "the context." When you ask whether a wall is an urban wall or a country wall, the subject (wall) is supposedly informed by the setting—a wall "in a field in the country" is a country wall.

This convention is baked into our official dictionary definitions. For example, the *Oxford English Dictionary* defines context as "the circumstances that form the setting for an event, statement, or idea, and in terms of which it can be fully understood." This definition contains essentially the same elements of most definitions of context:

Circumstances

The setting or situational factors that surround the subject.

Agent

The (implied) entity that is trying to understand the subject.* Note that in this book, you will see the term "agent" used at times, but also words such as "person," "perceiver," or "user" somewhat interchangeably, depending on the point being made. They all reference the same concept, except that agents are not always people, or what we normally think of as a "user."

Subject

The event, statement, or idea that is in the circumstances, and that is the focus of the agent's attempted understanding. From any particular point of view, there's always something that's nested within something else. But, as we'll see, that relationship is situationally dependent.

Understanding

An apprehension (or effort toward apprehension) of the meaning of the subject and its relationship to its circumstances.

So, the typical way of understanding context looks something like that presented in Figure 3-2.

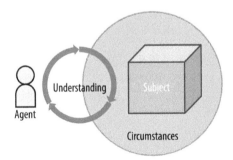

FIGURE 3-2
The conventional way we think of context

---

* Using the term *agent* gives us the ability to include nonpersons, such as software or other systems that try to determine context. It's also the term used most often in the scholarly literature for this element.

That's not a bad starting point. But the truth is, context is much more complicated. For one thing, as soon as something is "in a context," it changes the context. The same elements are present, but the number of the elements and their relationships are part of a multifaceted reality.

Perhaps the field has only a stone wall in it. But, the wall actually changes the nature of the field, which is now not just "a field" but "a field with a stone wall." Then, it's only a matter of time before more walls are built, roads are added, hotels and pubs spring up, and eventually it's a town with a road called "Field Avenue" as the only reminder that there was ever a field there at all.

As Malcolm McCullough explains in *Digital Ground*, context is bound up in our interaction with our environment.

> "Context" is not the setting itself, but the engagement with it as well as the bias that setting gives to the interactions that occur within it. "Environment" is the sum of all present contexts.[*]

Context isn't just the surrounding circumstances, because it includes and interacts with the subject that is surrounded, and the agent that tries to comprehend it all.

Paul Dourish, in his seminal paper on context and human-computer interaction, "What We Talk About When We Talk About Context," argues for a model in which, "Context isn't something that describes a setting; it's something that people do....It is an emergent feature of the interaction, determined in the moment and in the doing. In other words, context and...activity...cannot be separated. Context...arises from and is sustained by the activity itself."[†]

This is all sort of brain-bendy stuff, but unless we grapple with it, we run the risk of designing environments that assume too much about how agents understand them.

---

[*] McCullough, Malcolm. *Digital Ground: Architecture, Pervasive Computing, and Environmental Knowing*. Cambridge, MA: MIT Press, 2004: 48, Kindle edition.

[†] Dourish, Paul. "What We Talk About When We Talk About Context." *Personal and Ubiquitous Computing*. London: Springer-Verlag, February 2004; 8(1):19–30.

For example, my Google calendar via website has one set of information in it, including the TripIt calendar I've subscribed to, so that my travel information shows up among all my other scheduled events. However, that's only from my perspective. Others on my team can see only my main calendar, not my calendar subscriptions, a state of affairs that isn't clearly apparent to me. The only indication of this difference is a setting in Google Calendar that takes some effort to discover: it says "Anyone can: See Nothing."

Even though it's just one setting, the rule has implications that are harder to perceive—it means the circumstances are different depending on which agent is logged in and viewing the interface. The sort of place my calendar is to me is not the sort of place my calendar is to someone else.

As mentioned earlier, the contextual problems have to do not just with the calendar's settings or even its graphical interface, but the meaning of "calendar" itself. The label we use for the digital object sets an expectation that it is a singular calendar such as a paper calendar hanging on a wall, not a multidimensional, virtual object with many "calendars" in aggregate. The language we use for the environment is part of the environment as well.

So, we at least have to allow that the circumstances are not separate from the agent that's perceiving and trying to understand the subject; instead, the circumstances contain all these elements, as depicted in Figure 3-3.

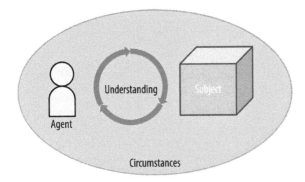

FIGURE 3-3
The agent is also part of the circumstances

But, what about circumstances in which the agent is also the subject (Figure 3-4)? For example, that's what I was trying to understand when I was at the airport, working out which label applied to me in the overall system of labeling. And it's what any of us are doing when we're navigating within a space, trying to get somewhere—whether on-screen or off.

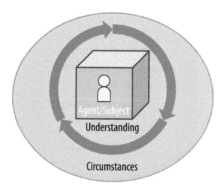

FIGURE 3-4
The agent is often also the subject

Add to this the fact that we're pretty much always trying to understand who and where we are in relation to our environment while simultaneously needing to understand the context of a lot of other things happening around us.

One moment, something is the *subject* but at another it's just background, part of the *circumstances*. In addition, we're almost never trying to take in only one subject at a time; instead, we're absorbing a shifting, roiling torrent of them, as illustrated in Figure 3-5. It all starts to get pretty overwhelming.

What a mess, right? Humans are pretty smart, but we're still finite creatures. We can really think hard about only one or two things at a time. So, a factor in all this complexity is the amount of attention we can summon and the cognitive effort we have to bring to bear on our environment and everything it's made of, including ourselves.

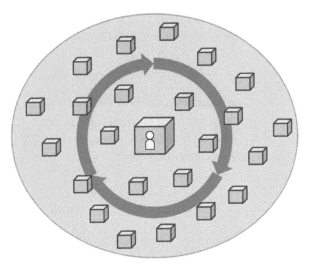

FIGURE 3-5
An agent in the midst of multiple subjects, and complicated circumstances

A New, Working Definition of Context

So, moving forward, we will stray from the conventional definition and use a new, working definition. It's just a bit more technical than the one we started with in Chapter 1:

> Context is an agent's understanding of the relationships between the elements of the agent's environment.

In this case, the parts of the definition are as follows:

Agent
A person or other object that can act in the environment. Not all agents are persons, and not all of them perceive or act the same way.

Understanding
An agent's cognitive engagement with, and making sense of, its surroundings. Although there are other non-agent-bound ways of thinking about context, our purpose here has to do with the subjective, first-person experience of the agent, even when it's not a person.

Relationships between the elements

Everything is made up of parts; context is all about how those parts relate to one another.

The agent's environment

Context is always about the entire environment, because the environment is what informs the meaning of anything the agent is trying to understand. Note we aren't saying "environment" in general—a setting observed from some omniscient, god's-eye view. It is "the *agent's* environment," because context is a function of the agent's own first-person perception. Perception is what undergirds cognition, experience, and understanding.

This definition makes context a function of how an agent perceives and understands the environment, not a property that exists outside of that understanding. It also doesn't specify that one element is the subject, special from everything else. Any element can be the subject at any moment and then drift or quickly switch to mere "circumstances."

So, does that mean we can't pin context down? Well, in a way, yes: if by pinning it down we mean we try to fix it in one state. That is, we can still map the elements out as agent, subjects, and circumstances; we just have to be careful that we aren't assuming that only one snapshot represents the whole contextual experience.

In my airport scenario in Chapter 1, we could do a pretty decent job of mapping the most important contextual relationships by identifying the elements:

- Each element that can reasonably be called an *agent*: myself, my coworker, each application on my phone that's making some kind of decision and taking action, and even the customer service representative.

- Each important element that at any moment could be a *subject* in the scenario: everything that's an agent, plus my boarding pass, the security queues, my calendar, and so on.

- Finally, the *circumstances*, which are basically each influential element of the environment, including (of course) the subjects and agents. Any element could be a circumstance or could be a subject, and vice versa. It's all a matter of what the agent needs to perceive and understand in order to act.

We can get a lot of value out of just listing out these different rela-tionships, and how they crisscross and overlap. There's no way to map every single factor in even a simple real-world environment, but it's possible to take snapshots from different perspectives, at various key moments, and bring them together into something more like a *collage* of snapshots that come nearer to telling the entire story. The important thing is to include more than a single, static perspective. What does the Passbook app understand about my situation that causes it to show a notification in the lock screen? What does my coworker understand about my calendar and the absence of any trip information there? And so on.

I offer this way of thinking about modeling context as a starting point. But, before anything else, we still have to get a handle on what we mean by things such as "understanding," "environment," and "agent." It turns out that understanding the elements of the environment depends on the way *information* works.

Modes of Information

Even though it's not listed in our working definition of context, *infor-mation* is required before any perceiving or understanding can occur. Before around 1960, people didn't use the word nearly as much as they do today.* The rise of computing technologies influenced how we talk about the way we communicate. Now, we say "information" a great deal. We use it as a catchall for just about anything that is intended to communicate a message or meaning or knowledge. It's not as general as a word like "stuff," but it's close. Is it expected to inform? Then it's information. Does it do a good job of informing? If it does, it's "good information." If not, it's "bad information."

And it would seem that bad information is everywhere, because the expectations we bring to information are often met with disappoint-ment. Most people would categorize the legalese in a software license or the instructions for a tax form as information—but they would be hard-pressed to agree they fully understand those texts. They just say, "this information is awful" or "I don't get this information at all."

---

* Based on a search for "information" in books from 1800 to 2000, using Google's Ngram Viewer (*https://books.google.com/ngrams/*).

It does seem odd that we'd even use the word "information" for something that doesn't effectively do the work of informing. In *Information Anxiety*, Richard Saul Wurman explains how the term gained an additional conventional meaning around the time of World War II, with the invention of information theories behind electronic transmission. The word "became part of the vocabulary of the science of messages. And, suddenly, the appellation could be applied to something that didn't necessarily have to inform. The definition was extrapolated to general usage as something told or communicated, whether or not it made sense to the receiver."* This slippage influenced our techno-fueled mid-twentieth-century culture to the point that we now talk of living in the "Information Age." Now, *information* can mean the coding of DNA, the credits at the end of a movie, or verbal instructions from a customer service desk. Like so many words that can mean so many things, information is now a muddle.

For regular people in everyday situations, rigorous definitions for the word might not be necessary. But for people whose job it is to make environments with information, a specialized understanding is called for. Psychologists need to understand what elements make up sadness so that they can help people who are troubled by it. Artists and art historians are responsible for creating and curating art, so they have to think about the materials, techniques, and cultural meanings behind what makes something "art." And game designers make a living from being deeply interested in what constraints, goals, and mechanisms make something "fun." Similarly, it's the responsibility of those of us who make "information things"—from software and digital gadgets to diagrams and newsletters—to have a practical, working model for how information works, and how it can meet the everyday expectations of its users.

You can find many sophisticated models and explanations of information in academic theories and scientific literature.† They all bring valid and valuable perspectives to bear. For our purposes here, though, I've developed a simple model that describes three different modes for

---

* Wurman, Richard Saul. *Information Anxiety*. New York: Doubleday, 1989: 38.

† I especially recommend Bates, M. "Fundamental Forms of Information." *Journal of the American Society for Information Science and Technology* 2006; 57(8):1033–45, and ongoing work on a taxonomy of information by Sabrina Golonka, (*http://bit.ly/1ySrrik* and *http://bit.ly/1CM2ti6*).

information that provide lenses for understanding how context works in the environments we design. We'll begin with a summary, here, but then delve more deeply into each mode in the next three parts of the book.

Figure 3-6 shows the three modes: Digital, Semantic, and Physical.

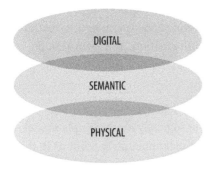

FIGURE 3-6
The three modes of information

Let's begin from the bottom and work our way up.

Physical

This is the information animals use to perceive their environment for purposes of taking physical action; of course, humans are a part of the animal realm, so we do this, too. It's information that functions "ecologically"—that is, in the relationship between a creature and its environment. It's about surfaces, edges, substances, objects, and the ways in which those things contain and relate to one another to support animals' behaviors and survival.

Semantic

This is information people create for the purpose of communicating meaning to other people. I'll often refer to this as "language." For our discussion, this mode includes all sorts of communication such as gestures, signs, graphics, and of course speech and writing. It's more fluid than physical information and harder to pin down, but it still creates environmental structure for us. It overlaps the Physical mode because much of the human environment depends on complementary qualities of both of these modes, such as the signage and maps positioned in physical locations and written on physical surfaces in an airport.

Digital

This is the "information technology" sort of information by which computers operate, and communicate with other computers. Even though humans created it (or created the computers that also create it), it's not natively readable by people. That's because it works by stripping out people-centric context so that machines can talk among one another with low error rates, as quickly and efficiently as possible. It overlaps the Semantic mode, because it's abstract and made of encoded semantic information. But even though it isn't literally physical, it does exist in physical infrastructure, and it does affect our physical environment more and more every day.

I should mention: like many other models I'll share, this one isn't meant to be taken as mathematically or logically exact. Simple models can sometimes work best when they are clear enough to point us in the right direction but skip the complexities of precision. So, for example, the overlapping parts of the modes are there to evoke how they are seldom mutually exclusive, and actually influence one another.

Starting from the Bottom

I began with the Physical mode for a reason. Context is about whole environments; otherwise, we are considering parts of an environment out of context. And when we take an environmental view, we have to begin from first principles about how people understand the environment, whether there are digital networks or gadgets in it or not. To illustrate this, Figure 3-7 presents another informal model that illustrates the layers involved in the discussion moving forward.

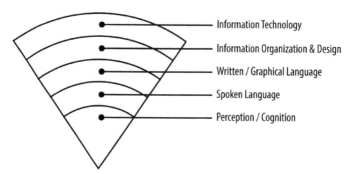

FIGURE 3-7
Pace layers of information

These are based on a concept known as *pace layers*—where the lower-level layer changes more slowly over time than the next, and so on. I've adapted the approach so that it also implies how one layer builds on another.[*]

- *Perception and cognition* change very slowly for all organisms, including humans, and these abilities had to evolve long ago in order to have a functioning animal to begin with. Perception here means the core faculties of how a body responds to the environment. This is the sort of perception lizards use to climb surfaces and eat bugs or that humans use to walk around or duck a stray football.

- *Spoken language* is next; as we will see, it has been around for a very long time for our species, long enough to at times be hard to separate from the older perception and cognition capabilities of our bodies and brains (as mentioned earlier, I'm lumping gestures in with speech, for simplicity's sake). Even though particular languages can change a lot over centuries, the essential characteristics of spoken language change much more slowly.

- *Written/graphical language* is the way we use physical objects—up until very recently, the surfaces of those objects—to encode verbal language for communicating beyond the present moment. Although spoken language is more of an emergent property of our species, writing is actually more of an ancient *technology*. Writing is also a way of encoding information, which is a precursor to digital code.

- *Information organization and design* arose as identifiable areas of expertise and effort because we had so much stuff written down, and because writing and drawing enabled greater complexity than is possible in mere speech. The ability to freeze speech on a surface and relate it to other frozen speech on the same surface opened up the ability to have maps, diagrams, broadsides, folios, all of which required organization and layout. Our methods for organizing and designing written information have also been precursors to how we've designed and organized digital information for computing.

---

[*] Borrowed and adapted from the work of Stewart Brand, particularly in *How Buildings Learn*, who adapted his approach from a concept called *shearing layers* created by architect Frank Duffy.

- Last, there's *information technology*, which is quite recent, and (as I'm defining it here) depended on the invention of digital software. We've seen this mode change rapidly in our own lifetimes, and it's the layer that has most disrupted our experience of the other two modes, in the shortest time. It didn't happen on its own, however; the ideas behind it originated in writing, linguistic theory, and other influences from further down the model.

If we place the three modes of information on top of these layers as demonstrated in Figure 3-8, it gives a rough idea of how these models relate to each other.

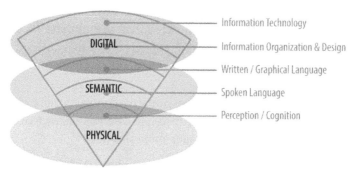

FIGURE 3-8
Modes and layers combined

In reality, the boundaries are actually much more diffuse and intermingled, but the main idea is hopefully clear: the ways in which we use and perceive information have evolved over time; some aspects are foundational and more stable, whereas other aspects are more variable and quick to change.

In my experience, most technological design work begins with information technology first and then later figures out the information organization and design and other communicative challenges lower down. Yet, starting with technology takes a lot for granted. It assumes X means X, and Y means Y; or that here is here, and there is there. What happens when we can no longer trust those assumptions? The best way to untangle the many knotted strands that create and shape context is to understand how the world makes sense to us in the first place—with bodies, surfaces, and objects—and build the rest of our understanding from that foundation.

[*Part II*]

Physical Information

The Roots of Context

THE PRODUCTS AND SERVICES WE DESIGN ARE PART OF A GREATER ENVI-
RONMENT, but they have the capacity to change that environment as
well as the behaviors of people who use them. Smartphones influence user behavior in a different way than older cell phones, which in
turn changed behavior from when only phone booths and land lines
were available. Obviously, right? But, did you know that the separation
between the environment, the object, and the user is mostly artificial
and that they're all part of one dynamic system? Have you also noticed
that when we use software, our perception seems to expect that environment to behave according to the same laws we rely on in the physical world?

The mechanics of physical life shape the way we understand abstractions such as language, social systems, and software. That's why we're
going to spend some significant quality time together looking at what
I'm calling *Physical Information*, the mode at the bottom of the diagram
shown in Figure II-1.

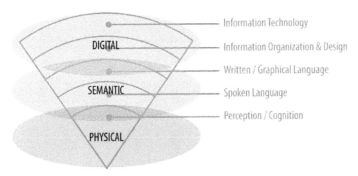

FIGURE II-1
Physical Information

Part II introduces some essential theories about perception and action. It explores what *affordance* really is, with special attention to how it was originally conceived by its creator, James J. Gibson. It also covers how the environment influences behavior, how memory and learning work, and offers models for breaking down the elements of any environment. Finally, this part shows how physical information principles translate into more-complex parts of our world such as social culture and organizations.

[4]

Perception, Cognition, and Affordance

In the Universe, there are things that are known, and things that are unknown, and in between there are doors.
—WILLIAM BLAKE

Information of a Different Sort

IF WE ARE TO KNOW HOW USERS UNDERSTAND THE CONTEXT OF OBJECTS, people, and places, we need to stipulate what we mean by *understand* in the first place. The way people understand things is through *cognition*, which is the process by which we acquire knowledge and understanding through thought, experience, and our senses. Cognition isn't an abstraction. It's bound up in the very structures of our bodies and physical surroundings.

When a spider quickly and gracefully traverses the intricacies of a web, or a bird like the green bee-eater on this book's cover catches an insect in flight, these creatures are relying on their bodies to form a kind of coupling with their environments—a natural, intuitive dance wherein environment and creature work together as a system. These wonderfully evolved, coupled systems result in complex, advanced behavior, yet with no large brains in sight.

It turns out that we humans, who evolved on the same planet among the same essential structures as spiders and birds, also rely on this kind of body-to-environment coupling. Our most basic actions—the sort we hardly notice we do—work because our bodies are able to perceive and act among the structures of our environment with little or no thought required.

When I see users tapping and clicking pages or screens to learn how a product works, ignoring and dismissing pop-ups with important alerts because they want to get at the information underneath, or keeping their smartphones with them from room to room in their homes, I wonder why these behaviors occur. Often they don't seem very logical, or at least they show a tendency to act first and think about the logic of the action later. Even though these interfaces and gadgets aren't natural objects and surfaces, users try using them as if they were.

This theory about the body-environment relationship originates in a field called *ecological psychology*, which posits that creatures directly perceive and act in the world by their bodies' ability to *detect information* about the structures in the environment. This information is what I will be calling *physical information*—a mode of information that is at work when bodies and environments do this coupled, dynamic dance of action and perception.

Ecological psychology is sometimes referred to as *Gibsonian* psychology because the theory started with a scientist named James J. Gibson, whose theory of information uses neither the colloquial meaning of information nor the definition we get from information science.* Gibson explains his usage in a key passage of his landmark work, *The Ecological Approach to Visual Perception*:

> Information, as the term is used in this book (but not in other books), refers to specification of the observer's environment, not to specification of the observer's receptors or sense organs....[For discussing perception, the term] information cannot have its familiar dictionary meaning of knowledge communicated to a receiver. This is unfortunate, and I would use another term if I could. The only recourse is to ask the reader to remember that picking up information is not to be thought of as a case of communicating. The world does not speak to the observer. Animals and humans communicate with cries, gestures, speech, pictures, writing and television, but we cannot hope to understand perception in terms of these channels; it is quite the other way

---

* I should note that in James Gibson's work, he never called this sort of information "physical information." He was careful to use "physical" specifically for describing properties of the world that exist regardless of creaturely perception. A more accurate term might be "ecological" or "directly perceived" information, but this is an academic distinction that I found unhelpful to design audiences. So, for simplicity, I've opted to call the mode "physical" instead.

around. Words and pictures convey information, carry it, or transmit it, but the information in the sea of energy around each of us, luminous or mechanical or chemical energy, is not conveyed. It is simply there. The assumption that information can be transmitted and the assumption that it can be stored are appropriate for the theory of communication, not for the theory of perception.[*]

Gibson often found himself having to appropriate or invent terms in order to have language he could use to express ideas that the contemporaneous language didn't accommodate.[†] He's having to ask readers to set aside their existing meaning of *information* and to look at it in a different way, when trying to understand how perception works. For him, "To perceive is to be aware of the surfaces of the environment and of oneself in it."[‡] In other words, perception is about the agent, figuring out the elements of its surroundings and understanding how the agent itself is one of those elements. And information is what organisms perceive in the environment that informs the possibilities for action.

Even this usage of "perception" is more specific than we might be used to: it's about core perceptual faculties, not statements such as "my perception of the painting is that it is pretty" or "the audience perceives her to be very talented." Those are cultural, social layers that we might refer to as perception, but not the sort of perception we will mainly be discussing in Part 1.

Even though we humans might now be using advanced technology with voice recognition and backlit touch-screen displays, we still depend on the same bodies and brains that our ancestors used thousands of years ago to allow us to act in our environment, no matter how digitally enhanced. Just as with the field and the stone wall presented in Chapter 3, even without language or digital technology, the world is full of structures that *inform* bodies about what actions those structures afford.

---

[*] Gibson, J. J. *The Ecological Approach to Visual Perception*. Boston: Houghton Mifflin, 1979: 242.

[†] ———. *The Ecological Approach to Visual Perception*. Boston: Houghton Mifflin, 1979: 239.

[‡] ———. *The Ecological Approach to Visual Perception*. Boston: Houghton Mifflin, 1979: 255.

I'll be drawing from Gibson's work substantially, especially in this part of the book, because I find that it provides an invaluable starting point for rethinking (and more deeply grasping) how users perceive and understand their environments. Gibson's ideas have also found a more recent home as a significant influence in a theoretical perspective called *embodied cognition*.

James. J. Gibson

James J. ("JJ") Gibson (1904–1979) was an American experimental psychologist, author, and theorist. He and his wife, Eleanor J. Gibson (1910–2002),—a major scientific figure in her own right—developed an extensive theoretical body of work on what they called ecological perception and learning.

FIGURE 4-1

James J. Gibson and Eleanor Gibson[*]

James Gibson developed his theories partly during research funded by the United States Air Force around the time of World War II while studying how pilots orient themselves during flight.[†] Gibson realized that his insight would mean overturning more than a century of established scientific research to get to the bottom of the problem, and insisted that a "fresh start" was required.[‡] What resulted was decades of work dedicated to changing the way science understood perception.

---

[*] Russ Hamilton, photographer. Cornell University Photo Services. Division of Rare and Manuscript Collections, Cornell University Library.

[†] Gibson, J. J. *The Ecological Approach to Visual Perception*. Boston: Houghton Mifflin, 1979: 148

[‡] ———. Sensory processes and perception. A Century of Psychology as a Science. *American Psychological Association*, Washington, DC, 1992: 224–230. (ISBN 155798171X)

Gibson particularly subscribed to the perspective of American Pragmatism, and the radical empiricism developed by William James.* As a radical empiricist himself, Gibson insisted on understanding perception based on the facts of the natural world, versus cultural assumptions or artificially contrived experiments.

Eleanor Gibson made major contributions to the science of childhood cognitive development as well as how people in general learn new knowledge. Her work has been foundational to later social science and psychology work on education and communities of practice. She was awarded the National Medal of Science in 1992. A famous experiment she created was the *Visual Cliff*, in which infants were placed on a wooden table whose surface was extended by a long portion of plate glass. She discovered that infants reacted to the perceived drop-off with caution or anxiety, but she also observed how they would adapt to their perceptions by patting the glass and learning about their environment through action.†

Most of the references to "Gibsonian psychology" in this book are specifically to James Gibson's work; but it's important to remember that this amazing couple jointly established some of the most important insights in psychological science in the twentieth century.

---

* James Gibson actually studied under a protege of William James, E.B. Holt. Burke, F. Thomas. *What Pragmatism Was.* Indiana University Press, 2013: 92.

† Gibson, E. J., and R. D. Walk. "The visual cliff." *Scientific American*, 1960; 202:64–72.

A Mainstream View of Cognition

Since roughly the mid-twentieth century, conventional cognitive science holds that cognition is primarily (or exclusively) a brain function, and that the body is mainly an input-output mechanism; the body does not constitute a significant part of cognitive work. I'll be referring to this perspective as *mainstream* or *disembodied cognition*, though it is called by other names in the literature, such as *representationalism* or *cognitivism*.

According to this view, cognition works something similar to the diagram in Figure 4-2.

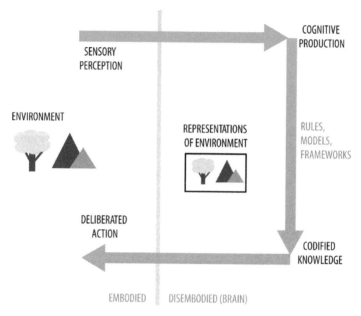

FIGURE 4-2

The mainstream model for cognition*

The process happens through inputs and outputs, with the brain as the "central processing unit":

1. The brain gathers data about the world through the body's senses.

2. It then works with *abstract representations* of what is sensed.

3. The brain processes the representational data by using disembodied rules, models, and logical operations.

4. The brain then takes this disembodied, abstract information and translates it into instructions to the body.

In other words, according to the mainstream view, perception is indirect, and requires representations that are processed the way a computer would process math and logic. The model holds that this is how cognition works for even the most basic bodily action.

---

* McCullough, Malcolm. [Based on a diagram in] *Ambient Commons: Attention in the Age of Embodied Information.* Cambridge, MA: MIT Press, 2013.

This computer-like way of understanding cognition emerged for a reason: modern cognitive science was coming of age just as information theory and computer science were emerging as well; in fact, the "cognitive revolution" that moved psychology past its earlier behaviorist orthodoxy was largely due to the influence of the new field of information science.[*]

So, of course, cognitive science absorbed a lot of perspectives and metaphors from computing. The computer became not just a metaphor for understanding the brain, but a literal explanation for its function. It framed the human mind as made of information processed by a brain that works like an advanced machine.[†] This theoretical foundation is still influential today, in many branches of psychology, neuroscience, economics, and even human-computer interaction (HCI).

To be fair, this is a simplified summary, and the disembodied-cognition perspective has evolved over time. Some versions have even adopted aspects of competing theories. Still, the core assumptions are based on brain-first cognition, arguing that at the center is a "model human processor" that computes our cognition using logical rules and representations, much like the earliest cognitive scientists and HCI theorists described.[‡] And let's face it, this is how most of us learned how the brain and body function; the brain-is-like-a-computer meme has fully saturated our culture to the point at which it's hard to imagine any other way of understanding cognition.

The mainstream view has been challenged for quite a while by alternative theories, which include examples such as *activity theory, situated action theory,* and *distributed cognition theory.*[§] These and others are all worth learning about, and they all bring some needed rigor to design practice. They also illustrate how there isn't necessarily a single

---

[*] Gleick, James. *The Information: A History, a Theory, a Flood.* New York: Random House, Inc., 2011: 4604–5, Kindle edition.

[†] Louise Barrett traces the origin of the brain-as-computer metaphor to the work of John von Neumann in the late 1940s. Barrett, Louise. *Beyond the Brain: How Body and Environment Shape Animal and Human Minds.* Princeton, NJ: Princeton University Press, 2011:121, Kindle edition.

[‡] Durso, Francis T. et al. *Handbook of Applied Cognition.* New York: John Wiley & Sons, 2007.

[§] Nardi, Bonnie. *Context and Consciousness: Activity Theory and Human-Computer Interaction.* "Studying Context: A Comparison of Activity Theory, Situated Action Models, and Distributed Cognition" pp. 35–52.

accepted way to understand cognition, users, or products. For our purposes, we will be exploring context through the perspective of *embodied cognition theory*.

Embodied Cognition: An Alternative View

In my own experience, and in the process of investigating this book's subject, I've found the theory of embodied cognition to be a convincing approach that explains many of the mysteries I've encountered over my years of observing users and designing for them.

Embodied cognition has been gaining traction in the last decade or so, sparking a paradigm shift in cognitive science, but it still isn't mainstream. That's partly because the argument implies mainstream cognitive science has been largely wrong for a generation or more. Yet, embodied cognition is an increasingly influential perspective in the user-experience design fields, and stands to fundamentally change the way we think about and design human-computer interaction.*

Generally, the embodiment argument claims that our brains are not the only thing we use for thought and action; instead, our bodies are an important part of how cognition works. There are multiple versions of embodiment theory, some of which still insist the brain is where cognition starts, with the body just helping out. However, the perspective we will be following argues that cognition is truly environment-first, emerging from an active relationship between environment, body, and brain.† As explained by Andrew Wilson and Sabrina Golonka in their article "Embodied Cognition Is Not What You Think It Is":

> The most common definitions [of embodied cognition] involve the straightforward claim that "states of the body modify states of the mind." However, the implications of embodiment are actually much more radical than this. If cognition can span the brain, body, and the environment, the "states of mind" of disembodied cognitive science

---

* Kirsh David. Embodied Cognition and the Magical Future of Interaction Design. *ACM Trans. On Human Computer Interaction* 2013.

† Including the entire environment as part of cognition has also been called "extended cognition theory." We'll just be using "embodied" as the umbrella term.

won't exist to be modified. Cognition will instead be an extended system assembled from a broad array of resources. Taking embodiment seriously therefore requires both new methods and theory.[*]

The embodied approach insists on understanding perception from the first-person perspective of the perceiving organism, not abstract principles from a third-person observer. A spider doesn't "know" about webs, or that it's moving vertically up a surface; it just takes action according to its nature. A bird doesn't "know" it is flying in air; it just moves its body to get from one place to another through its native medium. For we humans, this can be confusing, because by the time we are just past infancy, we develop a dependence on language and abstraction for talking and thinking about how we perceive the world—a lens that adds a lot of conceptual information to our experience. But the perception and cognition underlying that higher-order comprehension is just about bodies and structures, not concepts. Conscious reflection on our experience happens after the perception, not before.

How can anything behave intelligently without a brain orchestrating every action? To illustrate, let's look at how a Venus flytrap "behaves" with no brain at all. Even though ecological psychology and embodiment are not about plants, but terrestrial animals with brains and bodies that move, the flytrap is a helpful example because it illustrates how something that seems like intelligent behavior can occur through a coupled action between environment and organism.

The Venus flytrap (Figure 4-3) excretes a chemical that attracts insects. The movement of insects drawn to the plant then triggers tiny hairs on its surface. These hairs *structurally* cause the plant to close on the prey and trap it.

---

[*] Wilson, A., and S. Golonka. *Frontiers in Psychology* February 2013; Volume 4, Article 58.

FIGURE 4-3
A Venus flytrap—complex behavior without a brain*

This behavior already has some complexity going on, but there's more: the trap closes only if more than one hair has been triggered within about 20 seconds. This bit of conditional logic embodied by the plant's structure prevents it from trapping things with no nutritional value. Natural selection evidently filtered out all the flytraps that made too many mistakes when catching dinner. This is complex behavior with apparent intelligence underpinning it. Yet it's all driven by the physical coupling of the organism's "body" and a particular environmental niche.

Now, imagine an organism that evolved to have the equivalent of millions of Venus flytraps, simple mechanisms that engage the structures of the environment in a similar manner, each adding a unique and complementary piece to a huge cognition puzzle. Though fanciful, it is one way of thinking about how complex organisms evolved, some of them eventually developing brains.

In animals with brains, the brain enhances and augments the body. The brain isn't the center of the behavioral universe; rather, it's the other way around. It's this "other way around" perspective that Gibson continually emphasizes in his work.

Figure 4-4 illustrates a new model for the brain-body-environment relationship.

---

* Wikimedia Commons: *http://bit.ly/1xauZXB*

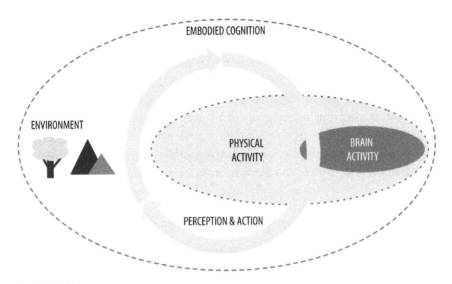

FIGURE 4-4

A model for embodied cognition

In this model, there's a continuous loop of action and perception in which the entire environment is involved in how a perceiver deciphers that environment, all of it working as a dynamical, perceptual system. Of course, the brain plays an important role, but it isn't the *originating source* of cognition. Perception gives rise to cognition in a reciprocal relationship—a resonant coupling—between the body and its surroundings.

This perception-action loop is the dynamo at the center of our cognition. In fact, perception makes up most of what we think of as cognition to begin with. As Louise Barrett puts it in *Beyond the Brain: How Body and Environment Shape Animal and Human Minds* (Princeton University Press), "Once we begin exploring the actual mechanisms that animals use to negotiate their worlds, it becomes hard to decide where 'perception' ends and 'cognition' starts."[*] Just perceiving the environment's information already does a lot of the work that we often attribute to brain-based cognition.

---

[*] Barrett, Louise. *Beyond the Brain: How Body and Environment Shape Animal and Human Minds*. Princeton, NJ: Princeton University Press, 2011:55.

Embodiment challenges us to understand the experience of the agent not from general abstract categories, but through the lived experience of the perceiver. One reason I prefer this approach is that it aligns nicely with what user experience (UX) design is all about: including the experiential reality of the user as a primary input to design rather than relying only on the goals of a business or the needs of a technology. Embodied cognition is a way of understanding more deeply how users have experiences, and how even subtle changes in the environment can have profound impacts on those experiences.

Using the Environment for Thinking

Designing for digital products and services requires working with a lot of abstractions, so it's helpful to bring those abstractions out of the cloudy dimension of pure thought and into the dimension of physical activity. This is why we so often find ourselves using our bodily environment for working out design problems and why it's emerged as a recognized best practice.

As an example let's consider how we use an office stalwart: the sticky note. By using sticky notes, we can move language around on a physical surface. As we'll see, language makes it possible for us to use bits of semantic information (labels, phrases, icons) as stand-ins for what they represent—anything from simple objects to large, complex ideas. By using the physical surface and the uncannily just-sticky-enough adhesive on the notes (Figure 4-5), we not only make use of the spatial relationships between notes to discover affinities and create structures, but also engage our bodies in thinking through the problem.

Sketching is another way we can externalize thought into bodily engagement with our environment—whether we're working through diagrammatic models to discover and rehearse abstract structural relationships, or we're informally playing around with representations of actual objects and interfaces. Sketching isn't only about what's being put on paper or drawn on-screen; sketching also engages our bodies in working through the contours of structure and potential action. Sketching can come in many forms, from chalk on a blackboard to CAD drawings or "wireframes" to making quick-and-cheap physical prototypes.

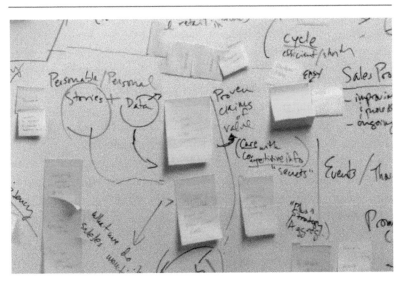

FIGURE 4-5
Using sticky notes to work through abstractions

FIGURE 4-6
Kate Rutter, live-sketchnoting Karen McGrane's closing plenary at IA Summit
2013*

---

* Photo by Jared Spool.

Action and the Perceptual System

As shown in the perception-action loop of Figure 4-4, we understand our environment by *taking action* in it. Gibson stresses that perception is not a set of discrete inputs and outputs, but happens as a *perceptual system* that uses all the parts of the system at once, where the distinction between input and output is effaced so that they "are considered together so as to make a continuous loop."[*] The body plays an active part in the dynamical feedback system of perception. Context, then, is also a result of action by a perceiving agent, not a separate set of facts somehow insulated from that active perception. Even when observing faraway stars, astronomers' actions have effects on how the light that has reached the telescope is interpreted and understood.

It's important to stress how deeply physical action and perception are connected, even when we are perceiving "virtual" or screen-based artifacts. In the documentary *Visions of Light: The Art of Cinematography*, legendary cameraman William Fraker tells a story about being the cinematographer on the movie *Rosemary's Baby*. At one point, he was filming a scene in which Ruth Gordon's spry-yet-sinister character, Minnie, is talking on the phone in a bedroom. Fraker explains how director Roman Polanski asked him to move the camera so that Minnie's face would be mostly hidden by the edge of a doorway, as shown in Figure 4-7. Fraker was puzzled by the choice, but he went along with it.

Fraker then recounts seeing the movie's theatrical premiere, during which he noticed the audience actually lean to the right in their seats in an attempt to peek around the bedroom door frame. It turned out that Polanski asked for the odd, occluding angle for a good reason: to engage the audience physically and heighten dramatic tension by obscuring the available visual information.

Even though anyone in the theater would have consciously admitted there was no way to see more by shifting position, the unconscious impulse is to shift to the side to get a better look. It's an intriguing illustration of how our bodies are active participants in understanding our environment, even in defiance of everyday logic.

---

[*] Gibson, J. J. *The Ecological Approach to Visual Perception.* Boston: Houghton Mifflin, 1979:245.

FIGURE 4-7
Minnie's semi-hidden phone conversation in *Rosemary's Baby* (courtesy Paramount Pictures)*

Gibson uses the phrase *perceptual system* rather than just "the eye" because we don't perceive anything with just one isolated sense organ.[†] Perception is a function of the whole bodily context. The eye is made of parts, and the eye itself is a part of a larger system of parts, which is itself part of some other larger system. Thus, what we see is influenced by how we move and what we touch, smell, and hear, and vice versa.

In the specific case of watching a movie, viewers trying to see more of Minnie's conversation were responding to a virtual experience as if it were a three-dimensional physical environment. They responded this way not because those dimensions were actually there, but because that sort of information was being mimicked on-screen, and taking action—in this case leaning to adjust the angle of viewable surfaces—is what a body does when it wants to detect richer information about the elements in view. As we will see in later chapters, this distinction between directly perceived information and interpreted, simulated-physical information is important to the way we design interfaces between people and digital elements of the environment.

---

* A frame captured from the streamed version of the film, reproduced under fair use.

† Gibson, J. J. *The Ecological Approach to Visual Perception*. Boston: Houghton Mifflin, 1979:244–6.

This systemic point of view is important in a broader sense of how we look at context and the products we design and build. Breaking things down into their component parts is a necessary approach to understanding complex systems and getting collaborative work done. But we have a tendency (or even a cognitive bias) toward forgetting the big picture of where the components came from. A specific part of a system might work fine and come through testing with flying colors, but it might fail once placed into the full context of the environment.

Information Pickup

Gibson coins the phrase *information pickup* to express how perception picks up, or detects, the information in the environment that our bodies use for taking action. It's in this dynamic of information pickup that the environment *specifies* what our bodies can or cannot do. The information picked up is about the mutual structural compatibility for action between bodies and environments.

In the same way a weather vane's "body" adjusts its behavior directly based on the direction of wind, an organism's biological structures respond to the environment directly. A weather vane (Figure 4-8) moves the way it does because its structure responds to the movement of air surrounding it. Similarly, the movements of the elbow joint also shown in Figure 4-8 are largely responses to the structure of the environment. When we reach for a fork at dinner or prop ourselves at the table, the specifics of our motion don't need to be computed because their physical structure evolved for reaching, propping, and other similar actions. The evolutionary pressures on a species result in bodily structures and systems that fit within and resonate with the structures and systems of the environment.*

---

* Gibson, J. J., *The Senses Considered as Perceptual Systems*. Boston: Houghton Mifflin, 1966:319.

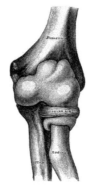

FIGURE 4-8
Weather vanes* and the human elbow joint† respond to their environments.

Information pickup is the process whereby the body can "orient, explore, investigate, adjust, optimize, resonate, extract, and come to an equilibrium."‡ Most of our action is calibrated on the fly by our bodies, tuning themselves in real time to the tasks at hand.§ When standing on a wobbly surface, we squat a bit to lower our center of gravity, and our arms shoot out to help our balance. This unthinking reaction to maintain equilibrium is behind more of our behavior than we realize, as when moviegoers leaned to the side to see more of Minnie's phone conversation. There's not a lot of abstract calculation driving those responses. They're baked into the whole-body root system that makes vision possible, responding to arrays of energy interacting with the surfaces of the environment. Gibson argued that all our senses work in a similar manner.

* Wikimedia Commons: *http://bit.ly/1rYwHIj*

† From *Gray's Anatomy*. Wikimedia Commons: *http://bit.ly/1CM8viC*

‡ Gibson, J. J. *The Ecological Approach to Visual Perception*. Boston: Houghton Mifflin, 1979:245.

§ It bears mentioning that Gibson's idea of "calibration" Norbert Wiener's cybernetics concept of "feedback." For more on Wiener, see: Bates, Marcia J. Information. In *Encyclopedia of Library and Information Sciences*. 3rd ed. 2010; Bates, Marcia J, Mary Niles Maack, eds. New York: CRC Press, Volume 3, pp. 2347–60. Retrieved from pages 4–5 of *http://bit.ly/1wkajgO*.

Affordance

If you've done much design work, you've probably encountered talk of *affordances*. The concept was invented by J.J. Gibson, and codeveloped by his wife, Eleanor. Over time, affordance became an important principle for the Gibsons' theoretical system, tying together many elements of their theories.

Gibson explains his coining of the term in his final, major work, *The Ecological Approach to Visual Perception*:

> The affordances of the environment are what it offers the animal, what it provides or furnishes, either for good or ill. The verb to afford is found in the dictionary, but the noun affordance is not. I have made it up. I mean by it something that refers to both the environment and the animal in a way that no existing term does. It implies the complementarity of the animal and the environment.[*]

More succinctly: Affordances are properties of environmental structures that provide opportunities for action to complementary organisms.[†]

When ambient energy—light, sound, and so on—interacts with structures, it produces perceivable information about the intrinsic properties of those structures. The "complementary" part is key: it refers to the way organisms' physical abilities are complementary to the particular affordances in the environment. Hands can grasp branches, spider legs can traverse webs, or an animal's eyes (and the rest of its visual system) can couple with the structure of light reflected from surfaces and objects. Affordances exist on their own in the environment, but they are partly defined by their relationship with a particular species' physical capabilities. These environmental and bodily structures fit together because the contours of the latter evolved within the shaping mold of the former.

---

[*] Gibson, J. J. *The Ecological Approach to Visual Perception*. Boston: Houghton Mifflin, 1979:127.

[†] This is a slight paraphrase from Golonka, Sabrina. "A Gibsonian analysis of linguistic information." Posted in Notes from *Two Scientific Psychologists* June 24, 2014. *http://bit.ly/1rYwsgm*.

And, of course, action is required for this information pickup. In nature, a tree branch has structural properties that we detect through the way light and other energy interact with the substance and texture of the branch. We are always in motion and perceiving the branch from multiple angles. Even if we're standing still, our bodies are breathing, our eyes shifting, and able to detect the way shadows and light shift in our view. This is an unconscious, brain-body-environment dynamic that results in our bodies' detection of affording properties: whether a branch is a good size to fit the hand, and whether it's top-heavy or just right for use as a cane or club.

Perception evolved in a natural world full of affordances, but our built environment also has these environmental properties. Stairs, such as those shown in Figure 4-9, are made of surfaces and materials that have affordances when arranged into steps. Those affordances, when interacting with energy such as light and vibration, uniquely structure that energy to create information that our bodies detect.

Our bodies require no explanation of how stairs work, because the information our bodies need is intrinsic in the structure of the stairs. Just as a hand pressed in clay shapes the clay into structure identical to the hand, affordance shapes energy in ways that accurately convey information about the affordance. Organisms rely on this uniquely structured energy to "pick up" information relevant to what the organism can do.

FIGURE 4-9
Stairs at City Lights Bookstore in San Francisco (photo by author)

For a person who never encountered stairs before, there might be some question as to why climbing up their incline would be desirable, but the perceiver's body would pick up the fact that it could use them to go upward either way. Humans evolved among surfaces that varied in height, so our bodies have properties that are complementary with the affordances of such surface arrangements.

For most of us, this is a counterintuitive idea, because we're so used to thinking in terms of brain-first cognition. In addition, some of the specifics of exactly what affordance is and how Gibson meant it are still being worked out among academics. The principle of affordance was always a sort of work in progress for Gibson, and actually emerged later in his work than some of his other concepts.[*] He developed it as an answer to Gestalt psychology theories about how we seem to perceive the *meaning* of something as readily as we perceive its physical properties; rather than splitting these two kinds of meaning apart, he wanted to unify the dualism into one thing: affordance.[†]

We won't be exploring all the various shades of theory involved with affordance scholarship. But, because there is so much talk of affordances in design circles, I think it's valuable to establish some basic assumptions we will be working from, based on Gibson's own work.

Affordance is a revolutionary idea

Gibson claimed in 1979 that affordance is "a radical departure from existing theories of value and meaning."[‡] And in some ways, it is still just as radical. As an empiricist, Gibson was interested in routing around the cultural orthodoxies and interpretive ideas we layer onto our surroundings; he wanted to start with raw facts about how nature works. If we take Gibson's theory of affordances seriously on its own terms, we have to take seriously the *whole* of his ecological system, not pick and choose parts of it to bolt onto mainstream, brain-first theory.[§]

Affordances are value-neutral

In design circles, there is sometimes mention of *anti-affordances*. But in Gibson's framework there's no need for that idea. Affordances offer the animal opportunities for action, in his words, "for good or ill." He

---

[*] Jones, K. "What Is An Affordance?" *Ecological Psychology* 2003;15(2):107–14.

[†] Gibson, J. J. *The Ecological Approach to Visual Perception.* Boston: Houghton Mifflin, 1979:138–9.

[‡] ———. *The Ecological Approach to Visual Perception.* Boston: Houghton Mifflin, 1979:140.

[§] Dotov, Dobromir G, Lin Nie, Matthieu M de Wit. "Understanding affordances: history and contemporary development of Gibson's central concept." *Avant* 2012;3(2).

writes of affordances having "positive" or "negative" effects, explaining that some affordances are inconvenient or even dangerous for a given agent, but they are still affordances.[*] An affordance isn't always good from the perspective of a particular organism. Water affords drowning for a terrestrial mammal, but it affords movement and respiration for a fish.[†] Fire affords comforting heat, light, and the ability to cook food, but it also affords injury by burning, or destruction of property. Affordance is about the structural and chemical properties that involve relationships between elements in the environment, some of which happen to be human beings. Separating what a structure affords from the effect on the perceiver's self-interests helps us to remember that not all situations are the same from one perceiver to the next.

Perception of affordance information comes first; our ideas about it come later

Gibson argued that when we perceive something, we are not constructing the perception in our brains based on preexisting abstract ideas. He states, "You do not have to classify and label things in order to perceive what they afford." When I pick up a fork to eat food, my brain isn't first considering the fork's form and matching it to a category of eating utensils and then telling my arm it's OK to use the fork. The fork affords the stabbing of bites of food and bringing them to my mouth; my body extends its abilities by using the fork as a multipointed extension of my arm. That is, my body appropriates the fork based on its structure, not its category. The facts that it is a *dinner* fork and part of a set of *flatware* are based on categories that emerge later, from personal experience and social convention.

Affordances exist in the environment whether they are perceived or not

One contemporary theoretical stance argues that we do not perceive real things in the world, but only our brain's ideas and representations of them. Gibson strongly disagreed, insisting that we couldn't perceive anything unless there were a real, physical, and measurable relationship between the things in the world and our bodies. He allowed room

---

[*] Gibson, J. J. *The Ecological Approach to Visual Perception*. Boston: Houghton Mifflin, 1979:137.

[†] ———. *The Ecological Approach to Visual Perception*. Boston: Houghton Mifflin, 1979: 21.

for a sort of "life of the mind" that might, in a sense, slosh about atop these real foundations, but it exists only because it was able to emerge from physical coupling between creature and world.

The properties that give something affordance exist whether they are perceived in the moment or not; they are latent possibilities for action. Affordance is required for perception; but an affordance doesn't have to be perceived to exist. I might not be able to see the stairs around the corner in a building, but that doesn't mean the stairs' ability to support climbing doesn't exist. This idea complicates the commonly taught concept that a mental model drives behavior. Affordance means the information we need for action does not have to be "mental" and is actually in the structures of the environment. I perceive and use the stairs not because I have a mental model of them; no model is needed because all the information necessary is intrinsic to the shape and substance of the stairs. Prior learned experience might influence my usage in some way, but that's in addition to perception, not perception itself.

Affordances are there, whether they are perceived *accurately* or not

A Venus flytrap exists because it can get nutrition. And it gets nutrition because it "tricks" its prey into thinking it is a source of food for the prey, rather than the other way around. For a fly, the affordance of the flytrap is being caught, dissolved, and absorbed by a plant. What the fly perceives, until it is often too late, is "food." Likewise, we might perceive ground where there is actually quicksand, or a tree branch that is actually a snake. Perception is of the information created by the affordance, not the affordance itself. This is an important distinction that has often been misunderstood in design practice, leading to convoluted discussions of "perceived" versus "actual" affordances. The affordance is a property of the object, not the perception of it.

Affording information is always in a context of other information

No single affordance exists by itself; it's always nested within a broader context of other affording structures. For example, even if we claim to "add an affordance" by attaching a handle to a hammer head, the hammer is useful only insofar as it can bang on things that need to be banged upon. Stairs afford climbing, but they're always part of some surrounding environment that affords other actions, such as floors and landings, walls, handrails, and whatever is in the rooms the stairs connect. In digital devices, the physical buttons and switches mean nothing on their own, physically, other than "pushable" or "flippable"— what they actually affect when invoked is perceived only contextually.

Affordances are learned

Human infants are not born understanding how to use stairs. Even if we allow that perception couples with the information of the stairs' surfaces to detect they are solid, flat, and go upward, we still have to learn how and why to use them with any degree of facility. Infants and toddlers not only inspect the stairs themselves, but also were likely carried up them by caregivers and saw others walking or running up and down them long before trying out the stairs for themselves. Learning how to use the environment happens in a densely textured context of social and physical experience. This is true of everything we take for granted in our environment, down to the simplest shapes and surfaces. We learned how to use it all, whether we remember learning it or not. In digital design, there is talk of *natural interfaces* and *intuitive designs*. What those phrases are really getting at is whether an interface or environment has information for action that has already been learned by its users. When designing objects and places for humans, we generally should assume that no affordance is natural. We should instead ask: is this structure's affordance more or less conventional or learnable—keeping in mind that "learnable" is often dependent upon how the affordance builds on established convention.

Directly Perceived versus Indirectly Meaningful

The Gibsons continued to expand their theories into how affordances function underneath complex cultural structures, such as language, cinema, and whole social systems. Other scholars have since continued to apply affordance theory to understanding all sorts of information. Likewise, for designers of digital interfaces, affordance has become a tool for asking questions about what an interface offers the user for taking action. Is an on-screen item a button or link? Is it movable? Or is it just decoration or background? Is a touch target too small to engage? Can a user discover a feature, or is it hidden? The way affordance is discussed in these questions tends to be inexact and muddled. That's partly because, even among design theorists and practitioners, affordance has a long and muddled history. There are good reasons for the confusion, and they have to do with the differences between how we perceive physical things versus how we interpret the meaning of language or simulated objects.

The scene from *Rosemary's Baby* serves as an apt example of this simulated-object issue. In the scene depicted in Figure 4-7, moviegoers can't see Minnie's mouth moving behind the door frame, even if they shift to the right in their seats, because the information on the screen only simulates what it portrays. There is no real door frame or bedroom that a viewer can perceive more richly via bodily movement. If there were, the door and rooms would have affordances that create directly specifying information for bodies to pick up, informing the body that moving further right will continue revealing more of Minnie's actions. Of course, some audience members tried this, but calibrated by stopping as soon as their perception picked up that nothing was changing. Then, there were undoubtedly nervous titters in the crowd—how silly that we tried to see more! As we will see later, we tend to begin to interact with information this way, based on what our bodies assume it will give us, even if that information is tricking us or simulating something else, as in digital interfaces.

Perception might be momentarily fooled by the movie, but the only affordance actually at work is what is produced by a projector, film, and the reflective surface of the screen. The projector, film, and screen are quite real and afford the viewing of the projected light, but that's where affordance stops. The way the audience interprets the meaning of the shapes, colors, and shadows simulated by that reflected light is a different sort of experience than being in an actual room and looking through an actual door.

In his ecological framework, Gibson refers to any surface on which we show communicative information as a "display." This includes paintings, sketches, photographs, scrolls, clay tablets, projected images, and even sculptures. To Gibson, a display is "a surface that has been shaped or processed so as to exhibit information for more than just the surface itself."* Like a smartphone screen, a surface with writing on it has no intrinsic meaning outside of its surface's physical information; but we aren't interested in the surface so much as what we interpret from the

---

* ———. *The Ecological Approach to Visual Perception.* Boston: Houghton Mifflin, 1979:42.

writing. Gibson refers to the knowledge one can gain from these information artifacts as *mediated* or *indirect*—that is, compared to direct physical information pickup, these provide information *via a medium*.

Depending on where you read about affordances, you might see "affordance" used to explain this sort of mediated, indirectly meaningful information. However, for the sake of clarity, *I will be specifying "affordance" as that which creates information about itself*, and I will not be using the term for information that is about something beyond the affordance. Images, words, digital interfaces—these things all provide information, but the ultimately relevant meaning we take away from them is not intrinsic. It is interpreted, based on convention or abstraction. This is a complex point to grasp, but don't worry if it isn't clear just yet. We will be contemplating it together even more in many chapters to come.

This approach is roughly similar to that found in the more recent work of Don Norman, who is most responsible for introducing the theory of affordance to the design profession. Norman updates his take on affordance in the revised, updated edition of his landmark book, *The Design of Everyday Things* (Basic Books). Generally, Norman cautions that we should distinguish between affordances, such as the form of a door handle that we recognize as fitting our hand and suited for pulling or pushing, and *signifiers*, such as the "Push" or "Pull" signs that often adorn such doors.* We will look at signifiers and how they intersect with affordance in Part III.

This distinction is also recommended in recent work by ecological psychologist Sabrina Golonka, whose research focuses on the way language works to create information we find meaningful, "without straining or redefining original notions of affordances or direct-perception." For affordance to be a useful concept, we need to tighten down what it means and put a solid boundary around it.[†]

---

* Norman does, however, explain that he is "appropriating" Gibson's concept and using it in a different way than Gibson intended. (Norman, 2013:14). My focus on affordance here has attempted to bring more Gibson into our understanding of the theory.

† Golonka, Sabrina. "A Gibsonian analysis of linguistic information." Posted in *Notes from Two Scientific Psychologists* June 24, 2014 (*http://bit.ly/1rYwsgm*).

That doesn't mean we are done with affordance after this part of the book. Affordance is a critical factor in how we understand other sorts of information. Just as a complex brain wouldn't exist without a body, mediated information wouldn't exist without direct perception to build upon. No matter how lofty and abstract our thoughts are or how complex our systems might be, all of it is rooted, finally, to the human body's mutual relationship with the physical environment.

As designers of digitally infused parts of our environment, we have to continually work to keep this bodily foundation in mind. That's because the dynamic by which we understand the context of a scene in a movie—or a link on a web page—borrows from the dynamic that makes it possible for us to use the stairs in a building or pick a blackberry in a briar patch. Our perception is, in a sense, hungry for affordance and tries to find it wherever it can, even from indirectly meaningful information. That is, what matters to the first-person perspective of a user is the blended spectrum of information the user perceives, whether it is direct or indirect. It's in the teasing apart of these sorts of information where the challenge of context for design truly lies.

Soft Assembly

Affordance gives us one kind of information: what I'm calling physical information. But, what we experience and use for perception is the information, not the affordance that created it. Cognition grabs information and acts on it, without being especially picky about technical distinctions of where the information originates.

Cognition recruits all sorts of mechanisms in the name of figuring out the world, from many disparate bodily and sensory functions. The way this works is called *soft assembly*. It's a process wherein many various factors of body-environment interaction aggregate on the fly, adding up to behaviors effective in the moment for the body.* Out of all that activity of mutual interplay between environment and perceiver, there emerges

---

* Barrett, Louise. *Beyond the Brain: How Body and Environment Shape Animal and Human Minds*. Princeton, NJ: Princeton University Press, 2011:172.

the singular behavior. Now that we can even embed sensors and reactive mechanisms into our own skin, this way of thinking about how those small parts assemble into a whole may be more relevant than ever.[*]

We're used to thinking of ourselves as separate from our environment, yet an ecological or embodied view offers that the boundary between the self and the environment is not absolute; it's porous and in flux. For example, when we pick up a fallen tree branch and use it as a tool—perhaps to knock fruit from the higher reaches of the tree—the tool becomes an extension of our bodies, perceived and wielded as we would wield a longer arm. Even when we drive a car, with practice, the car blends into our sense of how our bodies fit into the environment.[†]

This isn't so radical a notion if we don't think of the outer layer of the human body as an absolute boundary but as more of an inflection point. Thus, it's not a big leap to go from "counting with my fingers" to "counting with sticks." As author Louise Barrett explains, "When we take a step back and consider how a cognitive process operates as a whole, we often find that the barrier between what's inside the skin and what's outside is often purely arbitrary, and, once we realize this, it dissolves."[‡] The way we understand our context is deeply influenced by the environment around us, partly because cognition includes the environment itself.

In *Supersizing the Mind: Embodiment, Action, and Cognitive Extension* (Oxford University Press), Andy Clark argues that our bodies and brains move with great fluidity between various sorts of cognition. From moment to moment, our cognition uses various combinations of cognitive loops—subactive cognition, active-body cognition, and extended cognition, using the scaffolding of the environment around us. Clark explains that our minds "are promiscuously body-and-world

---

[*] Meinhold, Bridgette. "Bandaid-Like Stick-On Circuit Board Turns Your Body Into a Gadget." *Ecouterre* April 15, 2014 (*http://bit.ly/1nx6TYB*).

[†] Haggard, Patrick, Matthew R Longo. "You Are What You Touch: How Tool Use Changes the Brain's Representations of the Body." *Scientific American* September 7, 2010 (*http://bit.ly/1FrVPll*).

[‡] Barrett, Louise. *Beyond the Brain: How Body and Environment Shape Animal and Human Minds.* Princeton, NJ: Princeton University Press, 2011:199.

exploiting. They are forever testing and exploring the possibilities for incorporating new resources and structures deep into their embodied acting and problem-solving regimes."[*]

Clark also explains how an assembly principle is behind how cognition works as efficiently as it can, using "whatever mix of problem-solving resources will yield an acceptable result with minimal effort."[†] We might say that we use a combination of "loops of least effort."[‡] That's why audience members leaned to the right in a theater, even though there was no logical reason to do so. We act to perceive, based on the least effortful interpretation of the information provided, even though it sometimes leads us astray. That is, we can easily misinterpret our context, and act before our error is clear to us. Even though we might logically categorize the variety of resources the perceiver recruits for cognition, to the perceiver it is all a big mash-up of *information about the environment*. For designers, that means the burden is on the work of design to carefully parse how each element of an environment might influence user action, because the user will probably just act, without perceiving a difference.

"Satisficing"

Perhaps this loops-of-least-effort idea helps explain a behavior pattern first described by scientist-economist Herbert Simon, who called it *satisficing*. Satisficing is a concept that explains how we conserve energy by doing whatever is just enough to meet a threshold of acceptability. It's a portmanteau combining "satisfy" and "suffice." Its use has been expanded to explain other phenomena, from how people decide what to buy to the way a species changes in response to evolutionary pressures.[§]

---

[*] Clark, A. *Supersizing the Mind: Embodiment, Action, and Cognitive Extension* London: Oxford University Press, 2010:42.

[†] ———. *Supersizing the Mind: Embodiment, Action, and Cognitive Extension* London: Oxford University Press, 2012:568–569, Kindle locations.

[‡] "Loops of least effort" is not Clark's phrasing, but my own. This is an idea we'll return to later, when we see how users tend to rely on physical information before bothering with the extra effort required by most semantic information.

[§] Barrett, Louise. *Beyond the Brain: How Body and Environment Shape Animal and Human Minds*. Princeton, NJ: Princeton University Press, 2011:128, Kindle edition.

Satisficing is a valuable idea for design practice, because it reminds us that users *use* what we design. They don't typically ponder it, analyze it, or come to know all its marvelous secrets. They *act* in the world based on the most obvious information available and with as little concentration as possible. That's because cognition starts with, and depends upon, continual action and interaction with the environment. Users aren't motivated by first understanding the environment. They're too busy just getting things done, and in fact they tend to improvise as they go, often using the environment in different ways than intended by designers.*

Even the most careful users eventually "poke" the environment to see how it responds or where it will take them by clicking or tapping things, hovering with a mouse, waving a controller or phone around in the air, or entering words into a search field. Just the act of looking is a physical action that probes the environment for structural affordance information, picking up the minimum that seems to be needed to move and then appropriating the environment to their needs. We see this when we observe people using software: they'll often try things out just to see what happens, or they find workarounds that we never imagined they would use. It does no good to call them "bad users." These are people who behave the way people behave. This is one reason why lab-based testing can be a problem; test subjects can be primed to assume too much about the tested artifact, and they can overthink their interactions because they know they're being observed. Out in the world they are generally less conscious of their behaviors and improvised actions.

The embodied view flips the traditional role of the designer. We're used to thinking of design as creating an intricately engineered setting for the user, for which every act has been accounted. But the contextual meaning of the environment is never permanently established, because context is a function of the *active engagement* of the user. This means the primary aim of the designer is not to design ways for the artifact to be used but instead to *design the artifact to be clearly understood*,† so the user can recruit it into her full environmental experience in whatever way she needs.

---

* Dourish, Paul. *Where the Action Is: The Foundations of Embodied Interaction.* Cambridge, MA: MIT Press, 2005:170.

† ———. *Where the Action Is: The Foundations of Embodied Interaction.* Cambridge, MA: MIT Press, 2005:172.

Umwelts

We have a Boston terrier named Sigmund (Figure 4-10). He's a brownish-red color, unlike typical Bostons. When walking Sigmund, I notice that no matter how well he's staying by my side, on occasion he can't help going off-task. Sometimes, he stops in his tracks, as if the ground has reached up and grabbed him. And, in a sense, that's what is happening. Sigmund is perceiving something in his environment that is making him stop. It's not premeditated or calculated; it's a response to the environment not unlike walking into a glass wall. For him, it's something he perceives as "in the way" or even dangerous, like an angle of shadow along the ground that could be a hole or something closing in on him. It happens less as he gets older and learns more about the world around him. Stairs used to completely freak him out, but now he's a pro.

FIGURE 4-10
Sigmund

But often what affects Sigmund's behavior is invisible to me. Like many dogs, he's much more perceptive of sound and smell than hominids. In those dimensions, Sigmund's world is much richer than mine. If I bring him outside and we encounter even a mild breeze, he'll stop with his nose pointed upward and just smell the air the way I might watch a movie at IMAX. Certainly we make friends differently. At the dog park, I'm mostly paying attention to the visual aspects of faces around me, whereas Sigmund gets to know his kind from sniffing the other end.[*]

For Sigmund and me, much of our worlds overlap; we're both warm-blooded terrestrial mammals, after all. We're just responding to different sorts of information in addition to what we share. Sigmund might stop because of a scent I cannot smell, but I might stop in my tracks because I see a caution light or stop sign. Sigmund and I are walking in somewhat different worlds—each of us in our own *umwelt*.

Umwelt is an idea introduced by biologist Jakob Johann von Uexküll (1874–1944), who defined it as the world as perceived and acted upon by a given organism. Uexküll studied the sense organs and behaviors of various creatures such as insects, amoebae, and jellyfish, and developed theories on how these they experience their environments.[†]

As a result of this work, Uexküll argued that biological existence couldn't be understood only as molecular pieces and parts, but as organisms sensing the world as part of a system of signs. In other words, Uexküll pioneered the connection of biology with *semiotics*, creating a field now called *biosemiotics* (we will look more closely at signs, signification, and semiotics in Part III). His work also strongly influenced seminal ideas in phenomenology from the likes of Martin Heidegger and Maurice Merleau-Ponty.

If we stretch Uexküll's concept just a little, we can think of different people as being in their own umwelts, even though they are the same species. Our needs and experiences shape how we interpret the information about the structures around us.

For skateboarders, an empty swimming pool has special meaning for activities that don't register for nonriders; for jugglers, objects of a certain size and weight, such as oranges, can mean "great for juggling," whereas for the rest of us, they just look delicious.

---

[*] Interestingly, though, due to millennia of breeding, dogs depend on faces more than scent or body language for recognizing and relating to humans. Gill, Victoria. "Dogs recognize their owner's face" BBC Earth News October 22, 2010 (*http://bbc.in/1nx6Snh*).

[†] *http://en.wikipedia.org/wiki/Umwelt*

When you're looking for a parking place at the grocery store, you notice every nuance that might indicate if a space is empty. After you park, you could probably recall how many spaces you thought were empty but turned out to just have small cars or motorcycles parked in them. But, when you're leaving the store, you're no longer attending to that task with the same level of explicit concentration; you might notice no empty spaces at all. Instead, you're trying to locate the lot's exit, which itself can be an exercise in maddening frustration. The parking lot didn't change; the physical information is the same. But your perspective shifted enough that other information about different affordances mattered more than it did earlier.

In the airport scenario in Chapter 1, when I was conversing with my coworker about my schedule, my perception was different from his because the system for understanding the world that I was inhabiting (that is, my view of the calendar) was different from his, even though we are the same species, and even fit the same user demographics.

This idea of umwelt can also help us understand how digital systems, when given agency, are a sort of species that see the world in a particular way. Our bodies are part of their environment the way their presence is part of ours. New "smart" products like intelligent thermostats and self-driving cars—and even basic websites and apps—essentially use our bodies as interfaces between our needs and their actions. When we design the environments that contain such agents, it's valuable to ask: what umwelt are these agents living in, and how do we best translate between them and the umwelt of their human inhabitants?

[5]

Attention, Control, and Learning

Never memorize something that you can look up.
—ALBERT EINSTEIN

A Spectrum of Conscious Attention

CONTEXT IS A FUNCTION OF UNDERSTANDING THE ENVIRONMENT, which involves our consciousness. To what degree, however, are we really conscious of our environment, or even our consciousness? We like to think we're logical, rational beings that take action mainly out of higher-order thought. Yet, as is explored in Chapter 4, our bodies do a lot of the thinking for us. It turns out that the environment is also responsible for much of our decision-making, attention, and learning. Embodied cognition is part of a general trend in the past few decades in which new schools of thought are questioning long-held assumptions that go back at least as far as Rene Descartes' supposition that "I think, therefore I am."

Research has shown that much of our daily activity is driven by deep, preconscious impulses and primitive-brain emotions rather than logical, conscious analysis and decision-making. In *Descartes' Error: Emotion, Reason, and the Human Brain* (G.P. Putnam's Sons), neurologist Antonio Damasio shows how mind, body, reason, and emotion all work as a single system rather than separate entities. In fact, reason is an outgrowth of emotion; it is crippled without an emotional foundation to drive our decisions.[*]

In another major work on the subject, *Thinking, Fast and Slow* (Farrar, Straus and Giroux), psychologist and economist Daniel Kahneman shows how behavior exhibits two sorts of consciousness at work, which

---

[*] Damasio, Antonio. *Descartes' Error: Emotion, Reason, and the Human Brain.* New York: Penguin Putnam, 1994.

he refers to as *System 1* and *System 2*. System 1 is subconscious and emotionally driven; it works fast and automatically; it's frequently engaged and relies on stereotype. System 2 is conscious, working slowly with purposeful effort; it is engaged less frequently (in comparison to System 1), employing logical calculation.* A related distinction from behavioral economics calls these systems "Automatic" and "Reflective."†

There are other models exploring these different levels of consciousness, some of them breaking it down into more layers. One is Don Norman's three-level model of "Visceral, Behavioral, and Reflective," in which the first two are unconscious, and reflective is conscious.‡ Another, from the information sciences, is Marcia Bates' quadrant model for information seeking, in which one axis is Active/Passive and another is Directed/Undirected.§ I mention these models because they all provide equally useful perspectives on how much user action occurs without the same level of awareness or conscious thought. Don Norman stresses that "design must take place at all levels."¶

Here, I offer a simple model influenced by these others. Instead of presenting stages or levels, this model shows how these states of mind are not cleanly separated but instead function on a spectrum of conscious attention between *Explicit* and *Tacit*, as depicted in Figure 5-1.

Explicit is related to terms from other models such as *conscious, deliberate, reflective,* and *System 2*. It's a state in which we are reflecting, self-aware, and consciously thinking through our actions or considering the meanings in our environment.

---

* Kahneman, Daniel. *Thinking, Fast and Slow*. New York: Farrar, Straus and Giroux, 2011.

† Thaler, Richard H., and Cass R. Sunstein. *Nudge: Improving Decisions about Health, Wealth, and Happiness*. New Haven, CT: Yale University Press, 2008.

‡ Norman, Don. *The Design of Everyday Things: Revised and Expanded Edition*. New York: Basic Books, 2013:56, Kindle edition.

§ Bates, Marcia J. "Toward an Integrated Model of Information Seeking and Searching." (Keynote Address, Fourth international Conference on Information Needs, Seeking and Use in Different Contexts. Lisbon, Portugal, September 11, 2002.) *New Review of Information Behaviour Research* 2002;3:1–15.

¶ Norman, Don. *The Design of Everyday Things: Revised and Expanded Edition*. New York: Basic Books, 2013:53, Kindle edition.

Tacit   Explicit

Unconscious, Intuitive,   Conscious, Deliberate,
Automatic, "System 1"   Reflective, "System 2"

FIGURE 5-1

Explicit and tacit, along a spectrum

Tacit is related to other terms, such as *unconscious, intuitive, automatic,* and *System 1.* It's a state in which we take action implicitly without reflection, driven by unconscious impulse, resonance with the environment, and by habit or convention.

Again, these are not binary categories. They are part of a gradual continuum; and we can't count on someone being in just one side or another for everything they're doing—although satisficing through the loop-of-least-resistance principle means that people do as much as possible as far toward "Tacit" in this spectrum as they can. We evolved to conserve energy, and making conscious, explicit decisions burns a lot of fuel. In fact, research has shown we can suffer mightily from something called decision fatigue.* Our ability to make decisions deteriorates after too much deliberation, causing us to make worse or more impulsive decisions from the more tacit level of consciousness, even when we should be explicitly concentrating.

This spectrum also aligns with the Explicit/Tacit model for knowledge first described by Hungarian chemist and philosopher Michael Polanyi in the mid-twentieth century. Tacit knowledge is that which is hard or impossible to communicate through explicit means, such as written instructions. In Polanyi's terms, "We know more than we can tell."† Riding a bicycle can't be learned from a book; the body has to do the physical work of learning. A softball pitcher can't explain how she pitches in explicit terms; the knowledge is essentially embodied in the act of pitching. However, even tasks that aren't so physical are often tacitly driven. Language itself is eventually used tacitly after we learn it to the point of fluency.

---

* Tierney, John. Do You Suffer From Decision Fatigue? *New York Times Magazine.* Retrieved August 23, 2011 (*http://en.wikipedia.org/wiki/New_York_Times_Magazine*).

† Polanyi, Michael. *The Tacit Dimension.* Chicago: University of Chicago Press, 1996:4.

Context depends heavily on what level of conscious attention is being demanded of the agent (perceiver, user, person, and so on). Anything that doesn't accurately fit one's unconscious, tacit habits and conventions must be explicitly attended to and learned, or else it runs the risk of tricking the perceiver into an unintended consequence.

When we drive on a road at night, we assume by habit and convention that the road has enough friction to keep us safely moving forward, unless we detect something about the road's surface that would indicate otherwise. That's why the phenomenon called "black ice" is so dangerous: it appears to be one sort of structure, when it actually is the opposite: a slick of frictionless surface that doesn't reflect enough light to alert us to its presence, showing us only the dark asphalt underneath. When we see a variation in the road, we attend to it, slow down, drive more carefully. When we don't, we act tacitly, unconsciously.

As designers of environments, one of the biggest risks we run is putting black ice in front of people; we inadvertently trick them into thinking the environment affords one thing when it actually affords something else, possibly to the user's detriment. Facebook's Beacon created a wormhole of information, leaking personal actions into actively published feeds. By being too subtle (and in some ways, just confusing) about how the system indicated its actions, Beacon created a sort of black ice that wasn't perceived for what it would actually do. The few users who carefully paid explicit attention to it noticed what it was doing; but we can't expect users to do the digital equivalent of checking every inch of road for ice.

Environmental Control

Consciousness is something we think of as internal to the individual, but the external environment plays a powerful role in consciousness and behavior, as well. This idea was formulated in 1926 by psychologist Kurt Lewin, who created what is now called *Lewin's Equation*: $B=f(P,E)$. It's a heuristic formula (rather than a mathematical equation) that states, "Behavior is a function of the person and his or her environment." It was controversial at the time it was published because it emphasized the environment of the person *in the moment of perception* over the learned experience of the past. It has since become a foundational idea in the field of social psychology.[*] Although this equation predates the work of ecological psychology theorist James J. Gibson by quite a few years, the spirit of it is in line with Gibson's idea of the coupled relationship between the perceiver and the environment.

To a significant degree, *context controls conduct*. We like to think we actively decide our every action; isn't that what free will is all about? Yet, it so happens that the environment's structural constraints determine much of our daily behavior.

This doesn't mean that we have no agency whatsoever; a perceiver detects information in the environment and then has the ability to decide what to do about it, controlling the perceiver's motion.[†] But, environmental information is central to the very origin of the whole perceptual system, and it still exerts its structural pressures on our every act. Moreover, given that our cognition is bound up in action, our environment's constraints can shape how we think, as well. Certainly, we modern humans are able to control many of our behaviors and teach our bodies new ways to respond to environmental information, but we're doing it on top of a core organism—from limbs to limbic system—that was formed by the environment in which we evolved.[‡]

Nature is not the only force exerting this pressure. Technologies also alter our perception of our bodies and their abilities. In experiments during which full-sized adults were put into an apparatus where they perceived themselves as having a virtual child's body, the adults started to perceive the structures around them as a child might, including whether they could fit through openings or climb onto surfaces. The new body and the environment strongly influenced the adults' choices and behaviors, and even their emotions.[§] In a comparison between a room suited for adults and one more suited to children, the study found that "you see the world bigger, have more childlike attributes,

---

[*] *http://en.wikipedia.org/wiki/Lewin's_equation*

[†] Gibson, J. J. *The Ecological Approach to Visual Perception.* Boston: Houghton Mifflin, 1979:17.

[‡] ———. *The Ecological Approach to Visual Perception.* Boston: Houghton Mifflin, 1979:130.

[§] Banakou, Domna, Raphaela Groten, and Mel Slater. "Psychological and Cognitive Sciences: Illusory ownership of a virtual child body causes overestimation of object sizes and implicit attitude changes." *Biological Sciences* PNAS 2013;110(31):12846-51; published ahead of print July 15, 2013, doi:10.1073/pnas.1306779110.

and prefer a [child-suited] environment rather than an adult one."* The adults' brains didn't change; they were just estimating the world using a different sort of body than they were used to.

Some might argue that these adaptations mean the brain's "schema" or internal representation of the body has plasticity, meaning that it can adapt and change.† But an embodied argument could be more straightforward: just as stairs have intrinsic information that doesn't require a mental model for understanding their use, the brain doesn't need a representation of the body and its capabilities. It already has an actual body present, so the body can act as its own image. Thus, if the brain is given information that tricks it into thinking it has a different body, it uses the new one instead. If the "trick" is convincing enough that, even when moving and calibrating, the body can continue to believe the trick, it continues behaving accordingly.

A version of this adaptation affects us in all areas of life. The environment's information is soaked up by our bodies and changes our habits. Even our devices and applications affect our behavior, because new or different powers give us a different sense of what we can and can't do. When a desktop application starts remembering what documents we had open after we quit, we start opening the app to get back to those documents rather than hunting down the files on our hard drives. Gmail gave users a big Archive button and a more powerful way to search emails, and many users stopped sweating over filing away messages in folders. When our phones began remembering phone numbers as names, we stopped memorizing everyone's digits.

Our brains might not need a map or schema because all the information is right there in the environment. Of course, *past* experience is part of this dynamic as well, and we will look at that as part of memory and learning; but we tend to underestimate how much *present* information can shape our understanding and action.

---

* Hogenboom, Melissa. "Adults become more like children in a virtual world," (*http://bbc.in/1uuRqFl*).

† Shokur, Solaiman, Joseph E O'Doherty, Jesse A Winans, Hannes Bleuler, Mikhail A Lebedev, and Miguel AL Nicolelis. "Expanding the primate body schema in sensorimotor cortex by virtual touches of an avatar." *Biological Sciences – Neuroscience* PNAS 2013; published ahead of print August 26, 2013, doi:10.1073/pnas.1308459110.

This "nudging" effect is explored in the field of behavioral economics, which is largely about how environment influences behavior in complex cultural systems. One study showed that in the United States, when citizens have to "opt in" to be an organ donor, only about one-third do so. But in Austria, 99 percent are donors, partly because their government enlists all citizens in the program by default, giving them instead the choice to opt out. In both situations, people have a choice, but because of satisficing, this nudge in one direction versus another makes a huge difference.* The environment makes the initial, hard decision for them. Behavioral economists call these sorts of policy structures *choice architecture*. But this isn't architecture of stone or steel; it's architecture of rules and communications made of language.

We see environmental control in action in software environments, too. In the airport scenario in Chapter 1, when I assumed that my coworkers could see my travel schedule in my work calendar, it was because the affording information available in the interface didn't specify that other people couldn't see what I could see. The structures evident in the calendar app exerted control over what I perceived to be "my calendar."

Likewise, when Facebook users were taken by surprise by Beacon publishing private information to public feeds, it was because the environment's information didn't adequately specify what was going on behind the scenes. Software can all too easily trick our perception into assuming our environment has a particular stable structure that isn't really all that stable or universal.

When watching people use gadgets and software, we need to remember that the way they're making use of their context is largely being determined by the structures available to them. Often, I have heard e-commerce clients complain that their customers are using the online shopping cart improperly, as a sort of wish-list, even when the site provides a separate wish-list function. Though when you look at the environment neutrally as a cluster of environmental structures, it becomes clear that Add to Cart is usually a much easier and quicker function to find and use than Add to Wish-List—the button tends to be more prominent, more available, and the "Cart" itself is always represented

---

* Thaler, Richard H., and Cass R. Sunstein. *Nudge: Improving Decisions about Health, Wealth, and Happiness.* New Haven, CT: Yale University Press, 2008:181.

somewhere (normally as a concrete metaphor with a picture of a cart) regardless of where the user is shopping. Why wouldn't the user make use of such an available, straightforward environmental structure over a less-available abstraction?

Part of what we will continue to explore is how these semantic constructs—whether the "choice architecture" of civic policy or the "information architecture" of software—aren't merely metaphorical architecture, but real structure that exerts nudges and constraints on our behavior, similar to anything in the natural or built environment.

Memory, and Learning the Environment

Through all of this talk of perceiving environments and how the environment exerts control over our cognition, one might wonder, "yeah but what about *memory*? Don't we remember things about the environment? And, isn't that a sort of image or representation we store in our brains? If we're supposed to be designing context, doesn't it need to account for what people remember from previous experience?"

In short, the answer is yes; memory is a crucial part of how people experience context. However, the complicating factor is, no, we can't count on stable, fixed memory of our users in what we design. Because this is such a big issue for context, we should spend some time looking at it more thoroughly.

WHAT IS MEMORY?

The idea of "memory" is so deeply ingrained in our language and culture that it's a bit of a shock to learn that there is no universally accepted science or model for how it works.* The way we retrieve knowledge from ourselves is still, in its details, largely unknown and the subject of much scientific research and debate.

The prevailing idea of memory is the storage metaphor. We assume memory must be a place in our heads—like a sort of database or file cabinet—where our brains store experiences and then pull them out

---

* Schacter, Daniel. *Searching for Memory the brain, the mind, and the past.* New York: Basic Books, 1996.

when needed. Until about 20 or so years ago, even cognitive science assumed this to be accurate but has since acknowledged that memory is much more complicated.[*]

Still, the storage metaphor is the way we conventionally talk about memory, even though it's terribly misleading. If our brains actually stored everything away like cans of soup in a cupboard, we should be much better at remembering than we actually are. Memory is untrustworthy, and seems to hang onto only certain things and not others, often with little apparent rhyme or reason. In one study from 2005, people in the United Kingdom were asked if they'd seen closed-circuit television footage of a well-publicized bus bombing. Eighty-four percent of the participants said they had—some of them providing elaborate details in response to questions—even though no such footage existed.[†] More recent research has shown that even those who we popularly think of as having "photographic memory" (actually called *highly superior autobiographical memory*) are nearly as unreliable as those considered to have normal memory.[‡]

Of course, we know that we can recall some sort of information from our past, using neurochemical activity that makes it possible for our nervous systems to retain a kind of information about our environment and past experience.[§] Yet, in spite of all that modern science has at its disposal, "human memory remains a stunning enigma."[¶]

The question is, what do we need to know about how memory works to design appropriately for it, especially when it comes to the prior experience people bring to context?

TYPES OF MEMORY

From traditional cognitive science, there are many different models for how memory works, most of them variations on similar themes. Figure 5-2 presents a diagram showing one version.

---

[*] ———. *Searching for Memory the brain, the mind, and the past.* New York: Basic Books, 1996:4.

[†] McCall, Becky. "Memory surprisingly unreliable, study shows." *Cosmos* magazine, September 15, 2008. *http://bit.ly/1uDR42i*

[‡] Hayasaki, Erika. "How Many of Your Memories Are Fake?" *The Atlantic* (*theatlantic.com*) November 18, 2013

[§] Wilson, Andrew. "What Does The Brain Do, Pt 2: The Fast Response System." Posted in Notes from Two Scientific Psychologists, August 2, 2011 (*http://bit.ly/1FsoTWF*).

[¶] Malone, Michael S. *The Guardian of All Things: The Epic Story of Human Memory.* New York: St. Martin's Press, 2013:14.

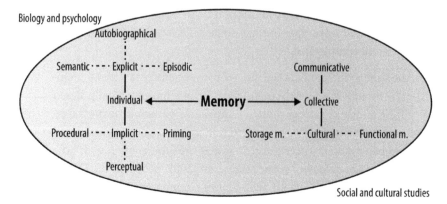

FIGURE 5-2

Various types of memory, related to the disciplines that tend to study them (source: Wikipedia)*

Such models have been built up over the years, based on the patterns researchers see in test-subjects' behaviors, and in the little we can learn from watching energy and blood moving in their brains. A model like this can mislead us into thinking there are distinct areas of the brain that perform each of these functions. In actuality, it's not so clear-cut.

AN EMBODIED PERSPECTIVE ON MEMORY

Embodied cognition theorists tend to question a lot of the received wisdom about memory. J.J. Gibson criticized the idea of memory as a "muddle"—a sort of "catchall of past experience" that lacks real evidence. He argues against the theory that what we experience in the present is mostly assembled from memories of the past: "the doctrine that all awareness is memory except that of the present moment of time must be abandoned."† Elsewhere, he points out that even the assumption that there is a clear distinction between present and past experience is somewhat of a fiction; perceiving and remembering are just two ways of looking at the same dynamic.‡

Louise Barrett's *Beyond the Brain: How Body and Environment Shape Animal and Human Minds* (Princeton University Press) shows how many seminal studies on memory—for example, Piaget's "A not B"

---

* Wikimedia Commons: *http://commons.wikimedia.org/wiki/File:Memory.gif*

† Gibson, J. J. *The Ecological Approach to Visual Perception.* Boston: Houghton Mifflin, 1979:202.

‡ ———. *The Ecological Approach to Visual Perception.* Boston: Houghton Mifflin, 1979:253.

test regarding infant memory—have since been undermined by newer research that accounts for an embodied dynamic.* Barrett explains that "memory is not a 'thing' that an animal either does or doesn't have inside its head, but a property of the whole animal-environment nexus; or, to put it another way, it is the means by which we can coordinate our behavior in ways that make it similar to our past experiences."† From this perspective, memory is really accumulated impressions from environmental perception. It's not something that begins in the mind, where some computer-like entity is recording sensory perception for later retrieval, or processing symbols and categories; rather it's built up from what our bodies-plus-brains retain from our ongoing activity in the perception-action loop.

Of course, if our perception didn't retain any information at all, we'd be poorly suited for survival. There is absolutely some form of retention and recall going on, and that can mean we have brain-centered experiences, thoughts, recollection.

Our friend J.J. Gibson allowed that we can have "internal loops more or less contained within the nervous system. There is no doubt but what the brain alone can generate is experience of a sort."‡ The difference between this allowance and the mainstream conception of memory is that embodied cognition *flips* the model, making the body the center of how memory works. The internal experience of remembering is more like a byproduct of aggregated, residual perception. Keep adding up these residual perceptions, and eventually you have an internal life of a "mind" where prior perception and thought (what scientists call "offline" experience) can be considered, inhabited, manipulated.§ But it doesn't begin in the mind—it begins in the body.

---

* Barrett, Louise. *Beyond the Brain: How Body and Environment Shape Animal and Human Minds*. Princeton, NJ: Princeton University Press, 2011:183, Kindle edition.

† Barrett, 2011:214, Kindle edition.

‡ Quoted by Barrett p. 238 [Gibson (1970), p. 426.] J. J. (1970). On the relation between hallucination and perception. *Leonardo* 3:425–427.

§ In cognitive studies, the terms "online" and "offline" refer to the difference between cognition about a situation that is at hand, in the present moment, versus cognition that's about a situation not at hand and remembered from some earlier experience. Climbing a tree to get at some apples in higher branches would involve cognition "online." Later, when away from the tree but planning how to get higher apples out of it the next time you're there requires "off-line" cognition.

LEARNING AND REMEMBERING VERSUS MEMORY

Memory is more verb than noun. It's more useful to think of memory as a dynamic that emerges from many different cognitive systems, one that is always in process. We're not accessing a memory so much as picking up perceptual experience and reconstructing what it means to us. Learning and memory are inseparable and are enmeshed with adaptive perception and action. As Eleanor Gibson succinctly put it, "We perceive to learn, as well as learn to perceive."[*]

In fact, there is no truly stable memory to be retrieved, because the act of remembering actually changes the content of what is remembered, in a process called *memory reconsolidation*.[†] Each time we recall a past experience, we alter it in some way, influenced by current circumstances; when we recall the experience again later, it's now the version that we reconstructed, interpreted yet again. It's not unusual to remember something that happened to you only to find it happened in a different way, or even to some other person whose story you've heard over the years.[‡]

LEARNING AND REMEMBERING ARE ENTANGLED WITH ENVIRONMENT

Some memories of our past have more to do with photographs we've seen and stories we've heard from relatives than some original representation stored in a brain-cabinet.[§] We naturally interpret environmental cues as part of our actual memory, to the point that we can actually be fooled into thinking things happened to us that never did; for example, in one study, subjects were convinced they had ridden in

---

[*] Baranauckas, Carla. "Eleanor Gibson, 92, a Pioneer in Perception Studies, Is Dead." *New York Times* January 4, 2003. Retrieved October 29, 2013.

[†] Alberini, Cristina M., ed. *Memory Reconsolidation*. Waltham, MA: Academic Press, 2013.

[‡] *http://www.radiolab.org/story/91569-memory-and-forgetting/*

[§] Lindsay, D. S., L. Hagen, J. D. Read, K. A. Wade, and M. Garry. "True photographs and false memories." *Psychological Science* 2004;15:149–154. doi:10.1111/j.0956-7976.2004.01503002.x.

a hot-air balloon because of manipulated photographs.* Our perception relies heavily on our current environment to inform what we think is true of past events.†

The structure of our physical environment is used by our brains to off-load some of the work of retaining prior experience, even when the content of memory isn't about our surroundings. One recent study tested subjects in both virtual and physical connected-room environments, and found "subjects forgot more after walking through a doorway compared to moving the same distance across a room, suggesting that the doorway or 'event boundary' impedes one's ability to retrieve thoughts or decisions made in a different room." Additionally, returning to the original room after passing through several other rooms didn't improve memory of the original information.‡ Memory doesn't just sit on a shelf ready to be accurately accessed again; it's always in flux, intermingled with our surroundings. Borrowing terms Don Norman often uses, "knowledge in the world" has a strong effect on whatever exists "in the head"—even what we think of as head-based knowledge.§

This makes sense, if we recall that our brains evolved to support our bodies, not the other way around. What else would memory have mainly evolved for other than recalling just enough about our surroundings to help us survive? Something like *factual accuracy* is an artificial idea we've invented in our culture. But organisms don't separate fact from interpretation; they just retain what is needed to get by, without clear lines between invention, environment, and remembering.

In digital interfaces, this principle is still at work. When using a search engine such as Google, the way the environment responds to our actions tacitly teaches us how to use that environment. When Google changes its results to reflect your search habits, learning from how

---

* Wade, K. A., M. Garry, J. D. Read, and D. S. Lindsay. "A picture is worth a thousand lies: Using false photographs to create false childhood memories." *Psychonomic Bulletin & Review* 2002;9:597–603. doi:10.3758/BF03196318.

† Gibson argues that "Information does not have to be stored in memory because it is always available" for pickup. Gibson, 1979:250.

‡ Guibert, Susan. "Walking through doorways causes forgetting, new research shows." *Notre Dame News* November 16, 2011 (*http://ntrda.me/1FsoXFX*).

§ I should point out that Norman is not an embodied cognition theorist; I am (I think, accurately) appropriating some of his more embodiment-compatible ideas.

you search for information, it's also simultaneously *teaching you* how to search Google, providing auto-suggested queries and prioritized results that create a sort of environmental feedback loop.*

ENVIRONMENT, AND EXPLICIT VERSUS IMPLICIT MEMORY

Sometimes we consciously, purposefully work at remembering information and experiences. One might memorize a poem or tell oneself to remember to take out the trash tonight. One might also try hard to recall a name of a friend or where they were on New Year's Eve two years ago. This intentional act of consciously working to remember something is *explicit memory*. It can be something we worked to remember on purpose, or something we've simply retained without much effort but that we're trying to pull up from the foggy depths of our minds and reconstruct in an explicit way.

Implicit (or in our model, "tacit") *memory* is essentially the opposite: it's the stuff we don't have to think about intentionally. Recalling when a parent helped us learn how to ride a bike would be explicit memory. But implicit memory (specifically, *procedural* memory) would be how our bodies just know how to ride a bike from previous experience.

What is important for context is that both of these sorts of memory depend on environmental interaction. Most of what we remember in our environment is learned tacitly, through repeated exposure to patterns of affordance, through action. The procedural "muscle memory" we employ when riding a bike exists only because we made our bodies ride bikes enough in the past that the ability to calibrate our body position was ingrained in us through repeated, physical activity.

Other tacit learning can happen almost immediately if the experience causes a high spike in our fear or other emotional response. (This is a property involving the brain's amygdala flooding the nervous system with hormones that mark the experience with sense-impressions of what the environment was like during the trauma.)† But, this is a highly unreliable memory resource when it comes to specific facts; for

---

* Osberg, Molly. "Hug it out: can art and tech ever be friends?" *The Verge* (theverge.com) May 8, 2014.

† McGaugh, J. "Involvement of the amygdala in memory storage: interaction with other brain systems." *Proceedings of the National Academy of Sciences* 1996. Available at http://www.pnas.org/content/93/24/13508.short.

evolution, it has to be only accurate enough to keep us from traipsing accidentally into another lions' den. It did not evolve to factually verify if another place has lions or not, or exactly what the lions looked like, or that the eucalyptus you smelled nearby during your early lion encounter isn't actually as dangerous as the lions themselves. These effects are blunt instruments that can actually have negative consequences; for example, they can cause us to react inappropriately to safe situations, which we can see manifest in post-traumatic stress disorders.

Explicit learning can result in accurately remembering a great deal of information, but it's a special case, and it always involves purposefully re-exposing ourselves to information until it "sticks," or using some environmentally tied mnemonic technique.

One example has to do with learning to type on a keyboard: how we have to explicitly think about where they keys are until we've done enough typing that we can do it by touch. A common argument goes that the knowledge of the keyboard has gone from our bodies into our heads. Saying "into our heads" might lead us to think there's a sort of representational map of the keyboard in the typist's brain, but it turns out that's not the case. In a recent study, it was found that skilled touch typists averaging 72 words per minute were unable to map more than an average of about 15 keys when asked to do so outside of the act of typing. If asked to type something, they can hit the right keys just fine, but it's their fingers that seem to "know" where to go. There's no explicit, readily retrieved representation in brain-storage. The body satisficed; it went straight to an embodied facility that translates words into "fingers making letters appear" without going to the trouble of constructing a conceptual map.

Likewise, when we get a little stuck trying to recall a phone number, we tend to do one of two things: we try to say it aloud to ourselves in sequence, as if recalling what it feels like in our mouths and ears, or we reach for phone to type it out, because our bodies seem to know which buttons to press (and in what order) better than our brains can remember the symbols alone.

Otherwise, we jot the number down someplace (on a napkin, a note, or the back of a hand). We use the environment to help us remember things all the time, even when we don't realize it. Of course, we're now a lot worse at remembering phone numbers because we seldom have to dial them with our fingers—we just tap a name in our phone's contact list. As always, cognition satisfices.

What Does All This Mean for Design?

Regardless of the differences in one theoretical perspective or another, the overall lesson is clear: we can't rely on an ability to invoke specific sorts of memory in users. We can't assume they will accurately retain anything from prior experience, and we especially can't expect them to explicitly memorize how to use a product. Even for the rare cases in which specialists are required to learn a complex system through repeated use, the system should do as much work as possible toward making its affordances clear without requiring memory. Perception satisfices, so it tacitly makes use of the environment around it *directly* as much as possible.

In Don Norman's conceptual model of "knowledge in the head" versus "knowledge in the world," he explains that we should always try to "provide meaningful structures...make memory unnecessary: put the required information in the world."* The environment is such a major player in how our brains function, "everything works just fine unless the environment changes so that the combined knowledge (between head and world) is no longer sufficient: this can lead to havoc."† If you've ever visited a country in which they drive on the opposite side of the road, or you've moved the furniture around in your bedroom only to bruise yourself on a chair in the dark until you get used to the new arrangement, you know about this havoc firsthand.

Of course, at a certain point of scale or complexity, it's impossible to put all the knowledge in the world so that it can all be perceived at once. This is why we historically rely on extensive menus in software; users can uncover for themselves what actions are available without the screen being overwhelmed with buttons. It's why an online retailer has to provide summary categories and search functions—you can't see the

---

* Norman, Don. *The Design of Everyday Things: Revised and Expanded Edition*. New York: Basic Books, 2013:100, Kindle edition.

† ———. *The Design of Everyday Things: Revised and Expanded Edition*. New York: Basic Books, 2013:79, Kindle edition.

entire inventory in one glance. And when software actions are happening beyond our perception, we simply don't know about them unless the environment presents us with detectable information.

This is why one of the most complex things to design in a device such as a smartphone is the notifications capability. In my iPhone's current iOS version, there are at least four different ways I can set various apps to alert me of events happening beyond my immediate view. We've created a world for ourselves in which we can't perceive much (or most) of what matters to us without these notification mechanisms.

As Jakob Nielsen explains, "Learning is hard work, and users don't want to do it. That's why they learn as little as possible about your design and then stay at a low level of expertise for years. The learning curve flattens quickly and barely moves thereafter."* With so much to learn, and such a low motivation and ability to learn it all, we have to rely more heavily on the conventions and implicit, structural affordances that users carry over from the physical world.

In the physical world, most important changes in the environment have perceivable signs that we learn to interpret: storm clouds or cold winds mean bad weather approaching; blooming flowers and longer days mean a warm season is coming; and if my neighbors can see what I'm doing in my house, it should be obvious to me that a window is uncovered or a wall has gone missing.

Software can disrupt these assumptions we've learned about how our environment works. When Beacon was launched, many users of Facebook had already become used to the structures of the platform as well as the structures implicit in how their browsers worked. If they were on a website in one browser window, it didn't share places and objects with a different website in a separate browser window. The only constant was the browser itself, plus whatever plug-ins and things were part of its function. Beacon broke this environmental convention, disrupting expectations from past experience by creating a conduit that automatically gleaned information from another context and publishing it without explicit approval from the user.

---

* Nielsen, Jakob "User Expertise Stagnates at Low Levels" September 28, 2013 (http://www.nngroup.com/articles/stagnating-expertise/).

So, what makes an environment easier to learn often has to do with whether or not its affording structures meet the expectations of its inhabitants, or if they do a good enough job at signaling disruptions of convention and teaching new expectations. Next, we'll look at the building blocks of environments and how we perceive them, which will give us some ideas about how to create understandable environments with language and software.

The PORT Elevator System

At a conference I attended in 2012, I and the other attendees encountered a new elevator system that the conference hotel had installed only a few months earlier.[*] Instead of calling for service by using a conventional set of Up and Down buttons, the PORT elevator system requires a guest to use a digital touch-screen to select a destination floor, as shown in Figure 5-3. The screen then displays which elevator the guest should use to get to that floor, requiring the guest to find that elevator and wait for it to arrive. Upon entering the elevator, the guest will find there are no floor-selection buttons inside. The elevator already knows the floors at which it should stop.

Technically, this is a brilliantly engineered system that corrects the inefficiencies of conventional elevator usage by calculating the logistics of which elevator will get each guest to his destination most quickly.

However, when attendees (including myself) encountered this system, there was widespread confusion and annoyance. Why?

People grow up learning how to use elevators in a particular way. You push a button to go up or down, watch for the first elevator that's going in your direction to open its doors, get in, and then select your floor. These are rehearsed, bodily patterns of use that become ingrained in our behavior. That is, we off-load the "thinking" about elevator usage to bodily, passively enacted habit. Unfortunately, these ingrained behaviors severely break the intended scenario for using the PORT elevators.

---

[*] "Schindler Installs PORT at Hyatt Regency New Orleans" schindler.com January 26, 2012 (*http://bit.ly/1wg5F4s*).

FIGURE 5-3

Part of an instruction booklet from the Schindler elevator company, explaining how to use its new PORT elevator system

- The touch-screen design assumes the guests will keep watching the screen to see which elevator they should use. But people are used to looking away immediately after pressing the up or down button, so they tend to look away in this case too—meaning they might never see which elevator they are assigned.

- People habitually step into whichever elevator opens first. In using the PORT system, however, chances are that the elevator that opens first or closest to you is actually not the elevator for your selected destination.

- After entering the elevator, guests realize there's no button panel and they have no control over floor choice. Even for people who follow the directions, discovering a lack of a button panel can be a surreal, upsetting surprise.

Throughout the event, we noticed hotel staff hovering around the elevators to explain them to guests—essentially acting as real-time translators between the unfamiliar system and people's learned expectations.

The PORT system is an apt example of how an excellent engineering solution can go very wrong when not taking into account how people really behave in an environment. Remember the perception-action loop: just as people behave in any environment, they will tend to act first and think later. Requiring them to think before acting in this context is a recipe for confusion.

This is another example of how environment controls action. It doesn't mean that this new system is a failure; it just tricked its users by presenting affording information that they were used to perceiving and acting upon without thought, and then pulled the rug out from under those assumptions. When people learn it as a new convention, it will result in more efficient and pleasant elevator experiences for everyone. There just needs to be an improved set of environmental structures provided to help "nudge" people toward stopping and thinking explicitly as they learn the new system, before using it improperly.*

---

* Much to my delight, many months after first drafting this passage, I learned that Donald Norman's new edition of *The Design of Everyday Things* also explores this elevator system (pp. 146–149). Norman comes to similar conclusions (though, as an engineer, he seems to find more to like about the system than I did as an annoyed conference attendee).

[6]

The Elements of the Environment

The earth is not a building but a body.
—**WALLACE STEVENS**

Invariants

WE'VE LOOKED AT HOW our basic functions of perception and cognition work in an environment and how affordances form that environment. Given that context is largely about how one thing relates to another thing, let's now look at how we perceive elements and their relationships.

Luckily, our friend James J. Gibson, the ecological psychology theorist, created an elaborate yet straightforward system describing the structures that make environments. We won't be exploring all its details, but there are some major portions we can borrow for making a sort of building-block kit for purposes of design. These elements start with the most basic: what Gibson calls *invariants*.

Invariants are persistently stable properties of the environment; they persist as unchanging, in the midst of change.[*] These are not *permanent* properties in the scientific sense of permanence.[†] A hill might erode; a fallen tree might rot; the sun will eventually burn out, but they still involve invariants because they have properties that have been "strikingly constant throughout the whole evolution of animal life."[‡] Invariance is, then, about the way the animal perceives the environment, not an objective measurement of permanent structure.

---

[*] Gibson, J. J. *The Senses Considered as Perceptual Systems.* Boston: Houghton Mifflin, 1966:201.

[†] ———. *The Ecological Approach to Visual Perception.* Boston: Houghton Mifflin, 1979:13.

[‡] ———. *The Ecological Approach to Visual Perception.* Boston: Houghton Mifflin, 1979:18–19.

The only reason we can do anything is because some parts of our environment are stable and persistent enough to afford our action. The laptop keyboard I'm typing on right now is solid, with little square keys that spring up and down in response to my fingers. The keys wouldn't be able to do this if the body of the laptop and the bed of the keyboard were made of, say, helium. Only because it's a solid surface with a particular kind of shape can this activity take place.

Likewise, when I get up from my writing spot and go to make a cup of coffee, I can get to the kitchen because the surface of my floor is made of wood, which is solid and supportive of my weight. That is, it's enough like the ground my species evolved on that I can walk on it, as well.

There are also walls around me, and they have openings that are windows and doors. The doorway between my current writing spot and the kitchen is large enough for me to walk through; I know this because I've walked through many other doors and have a good feel for which ones will afford passage and which ones won't. I've also grown up in a culture where conventional doorways afford walking through for someone of average size such as myself. I take them for granted as persistent structures in the built world, the way a squirrel takes for granted that trees will afford climbing.

Perception itself originates with our perceiving of invariants.[*] "The persisting surfaces of the environment are what provide the framework of reality."[†] We can intellectually know that an earthquake or a hurricane isn't actually changing "reality," but at an ecological level, these rare events disrupt our most deeply embodied knowledge of how reality should work.

Invariants exist along a wide scale of the environment, from the most basic components to large structures. The invariant properties of stone are such that a human can pick up a fist-sized rock and throw it at a bird's nest or use it to bash open a walnut. The same properties of stone make it so that a mountain serves as a landmark for generations

---

[*] ———. *The Ecological Approach to Visual Perception*. Boston: Houghton Mifflin, 1979:254.

[†] ———. *The Ecological Approach to Visual Perception*. Boston: Houghton Mifflin, 1979:100.

of people, not to mention a source of fresh water and a habitat for millions of creatures that evolved there. But, invariance is ultimately about individual perceiving agents and how structure persists in their environment.

Context is impossible to comprehend without invariants. We understand something only in relation to something else, and the "something else" has to be invariant enough to be "a thing" to begin with. (Or, as Richard Saul Wurman so often says, "You only understand something relative to something you already understand.")[*]

I know I am outside my house when I can see the outside of the structure and look up and notice that I am on uncovered ground, and the sky is above me. If these structures were not invariant, I'd have no idea where I was (not to mention they would no longer be structures).

Invariance is a simple idea that we don't think about much because it's so intrinsically a part of our world. It's why we can say something "is" or that we are "here." Our cognition evolved in a world in which invariance just comes along, automatically, with the places and objects we experience.

EXAMPLES OF INVARIANTS

There are dozens of invariants explored in Gibson's work, but here are just a few:

Earth and sky

> The earth "below" and the air "above." The ground is level, solid, affording support for walking, sitting, lying down. The air is the opposite of the ground, affording locomotion, allowing light and sound to penetrate, and giving room for living things to grow and breathe. In Gibsonian terms, this earth/sky pairing forms the most basic invariant human-scale structure, a shell within which all other structures are structured, comprehended, and acted upon. Humans didn't evolve in outer space, so like it or not, we have ingrained in us these structures of earth and sky, and what is up or down.

---

[*] Epstein, Nadine. "In Search of the God of Understanding." *Moment* (momentmag.com) September-October 2013.

Gravity

We tend to think of gravity as a mathematically expressed property of physics, but our bodies don't comprehend gravitation as a scientific concept. Long before Newton, our bodily sense of up and down was written into our DNA through natural selection. Our embodied experience of gravity isn't concerned with purely elastic elementary bodies interacting in space; the planet's actual environment is made mostly of surfaces that don't behave much at all like the mathematical ideals of Newtonian physics.[*]

The occluding edge of one's nose

Human vision is framed most of all by the edge of the human nose; "of all the occluding edges of the world, the edge of the nose sweeps across the surfaces behind it at the greatest rate whenever the observer moves or turns his head" providing an "absolute base line, the absolute zero of distance-from-here."[†] In English, we often turn to an embodied verbal expression to describe something as "right in front of my nose" as a way to mean it's as present and obvious as possible (even though we may not notice it). The edge of the nose is, to our vision, the purest instantiation of what "here" means. This reminds us of how our bodies are a crucial element of our environment. The perception-action loop depends on the "landscape" of the body as much as any other of the invariant features in the experienced world.

Other, more complex invariants Gibson describes run the gamut from "the unchanging relations among four angles in a rectangle" to "the penumbra of a shadow" and "margins between patches of luminance."[‡] These are as important as the aforementioned more basic invariants, because they set the foundation for how we know a table is within our reach or whether we can fit through a doorway. A more detailed inventory of Gibson's invariants is beyond our scope here, but they are central to the key challenges of much industrial and interaction design.

---

[*] Gibson, J. J. *The Ecological Approach to Visual Perception*. Boston: Houghton Mifflin, 1979:15.

[†] ———. *The Ecological Approach to Visual Perception*. Boston: Houghton Mifflin, 1979:117.

[‡] Goldstein, E. Bruce. "The Ecology of J. J. Gibson's Perception." *Leonardo* Cambridge, MA: The MIT Press, 1981;14(3):191–195. Stable URL: *http://www.jstor.org/stable/1574269*.

Invariants significantly affect how learnable an environment is. They are what contribute to what we tend to call "consistency." In the natural world, we come to depend on the patterns we learn about with respect to what different substances and objects do and don't do; we quickly pick up on the rules of cause-and-effect. It's crucial to reemphasize, though, that invariants are not necessarily permanent, "frozen" structures; they are invariant because they are experienced that way by the perceiver, in contrast to the changing parts of the environment: variants.[*]

VARIANTS

In contrast to invariants, *variants* are the environmental properties that tend to change in our perception. The shadows cast by a tree will change as the direction of sunlight changes through the day. The shape of water changes as wind interacts with it, or as it is poured into a differently shaped container. Although these changes might be predictable and follow some consistent patterns, we perceive them as changing in relation to the relatively invariant surfaces and objects around them. Elements all around us have variant properties that we don't count on for affording action. Imagine a tribe of humans that lived for generations on an island where most of the ground was actually quicksand that was impossible to perceive as such without stepping on it. One could be sure they would walk differently than the rest of us, testing each step as they went.

COMPOUND INVARIANTS

Invariants can be simple properties of simple structures, such as the hardness of a substance. But, there are also combinations—or *compound* invariants—that we experience as a singular "unit" of invariant properties.[†] A bicycle is a combination of invariants providing many affordances: pedals support feet, but they also move to pull a chain, and the chain turns a wheel; the seat supports my weight; the handlebars support my body leaning forward, but also afford turning the front wheel for steering. Yet, as soon as I've grown used to riding a bicycle, I don't approach the vehicle as a pedal-handlebar-seat-wheel-turning-etc.

---

* Gibson, J. J. *The Ecological Approach to Visual Perception*. Boston: Houghton Mifflin, 1979:87.

† ———. *The Ecological Approach to Visual Perception*. Boston: Houghton Mifflin, 1979:141.

object, but as an object that affords "riding a bicycle." The invariant affordances combine into a unit that I learn to perceive as a single invariant entity.

In the science literature, this idea of compound invariants is still being debated and fleshed out, but I think it's safe for us to think of it as a basis for much of what we make with technology. Most of what we design is more complex than a stone or stick; it combines invariants and variants in multiple ways. As we'll see, with language and software, invariants can be compounded to the point that they're not *directly* connected to physical properties at all; rather, they're part of a self-referential system distantly derived from our physical-information surroundings.

INVARIANTS ARE NOT ONLY ABOUT AFFORDANCE

Here's an important point to make regarding invariants and affordances: although affordance involves perception of invariant information, not all invariant information is about affordances. We are using "affordance" for physical information. Yet, we encounter all sorts of other invariant information that is meaningful to us without being directly perceived. A stop sign means "stop," but its affordances have only to do with how the object is visible or how it is sturdy enough to lean against while waiting to walk across the street. The meaning of "stop" is one of the most stable invariants in English (and red, octagonal stop signs have a conventional, invariantly informative presence in many non-English-speaking places, as well). But the most important meaning of the stop sign is not its physical affordances. Because digital environments depend on such continuities of meaning, this distinction between language-based invariants and physical invariants is central to the challenges of context in a digital era.

DIGITAL INVARIANTS

In digital interfaces and objects, we still have need of invariants because perception depends on them. However, this sort of information doesn't naturally lend itself to the stability we find in physical surfaces and objects. The properties of user interfaces need to be consistent for us to learn them well. We hunger for stable landmarks in the often-ambiguous maze of digital interfaces.

The Windows operating system's innovation of a Start button was, in part, a way to offer an invariant object that would always be available, no matter how lost users might become in the complexities of

Windows. Likewise, websites have retained the convention of a Home page, even in the age of Google, when many sites are mainly entered through other pages. It provides an invariant structure one can cling to in a blizzard of pages and links.

These examples exist partly because the rest of these environments tend to be so variant and fluid. Digital technology gives us the capability to break the rules, in a sense, creating variants where we expect invariants. There are huge benefits to this physically unbound freedom; we can handle scale and make connections that are impossible in the physical environment. Folders can contain more folders to near-infinite capacity; a desktop can multiply into many desktops. But there are equally substantial dangers and pitfalls.

For example, across platforms, actions can have significantly different consequences: in one mobile app, double-tapping a photo zooms in on it, whereas in another, the same gesture marks the photo as "liked," even if you find the photo horrible or offensive. Even within a single platform, the rules can radically change. In Facebook, it seems every few months the architecture of privacy morphs again, disrupting the invariants users learned about who could see what information and when. This is not unlike waking up one day to find the roof removed from one's house. If these invariants were created by physical affordances, they couldn't change so radically. We know software isn't physical. But because perception depends upon invariant structure, we see it and use it whenever it seems to be offered to us, even if a software code release can upset those invariants in a moment's time.

These differences and disruptions are not the sorts of behaviors we evolved to perceive with any accuracy. They are instead the black ice, or quicksand, of digital objects and places.

The Principle of Nesting

All these invariant components of the environment are perceived in relation to one another, and the principle by which we perceive these relationships is the *ecological principle of nesting*. Animals experience their environment as "nested," with subordinate and superordinate structures.

Nested invariants establish the persistent context within which motion and change happen, both fast and slow. As Gibson says somewhat poetically, "For terrestrial animals like us, the earth and the sky are a basic structure on which all lesser structures depend. We cannot change it. We all fit into the substructures of the environment in our various ways, for we were all, in fact, formed by them. We were created by the world we live in."[*] The way the world is nested forms a framework for how we understand it.

Within the earth and sky, at subordinate levels, there is more nesting: "canyons are nested within mountains; trees are nested within canyons; leaves are nested within trees. There are forms within forms both up and down the scale of size."[†] Nesting provides a framework for the agent to pick up information about the environment at different levels of scale, focusing from wide to narrow, huge to tiny.

Even without telescopes and microscopes, humans have a great deal of environmental information to pick up; the ability to learn an environment (and therefore, learning in general) might be largely due to the ability to break it down into loosely defined tiers and components, none of which exists discretely in a vacuum.[‡]

NESTING VERSUS HIERARCHY

Nesting is not the same as hierarchy (see Figure 6-1), because it is "not categorical but full of transitions and overlaps. Hence, for the terrestrial environment, there is no special proper unit in terms of which it can be analyzed once and for all."[§] Again, this is a property of how terrestrial creatures such as humans perceive the environment, not an artificially defined property like "meter" or "kilogram." It isn't about logically absolute schemas such as the periodic table of elements, or the mutually exclusive branching we see in strict hierarchies.

---

* ———. *The Ecological Approach to Visual Perception.* Boston: Houghton Mifflin, 1979:130.

† ———. *The Ecological Approach to Visual Perception.* Boston: Houghton Mifflin, 1979:9.

‡ Wagman, Jeffrey B., and David B. Miller. "Animal-Environment Systems: Energy and Matter Flows at the Ecological Scale." Wiley Periodicals, 2003 (*http://bit.ly/1vX9Zr*).

§ ———. The Ecological Approach to Visual Perception. Boston: Houghton Mifflin, 1979:9.

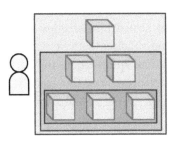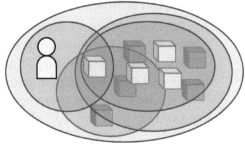

FIGURE 6-1

Hierarchies (left) are categorically defined, with in an objective parent-child tree structure, separate from the perceiver. Ecological "nesting" (right) has elements contained within others, but in perceiver-dependent fashion that can shift and overlap depending on the present perceptual needs of the individual.

A conventional hierarchy is about categorical definition that's true regardless of context, whereas our ecological experience of the environment shifts depending on circumstances. A geological definition of "cave" doesn't change with the weather. For an animal, however, a cave that provides excellent protection in dry weather might be useless during the rainy season, if its opening is angled to let water in: suddenly "inside" feels like "outside."

Likewise, the way we think of "here" and "there" can shift—which on the face of them seem like clear opposites. But, these designations are dependent on the nested context. You might be sitting at home, in a comfortable reading chair, from which you can see a bookcase on the far wall. You're trying to remember if you left a particular book at work and wonder if the book is *there* or if it is *here* at home—which could mean anywhere in the house. You look up to the bookcase and see it, and realize with relief that, yes, not only is it here at home but *here* in the room with you, not *there* in some other room. Still, when you decide you want to read the book, it's no longer *here* but *there* on the bookshelf, because now here and there are defined not by mere location but by the factor of human reach. From a geometrical point of view, nothing changed, but from an ecological point of view, many shifts in perceived structure happened in a matter of a few moments.

DIGITAL ENVIRONMENTS AND NESTING

Interfaces can graphically represent these nested relationships with boxes and panels, outlines and background shading, with one set of information contained by another, and so on. Information architectures (which depend in part on interfaces representing this containment) also present nested structures through categories and semantic relationships.

Yet, interfaces need ways to provide invariants while still allowing users to move through structures from various angles based on need; a user might shift between different nested perspectives in the course of only a few minutes.

For example, Figure 6-2 presents a scenario in which an office worker might need to gather information about a prior project, including its documentation, personnel, and manager involvement. The worker might begin with his focus mainly on finding a related document, from which he discovers the name of the document's author. He then uses the author to find who the team manager was, in order to find others who might have past knowledge of the project.

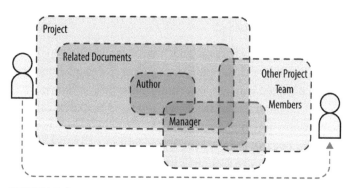

FIGURE 6-2

Information is nested from different perspectives for the same user, at different points in an activity

In this case, the user's information pickup organizes itself around documents and projects first, then finding people by name, and then finding people by organizational relationship. All these structures overlap in various ways: a document can be just a document or part of a project, and the project might be related to a larger ongoing enterprise program but also related to various teams in several departments, which themselves can shift in importance depending on a worker's cognitive activity from one task to the next.

In particular, for the work of information architecture, we have to remember that users might comprehend an information environment in a nested way, but that doesn't mean they naturally comprehend artificial, categorical hierarchies. Learning a new hierarchy of categories depends on explicit, conscious effort. But an information environment that works well at an ecological, embodied level might seem incoherent through the lens of logical hierarchy. When online retailers add holiday-specific categories to their global navigation menus, it upsets the logic of hierarchy, but it makes perfect sense to the many shoppers who are seasonally interested in holiday gifts.

Facebook users experienced disorientation, especially in its early years, as it expanded from being nested within a single university to multiple universities, and then to high schools, and finally opened up to everyone. Likewise, its internal structures (and its invisible reach into other contexts, such as with Beacon) are continually "innovated" to the point at which users struggle to grasp where they and their actions are nested in the shifting fun-house of illusory invariants.

Surface, Substance, Medium

When we perceive information in the environment, we're largely perceiving information about its *surfaces*, which are formed by "the interface between any two of these three states of matter—solid, liquid, and gas." Where air meets water is the surface of a pond. Where a river meets earth is a surface is a riverbed. Where air meets earth is a surface—the ground—which, for terrestrial animals, is "both literally and figuratively" the ground of perception and behavior.* The structure of the environment is, in essence, its "joinery" between surfaces and substances. These are the "seams" of our world. If it were "seamless," there would be no structure, and no perception.

---

* ———. *The Ecological Approach to Visual Perception.* Boston: Houghton Mifflin, 1979:16.

These surfaces are made of *substances* which are substantial enough that, when environmental energy (sound, light, and so on) interacts with them, the resulting information can be perceived. We didn't evolve to readily perceive invisible things or things that are too tiny or huge to apprehend, at least as far as physical information is concerned.

Medium refers to the substance through which a given animal moves. For a fish, it's water. For terrestrial creatures, it's air.[*] Another quality of a medium is that it physical information can be detected through it. Solids do not allow the full pickup of information because they impede ambient energy.[†] Sure, we can sometimes hear noise through a solid wall, but only because there is air on both sides of the wall that reverberates the sound. Fill our ears and the room around us with wall plaster, and we'll hear a great deal less.

DIGITAL EXAMPLES

In software, we see users trying to figure out what parts of a system they can move through (medium) versus parts that do not afford action (impeding substances/surfaces). An understandable interface or information architecture provides invariant indications of where a user can go and how. Perception evolved among actual substances and surfaces, made of atoms, so even in the insubstantial realm of language and bits, it still reaches for substantial information, hoping something will catch hold.

Objects

An *object* is a "substance partially or wholly surrounded by the medium." Objects have surfaces but with a topology that makes them perceivable as distinct from other surfaces.

Some objects are *attached* and others *detached*. An attached object is a "protuberance" that has enough of its own independent surface that it can be perceived to "constitute a unit."[‡] It's topologically closed up to the point at which it is attached to a surface. An attached object can be counted, named, thought of as a thing, but still understood to be a persistent part of the place to which it's attached. An attached object can't be displaced

---

[*] ———. *The Ecological Approach to Visual Perception.* Boston: Houghton Mifflin, 1979:307.

[†] ———. *The Ecological Approach to Visual Perception.* Boston: Houghton Mifflin, 1979:17.

[‡] ———. The Ecological Approach to Visual Perception. Boston: Houghton Mifflin, 1979:241.

unless it's detached by some kind of force (which, once applied, then results in a detached object). Attached objects are in an invariant location, so they make up part of the invariance of the surrounding information.

Detached objects are topologically closed, independent entities. Learning to perceive a detached object is different from perceiving an attached one because it has different properties and affords different actions. A tree branch might be attached to a tree, but when we break it off, it is now detached, affording actions unavailable in its attached state. The many bumpers of a pinball machine and other structures are attached objects; the pinball is detached.

Recall how we established earlier that when we pick up an object and use it as a tool with which we extend our body's abilities, we perceive it as an extension of ourselves.* A tree branch can go from being an attached object, to a detached object, to part of "me" with great ease.

PHENOMENOLOGY AND OBJECTS

In some ways, embodied-cognition science has been catching up to ideas that have been explored in other disciplines for at least a century. For example, phenomenologist Martin Heidegger famously described three modes of experiencing the world:

Readiness-to-hand

> When an experienced carpenter is using a hammer, the carpenter doesn't think consciously about the hammer. Instead, the hammer becomes a natural extension of the carpenter's action, and the carpenter "sees through" the tool, focusing instead on the material being affected by hammering. In our levels of consciousness spectrum, this is tacit, unconscious action, in which there's no explicit consideration of the tool any more than explicitly considering our finger when we scratch an itch.

Unreadiness-to-hand

> When the action of hammering is disrupted by something—a slippery handle, a bent nail, a hard knot in the wood—the hammer can become "unready-to-hand." Suddenly the carpenter must stop and think explicitly about the tool and the materials. The hammer

---

* Bodies and Environments; earlier this chapter.

can become less of an extension of the self at this point—no longer "seen through" but considered as an object with a frustrated or interrupted potential as a natural extension of the body.

Presence-to-hand

When looking at a hammer as "present-to-hand," we remove it from its context as a tool or a potential extension of the self; instead, we consider it neutrally as an object with properties of size, density, color, and shape.[*] This is explicit consideration outside of the cycling between the "unreadiness" and "readiness" in the context of the tool's affording functions. As designers, we often need to switch into this level of awareness of what we are designing: its form and specification and other aspects that the user doesn't (or normally shouldn't) have to worry about.

MANIPULATING AND SORTING

A detached object can also be manipulated, considered, and organized in ways that attached objects can't. It can be compared with another object, grouped with similar ones, and sorted into classification schemes, allowing counting and assignment of a number.[†] As we'll see, this is what we do with the abstractions of language, with which we use words or pictures to categorize and arrange the world with signifiers rather than the physical elements themselves.

OBJECTS WITH AGENCY

Among the world's detached objects are animals, including humans.[‡] We evolved to comprehend that these objects are special, and have a sort of agency of their own, an *animus* evident in their physical actions, signals, and (for humans) symbolic language. In modern life, many of us don't encounter a lot of wild animals, but we're familiar with pets as independent agents in our midst. Other humans interface better with us than animals (usually...), because we share more of an *umwelt* (environmental frame) with them, including the full capabilities of human

---

[*] Dotov D. G., L. Nie, A. Chemero. "A Demonstration of the Transition from Ready-to-Hand to Unready-to-Hand." *PLoS ONE* 2010;5(3):e9433. doi:10.1371/journal.pone.0009433.

[†] Gibson, J. J. *The Ecological Approach to Visual Perception.* Boston: Houghton Mifflin, 1979:241.

[‡] ———. *The Ecological Approach to Visual Perception.* Boston: Houghton Mifflin, 1979:307.

language. Regardless of human or animal, we spend a lot of energy figuring out what these agents are up to, what they must be thinking, or what they need.

Of course this means we ourselves are detached objects, and in moments of objective consideration, we sometimes perceive ourselves as such. Typically, though, we don't see ourselves with the objectivity that other agents perceive us. So, a human agent might be puzzled or troubled when an environment treats him like another object rather than as a "self." When we find ourselves in bureaucratic labyrinths, shuttled along as if on a conveyor belt, it feels "dehumanizing"; we feel the same when digital systems communicate with abrupt sterility, or coldly drop us from what felt like a meaningful exchange. Technological systems tend to lack contextual empathy.

DIGITAL OBJECTS

Digital objects might be simulated things on screens or physical objects with digitally enabled properties.

Simulated objects are, for example, icons in a computer's interface. From early in graphical-user-interface (GUI) design, the convention has been that these should be able to be moved about on a surface (such as the desktop) or placed in other container objects (folders). However, these are flat simulations on a flat screen. If they were physical objects, we would be able to determine through action and various angles of inspection whether they were attached or detached, or if they were merely painted on a surface. Digital displays don't give us that luxury, so we have to poke and prod them to see what they do, often being surprised when what seemed an interactive object is really a decorative ornament. Like Wile E. Coyote in the Road Runner cartoons, we slam into a wall where the tunnel is only painted on.

Software also uses text as objects of a sort. Labeling our icons means we're attaching word objects to the picture objects. But even in something like a text-based email application, or a command-line file-transfer-protocol (FTP) interface, for which there's little or no graphical simulation, there are still commands such as "put" and "get" and "save" that indicate we are treating chunks of text as singular objects to be moved about, modified, put away, or retrieved from storage.

Sometimes, we perceive an entire interface as an object, with buttons and things that we are manipulating the way we would manipulate a physical object such as a microwave or typewriter. These objects are made up of other, smaller objects, nested together into compound objects (with compound invariants). Other times, we perceive an interface as a place (which we will discuss shortly). And often, because of the weird nature of digital information, we perceive a digital thing as both object and place at the same time, which can be just fine or very confusing, depending on how appropriately it's expressing itself as one and the other, or the perspective the user brings to it.

As David Weinberger explains in *Small Pieces Loosely Joined: A Unified Theory Of The Web* (Basic Books), this has been the case with the Web for a long time: "With normal documents, we read them, file them, throw them out, or send them to someone else. We do not go to them. We don't visit them. Web documents are different. They're places on the Web....They're there. With this phrase, space—or something like it—has entered the picture."* Our everyday language shows how this works: we find ourselves using prepositions interchangeably in digital environments, such as "you can learn more *on* Wikipedia" or "I'm *in* Facebook right now" or "find my book *at* Amazon.com!" Physical structures tend to constrain the prepositional phrasing that makes sense for them. I don't say I am "on" my house if I am inside it, but I might say I am "in" or "at" my house. Digitally driven structures are more fluid, allowing us to use words with more flexibility, based on the context of the interaction.

Other times, it's clear that what we are using is an object, but it conflates not with place but with our bodies. When we use a desktop computer with a mouse, our cursor becomes an extension of the arm as much as our finger is an extension of our hands-on touch screens. Our bodies have an appetite for environmental extension, always working to find equilibrium that allows us to be more tacit than explicit, more "ready-to-hand" than otherwise.

Digital objects are also physical objects with digital information driving some of their affordances and agency. We are increasingly surrounded by these, in our burgeoning *Internet of Things*. When we perceive these objects and interact with them, we're tapping into ancient cognitive functions to comprehend what they're up to in relation to ourselves.

---

* Weinberger, David. *Small Pieces Loosely Joined: A Unified Theory Of The Web.* New York: Basic Books, 2002:39.

But, we don't always know if an object has agency or not, and they're often harder to comprehend than any natural creature. One wouldn't expect one's computer to whisper secrets to one's friends about buying a private item from Amazon or cranking up a game on Kongregate during business hours. The information readily perceived by the user was not clearly indicative of those behaviors. Yet, when Beacon posted news items on behalf of Facebook users, it was doing just that as a digital agent making a decision not directly controlled by the human agent, and without clearly informing its intentions and rules of cause and effect.

How well we perceive context in digitally affected environments is often a matter of how well the environment clarifies what is an object that is detached or attached, what sort of object it is, whether it has agency of its own, and what rules it follows.

Smartphones "at-hand"

Recent research into how we use our smartphones shows that we tend to use them—in Heidegger's terms—as "ready-to-hand" objects, extensions of ourselves.

FIGURE 6-3
An honest bit of graffiti in the San Francisco Mission District (photo by Jeff Elder)*

---

* https://twitter.com/JeffElder/status/431673279128936449

In one study, over 50 percent of smartphone owners kept their devices close to them when going to bed at night.[*] In another study, for well over 80 percent of days tracked, the smartphone was the first and last computing device used by participants—bookending their days more pervasively than laptop and desktop computers. Generally, users "always" kept their phones with them, defaulting to desktop and laptop devices only "when absolutely necessary." The study concluded that "the phone is emerging as a primary computing device for some users, rather than as a peripheral to the PC."

Of course, for many populations in the world—those who missed out on the personal-computer revolution—phones are their first and only computing devices. And according to a World Bank report, "About three-quarters of the world now have easier access to a mobile phone than a bank account, electricity, or clean water."[†]

Mobile phone devices have many characteristics that, taken together, make them a sort of "perfect storm" object for extending our cognitive abilities—and the dimensions of our personal context. Here are some of those characteristics:

- For over a century, the telephone has been one of our most intimate modes of communication, allowing us to whisper to each other—lips to ears—in private conversations.

- Mobile phones are small, portable, and more easily treated as "ready-to-hand" extensions of ourselves than other, larger devices.

- They're always connected, often through multiple networks.

- Phones are more likely to be geolocation capable, providing extended-cognitive situational awareness.

- Because we carry phones on our person, they can communicate with us through touch—vibrating our skin, asking for attention.

Considering all these factors, it makes sense that adoption of mobile phones is outstripping all other devices by leaps and bounds. [‡]

---

[*] Smith, Aaron. "The Best (and Worst) of Mobile Connectivity." *Pew Internet & American Life Project*, November 30, 2012 (*http://bit.ly/10neutq*).

[†] Mlot, Stephanie. "Infographic: Mobile Use in Developing Nations Skyrockets." *PC Magazine* July 18, 2012 (*http://www.pcmag.com/article2/0,2817,2407335,00.asp*).

[‡] Karlson, Amy K.,1 Brian R. Meyers,1 Andy Jacobs,1 Paul Johns,1 and Shaun K. Kane2. "Working Overtime: Patterns of Smartphone and PC Usage in the Day of an Information Worker," (*http://research.microsoft.com/pubs/80165/pervasive09_patterns_final.pdf*).

Layout

Layout means "the persisting arrangement of surfaces relative to one another and to the ground."[*] It's the invariant relationship of elements such as objects and other features in a particular setting.[†] Each arrangement provides a particular set of affordances that differs from some other layout; one layout involving trees might afford one sort of behaviors for a squirrel and different behaviors for a bird.[‡]

Perceiving layout depends on both perception and action. We tend to use the word "layout" for static two-dimensional artifacts such as newspapers or posters, which have pictures and text. However, our perception of layout evolved in three dimensions, which we come to understand by moving through an area and seeing things from different angles, touching them, smelling, and hearing. The layouts we see in two-dimensional surfaces such as paper and screens are representational, artificial layouts. They borrow some properties of the three-dimensional environment but are not as physically information-rich.

Layout affects the efficacy of action and an environment's understandability. The layout of a kitchen in a restaurant can make or break its success—you don't want wait staff bumping into the sous-chef, or the baker's oven opening over the head of the saucier. Likewise, an airport ideally has a layout that clearly informs us about the rules and expectations of the space.

Related to layout is *clutter*, which are objects that obscure a clear view of the ground and the sky for a given perceiver.[§] Yet, when one of those objects becomes the subject of the perceiver's attention, it's no longer perceived as clutter but as an affording object in its own right. A stone on the ground is part of the clutter that obscures a full view of the ground; but the stone can also be an object that affords picking up and using as a tool or placing as part of a wall. A room might be full of

---

[*] Gibson, J. J. *The Ecological Approach to Visual Perception.* Boston: Houghton Mifflin, 1979:307.

[†] ———. *The Ecological Approach to Visual Perception.* Boston: Houghton Mifflin, 1979:148.

[‡] ———. *The Ecological Approach to Visual Perception.* Boston: Houghton Mifflin, 1979:128.

[§] ———. *The Ecological Approach to Visual Perception.* Boston: Houghton Mifflin, 1979:307.

furniture that is clutter to the person trying to get as quickly as possible from one end of the room to the next; but when the same person is tired from all that jumping about, a chair affords respite.

Sometimes, a cluttering object acts as a barrier, which hinders further movement. A barrier's affordance is that it blocks our movement. Remember, all affordances are just affordances, not anti-affordances—whether an affordance is positive or negative for the perceiver is a matter of context.

What is clutter or not is a nested property of the perceiver's current experience. Again, this isn't a permanent categorical hierarchy. Contextually, anything can change its role in the layout depending on current behavioral needs.

DIGITAL LAYOUT

Digital interfaces and linked environments likewise have these layout concerns. Some are about efficiency of action, such as with guidelines like Fitts' law, which concerns the relationship between size of target and distance to target. Some are about comprehending the relationships of the elements on the screen and between different "places" in the software environment. Users must understand the difference between an underlying surface and what is an attached or detached object and what these things allow the user to do: Can I move a document into a folder? Can I edit or erase a string of text? Is a drop-shadow under an object an indication of its movability, its press-ability, its priority in the visual hierarchy, or is it just decoration? These treatments are all clues as to the relationship of a particular entity to other entities, in an overall layout.

Clutter is a factor for digital interfaces, as well. We often hear users say "there's so much clutter" in an interface. Yet, everything in an interface was put there by someone for some reason, whether warranted or not. One user's trash is another user's treasure. One shopper's clutter is a marketer's sale promotion insert.

Events

An *event* is a change in the invariant structures of the environment, such as a change in substance, object, or layout.[*] Gibson offers a thorough classification of terrestrial events, which we won't cover fully, but it includes three major categories:

- Changes in the layout of surfaces (and by extension, objects, and so on)
- Changes in color and texture of surfaces
- Changes in the existence of surfaces[†]

Examples of these could include things such as a ball being thrown from the pitcher's mound to home plate; the movement of a rabbit from "in range" for catching to "out of range" down a hole; or the changes observed in substances as they transition, such as from ice to water or as soft clay hardens. Changes in existence can be due to burning in fire, or decay, or in an animal that was once not in existence being born and now in the environment as a detached object.

Like other structural elements of the environment, events can be nested and interdependent.[‡] A place can change from "cool shade" to "hot and bright" if a tree (an attached object) falls (another event, changing the tree to a detached object). Most natural events contain so many small events that it's impossible to identify them all. We perceive these complex events in a compound way, not having to keep cognitive track of every observable change. We don't have to perceive every single raindrop to know that it's raining.

Events are related to a psychological phenomenon called *change blindness*. This occurs when something in the environment changes without our noticing it. We can easily overlook events if they're not perceived as part of what is relevant to our current action. In a well-known video demonstrating this effect, the viewer is asked to keep track of how many times a group passes a basketball between its members. Most viewers don't notice the weird, costumed "dancing bear" among them. Facebook's Beacon presented only a small indicator of its activity that

---

[*] ———. *The Ecological Approach to Visual Perception*. Boston: Houghton Mifflin, 1979:242.

[†] ———. *The Ecological Approach to Visual Perception*. Boston: Houghton Mifflin, 1979:94.

[‡] ———. *The Ecological Approach to Visual Perception*. Boston: Houghton Mifflin, 1979:110.

was easily overlooked in the busy events happening on a kinetic site such as Kongregate. These change-blindness issues are even more of a danger in screens and displays, because the information available for pickup is so limited compared to a three-dimensional, object-laden environment.

AFFORDANCES AND LAWS FOR EVENTS

Events can have affordances of their own. A campfire can afford keeping us warm; rain affords watering our crops. These events are, of course, nested in particular contexts; the campfire can also burn our bodies, and rain can flood our fields.

Perception evolved in a world in which events tend to follow natural laws that can be learned. The motion of water can be variant as a substance, but its behaviors are invariant in that water will always behave like water. The sun moves across the sky through the day, but it does so every day, following an invariant pattern.

EVENTS AND TIME

We actually perceive time as *events* rather than as abstractions such as seconds or minutes.[*] We feel time passing because things are changing around us. Until only a century or so ago, most people still thought of "noon" as when the sun was directly overhead. Even though clocks were already fairly common, they were thought of as approximations within a given locality, not synchronized with any global standard. It was the rise of railroads that brought absolute, standardized time to the general public; railways couldn't have one town's noon be different from another's; otherwise, trains would never be on time anywhere, or (at worst) they might collide at junctions.[†]

We now live in an artificially mechanized sort of "time." Our culture regulates the events around us to the point at which our surroundings tick to the same rhythm as the clock, no longer tied to the relatively fluid event of the sun rising and setting. Even when it's a mechanical structure, though, it's the environment that creates information marking time, not the abstract measurement of seconds or hours.

---

[*] ————. *The Ecological Approach to Visual Perception*. Boston: Houghton Mifflin, 1979:100.

[†] Kuniavsky, Mike. *Smart Things: Ubiquitous Computing User Experience Design*. Burlington, MA: Morgan Kaufmann, 2010:3.

This is why time can feel so relative to us, no matter how many seconds are measured.* A bad and boring 90-minute movie feels interminable; an exciting, quality 90-minute movie feels like it flies by. In digital design, we might want to judge the efficacy of a website, for example, by how long it takes a user to get from one page to another, either in terms of seconds or mouse clicks—but we find the user perceives the passage of that time differently depending on context. User perception is important to consider when looking at the results of analytics and other performance measurements. Ten clicks might be fine, if the user is getting value out of each one (and feels like she's getting where she needs to go); three clicks can feel like forever if the user is floundering in confusion.

DIGITAL EVENTS

There are many sorts of events we perceive in digital interfaces. There are rich-interaction transitions (windows zooming in and out; swiped objects disappearing in a puff of animated smoke) that make clear where simulated objects have gone or where they came from. There are also system processes, including backing up a file or establishing a wireless connection. These can be initiated by us or initiated by the system's own digital agency.

Users often struggle to comprehend the events that occur in software environments, where cause-and-effect does not have to follow natural laws. This can be especially true when the system is doing something on its own, outside of our immediate perception. The more complex our digital infrastructure becomes, the greater role these invisible, automated events play in our environment.

Place

Place is the last element we will cover in this summary. It's especially important to context because so much of context has to do with how we perceive our environment as organized into places. Here are the key factors that describe place:†

---

* Popova, Maria "Why Time Slows Down When We're Afraid, Speeds Up as We Age, and Gets Warped on Vacation," *brainpickings.org* July 15, 2013.

† The points following all come from Gibson, 1979, pp. 240–241.

- A place is a location or region in the environment that has a particular combination of features that are learned by an animal. An animal experiences its habitat as being made up of places.

- Unlike an object, in nature, a place has no definite boundaries, which might overlap in a nested fashion depending on the current action of the perceiver, and other factors. Sometimes, however, there are in artificial boundaries like fences, walls, or city blocks. These are layout structures that nudge us into perceiving them as places, because of how they constrain and channel action. It's still up to the perceiver to distinguish a city block or the inside of a building as a place, but the environment exerts great control over that perception.

- Places are nested—smaller ones are nested within larger ones, and they can overlap or be seen differently from various points of view, depending on the particular actions and perceptual motivations of the perceiver.

- Movement in the environment is movement among places, which can be reached via one or more paths (which themselves go through other places). Even a path through the woods can be experienced as a place—it's a layout in the environment that affords motion between other places. Yet, the path is meaningful because of the places it connects.

- We don't perceive "space." Instead, we perceive places. Space is a mathematical concept, not an embodied one. Space is undifferentiated; but just by perceiving and moving within an area, the perceiver's presence is already coming to grips with the area as one or more places.

- Place-learning is "learning the affordances of places, and learning to distinguish among them." It is an especially important kind of learning for all animals, including humans. As we saw earlier, place has a function in how our extended cognition learns and recalls information, such as when people had more accurate recollection when staying in the same room.

- Place-learning and orienting oneself among places is what we call *wayfinding*—knowing where one is in relation to the entire environment, or at least the places that matter to the agent.

- Places persist from the point of view of the perceiver—they cannot be displaced the way objects can. Our perception counts on places being where they are, from one day to the next.

The persistence of places and the way we learn them is especially important to point out. A place can be altered, such as by fire or a destructive storm, but it is still in the same location in relation to other places. Place-learning depends on this persistent situated quality.

DIGITAL PLACES

This issue of persistence is especially important when we look at software environments. Our perceptual system relies on the persistent properties of place, and can be confounded by environments that don't meet those expectations. Yet, software can create the useful illusion of persistent places and then obliterate or move them or change them fundamentally in ways that cannot occur through the natural laws that govern physical information.

A website can feel like a place, but it can also feel as though it has places within it. Likewise, a portal that gathers articles from many sites can be its own place, even if all the content is from elsewhere. An application can be a place nested in an operating system. A document is an object until it's opened and, in a sense, "dwelled in," and feels like a place again. Likewise, digital technology can change the way we experience physical places, such as when we use something like a "geo fence" to teach a smartphone to present home-related information when it's near our home address.

Places, and "placemaking," will figure centrally in our exploration as we continue through semantic information, digital information, and the vast systems of language we inhabit. For humans, it turns out that place is as much about how we communicate as what we physically perceive.

[7]

What Humans Make

Civilization is a limitless multiplication of unnecessary necessities.
—MARK TWAIN

The Built Environment

AS HUMANS, WE ARE the source of much of the environment we live in, including roads, buildings, and cities, as well as the social interactions and relationships we have, which influence our choices and behaviors every day. Architects and engineers refer to the human-made structures as *the built environment*. Although there are certainly big differences between the built environment and the natural one, our perception of context comes from the same cognitive capabilities, whether we're surrounded by towering skyscrapers or giant redwoods. From the human point of view, the products of our culture are separate from nature, but from the planet's point of view, our environments emerged from the activity of our species not unlike an ant hill or bee hive. "There is only one world, however diverse, and all animals live in it," says J. J. Gibson.* No matter how much plastic and electricity we use, our built environment is still made of substances, surfaces, objects, and events.

Even though people have been building things for a long time, the study of how cognition works among these structures is fairly recent. One landmark work is the 1960 book by Kevin Lynch, *The Image of the City* (MIT Press), which presents a framework for analyzing the contours of urban environments and understanding them in human terms. It was the result of a five-year study interviewing and observing

---

* Gibson, J. J. *The Ecological Approach to Visual Perception*. Boston: Houghton Mifflin, 1979:130.

inhabitants of several American cities. Lynch's focus was on the *form* of built urban environments—their physical, structural properties and the clues they provide.

Even though it was not an expressly ecological-psychology work, there are strong parallels between Gibson's concepts and those of Lynch, whose elements of urban form (Paths, Edges, Districts, Nodes, Landmarks) are preoccupied with how people navigate and learn the surfaces, objects, layouts, and places of a city. As a way of talking about coherent invariant cues, Lynch proposes the concept of *imageability*— the "legibility," or understandability, of the urban landscape. Lynch also introduces a new use of an older term (previously used mainly for things such as navigation by compass and maps), *wayfinding*, for how people use sensory cues from the environment to work their way through it.

Lynch points out that "the image of a given physical reality may occasionally shift in its type with different circumstances of viewing. Thus an expressway may be a path for the driver, and edge for the pedestrian."[*] This idea is similar to the shifting nested quality of the environment in ecological terms, and also similar to the idea of a creature's *umwelt*. Lynch also found that, as people lived in a city longer, the elements in the environment they relied upon might shift from, for example, particular paths to a broader set of landmarks and nodes; in a sense, their umwelt changed over time, as their perception learned and internalized patterns.[†] Lynch also found that, even though his framework breaks the city down into components, people don't rely on that sort of parsing; rather, they take it all in as one integrated environment.[‡] More recent research reinforces that wayfinding is tied to embodiment, finding that people could remember more accurate details about their environment if they were more "cognitively active" way-finders versus

---

[*] Lynch, Kevin. *The Image of the City*. Cambridge, MA: MIT Press, 1960:48.

[†] ——. *The Image of the City*. Cambridge, MA: MIT Press, 1960:49.

[‡] ——. *The Image of the City*. Cambridge, MA: MIT Press, 1960:49.

"cognitively passive." This means that people who drive or walk themselves places tend to remember more about the built environment than those who ride in vehicles that others are driving.[*]

Built environments might be perceived with the same principles that drive perception of the natural world; artificial structures can exert great influence on how people perceive a layout as a place or not. Recall the field and the stone wall in Chapter 3: in a sense, the wall makes a strong argument about what the perceiver should experience, splitting parts of the field into one place separated from another. We could do the same with just signage and names, as with a parking sign that indicates parking is legal on the left, but illegal on the right. And as we will see, in software, the language establishes the structure of the territory itself.

Over the years, wayfinding has become a design field in its own right. For example, a classic text by Paul Arthur and Romedi Passini, *Wayfinding: People, Signs, and Architecture* (McGraw-Hill), takes some of the essential ideas from Lynch and runs with them, adding more insights on how people learn urban places. Unlike Lynch, they add significant content focused on how signage in the built environment shapes how people understand it.

Alas, their book is now out of print. The bulk of books and materials on wayfinding now focus mainly on the design of signage rather than the intrinsic, physical-information qualities of buildings and cities. I bring this up because it's important to realize that, for context design, physical information—the surfaces and objects of the environment—are core to how all creatures find their way and learn places. Signage is part of the semantic information we will look at in Part III. In the built environment as well as in virtual environments such as digital interfaces, the physical shape of our surroundings is what we perceive most directly, with the least *explicit* effort.

---

[*] Mondschein, Andrew, Evelyn Blumenberg, and Brian D. Taylor. "GOING MENTAL: Everyday Travel and the Cognitive Map." *Access* 2013;43:2–7. *http://www.uctc.net/access/43/access43_goingmental.shtml*. (Thanks to Bogdan Stanciu for this reference.)

The Elusive "Cognitive Map"

Kevin Lynch's pioneering work on wayfinding relied heavily on a psychological concept called a *cognitive map*, a phrase that you will see often in research literature, usability guides, and experience-design textbooks and articles.

The phrasing is actually unfortunate, because it can lead practitioners to assume that users have something like a map in their heads that gets filled in as they explore an environment, or that they have a stable "mental model" formed in their brains. Even according to traditional cognitive psychology, these maps are not stable or necessarily accurate, and can be distorted depending on many factors. And yet, the metaphor of a "map" in the brain persists. But there is no literal cognitive map we can point to inside people's brains, just as there are no representational "pictures" in the brain—and no brain-dwelling observer to look at them with tiny eyeballs.

It's possible to *memorize* maps and make use of explicitly recalled semantic structures, but the typical wayfinding individual is using the environment itself more for recognition than recall, and attending to only the minimum information necessary. The body is significantly involved in the process of that learning. That's why people don't remember details of a traveled route as well if riding in a car compared to walking or jogging to their destination.[*]

One problem with many wayfinding studies is that they rely on recollection after the fact, using verbal and written data from interviews and surveys. By the time interview subjects have articulated answers into language, they've moved from *tacit* awareness to *explicit* deliberation, which might not accurately describe their actual perception-and-action during wayfinding. For the same reasons, this distortion can also be a problem for user-testing in software design: asking users "Why are you doing that?" often causes them to invent a reason they convince themselves is real.

Brains are, of course, involved in wayfinding and environmental learning, like all action, but it's a matter of degree. When it's crucial to memorize a map, the brain works overtime. Evidence shows that memorization of massive wayfinding data, such as what London cab drivers are required to do for their licenses, can actually cause the brain's hippocampus to grow to an unusual size.[†] However, that is deliberate, purposeful memorization, as opposed to tacit engagement with familiar surroundings.

---

[*] See reference in main text to GOING MENTAL: Everyday Travel and the Cognitive Map.

[†] Jabr, Ferris. "Cache Cab: Taxi Drivers' Brains Grow to Navigate London's Streets" Scientific American (scientificamerican.com) December 8, 2011

The environment itself serves as an external map of physical and semantic information cues, most of it beyond our conscious awareness. A city's layout, culture's language, and the ever-present activity of other people serve as extended-cognitive scaffolding that have the models already in them, without our having to keep them in our heads. The environment that makes up someone's context is inseparable from their ability to understand, learn, and navigate that environment. All the more reason why we have to make environments that are coherently structured so that user perception can make sense of them based on what they present to the perceiver in the moment, rather than some hoped-for map in the user's head.

The Social Environment

The built environment isn't made by or for just one person. Look around you; almost everything you'll see that's made by someone was made in a social context that involved conversation or collaboration of some kind. Humans are deeply social creatures, and other people are a critical part of our environment.

For humans, other humans are a special class of animal—objects that are animate in the environment. Recognizing animals (and humans) as distinct and different from other objects is one of the first things human infants learn. As Gibson points out, they provide the "richest and most elaborate affordances" in our environment; "When touched they touch back, when struck they strike back; in short they *interact* with the observer and with one another. Behavior begets behavior."[*] When things in the environment "touch back," they are "interactive." And human interaction is the standard against which we compare and comprehend all other interaction.

We tacitly attend to our social context all the time to see how others are behaving or where they're going, to gauge our actions against what feels like the normal behavior. You've probably had an experience in which you find yourself standing in a line unnecessarily because you assumed you were supposed to line up with everyone else, or you went to dinner with friends with a resolution to skip dessert, but ended up eating one anyway because everybody else was getting one.

---

[*] Gibson, J. J. *The Ecological Approach to Visual Perception.* Boston: Houghton Mifflin, 1979:135.

We also rely on other humans for much of our extended cognition and memory. A lot of what we assume to be objective reality is actually just what we absorb from the collective assumptions and perspectives of our respective societies; but like so many things that are deeply part of human life, we're typically unaware of just how strongly the social environment affects our own thinking and behavior.

Classic social psychology studies, such as the Asch Conformity Experiments in the 1950s, have shown social pressure can cause people to believe obviously incorrect "facts." In one famous example, subjects were convinced by participants (who were secretly part of the study) that the line on the left card depicted in Figure 7-1 was not the same length as line C on the card on the right, even though it was.[*]

FIGURE 7-1
Cards and lines like those used in the Asch Conformity Experiments

More recently, studies have been showing that people are influenced in a more passive way, just by social behavior going on around them. One well-known finding from a few years ago discovered that obesity tends to be "contagious," in the respect that the eating and activity behaviors of the people around us tend to affect our own daily habits.[†] This effect was later found to vary across cultures. Some were more prone to group pressure than others, but the principle still held.[‡]

---

[*] Wikimedia Commons: *http://commons.wikimedia.org/wiki/File:Asch_experiment.png*

[†] Stein, Rob. "Obesity Spreads In Social Circles As Trends Do, Study Indicates." *Washington Post*, July 26, 2007.

[‡] Watters, Ethan. "We Aren't the World," *Pacific Standard* (psmag.com) February 25, 2013.

In another example, passersby dropped money in a street musician's hat eight times more often when they observed another person donating. When asked afterward why they donated, none of them said it was because they'd seen someone else do it. They all constructed reasons on the fly, such as "I liked the song he was playing" or "I felt sorry for the guy."* These discoveries underscore the fact that we're mostly not consciously aware of what our environment is influencing, socially or otherwise.

Just using language describing the social behavior context can have a strong effect. In the United Kingdom, in an attempt to improve collections on delinquent taxes, the tax agency tried providing some social context:

> In one letter HMRC appealed to people's sense of civic duty. "We collect taxes to make sure that money is available to fund the public services that benefit you and other UK citizens," it read. "Even if one person fails to pay their taxes it reduces the services and resources that are provided." Another used actual statistics: "Nine out of ten people in Britain pay their tax on time."

The results were dramatic: collections rates increased from 57 percent in 2008 to 86 percent in 2009, within similar portfolios of debt.† It bears repeating: these people were not physically watching others' behavior; they were only reading about it, and yet that environmental pressure tacitly nudged them toward behaving differently in vast numbers.

There's a seemingly endless stream of studies like these from the social sciences. I think we're fascinated with them because we are consistently taken by surprise by how little truly independent agency we actually have. Of course, lots of what we respond to in the social environment isn't physical information but the social narrative in which we're immersed—things we hear or read about or the belief systems in which we're raised.

---

* Cialdini, Robert B. "Basic Social Influence Is Underestimated." *Psychological Inquiry* 2005;16(4):158–161. Copyright © 2005 by Lawrence Erlbaum Associates, Inc.

† Martin, Steve. "98% of HBR Readers Love This Article," *Harvard Business Review* (hbr.org) October 2012.

Meaning, Culture, and "Product"

The built environment and the social environment are all part of what we loosely refer to as *culture*. Culture is something we don't normally think about *as culture*. We take its cues and meanings for granted the way we take a tree or mountain for granted—it's just there. Studying one's own culture in an objective manner is a fairly recent concept.

Culture brings with it environmental invariants that aren't always physical. In fact, the parts of our environment that we think of as culture are mostly nonphysical, even when they're about physical things. Figure 7-2 shows the famous Bilbao Guggenheim Museum in Spain, which is a functioning edifice made of physical materials, but most people who have heard of it or seen pictures of it understand it as uniquely shaped with cultural meaning far beyond its physical form.

FIGURE 7-2

The Bilbao Guggenheim Museum, designed by Frank Gehry*

Even a mundane object such as a mailbox has meaning to us that is mostly about cultural concepts. J.J. Gibson uses the mailbox as an example of something that affords action beyond its intrinsic qualities. From its physical information alone, a mailbox, such as the one presented in Figure 7-3, affords a simple concavity that can hold objects of a certain size, and that's all. But, for a human who is "encultured" in using postal services, a mailbox offers the possibility of a more complex

---

* Wikimedia Commons: *http://bit.ly/1xaxMA2*

action—putting an addressed object into it, and expecting that the cultural system of postal services will take that object to the specified address. This is where cultural constructs and affordance overlap, from the first-person perspective of the perceiver.

FIGURE 7-3
A mailbox in Denmark[*]

This rich bundle of compound invariants requires the existence of many social systems working together, from educational (people need to know how to read and write letters and address them) to infrastructural (there needs to be some organized mechanism for moving mail around, even if it's just carriers riding horses), not to mention economies that offer the purchasing and using of stamps and other forms of payment. The complex systems of our cultural environment are built up from information that eventually traces back to affordances, which undergird all of our activities, no matter how brain-based and abstract they have become.

---

[*] Wikimedia Commons: *http://commons.wikimedia.org/wiki/File:Postkasse_ubt.jpeg*

When designing a product, we are designing a new part of the human environment that will be placed within existing, living contexts made of other informing systems, whether those systems are towns and cities, or people, or other products.

If we think of the product as a newly introduced set of capabilities, nested within the environment, it helps to clarify how we should design the product. Does it add capabilities that complement those that already exist? Does it present itself as clearly relevant to potential users who can understand new things only in the context of what they already understand?

John Seely Brown, one-time technology chief for Xerox's famed Palo Alto Research Center, better known as PARC, tells the story of how the early market for photocopiers was miniscule. Office workers were already making copies by using carbon sheets between pages in typewriters. They made all the copies they needed as they were typing the documents, simultaneously. A photocopier actually seemed to add complexity, requiring that you type the document first and then make copies of it on another machine altogether.

What the market didn't grasp yet was the potential value of being able to make unlimited copies from a single original, and even copies of that copy, and so on, having created the document only once. Seely Brown explains that it took great marketing work to create the right cultural interface between the technical innovation and the market.* People had to be told a story that reframed how they understood copying to begin with. The structures of the existing environment that constrained the number of copies one could make had set cultural expectations about what copying business documents meant. It created intrinsic, tacit constraints on the value people could see. It wasn't just the object that mattered, but the object plus the language about it.

Conversely, in a more recent example, consider the One Laptop per Child program. Founded on many laudable ideas, the program sought to put network-enabled, inexpensive, durable laptops in the hands of children in less-developed parts of the world.

---

* One example of this story is found in JSB's essay "Changing the game of corporate research: Learning to thrive in the fog of reality" *Technological Innovation*. Oversights and Foresights. Edited by Raghu Garud, Praveen Rattan Nayyar, and Zur Baruch Shapira. New York: Cambridge University Press, 1997:95–110.

But the product's designers made the mistake of developing the OLPC laptop—the XO—based on sound-yet-unconventional concepts about learning, community, and computing. Even though the product won many design awards, it found low acceptance in its intended populations. Why? Because the product wasn't really suited to find a niche in the nested ecologies of its intended market. These societies were already adopting mobile phones as their personal-computing device of choice, where marketplace conventions and community norms had already emerged around using SMS and other simpler cell-based communications.[*] If their children were going to learn how to use a laptop, they wanted kids to learn the device as a business and workplace computer. So, they preferred that children learn Microsoft Windows and other conventional business software, rather than the elegant, theoretically sound Sugar operating system of the XO.[†]

Writing about innovation, products, and business practices, John Seely Brown says, "Context has its own dynamics. It's just like a garden. You can't pick up a set of plants and just move them without understanding how the chemistry could be different, how the sun shining on the garden could be different. The whole notion of portability of best practices has been a major setback for understanding how situated technologies must be and how it is the content coming together with the context, and the interaction between the thing and the context, that produces value."[‡]

---

[*] Nussbaum, Bruce. "It's Time To Call One Laptop Per Child A Failure," *Bloomberg Businessweek* (*businessweek.com*) September 24, 2007.

[†] Gaurav Chachra "Who Actually Needs Windows XP on the XO Laptop?" *OLPC News* (*olpcnews.com*) May 2, 2008.

[‡] *http://www.johnseelybrown.com/evolutioninnovation.pdf*

FIGURE 7-4
The beautifully designed but contextually mismatched, OLPC XO laptop[*]

Affordances create information that makes sense for action only in the context of interdependent, nested layers. A product—whether it takes the form of a mobile app, a "smart" device, or just a plain, old website—is more than a list of features. It's part of a whole, just as vision isn't only the parts of an eyeball, but an organically nested system throughout the body. A uniquely human dimension that we so often ignore is culture. And culture's interface with human life is ultimately *language*, which we will explore in Part III.

---

[*] Wikimedia Commons: *http://bit.ly/1xaxUzF*

Part III

Semantic Information

Language as Environment

SEMANTIC INFORMATION IS WHAT WE ADD TO THE ENVIRONMENT TO MAKE IT EVEN MORE RELEVANT AND USEFUL FOR HUMANS; it's a mirror we use to reflect upon our experience and create narratives for explaining our environments to ourselves; it's the primary interface between humans and the complex systems that humans create. As we will see, semantic information is an inseparable and crucial part of how context is shaped in the human environment.*

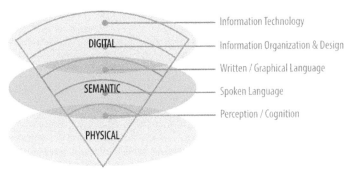

FIGURE III-1
Semantic information

In Part III, we cover basic concepts about what language is and how it works. We will see how symbols give us amazing flexibility in our environment but also how they come with challenges. We'll also see how language works as a kind of environment, functioning in ways similar to but different from physical information, and how writing enhances

---

* Moving forward, I'll be using *semantic information* and *language* interchangeably; this would not work in a linguistics classroom, but for our purposes here, it will suit fine.

and changes those properties. Finally, we'll look at how physical and semantic information intersect and how technology adds even more flexibility to the mix, with more challenges to overcome.

[8]

How Language Works

Thought is made in the mouth.
—TRISTAN TZARA

Looking at Language

To understand how language functions as such a crucial part of our environment, we need to look at how it manages to mean anything to begin with. That means understanding some basics about signs and symbols, the mechanisms of signification.

Language is so much a part of human life, we hardly ever think about it explicitly. Like fish in water, we just use it as a sort of natural human medium. That's one reason language works so well. If we had to ponder the depths of meaning for every utterance, we wouldn't get much done. In everyday usage, we frankly treat language in much the same way scholars of the sixteenth century believed language to be: that words are essentially copies of the objects they name.[*]

Eventually, though, the question of how language means anything became an obsession that nearly consumed the philosophical work of the twentieth century, and especially energized the field of linguistics. Over the years, linguistics experts have broken down the study of language into layers, as pictured in Figure 8-1.

---

[*] Chandler, Daniel. *Semiotics: The Basics.* New York: Taylor & Francis, 2007:71.

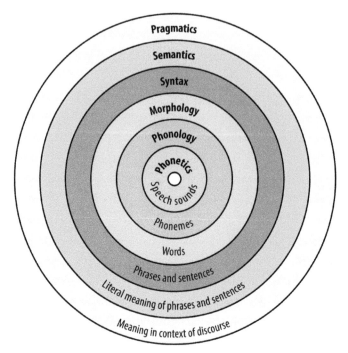

Pragmatics
Semantics
Syntax
Morphology
Phonology
Phonetics
Speech sounds
Phonemes
Words
Phrases and sentences
Literal meaning of phrases and sentences
Meaning in context of discourse

FIGURE 8-1

Major levels of linguistic structure, from raw spoken sounds to the complexities of meanings influenced by context*

There is physical, ecological information involved in language, but only at the level of the center circle. (For writing, the equivalent is just the physical marks on a surface.) That is, we make phonetic sounds or physical marks, and those sounds and marks are physical structures, but they have meaning only because of the context in which they're nested.

Language has meaning not because of its phonetic physicality but because of semantic convention. Meaning emerges from densely webbed systems of communication that have grown over millennia, built up in layers like the concentric circles of this diagram. Language is challenging to study partly because we have to use language to do so; it takes practice to pull ourselves out of the immersion within language to look at it objectively and parse its layers in this way.

---

* Wikimedia Commons: *http://bit.ly/1xay75J*

Notice especially that outer layer—Pragmatics—which is the linguistic study of meaning in the context of discourse. The word "fire" literally means a number of different things, depending on where and how it is said. In the United States, there's legal precedent constraining free public speech such that you're not allowed to "yell fire in a crowded theater" (as the colloquial version goes), because yelling it loudly when there's no fire can cause people to unnecessarily panic and cause injury. Ironically, many movies have people yelling "fire" in them, and it's not a problem—same sound, same place, different context. Yelling it loudly is another factor, of course; merely whispering the word to your neighbor wouldn't have the same effect.

Even though all of these layers are important for making understandable environments, in design work, it's the pragmatics of linguistic meaning that often brings the biggest challenges.

Signs: Icons, Indexes, and Symbols

In the fields of linguistics and semiotics, a *sign* is something that can be interpreted as having a meaning other than its own form. Semantic information depends on references between a thing and what that thing means. In contrast, physical information has intrinsic meaning. Stairs mean, to my body, that I can walk up them: that relationship is directly perceived. But when I say the word "stairs," the form of the word is not the same as the object; it only *refers* to the object. You can't walk up the word "stairs."

When we communicate with one another, we must use something other than the objects around us to make ourselves understood. Although signs exist that aren't made by humans—for example, smoke coming from a forest is a sign that there is a fire—everything humans make to communicate meaning is a sign of one sort or another.*

Generally speaking, according to linguistics, there are three modes for signification—three ways in which human expression means what it means. It's important to note that all the signifiers in the subsections

---

* For clarity's sake, we are skipping a lot of background here about the different schools of thought behind signification, particularly the difference between Saussure's *dyadic* approach and Pierce's *triadic* approach, and plenty of other important details. Beyond our scope here, these are still valuable details that I recommend curious readers investigate, because they help us think more rigorously how we design for meaning.

that follow work, in part, because of their dependencies on other signifiers in an object or device, with icons, indices, and symbols all in the mix. Just as our environment is nested and contextual, our language use also never works as isolated parts.

ICONS

The signifier in an *icon* has some physical resemblance to its referent—it looks or behaves as portrayed by the signified. Many buildings have signage that depicts the shape of a stairway to mean there are stairs nearby, important for emergencies when the elevator isn't working.

FIGURE 8-2
The standard icon for "stairs" from the AIGA "Symbol Signs" collection*

Iconic signifiers can be more or less realistically detailed. This book has a picture of a bird on the cover. That picture is an iconic reference to the type of bird—a green bee-eater. However, even a less detailed icon would work, such as a stick-figure bird, but it wouldn't be sufficiently specific to iconically represent a particular species. Figure 8-3 demonstrates that a detailed drawing of a tree can resemble its subject down to the tiniest branch, but a simple pictograph with a green triangle and a descending brown rectangle also looks enough like a tree to be an effective iconic signifier, depending on the level of specificity required.

---

* *http://www.aiga.org/symbol-signs/*

FIGURE 8-3

A line drawing of a tree represents that object iconically,[6]* but so can a simple, abstract shape

INDEXES

A sign that involves a direct temporal or spatial connection between signifier and signified is working as an *index*. An easy way to remember this one is to think of how we point at things with our *index* fingers. If you were to ask me where I found a pine cone, I might answer by pointing at a pine tree. My pointing at the tree is a spatial relationship between the direction of my pointing and the location of the tree. For objects small enough, we can actually pick up the object and show it; the act of showing it *indicates* that we are directing attention to the object. So, in answer to "which hammer did you use to repair the window?" I can grab the hammer and show it to you. In the famous World War I poster (Figure 8-4), Uncle Sam is pointing at the viewer. There are many signifiers at work in the image, but the finger pointing at the viewer indicates "You" as a potential recruit.

There can be temporal indices as well, which normally involve cause-and-effect relationships. When we see smoke, it is often an indexical signifier of a related fire. When we see a footprint in mud, we can surmise that a foot was once in that spot. And automobiles have fuel gauges, such as that illustrated in Figure 8-5, directly indicating the level of fuel in the tank—the level of fuel causes the effect of a change in the needle's position on the gauge.

---

* Wikimedia Commons: *http://bit.ly/1yufln2*

FIGURE 8-4
The famous World War I poster of Uncle Sam[*]

FIGURE 8-5
An automobile's fuel gauge[†]

Like all signifiers, a fuel gauge means something because of its context. I can't actually see the mechanism that is connecting this indicator with the level of fuel in my car's tank; I have to interpret the connection. Also, the letters "F" and "E" are significant here because they are situated spatially along a continuum, with a needle that moves, in a car's dashboard, and with a fuel-pump icon nested in the layout.

---

[*] Wikimedia Commons: *http://commons.wikimedia.org/wiki/File:Unclesamwantyou.jpg*
[†] Photo by author.

Indexical and iconic signification both rely on some direct physical connection, either between the "pointer" and an object or between the physical form of a depiction and the physical form of what it portrays. In both of those modes, the signifier is specific to a particular signified referent. When I point at a pine tree, I'm not pointing at anything else. The fuel gauge is in a specific car, indicating a specific amount of fuel.

SYMBOLS

Symbols are different, in that they are signifiers that could mean anything, but have specific meaning only because of conventional usage in a given culture. We know what they mean only by experiencing their use in a system of other symbols and contexts, such as the "heart" symbol in Figure 8-6.

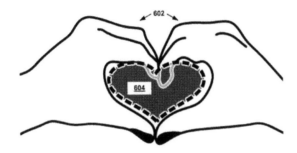

FIGURE 8-6
A gesture forming the symbol of a "heart" for "liking" something in the visual field of Google Glass (from Google's 2013 patent)[*]

Back to our example of the stairs: I can point at a stairway in answer to the question, "Where are the stairs?" and be performing an indexical sign. Or I might see a picture that iconically represents the form of stairs, giving a clue that stairs can be found near the picture.

But if I say the word "stairs," there is nothing in that phonetic sound that is intrinsically connected to an actual stairway; it has no uniquely bound connection other than through general agreement. Other languages don't have to use the same words used in English; they have their own conventional combinations of different sounds, as shown in Figure 8-7.

---

[*] *https://www.google.com/patents/US8558759*

stairs σκάλες 계단 سیڑھیاں

FIGURE 8-7

The symbolic written signifiers for stairs, from English, Greek, Korean, and Urdu, respectively (captured from Google Translate)

The essence of a symbolic sign is that the signifier is essentially arbitrary. Any sound could have ended up as our term for stairs. Even within the same language, we have synonyms: "steps" or "stairway" or "flight," as in, "I ran up 10 flights to get here!" That's not to say that language is just generated randomly, like rolling dice. Etymologies often point to onomatopoeic origins, imitating the sounds of nature, such as "buzz" or "zap" or even "scream." But most symbolic language is unmoored even from these tenuous literal connections.

The Superpowers of Symbols

Symbols are what make language so terrifically powerful: they can be variables that we can use with great flexibility to create new sorts of meaning. Here are just a few of the superpowers symbols give us:

Evocative expression

> The symbolic mode gives us the capability to use words in evocative, novel ways as similes and metaphors. This can make communication much more efficient: if I say I saw a truck "jackknifed" on the freeway, it conveys a lot of meaning about the truck's folded state that I would have otherwise needed to explain in detail. Symbols can also help us be more descriptive with language: I can describe an encounter with an attorney by saying, "That guy negotiates like a bulldog. I hate it that I got ripped off, but I swear I felt like I'd brought a banana to a knife fight." Of course, there were no actual animals, ripping, fighting, fruit, or sharp objects involved in this situation. If all those words were confined to their more literal meanings, such a sentence would be impossible, and its replacement would be far less expressive.

Categories

> Because they're often used to point at physical objects, categories can still have an indexical flavor, but they're freed from the tethers of specific reference. This allows us to combine concepts with other concepts. The word "mango" can mean the type of fruit rather than a specific mango I'm holding in my hand.

Categories have allowed us to organize the world around us to a scale that would've been impossible otherwise. The categorical label of an item makes it possible for us to find it more easily, but it can also change the way we perceive and understand that item, for good or ill.

Concepts

Symbols also allow us to work with concepts that are not categories of physical referent-objects but are new things that exist only in the realm of language and ideas. This might be the most super of our symbolic superpowers; we can create whole new environments of language-based things that we can use to solve problems, imagine new possibilities, and establish social agreements, boundaries, and expectations. In other words, symbols are the means by which we create new contexts out of nothing but language.

Reification

When we *reify*, we take an abstraction and treat it as if it were singular and concrete. For example, we often speak of "the economy" as if it were a monolithic object we could go and touch, measure, and understand in all its dimensions. But the economy is actually made up of many millions of transactions that don't necessarily have anything to do with one another. We do the same with concepts such as "nature," "the media," or "society."

Reification is a sort of cognitive quirk that allows us to understand, communicate about, structure, and act upon the world with categories and symbols rather than having to ponder every scattered facet every time. It's partly responsible for our ability to have language at all.

Still, like so many of our cognitive superpowers, it can also have a downside as a cognitive fallacy (called, you guessed it, the *reification fallacy*). We often confuse symbols or models we have created as the reality they represent. Treating the "economy" like it's a singular thing can lead us to assume one part of it, such as the stock market, is the whole, to the detriment of all the other factors that contribute to a healthy economy, such as infrastructure, education, and healthcare. Likewise, treating "design" as a single entity with solid boundaries results in endless debates among designers online and elsewhere.

Or, take the Facebook Beacon example: here was a situation in which the idea of "friend" was reified by Facebook to mean just one narrowly defined entity. (In fact, reification is a term of art in computer science for doing pretty much this very thing.) In fact, "friend" is not unlike the idea of "the economy" or "work"—when you try pinning it down with any precision, it dissolves under your fingers, because "friend" is an abstraction we use as shorthand to describe many different sorts of relationships in many different contexts. But defining that abstraction so narrowly resulted in collapsing the contexts of many real-life relationship dimensions to a single point.

Reification is inevitable; it's a core dynamic in how humans make meaning. So the trick is to pay attention to where it happens and ensure that it's establishing meaning in the way we need it to.

Signification Conflation

The modes of signification help us understand how the artifacts we design can mean something to users. But in everyday life, we and our users conflate these modes all the time. We use language so naturally, with so little conscious thought, that we tend to use symbolic signs as if they were indexical or iconic.

In actual experience, we tend to reify symbols as real things because it's quicker and easier. This is crucial to remember when we think about how we experience context: people make do in the world by *satisficing*. We reach for whatever tool, object, method, or mode of understanding that will get the job done with the least effort. This isn't laziness so much as an evolutionary feature of all natural things.

This is why scholars until the sixteenth century tended to think of words as copies of what they signified; it seems obvious in the same way that it seems obvious that the sun orbits the earth. In daily life, we talk about a "sunrise"; we don't say, "Let's go out to the beach and watch the earth turn!" It's only through thinking objectively about the whole system that we understand how something is actually working, rather than how we immediately perceive it. But that's a lot of work. In the systems we design, it's the designer's responsibility to do that work as much as possible, so the user doesn't have to. We want our users to be able to say "sunrise," even if it doesn't accurately reflect the "business rules" of how the solar system actually works. It wasn't the users' responsibility to comprehend the complexities of Beacon; and it wasn't my responsibility as a user of Google Calendar to comprehend that others in my company could see some parts of my calendar but not others. It was the system's responsibility to make its environmental invariants clear to the user.

Understanding signification can help us work through everyday design issues, because digital interfaces are essentially language constructs, wherein one of the most important tasks is to disambiguate the meaning of symbols. For example, in the version of the Zimbra email interface presented in Figure 8-8, it can be hard to determine which of the red X icons one should click, if trying to do so in a hurry.

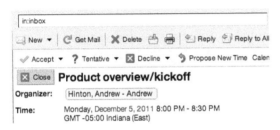

FIGURE 8-8
A version of the Zimbra email interface, showing an example of an email detail view

If you look at the interface closely enough and consciously ponder the layout and labels, it's not too hard to figure out. The nested position of each X icon gives clues to its meaning, but that's only when we pay explicit, deliberate attention. But in the heat of the workday, I found myself deleting or closing when I meant to decline an invitation, causing confusion between me and coworkers.

What was especially frustrating was that I didn't get better at this over time, I actually got worse. Why?

My cognition's "loop of least resistance" bends toward needing to learn an environment to the point at which I can do most or all of the actions tacitly, especially if it's an environment I use a lot. Yet, this interface has invariant structures that look too much like one another, keeping me from being able to just mindlessly click the correct object. This environment resists learning, keeping the user in a frustrating oscillation between tacit and explicit action.

In nature, things can masquerade as other things, but it's done for deception, allowing prey to better hide from predators, or for predators to fool their prey. Most flowers are actually flowers, not fly traps; most tree branches on the ground are wooden, not a snake. Our perception-action loop works best, and with the least confusion and explicit effort, when the environment allows us to conflate signifiers without having to solve referential puzzles.

Language Is Contextual

The contextual nature of language is something that makes semantic information fundamentally different from physical information. Language works entirely because of the context of what is said in relation to everything around it. We understand what a word means because we understand its relationship to its sentence, or the surface on which it is inscribed, or the character of the person talking. And, just as with our early diagrams of contextual relationships in Chapter 1, everything "around" a word also depends on context for its own meaning. We define words with other words or pictures of the things they name.

Shouting "fire" in a crowded theater is not the same as shouting "fire" during a military engagement. The phrase "Meet me on the bridge," spoken by *Star Trek*'s Captain Kirk has a particular meaning involving space adventures and ship commands; but if spoken by Jimmy Stewart's character in the movie *It's a Wonderful Life*, "meet me on the bridge" would involve dark emotions and whimsical angels earning their wings.

Language isn't just about words or pictures. It consumes much of what it touches, including many of the objects and surfaces in our environment. Take, for example, a simple object like the name tag in Figure 8-9.

If you see my name on a sticker affixed to my shirt, you can surmise that name is labeling me, not because of any *intrinsic* connection between the name and myself but through other means. There seems to be a direct indexical relationship between the written name "Andrew" and myself, because the name is "on me." It's one of the most straightforward ways we use language in everyday life. Yet, even that seemingly direct connection is constructed of many other elements in our surroundings:

FIGURE 8-9
Hello, my name is Andrew

- The sticker is a common object for displaying one's name at particular kinds of social functions at which strangers tend to meet and are expected to call one another by name.

- The sticker's layout fits a convention in which "Hello my name is" is pre-printed on the object, and participants write in their names (or the host runs the stickers through a printer, if neatness and RSVPs are high priorities).

- If the "name" part of the sticker said "cantaloupe" and not "Andrew," it would be ironic, because cultural convention dictates that name tags show people-names, and most people-names aren't lowercase categories of melon.

- At some gatherings, the cultural norm is that only newcomers wear temporary sticker name tags, which adds more context to the meaning of the object. Even these cultural norms are largely established through language use and then embodied in active ritual.

Here's the bottom line: a name written on a person's surface does not always mean that is the person's name. Wearing a T-shirt that says only "Bob Dylan" on it would more likely be a minimalist concert souvenir. The words-on-person construct needs a lot more context in order to even mean something as simple as "this is my name."

Yet, every time I see someone with a name tag, I don't have to calculate all of this explicitly. It's a learned feature of my environment. The name-tag object is an invariant cultural convention, learned in a system of other signifiers, just like language itself.

The Facebook "Like" is an example of a decontextualized gesture that lacks the clues I mentioned for the name tag. It's a blunt instrument that can mean almost anything depending on what is being liked, by whom, at what time, and with what commentary. Yet, complicating it with more choices would certainly constrain user expression more than help it. In that sense, the "Like" works the way any language does.

As we will see in other examples, much of the human-made environment makes sense only because of the language that stitches its meanings together. Our physical-information environment is contextually transformed by the way we communicate about it.

[9]

Language as Infrastructure

*If I feel physically as if the top of my head were taken off, I know that
is poetry.*
—EMILY DICKINSON

Language and the Body

LANGUAGE IS PHYSICAL. WHEN we speak, we're using our bodies to
breathe and create the sound vibrations for articulation, not to mention
gesturing and "body language." When we write, we add to the environment physical information that we assume a reader will interpret.

Broca, the French physician for whom the language center of the brain
is named (*Broca's area*), argued that we have "not a memory of words,
but a memory for the movements necessary for articulating words."[*]
We don't recall language-expression as a disembodied set of abstracted
concepts; it is rehearsed bodily action, eventually internalized over
time. Recent research has demonstrated Broca's argument: the more
scientists observe the neural mechanisms at work when we use language, the more they find that language and bodily action are not separate systems, as once assumed, but part of a single connected system.[†]
Even when we read silently, our bodies are firing neurons that we use

---

[*] Barrett, Louise. *Beyond the Brain: How Body and Environment Shape Animal and Human
Minds.* Princeton, NJ: Princeton University Press, 2011:214, Kindle edition.

[†] Pulvermüller, Friedemann. "Brain mechanisms linking language and action." *Nature
Reviews Neuroscience* July, 2005;6:576–82 (*http://bit.ly/10eMjlB*).

when reading aloud.* This *subvocalization* has been used by NASA in new technologies with which users can give commands without having to literally say them.†

There is mounting evidence that sophisticated, symbolic language has been with humans since before we were Homo sapiens and that it has been a factor in shaping the evolution of our species. Patients with brain injuries to the main language-related areas of the brain are often still able to relearn language, an ability requiring extreme redundancy in brain structures that takes millions of years of evolution to develop.‡ Anthropologists have established a strong connection between language and the sophistication of complex tools and weapons; and they have discovered evidence of such tools from many thousands of years before Homo sapiens emerged 200 thousand years ago.§

Like those ancient tools, language is something we add to our environment to extend our abilities. But, as established earlier, the meaning of language depends on context and convention. As ecological psychologists Sabrina Golonka and Andrew Wilson explain, "Conventions can change and so can the meaning of words; language is much less stable than [physical-information] perception."¶ We will keep coming back to this unstable nature of symbolic language, because it's central to how this kind of information adds ambiguity to context.

Structure of Speech

We use more than single words or short phrases when we communicate; we need to string together sets of symbols to convey even simple concepts. So a big part of how language works is through its

---

* Perrone-Bertolotti, Marcela, Jan Kujala, Juan R. Vidal, Carlos M. Hamame, Tomas Ossandon, Olivier Bertrand, Lorella Minotti, Philippe Kahane, Karim Jerbi, and Jean-Philippe Lachaux. "How Silent Is Silent Reading? Intracerebral Evidence for Top-Down Activation of Temporal Voice Areas During Reading." *The Journal of Neuroscience* December 5, 2012;32(49):17554–62 (*http://bit.ly/1wujhIr*).

† Braukus, Michael, and John Bluck. NASA Develops System To Computerize Silent, "Subvocal Speech." *NASA News* March 17, 2004 (*http://1.usa.gov/1FsgmWJ*).

‡ Deacon, Terrence W. *The Symbolic Species: The Co-evolution of Language and the Brain*. New York: W.W. Norton & Company, Inc., 2011, Kindle edition.

§ Meyer, Robinson. "Researchers Discover the Hot New Technology: Throwing Javelins." *The Atlantic Online* December 2, 2013 (*http://theatln.tc/1ybTOVw*).

¶ Wilson, Andrew D., and Sabrina Golonka. "Embodied cognition is not what you think it is." *Frontiers in psychology* February 12, 2013. doi: 10.3389/fpsyg.2013.00058. See more at *http://bit.ly/1shEeC8* and *http://bit.ly/1shElO6*.

grammatical structure. Without environmental context and the interior structure of language grammar, spoken words are just sounds if they are without significance.

The order of words in a statement determine the statements' meaning as much as the words themselves. For example, let's take a look at Groucho Marx's famous joke from the movie *Animal Crackers*:

One morning I shot an elephant in my pajamas.

How he got into my pajamas I'll never know!

It's old-fashioned humor, and funnier with Groucho's delivery. But hang on; I'm going to spoil the joke even more:

The poorly structured grammar is what makes the joke funny. It sets us up with a verbally sketched situation that we think we understand to mean he shot an elephant while wearing his pajamas—because that's the most likely meaning. In the cultural context of the joke, it's an *invariant* fact that pajamas are worn by people more than by elephants.

FIGURE 9-1
An elephant in pajamas (illustration: Madeline Hinton)

The joke works by playing with that cultural invariance, and by structuring the first sentence with what's called a *misplaced modifier*—"in my pajamas" is placed in closer proximity to the word "elephant" than the word "I." We *satisfice* the way we hear and assume the meaning of the first statement, based on cultural invariance, rather than the index-ical proximity between "elephant" and "in my pajamas." The punch line then completes the statement by shifting the context of the first statement—it turns out the elephant is the one in the pajamas, which is an absurdly silly image that "clicks" into recognition as the correct logical interpretation of the first statement. If he'd said "One morning, in my pajamas, I shot an elephant," it would have been more accurate, but wouldn't have been comedic.

Doing such a close reading and analysis of Groucho's quip certainly takes some fun out of it. However, the exercise illustrates the degree to which meaning depends on context, and how context depends on meaning. It also shows how it's hard to overthink context—getting it right demands some rigorous analysis.

Understandable language follows invariant conventions of structure, not unlike the physical environment. Language's emergent structures came from nature the way trees and flowers did; it's just that humans are the soil where language grows.

Keep in mind that grammatical rules were not bestowed upon us by grammar deities. Syntax emerges from bodies and environments.[*] Our language's structure is resonant with the structures of human action. The grammatical rules we learn in school are just the patterns that have coalesced over millennia, identified and codified, the same way words emerge from popular usage and are only later identified as new conventions and added to official dictionaries. Language evolves, mor-phing to meet the changing pressures of its environment.

Just as physical structure happens when two kinds of matter inter-sect, and layout occurs when there's a meaningful spatial relationship between various surfaces, language's structure happens in the inter-sections and arrangements of parts of speech.

So, it makes sense that language is structured not unlike the ele-ments of the environment we learned in Chapter 6. All languages have the equivalent of *object* and *event*—that is, some form of noun and

---

* Deacon, Terrence W. *The Symbolic Species: The Co-evolution of Language and the Brain.* New York: W.W. Norton & Company, Inc., 2011:354, Kindle edition.

verb.* Statements are *nested* within longer statements and narratives. Depending on the language, syntax (word order and proximity) can be more or less critical for understanding. Yet, all languages depend on some sort of structure, whether it's provided by modulation of voice, bodily gesture, or grammatical pattern.

Language has to follow its own emergent laws within a given linguistic system; the success of a given utterance depends on its structure and context, its place nested in an environment. Grammar is often behind the most egregious contextual errors in modern life. What works well for Groucho Marx doesn't work so well in a legal contract or a conversation with your boss. It especially doesn't work well when we try telling computers what to do—they depend on literal structure even more than we context-interpreting humans.

So much of what we design depends on well-structured language that it doesn't hurt to consider grammar an important element of good design. Still, the ultimate point I'm making is broader and deeper. We're now immersed in ambient and pervasive technologies that are essentially made of language. Outside of a carnival fun-house, irony and infrastructure shouldn't mix. A misplaced modifier can be the equivalent of a bridge collapse.

The Role of Metaphor

An important body of work in the last few decades has been about the connections between the body and language, especially how much of language uses bodily and spatial metaphors. In fact, one of the earliest works connecting language and embodiment theory is the 1980 book by George Lakoff and Mark Johnson, *Metaphors We Live By* (University of Chicago Press). At the time the book was published, the standard theory (originating in part from linguist Noam Chomsky) was that humans had universal, deep structures that gave rise to language; these structures gave language a formal logic, using repeatable

---

* There are exceptions, depending on how we define noun and verb. The language of Tonga, for example, has a different morphology, but still can be mapped within a noun/verb "prototype framework." Broschart, Jürgen. "Why Tongan does it differently: Categorial distinctions in a language without nouns and verbs." *Linguistic Typology*, de Gruyter, January 1, 1997;1(2) (*http://bit.ly/1rnQHEk*).

patterns, much like a computer.* Language was thought of as disembodied function, and metaphor was considered to be decorative, poetic speech that wasn't part of language's core function.

Lakoff and Johnson argued the opposite, positing that language is "fundamentally metaphorical in nature."† Language is the emergent set of behaviors, or techniques, we've developed to help us work through and communicate abstractions. The more abstract the concept being expressed, the more that expression relies on metaphor.

Lakoff and Johnson point out many metaphorical uses of the body, such as "give me a hand," "do you grasp what I'm saying?" or "I need your support; can you get behind me on this?" They explore more sophisticated metaphors involving cultural categories, including how we tend to talk about argument in terms of war metaphors ("Defend your claims"; "Her attack targeted my plan's main weakness.").

Of course, there are other metaphors we use in design that aren't so closely tied with the body, but still make use of conventions learned through nondigital, bodily experience. The personal computer "desktop"—with roots going back at least as far as the 1960s—is a foundational metaphor in graphical user interface design. Even though the desktop doesn't literally behave in every way like a physical desk, it still provides enough concreteness to help users get started.

Sometimes, though, a metaphor doesn't quite survive the translation. If we use metaphors inappropriately, it can be confusing. In Apple's iOS, the category structure for organizing photos borrows from pre-digital camera-and-film photography. At one level, it nests pictures into the larger container of Albums, and then puts photos into categories within the Albums container, as depicted in Figure 9-2.

---

* Chomsky's theories argue, in part, that the "deep structure" of universal grammar has a logical purity that isn't always translated to the messy "surface structure" of actual language use. This Platonic-forms approach runs counter to an embodied understanding of cognition, which unifies everything into one, nested, naturally messy system.

† Lakoff and Johnson, *Metaphors We Live By*. Chicago: University of Chicago Press, 1980:3.

FIGURE 9-2

The iPhone "Albums" structure in iOS 6 that somehow contained a "Camera Roll"

The categories, however, don't align with how we expect the metaphor of "Albums" to work. For example, the "Camera Roll" is nested under "Albums," but the metaphor has nothing to do with photo albums; it refers to film cameras that used physical rolls of film in canisters. Film rolls have a limited number of frames to use, and then you have to swap out the used film for a fresh roll. But that's not how the iOS Camera Roll works either—it has no frame limit other than the memory of the device, and you don't "swap it out" for a new roll at any point. It just continues to store whatever pictures you leave on the phone.

Interface metaphors don't need to slavishly copy the physical world, but neither should they appropriate meanings only in the name of seeming familiar, without also behaving according to the expectations they set. When the labels present a nested structure that's actually the opposite of the physical referents they borrow from, one wonders why use the metaphors at all.

Visual Information

Graphical information is also semantic but uses iconographic and indexical approaches in ways for which words are not as well suited. Visual information is especially good at borrowing from the objects of the physical environment to create explanations, metaphors, and spatial arrangements for conveying meaning.

Sometimes, graphics are used in strictly an iconic manner. Photographs, realistic paintings, and even abstract images, such as the stairs sign illustrated in Chapter 8 (Figure 8-2), can be used as icons for what they depict. Graphical user interfaces make heavy use of iconography, often more as symbols than strict icons. Some visual metaphors are for functions that have no present, physical referent. Figure 9-3 presents an example from a Macintosh computer: a padlock's open or closed state represents whether an administrator has unlocked settings so that she can make changes to settings.

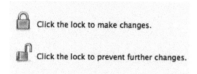

FIGURE 9-3
The locked and unlocked states in an OS X dialog box

The icon (and the mechanical sounds the computer makes when activating it) brings a representation of physical information into a semantic display. It clarifies, with body-familiar imagery, the state of locked versus unlocked. Of course, there is no actual padlock in the computer. Digital information is abstract by nature. Therefore, it requires translation, such as these metaphors. Even before the invention of graphical interfaces, computers used similar metaphors but with typed commands, such as "get," "put," and "set."

We also use graphics in less literal ways to physically represent abstract ideas. An early example is a diagram called the *tetragrammaton* (see Figure 9-4), which represented the Christian Holy Trinity.

FIGURE 9-4

A tetragrammaton from the twelfth century*

It takes something that people could not see in the physical world—the relationships between the Father, Son, and Holy Spirit, together in a single deity—and puts those together into a shape illustrating how the Christian God can be three beings and one being at the same time.

Even now, we use similar diagrams to explain abstract concepts, because making the ideas into representations of physical objects makes them easier to grasp. For example, the Venn diagram shown in Figure 9-5 shows the intersection of mathematical sets, or the shared qualities among multiple entities. It does a great job of making the invisible visible, working with otherwise disembodied ideas as if they were concrete objects.

Graphics are especially useful for giving form to the abstractions of mathematical measurement. The first known usage of visual explanation for data was by William Playfair in the late eighteenth century, as shown in Figure 9-6. The figure shows a trade balance relationship over time, involving England, Denmark, and Norway.

---

* *http://commons.wikimedia.org/wiki/File:Tetragrammaton-Trinity-diagram-12thC.jpg*

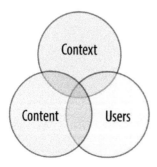

FIGURE 9-5

The "three circles of information architecture" introduced by Rosenfeld and Morville in the 1990s*

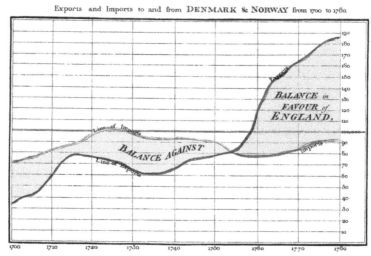

FIGURE 9-6

William Playfair's time series of exports and imports of Denmark and Norway†

---

* Used in their consulting practice since the mid-1990s, but first mention in print in *Information Architecture for the World Wide Web.* Morville, Peter, Louis Rosenfeld. *Designing Large-scale Web Sites.* Sebastopol, CA: O'Reilly Media, 1998.

† *http://commons.wikimedia.org/wiki/File:Playfair_TimeSeries-2.png*

In addition to this line-graph method, Playfair went on to invent the bar chart, the pie chart, and the circle graph—essentially creating the field of graphical statistics.

A recent practical example is the concept for a parking sign portrayed in Figure 9-7. Instead of the confusing jumble of words and numbers we usually see, the designer represented time spatially.

Visual information lets us model abstraction and work with thoughts and concepts symbolically, while managing to provide objects we can see, manipulate, and arrange. Like writing, this capability makes it possible for us to work with more-complex systems, over greater scale and longer periods of time. Even though our main focus is how words create information, they are often assisted by graphics, and vice versa. All of it is semantic information, and all of it functions as structure we add to our environment.

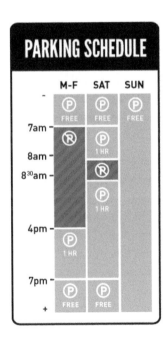

FIGURE 9-7
A graphical parking sign, by designer Nikki Sylianteng[*]

---

[*] Posted at *toparkornottopark.com* by Syliantent, Nikki, June 24, 2014 (*http://bit. ly/1CMoWvl*).

Semantic Function

How does semantic information work for perception and cognition? If we reserve "affordance" to mean physical information's direct specification of physical opportunities for action, where does language fit into the model?

Language is fundamental and clearly affects our behavior and experience far beyond mere abstraction. Signifiers are all fine and good, but *signification* is too easily construed as a cloudy, disembodied concept. Although accurate, it runs the risk of detaching how we think of language from its truly visceral effects. At the same time, language is not the same as physical information. The word "hammer" doesn't budge a nail, not even a smidgen.

I'll be using the phrase *semantic function* to indicate the way we use language as part of our environment (see Figure 9-8). What I hope it conveys is that semantic information has a *real, functional* role as invariant structure in our surroundings. Even though language can be exceedingly abstract—as in a word like "love"—it can have real, physical consequences—as when our hearts can suddenly race when we hear, " I love you." Language can be a sort of civil machinery, such as laws and contracts. It functions as instruction, like virtual guardrails for baking a cake or driving a car. So, semantic function is the near-equivalent of physical affordance but for semantic information.

From the perspective of the human agent, language and semantic conventions can become tacitly understood parts of the environment, to the point where the agent uses them with nearly the same familiarity and facility as the physical parts of the world.* In other words, to the agent, there is only *information from the environment*. The soft assembly of the agent's experience uses semantic function and physical affordance indiscriminately, in whatever combinations necessary.

---

* I have previously used the phrase "semantic affordance" for this idea, both in early drafts of this book and in "What We Make When We Make Information Architecture" (Resmini, Andrea (Ed.) Reframing Information Architecture Springer, 2014) and various presentations. I have since changed course, to avoid muddling the core value of Gibson's affordance theory.

As designers, we have to assume that for users there is no meaningful affordance-versus-function separation.* From the user's point of view, the main differences are along the explicit-to-tacit spectrum. But, to make something that users can easily use, we have to do the hard work of understanding these distinctions between affordance and semantic function in the work of design. Designers will likely continue using the term "affordance" more broadly than I am specifying here. But if these physical-versus-simulated dimensions are not clarified in the work of design, it can lead to dangerous assumptions about what users perceive and understand.

FIGURE 9-8
Semantic function surrounds human perception and augments physical affordance

The red stoplight in Figure 9-9 is a physical object that emits light in three colors. In the context and learned conventions of roadway driving, its red mode means *Stop*. Most of us respond to it physically, stopping in front of it. When learning to drive, we have to think about it more explicitly, but eventually we respond to it with little or no conscious attention. It becomes tacitly picked up, *indirectly* controlling part of our environment. Is it as directly perceived and controlling as a *physical* barrier? No, but it's about as close as a semantic sign can come to being such a barrier.

---

* Wilson, Andrew D., and Sabrina Golonka. "Embodied cognition is not what you think it is." *Frontiers in psychology* 2013;4(58).

FIGURE 9-9
A traffic light, displaying red to mean "stop"[*]

For a twenty-first-century person in the developed world, a huge portion of the environment is made up of these signs and symbols. They surround us as bountifully as trees, rocks, and streams once surrounded our ancestors.

Software interfaces are made entirely of semantic conventions. The only truly physical affordance on a digital device's screen is the flat surface of the screen itself. The only way it can interact with us is through signs and symbols—words with simulated surfaces and objects on the screen, or sounds whose meanings also require learning as language. There is ongoing research to create haptic interfaces that mimic the contours of three-dimensional surfaces, but they will only enhance the simulation. We will still need to learn what the simulated button, edge, or other object actually does.

That's because any object that controls something beyond its present physical form works a lot like language. Consider a typical light switch, such as the one in Figure 9-10. Even this simple mechanism might not be immediately clear in its function to someone who has never encountered one before. But for those of us who grew up around the use of such switches, there is intrinsic physical information that specifies the affordance of "flipping" up or down. That is all we know from looking at the object alone. What does the switch turn off or on? Is that even what it does? The answers depend on contextual relationships.

---

[*] Wikimedia Commons: *http://commons.wikimedia.org/wiki/File:Redtrafficlight.svg*

FIGURE 9-10
A domestic light switch*

To know what this switch will do beyond its intrinsic structure, I have to either be told, or I have to flip the switch to learn what happens. I've often been startled by the angry growl of a garbage disposer in a sink when I expected to illuminate the kitchen. To really understand controls like this, we often resort to adding labels, or otherwise creating semantic context between the object and its ultimate effect.

The switch is acting as a symbol. It's a signifier that could mean almost anything. Like language, our technological systems depend on contextual learning and associations. Yet, as we do with all familiar language, we conflate these elements. If you asked, "What does that switch do?" and I answered, "It flips up and down," you'd think I was joking around. "Of course it flips up and down, but what does it do when you flip it?" you'd counter.

When we point at a switch to ask someone "can you turn on the light?" when the light is actually above our heads, we've merged the *signifier* and *signified* across space. We're using one context to talk about and control another, essentially making them one. If we were designing a new light-control system, we would want to untangle the semantic function and physical affordance dynamics at work here, because they would inform how we might improve the system for use. At some point, though, we would have to again see it as one conflated, intermingled, nested system, because that's how its users will need to perceive

---

* Photo by author.

it, as well. This conflation happens when we learn anything, from how to use a computer mouse or game console controller, to how we learn to swipe left to right to unlock our smartphones.

We are a symbol-laden species, so the way we talk about the world pervades the world, affecting how we *understand* it and *use* it, regardless of how our bodies *perceive intrinsic* affordances. Just as a fallen branch might have an affordance of being picked up and held in the hand and then used as an extension of one's arm, a word for the fallen branch—like "club" or "kindling"—offers a new dimension of meaning for the branch, a semantic function implying certain kinds of action. And, it does this without anyone having to actually pick up the stick and use it.

In that sense, for language-comprehending humans, a label can alter *what the object actually is*. It doesn't change the physical form of the object, but for all practical purposes in human life, it's a different object. When we design products and services, we are designing in the "for all practical purposes" realm. In that realm, language functions as environment. That's because semantic function is not merely abstract; it shapes our very reality.

Tools for Understanding

Semantic function allows us to use words to name and organize our world. Gibson saw language as something that transforms the way knowledge works; it makes "knowing explicit instead of tacit. Language permits descriptions and pools the accumulated observations of our ancestors."[*] It turns knowledge into environment that can persist with us across time, even if only as stories imperfectly told from one generation to the next.

Andy Clark calls language "a form of mind-transforming cognitive scaffolding: a persisting, though never stationary, symbolic edifice [playing a] critical role in promoting thought and reason."[†] We use language to add structures to our environment, structures that inform us in ways that wouldn't exist without language. A conversation creates

---

[*] Gibson, J. J. *The Ecological Approach to Visual Perception.* Boston: Houghton Mifflin, 1979:263.

[†] Clark, Andy. *Supersizing the Mind: Embodiment, Action, and Cognitive Extension (Philosophy of Mind)* London: Oxford University Press, 2010:44.

environmental structures that we pick up as having meaning that supports collaborative action. A set of written instructions guides us in building a house or a piece of furniture, which we would not know how to create without those plans.

What this means is, *language is infrastructure.* Language can actually create new invariants for us to interact with and inhabit. It can have the effect of creating new elements in the environment—and even new environments. Symbolic language affords fluid usage of words for the things around us. Because there's not a necessary one-to-one, never-changing relationship between word and object, we can label things in many ways. This labeling function is one of language's most powerful abilities. Labeling is how we bring stability to our experience and make explicit sense of the world as humans.*

Clark describes this as language creating "a new realm of perceptible objects."† Here are the key points he makes about labels in particular:

- Labeling "functions as a kind of augmented reality trick," where we supplement our surroundings with new structure.

- Labels are "cheap" ways to group objects without having to actually move items around (and in some cases group things that we couldn't physically move into piles anyway).

- Labels are open-ended in the sense that we can group things that have no physically evident affordance for doing so.

- Labels behave much like physical tools for piling (and, for the piles they create), and our cognition treats them much as we treat the physical equivalent.

- Labels are, themselves, new objects added to the environment, for which we can then create new labels and pile at even higher levels of abstraction.

All these points have major implications for what language is to us, especially the last one: our cognition moves from physical-object to abstract-label-object with ease. We create systems with language that

* Weick, Sutcliffe, Obstfeld. "Organizing and the Process of Sensemaking Organization Science." *INFORMS* 2005;16(4):409–421.

† Clark, Andy. *Supersizing the Mind: Embodiment, Action, and Cognitive Extension (Philosophy of Mind)* London: Oxford University Press, 2010:45–46.

we use as additional "built environments." Labels and categories are certainly enabled by our brains, but they're not confined there. They are the trellises that shape the way our understanding grows. They are part of the environment that surrounds us, where we recognize them and orient ourselves around them the way we recognize and orient ourselves around landmarks.

The structure of our language can affect our ability to think through problems and articulate complex ideas. In recent work in composition education, teachers discovered that students were struggling to work through complex subject matter. It was partly because they lacked the linguistic scaffolding for doing so, especially the structural parts of speech that enable complex sentences: words such as "although," "unless," and "if." After those traditional elements were reintroduced, students showed improvement in synthesizing a thoughtful, complex response to an instructor's questions.[*]

This further reinforces the idea that language really is infrastructure for us. It gives us the "joints" for bending our thoughts in new directions and connecting them together into new concepts. We use language as part of our cognitive loop to reflect upon and come to new understandings about our environment and ourselves.

Semantic Architecture

Language provides not only a scaffolding for the physical world, but another world of language's own making, created from abstractions that aren't directly indicative of anything literally in the world at all. We live within the structures and constraints provided by those abstractions just as fully as we do among physical structures.

Gibson saw language as part of a continuum from simple affordances to highly complex "reciprocal affordances," saying that when the affordances of vocalization become the semantics of speech—and "manufactured displays become images, pictures, and writing, the affordances of human behavior are staggering."[†] Affordance of physical information undergirds and enables the workings of semantic function, which then introduces massively higher opportunities for complexity.

---

[*] http://theatln.tc/1ybUhH6

[†] Gibson, J. J. *The Ecological Approach to Visual Perception*. Boston: Houghton Mifflin, 1979:137.

Clark echoes Gibson in saying, "The cumulative complexity here is genuinely quite staggering. We do not just self-engineer better worlds to think in. We self-engineer ourselves to think and perform better in the worlds we find ourselves in. We self-engineer worlds in which to build better worlds to think in."[*] We don't have two separate brains—one for language and one for physical things. Even though there is a big difference in the intrinsic nature of physical information versus the mediated nature of semantic information, our cognition does its best to take it all in as one environment.[†] When we say we're trying to "clarify" a point or "make the complex clear," it's not just a metaphor; we're trying to make an environment's semantic function make coherent sense to our bodies.

It can surprise us, the degree to which language establishes structures that change the meaning of our behavior. Take for example an activity many of us encountered in childhood: the staring game.[‡] Two people agree on simple rules: "We have to stare at each other, and maintain eye contact, without breaking it; whoever breaks it first loses." Then, they begin staring at each other, probably trying various tricks to get the other to break contact, like telling a joke or making silly faces. Eventually someone breaks the stare, and the game is over.

If I walked up to you and just started staring, without this prior agreement, it would be...awkward. But, if we just have a quick verbal exchange about the rules, we create an information structure that we temporarily inhabit together. We've built a sort of place that gives us a new context for behavior. Even though it's only a simple game with a simple rule, it requires mountains of contextual meaning to exist at all.

Language makes places on its own, but also participates in making and remaking all the other human places we inhabit. The built environment and language are all part of an interconnected system of human meaning-making through using and dwelling.[§] William Mitchell

---

[*] Clark, Andy. *Supersizing the Mind: Embodiment, Action, and Cognitive Extension (Philosophy of Mind)* London: Oxford University Press, 2010, Kindle locations 1424–28.

[†] Golonka, Sabrina. "Language: A task analysis (kind of)." Posted in Notes from Two Scientific Psychologists, May 25, 2012 (*http://bit.ly/1x1ua4A*).

[‡] I owe Frederick van Amstel for this example, which he used as an instance of an "interaction" during his presentation at the 2012 Interaction conference in Dublin, Ireland.

[§] Mitchell, William J. *Placing Words: Symbols, Space, and the City.* Cambridge, MA: MIT Press, 2005:11, Kindle edition.

proposes that architecture is as important to language as language is to architecture. "The cognitive function of architecture (distinct from its function of providing shelter) is to create a rich environment for symbol, language, and discourse grounding, and act as the glue of communication that holds communities together."[*] Language is part of the human-made environment like everything else we build. It establishes structures and rules that we live in together. It creates architecture.

---

[*] Mitchell, William J. *Placing Words: Symbols, Space, and the City.* Cambridge, MA: MIT Press, 2005:12, Kindle edition.

[10]

The Written Word

To imagine a language is to imagine a form of life.
—LUDWIG WITTGENSTEIN

The Origins of Writing

MOST OF WHAT WE DESIGN INVOLVES WRITING IN ONE WAY OR ANOTHER, and writing has properties that are different from aural communication. Writing is much newer, but it's no less fundamental to our daily reality.

Writing as we know it emerged as an elaborate game of charades using scribbled and imprinted signs to create a mélange of evocations—some representational pictures, some phonetic, some a combination of both. Eventually writing became much more about encoding the richness of verbal language than mere pictorial representation, because the pictures were quickly co-opted into representations of the *sounds* of oral language, instead.[*] That is, pictograms were transformed into phonograms. After all, oral language was already a much more sophisticated and capable ability: why keep using clunky pictures strung together when so much nuance was possible by mimicking the sound of just talking?

Enter the use of phonetic writing. For example, a picture of a bull with horns might be co-opted to stand for a spoken sound that means "king." When that innovation happens, the flood gates open: writing starts being used mainly as a way to *encode verbal language.*[†] Chapter 9 relates how research has shown that our nervous systems fire sig-

---

[*] Boulton, David, Interview with Terrence Deacon, *childrenofthecode.org.* September 5, 2003 (*http://bit.ly/ZDcsJq*).

[†] This way of interpreting signs is called the "rebus principle." Even literal pictographic representations were quickly co-opted, transforming pictograms into what are called phonograms. A nice summary of these ideas is provided by the Metropolitan Museum of Art at *http://www.metmuseum.org/toah/hd/wrtg/hd_wrtg.htm.*

nals for reading aloud even when we're reading silently. When we read the written word, we are picking up information from the marks on a surface representing the bodily sounds we make when speaking; and because we've been taught (usually from an early age) how to decipher these marks, we have learned how to translate the physical affordance of "seeing marks on a surface" into the mediated meaning we get from "reading." As we become more practiced readers, we hardly notice that this sound-deciphering is going on. It feels as if we are directly perceiving the meaning on the page.

What Writing Does

In the terms of environmental elements, writing changes language from an oral *variant* event to a written *invariant* object. And that affords abilities that did not exist previously.

Oral language is trapped within an event-based, physically constrained mode of experience. Prior to writing, the only way to store and retrieve semantic information was to memorize it. In *The Art of Memory* (Pimlico), Frances A. Yates famously explains that orators developed elaborate mnemonic methods for retaining long speeches.

They imagined a huge house with many rooms, and then placed images or objects in the rooms that reminded the orator of the language that is to come next in the oration. "We have to think of the ancient orator as moving in imagination through his memory building whilst he is making his speech, drawing from the memorized places the images he has placed on them."[*] This strategy of using imagined rooms—physical information about places and connections between them—makes sense, given that we know memory is built up from physical experience of structural patterns in the environment. Yet, even for these incredibly adroit memorizers, the information was only "inside their heads" and could be expressed only orally, part of a linear narrative, spoken as an event of sound vibrating the air and disappearing.

---

[*] Yates, Frances A. *The Art of Memory* London: Pimlico, 1966:18.

Eventually some of these orators wrote down what they had memorized, which moved the cognitive work from the body to the surfaces of the environment. Writing meant that language wasn't just a stream of sounds that came and went; it allowed communication to be encoded into actual objects.

Even in the most advanced digital devices and software, spoken words are under event-based, linear constraints. When I use my car's GPS, the device speaks the directions, but if I'm distracted and don't hear them clearly, too bad—they're gone. I have to look at the written information on the screen (as well as the graphical semantic information, such as the map and status icons) to reference and analyze where I'm going. The entire concept of referencing information or "looking it up" wouldn't exist without writing.

Writing enabled us to freeze our ideas in time and space and then dissect and study them.* By separating the communicated thought from the moment, we can organize our experience in a different way. Writing brings the ability for us to be "meta" about our experience; to not just share knowledge but to *make* knowledge, and then make knowledge about knowledge itself. This turn brings with it the ability to organize information in completely new and innovative ways, untethered from the tyranny of linear, ephemeral speech.

The practical implications of this shift are significant. Here are some of the abilities with which writing imbues us that we did not have before:

Categories, and categories of categories
Oral language already uses categorical concepts. As philosopher and author Andy Clark told us in Chapter 9, labels give us "cheap" ways to group elements of the environment without having to actually move them physically, and to group things together that we wouldn't be able to move to begin with. But with writing, categorization really comes into its own. Classification moves from being something we use for organizing language about elements of our environment (animals, plants, and so on) to also being a way for us to organize the objects we've written upon, and even the ideas written about.

---

* Gleick, James. *The Information: A History, a Theory, a Flood.* New York: Random House, 2011, Kindle locations: 622–3.

Abstraction

Categorization introduces a whole new dimension of abstraction; the power it gives us to organize also results in further distancing information from its original signification. Classifying ideas produces semantic information that's even more abstract. We can make symbols for classes of symbols, which can then be classified yet again, ad infinitum.

Proliferation

Writing means that the semantic information we create persists in the environment; it doesn't go away unless its medium decays or we lose it or destroy it. Before long, the written artifacts really start to pile up. We eventually have a big challenge for what to do with all this written information that would have previously vanished into the air.

Storage and retrieval

Classification helps us devise ways to organize all these artifacts so that we can find them later. But the manner in which we classify information into categories is, in and of itself, a new sort of infrastructure that adds new information—new *environment*—to what already exists. Semantic information ushers in new activities of *storing*, and then *retrieving* (by first finding) information. These were activities humans previously performed only with physical elements of the environment. Hunting, gathering, storing, consuming—all the embodied actions we used for millions of years for survival, now being employed in the meta-dimension of the information we created for ourselves. But instead of objects being nested within features of the terrain, *we create our own nested terrain made of lists and categories*. The way in which we organize information in mechanisms such as databases matters with respect to how we can interact and have conversations with it, and how it can help us understand the world it represents.*

---

* Dourish, Paul, and Melissa Mazmanian (Department of Informatics, University of California, Irvine Irvine, CA). "Media as Material: Information Representations as Material Foundations for Organizational Practice." Working Paper for the Third International Symposium on Process Organization Studies Corfu, Greece, June 2011. *jpd@ics.uci.edu*, *m.mazmanian@uci.edu*.

Logic

The ability to write down ideas and analyze them, seek out their structures and reconfigure them into new combinations is a necessary condition for formal logic. Author and historian James Gleick explains, "Logic descended from the written word, in Greece as well as India and China, where it developed independently. Logic turns the act of abstraction into a tool for determining what is true and what is false: truth can be discovered in words alone, apart from concrete experience."* The ability to embody logical operations in language also helps set the stage for digital information—abstractions used as building blocks for new structural realities.

Complexity of thought

Being able to put our thoughts into the world as marks on surfaces gives us the ability to reflect on what we've written as reified objects. We can forget about them and come back to them, or we can add to them later. It supercharges our ability to create elaborate, vast conceptual systems. And it makes it possible for us to have thoughts that simply wouldn't have been possible otherwise.†

Transmission

Rather than sending a human with a memorized oral message, writing facilitates the message to be sent as an object, like any other cargo. It can be written in someone's "own hand" and sealed with a representation of their physical presence. That is, it affords a person the ability to be represented more intimately and directly to another, across time and space. And it allows these messages to take the form of infrastructure, stitching together cities and towns with invariant structures rather than variant events.

Writing enables us to create logically structured, transmittable, stored and retrieved semantic information. It brings a whole new dimension of communication and understanding, and gives us the capability to create persistent linguistic scaffolding for enhancing the natural and built physical environment. The ability to label, direct, and instruct

---

* Gleick, James. *The Information: A History, a Theory, a Flood.* New York: Random House, 2011, Kindle locations: 672–4.

† Barrett, Louise. *Beyond the Brain: How Body and Environment Shape Animal and Human Minds.* Princeton, NJ: Princeton University Press, 2011:194–5.

through written language and semantic graphics is a huge boon to creating the context of inhabited environments; it is part of what makes civilization possible.*

But writing also opens a sort of Pandora's box of environmental abstraction because it allows us to (in a sense) create scaffolds for scaffolds: environments that are mostly language referring to language—and ideas built on top of ideas—where there's little (if any) physical information to orient us to something concrete. The less physical information available to us, the less we can rely on the most ancient and capable aptitudes of our perceptual systems. It's this quality of writing that eventually leads to the characteristics of the digital mode of information, which we will explore in Chapter 11.

Lists

> The list is the origin of culture. It's part of the history of art and literature. What does culture want? To make infinity comprehensible.

—UMBERTO ECO*

Plain, mundane lists are one of the oldest (see Figure 10-1) and most useful forms of written language ever invented—and a prime example of how we use language as environmental infrastructure. They make labels—names of things—into structures that allow us to move the world around with only a pencil and paper (or a stylus and a slab of clay). Lists were among the first written artifacts ever made, and were possibly a main driver behind the invention of writing in the first place.

---

* Beyer, Susanne and Gorris, Lothar. "Spiegel Interview with Umberto Eco: 'We Like Lists Because We Don't Want to Die'," *Spiegel Online International* (*spiegel.de*) November 11, 2009 (*http://bit.ly/ZLUzc1*).

---

* Wiener, Norbert *The Human Use of Human Beings: Cybernetics and Society* Boston: Houghton Mifflin, 1954.

FIGURE 10-1

A cuneiform tablet listing a temple's possessions (shown at the Louvre, Paris)[*]

We take them for granted, but they still have an important role in everything we do. Especially in complex, high-stress situations, lists can literally save lives. In 1935, the United States Army was losing a depressing number of the new, complex Boeing B-17s—not to mention its pilots—to human error during takeoff and landing. Then, bomber crews were required to use procedural checklists: accident rates dropped to nearly zero. The requirement eventually had a major effect on Allied efforts in World War II.

Skip to 50 years later, and this ancient bit of infrastructure saved the day yet again, this time in hospitals, which were suffering from high infection rates and mortality due to infections from routine procedures. In a single initiative within Michigan alone, requiring checklists for such procedures saved "an estimated hundred and seventy-five million dollars in costs and more than fifteen hundred lives."[†]

In both of these cases, the people who were making life-endangering errors were experts. The army pilots, doctors, and nurses all had thousands of hours of experience. Ironically, it was their experience that was the problem: the more we do something, the more we *satisfice*, taking shortcuts without realizing it.

---

[*] Wikimedia Commons "List of possessions of a temple," (*http://bit.ly/1wkj4HO*).

[†] Gawande, Atul. "The Checklist," *The New Yorker,* December 10, 2007.

For simple physical tasks, where any harm is evident immediately through feedback, negative consequences can be calibrated against by our bodies. But when complex systems are involved (whether vast, complicated bomber aircraft or organic, invisible systems such as bacteria)—systems we can't perceive all at once and react to naturally—we need to add environmental structure to keep us on track.

The Structure of Writing

Oral language relies on the rhythms of speech for a lot of its context, and its form comes from how we express it with our bodies—our breathing, pitch, gestures, and more. Thus, writing requires even more care with how we structure sentences to ensure that we convey the full meaning of a message.

This is why many languages developed more standardized grammatical conventions. At one time, it was common practice for schools to teach grammar by using sentence diagrams, such as that shown in Figure 10-2.

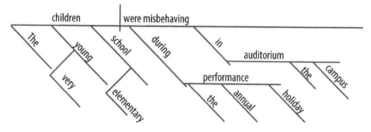

FIGURE 10-2

A sentence about elementary school children misbehaving in a performance, broken into a standard English sentence diagram format*

Writing gives us the ability to put what we say onto a surface and analyze it in a way that wasn't possible with oral speech. It makes it possible for us to have invariant objects that show these patterns, so we can point to them and agree on not just the structure, but what names we

---

* Based on an example from Wikimedia Commons: *http://bit.ly/1DtzCkI.*

use to categorize the parts. Standardization is possible only because writing takes the tacitly nested parts of oral speech and makes them into explicitly manifested objects.

Eventually, many languages also had to develop punctuation, which brings bodily context to writing, indicating where we should pause, breathe, modulate tone up or down to indicate a question, statement, or exclamation. It adds environmental information that provides needed context that we lose without hearing it spoken.

The following joke about a panda is an often-referenced example of how punctuation changes the meaning of a statement:[*]

> A panda walks into a café. He orders a sandwich, eats it, and then draws a gun and proceeds to fire it at the other patrons.
>
> "Why?" asks the confused, surviving waiter amidst the carnage, as the panda makes toward the exit. The panda produces a badly punctuated wildlife manual and tosses it over his shoulder.
>
> "Well, I'm a panda," he says, at the door. "Look it up."
>
> The waiter turns to the relevant entry in the manual and, sure enough, finds an explanation. "Panda. Large black-and-white bear-like mammal, native to China. Eats, shoots and leaves."

Like the quip in Chapter 9 by Groucho Marx about the elephant in pajamas, this works pretty well as joke, but it's also a surreal and silly contrivance that doesn't quite mirror real life. Pandas don't talk, for one thing. And even though they have thumbs, they would have trouble getting guns into cafés.

We know the phrase "eats, shoots and leaves" is silly because we're reading it in the context of the joke. But remove that context and put the written phrase under the pressure of *literal* interpretation, and it's not unreasonable for a reader to assume it describes someone eating something, shooting something (a gun? A basketball? Or slamming back a dram of whiskey?), and then departing the premises. The more decontextualized an expression, the more important grammar becomes, meaning that a single comma—something that could be mistaken for

---

[*] Truss, Lynne. *Eats, Shoots and Leaves: The Zero Tolerance Approach to Punctuation.* New York: Penguin, 2003.

a bit of lint—*changes the nature of the world that phrase describes.* This is true for human readers, but it's especially true for language-parsing computers, which rely heavily on standard structural patterns for comprehending text.

Turning language into the infrastructure we live in, whether laws or digital systems, puts a great deal of pressure on contextual meaning. Writing is a sort of proto-technology beneath all information technology. It's with writing that humans invented a way to encode speech for consumption outside its initial utterance. Now that we're encoding so much of the rest of the world we live in, we find that what's true for the context of language is also true for these other encoded "meanings"— everything from the labels on an entry form to the implied privacy of a social media conversation.

Language is not "extra"—it is central and vital. I've seen large corporations nearly crippled operationally because the categories used for incoming customer calls were poorly designed, and entire product categories fail because of fanciful labeling. When we sweat over content inventories and taxonomies, or we devise iconography standards and style guides, we are actually working with the beams, girders, ducts, and panels that create invariant structure for organizations, markets, and user experiences.

Rules and Systems

The structures we create with language are not only static frameworks and foundations, but conditional systems of logic and cause-and-effect that guide our actions, individually and collectively. We use them to construct cultural machinery made of rule-systems. Whether it's the "Terms and Conditions" listed on an e-commerce website, or the way a social network platform gives us the option to "like" something but provides no equivalent function for "hating" it, rules form essential functional elements of semantic environments.

When I was a kid, I played various sorts of stickball with neighborhood friends. Each time we played, we would need to have a discussion to decide on the rules. We'd either use the rules we'd agreed upon already, or we would adjust them. We'd go over them for new players and take suggestions on improving the structures of the game. We'd inhabit that rule system together for a while, play some innings, and then break off to do something else. We didn't have to write any of it down, because the group kept a collective recollection of the system well enough, and it kept adjusting and iterating anyway, adding to the fun.

But, what if we wanted to expand the game to other neighborhoods and have some kind of official tournament? That's how baseball emerged as a professional sport, with officially defined rules, such as those illustrated in Figure 10-3, which facilitated the game's scaling far beyond a group of kids playing stickball.

Writing allows us to officially record rules and share them as copies far and wide. It's the only way we can now have what we call "organized sports" at all.

Ever-expanding scale is something writing can accommodate nicely. As trade expanded thousands of years ago, it required writing to record inventories, prices, and negotiated transactions. Cities, commerce, expanding empires—all these reached a tipping point at which the "fittest" groups developed ways of keeping records, not only tallies but the agreements around the tallies as well as lots of other contextual information such as timelines and important stakeholders. Writing isn't just a by-product of wide-scale commerce; it's a necessary condition for having that level of commerce to begin with.[*]

Through writing, agreements can be taken out of immediate oral expression and fragile memory and made into actual, physical objects that not only contain but embody the agreements in documents. Furthermore, because documents can be copied, writing provides an infrastructure that can scale across great reaches of time and space, to an unlimited number of people, over generations.

---

[*] Gleick, James. *The Information: A History, a Theory, a Flood.* New York: Random House, 2011, Kindle locations: 759–60.

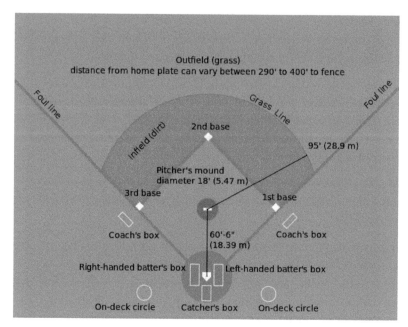

FIGURE 10-3

A diagram describing the semantics of physical layout for a baseball field*

When you watch a team play a game of cricket or baseball, just imagine the invisible mechanisms out on the field that form the boundaries for where players can run, when they can hit the ball, and how they can throw it, what constitutes a "point" in a team's score and what doesn't. There's almost nothing physical dictating these constraints—hardly any walls to speak of, no limb-restricting armatures, no team-switching mechanical apparatus. It's just people co-inhabiting a shared understanding of a set of rules. We're so used to it that it's hard to realize what a miraculous and amazing invention this is.

Like perception, symbols, and context itself, this shared environment exists because of people's actions. The teams, scorekeepers, umpires, and the rest are what make these games real. The rules in the rulebook stand as the definitive conceptual structure—a map defining the architecture for play. The game is an embodiment of the structures the rules describe. So, it doesn't take advanced technology to blur the lines between physical and semantic information; organized sports have

---

* Wikimedia Commons: *http://commons.wikimedia.org/wiki/File:Baseball_diamond.svg*

been around at least as long as Olympians, and they're still an example of how the semantic system of the *map* and the embodied action of the *territory* overlap.

This overlapping and integrated reality of written language and physical action is why semantic information is so thoroughly, inseparably part of context. For humans, there's effectively no environment that isn't fundamentally semantic.

[11]

Making Things Make Sense

Thoughts exchanged by one and another are not the same in one room as in another.
—LOUIS KAHN

Language and "Sensemaking"

WE CAN ACCOMPLISH A LOT OF PHYSICAL ACTIVITY WITHOUT HAVING TO CONSCIOUSLY MAKE EXPLICIT SENSE OF IT. We just do it. But sensemaking is a special sort of activity that brings another level of coherence with which we knit together our experiences, think about them, and understand them at a more abstract level.

When we consciously try to make sense of our experience, it is an expressly linguistic activity.* Like perception itself, language is enacted; it is something we "do."† We communicate with each other to develop a mutual understanding of our shared environment. Likewise, as individuals, we engage in a dialogue with ourselves about the environment and our choices in it, putting the mirror of language in front of us to "reflect" on our actions.

The term *sensemaking* generally refers to how people gain meaning from experience. More specifically, it has been the term of art for several interdisciplinary streams of research and writing, starting in the 1970s, including human-computer interaction, organizational studies, and information science. Much of the academic work on sensemaking has been about how people close the gap between their learned experience and a newly encountered technology or corporate environment.

---

* Weick, Sutcliffe, and Obstfeld. "Organizing and the Process of Sensemaking Organization Science." *INFORMS* 2005;16(4):409.

† Dourish, Paul *Where the Action Is: The Foundations of Embodied Interaction*. Cambridge, MA: MIT Press, 2001:124, Kindle edition.

When we study nature and strive to understand its complexity, we use language to create and reflect on that knowledge. The same goes for human-made environments, which are largely made of language to begin with. As one seminal article on sensemaking puts it, "When we say that meanings materialize, we mean that sensemaking is, importantly, an issue of language, talk, and communication. Situations, organizations, and environments are talked into existence."[*]

Our conscious engagement with context requires our use of language. When we experience new situations—whether a new software application or a new job at an unfamiliar company—we use language as an organ of understanding, calibrating our action to find equilibrium in our new surroundings. This activity involves the whole environment, including other people and the semantic information woven into the physical.

Like basic perception of the physical environment, this sensemaking activity happens at varying levels between explicit and tacit consciousness. Somewhere between fully conscious thinking and mindless action, we perform a nascent kind of interpretation but without explicit labeling, because no name has yet emerged for the new thing we encounter.[†] It's in the ongoing perception-action cycle that we have to exercise conscious attention and begin making explicit, thoughtful sense of the experience.

We can perhaps think of this as a dimension added to our earlier diagram showing the perception-action loop (refer to Figure 11-1). As we make sense of our environmental context, the many "loops" of cognition that make up the overall loop are cycling not just among brain, body, and environment, but at different levels of conscious attention across the explicit/tacit spectrum.

In each thread of sensemaking, there's a building of understanding that takes place. Tacit, passive awareness transitions to purposeful consideration, which then (for humans) leans on the infrastructure of

---

[*] Weick, Sutcliffe, and Obstfeld. "Organizing and the Process of Sensemaking," *Organization Science Vol. 16, No. 4, Frontiers of Organization Science*, Part 1 of 2 (Jul. - Aug., 2005), pp. 409-421.

[†] Weick, Sutcliffe, and Obstfeld 2005.

language to figure out "what is going on?"—which is then followed by "what do I do next?" This then spurs action that might go through the cycle all over again.

We carve understanding out of the raw stream of experience by eventually naming and conceptually "fixing" the elements of our environment. This creates conceptual *invariants* around which we orient our sensemaking. Eventually, these newly identified invariants become part of the "common currency" for social engagement.* In other words, this individual cycle is also woven into the fabric of *social* sensemaking, where we all collectively add to the environment for one another, causing shared conceptual structures to emerge in our common culture.

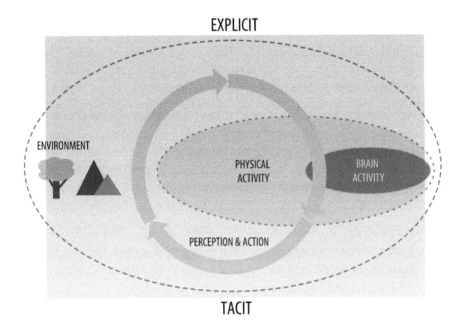

FIGURE 11-1
Explicit and Tacit spectrum over the perception-action loop

There's an awful lot going on in the preceding paragraphs, so here's an example to illustrate: imagine pulling up to a fast-food restaurant's drive-through menu. You're hungry, and just wanting something to eat, but you're also trying to eat more healthy fare lately, so you're

---

* Weick, Sutcliffe, and Obstfeld 2005.

looking for better nutritional choices. Your hungry body (and emotional brain) is getting in the way of your more explicit health-goal-driven thoughts, all while trying to figure out what food is represented in the menu while an attendant is squawking, "What's your order?" through a scratchy audio speaker.

A lot of your decision-making is being driven tacitly: your hungry body and the emotional centers of your brain are body-slamming your ability to thoroughly parse and understand the menu, while another hungry driver revs his engine behind you.

The convoluted menu doesn't help much: clever labeling of a "Prime Deluxe" and a "Premium Choice Grill" doesn't provide much distinguishing information. And the most-popular options (because they're the most tasty and least healthy) have the biggest pictures and easy-to-order numbering schemes—like a magician forcing a card to you on stage—nudging you further toward taking the quick option rather than having to make a more difficult decision.

To avoid slipping into the path of least resistance, you have to begin reading the menu aloud to yourself, working hard to find the specific trigger terms you're looking for—"salad" or "heart-healthy," or whatever—and doing the math of calorie counts. Otherwise, you know you'll just give up and say, "Gimme a number three," and then drive away with a sloppy burger and a bag of greasy fries.

It's challenging to make sense of the environment well enough to make a different choice and avoid the less-thoughtful, default "grooves" provided by the menu (and the stressful pressure to "order now" while others wait behind you). You have to stop and think, calculate, and drag your brain into explicitly reflecting with language.

This insight about how people make sense of their experience is crucial to designing context in any environment. Users gain coherent understanding of what they're doing, where, and with whom, through individual and communal activity and communication. What something or somewhere "is" depends on all those factors, not just the discrete interaction of one person with one object or place. Nothing we make for others to use is experienced in a vacuum; it will always be shaped and colored by its surrounding circumstances.

Even the labels we put on products can alter our physical experience of them. In a well-known series of experiments, neuroscientists had subjects sample wine with differently priced labels—from cheap to expensive. The subjects didn't know it was the same wine, regardless of price. Even though the semantic information specifying price was the only difference between the wines, functional Magnetic Resonance Imaging (fMRI) brain scans showed significant differences in activation of pleasure centers in the subjects' brains—they literally enjoyed the "expensive" wine more than the "cheap" one, even though there was no physical difference in the wines.[*] Again, our perceptual systems don't spend a lot of time parsing semantic from physical information. These subjects took price as a face-value framing for the wine, knowing nothing else about it. It's another example of how our immediate experience of the environment is a deeply intermingled mixture of signification, affordance, cultural conditioning, and interpretation. Similar studies confirm that the aesthetic styling of websites can strongly affect users' opinions of their value.[†]

In the airport example from Chapter 1, much of my activity was nudged and controlled by the semantic information that surrounded me, in concert with the social context: I tended to gravitate toward actions that were similar to what others around me were doing; and most of what I did was almost completely tacitly driven, until I had to stop and think about it explicitly. And even then, I found myself asking another person about what to do, and talking to myself about the labels and physical layout I was trying to understand. There was no separating the language from the physical layout of the airport; they were both intermingled as "environment" for my perception-and-action.

[*] Plassmann, Hilke, John O'Doherty, Baba Shiv, and Antonio Rangel. *Marketing actions can modulate neural representations of experienced pleasantness.* Published online before print January 14, 2008. doi: 10.1073/pnas.0706929105. PNAS January 22, 2008;105(3):1050–4.

[†] Reinecke, Katharina, Tom Yeh, Luke Miratrix, Rahmatri Mardiko, Yuechen Zhao, Jenny Liu, and Krzysztof Z. Gajos. "Predicting Users' First Impressions of Website Aesthetics With a Quantification of Perceived Visual Complexity and Colorfulness." Proceeding CHI '13 Proceedings of the SIGCHI Conference on Human Factors in Computing Systems New York: ACM, 2013:2049–58 (*http://bit.ly/1FwSxNz*).

Physical and Semantic Intersections

In a sense, ever since we started naming places together, we've been living in a shared "augmented reality," in which language, places, and objects are impossible to separate. Semantic and physical information are now so intertwined in human life that we hardly notice. Consider just a few ways that they work together:

Identification

> We name things and people so that we can talk about them and remember what and who they are. Recall that labels give us the ability to move things around in our heads (or "on paper"), piling, separating, juxtaposing. Anything of shared human importance has a name.

Clarification

> Sometimes, we can already tell what something is, but we still need more context. I can ascertain that an egg is an egg, but information on the carton informs me if it's organic or cage-free as well as when the eggs will expire.

Orientation

> A typical door has clear physical information for affordance, but without more information we don't know why we would use that door rather than another. Especially in built environments where manufactured surfaces can all look nearly alike, there's little or no differentiation (unlike in nature) to distinguish one layout from another. So, we need supplemental orientation to tell us "long gray hallway A goes to the cafeteria, and long gray hallway B goes to the garage." Likewise, stairways clearly go upward, but their destination is often obscured. A wider view of our stairs example from Chapter 4 reveals that a step has the label "Poetry Room" painted on it (Figure 11-2). The label adds orienting information about where we will be after we climb the stairs—semantic scaffolding that signifies the context of the physical affordance.

FIGURE 11-2

The wooden stairs in the famous City Lights Bookstore in San Francisco, this time showing a label*

Instruction

Even if we know what something is, we often need help knowing how to use it. In recent years, many public bathrooms have been outfitted with automated fixtures. The invariants that many of us grew up around in bathrooms have been scrambled, so we have to figure out each new bathroom anew. In one, the sink might be automated, whereas the toilet is not, and in the next it can be the opposite. Anything that doesn't have clearly intrinsic affordances requires some kind of instruction, even if it comes from instructing ourselves through trial and error. Instructions are an example of how all these sorts of semantic-and-physical intersections can overlap and work together. Sometimes, instructions help identify, clarify, and orient us all at once.

DIGITAL INTERSECTIONS

As we are called upon to create more physically integrated user experiences, these intersections between language, objects, and places are increasingly critical for us to design carefully. In software, it can be even more challenging, because the objects and places we simulate with graphical interfaces can so easily break the expectations we've

---

* Photo by author.

learned from the physical environment. Recall from the Chapter 1 how hyperlinks introduced an unprecedented flexibility in connecting digital places but also introduced new opportunities for contextual confusion.

On the City Lights Bookstore website in Figure 11-3, we see labels, but no physical information other than what is simulated with graphical elements (color blocks, lines, arrow-triangles, negative space) and layout (spatial relationship of elements to one another) telling us that the label "POETRY" is something we can touch, and that it will take us to what we expect to be another place, about poetry. The function of a hyperlink is learned through experience and established through convention, like language itself.

FIGURE 11-3

The Poetry link on the City Lights Bookstore website

If we walked up the stairs of the store, only to find that there was no "Poetry Room" but instead some other sort of room, or no room at all, we'd be disoriented. Similarly, tapping or clicking the hyperlink takes us to a place that we expect to fulfill the promise of the label. In a digital interface, however, so much of the information is semantic that the interface has to be designed with great care to reduce ambiguity, because the meanings of the labels and the subtle hints of visual layout are all we have work with as guiding structure for users.

In the built environment of cities, we've created such complex structures that we struggle to rely on the shapes of surfaces alone to give us contextual clues about where to go. So, the field of architectural wayfinding has expanded over the years to be almost exclusively about using semantic information to supplement the physical. The way icons and text help us get around in a city or building can make a huge difference in our lives. For example, in hospitals, research shows that good wayfinding promotes better healing, medical care, and even improved fiscal health of the organization.[*]

We can look at any modern city intersection and see how much semantic information is required to supplement human life there. In the image from Taipei City shown in Figure 11-4, nearly every surface has semantic markings, from the advertising to the street signs, traffic signals, and even the arrows, crosswalk markings, and street boundary lines painted on the city's streets.

When we say *city*, we are talking about all of these modalities, all at once. In fact, it's hard to say that language is merely scaffolding here, because in some instances the buildings are there to support the cultural activity of language-use to begin with. That is, the language environment came first, and the built environment emerged to support its growth and evolution. Language is more our home medium than steel and concrete. We've been speaking sentences longer than we've been building roads.

To understand and improve these environments, we should know how to distinguish physical from semantic, but we should not forget that the denizens of such a city can't be expected to parse them. They are intermingled in what information architect Marsha Haverty suggests is a "phase space"—just as water can undergo a phase transition from solid (ice) to liquid (water) to gas (steam), information can move across a similar spectrum.[†]

[*] Huelat, Barbara J., AAHID, ASID, IIDA. "Wayfinding: Design For Understanding." A Position Paper for the Center for Health Design's Environmental Standards Council, 2007 (http://www.healthdesign.org/chd/research/wayfinding-design-understanding).

[†] Haverty, Marsha. "Exploring the Phase-Space of Information Architecture" Praxicum (praxicum.com) May 8, 2014 (http://bit.ly/1t9pLgP).

FIGURE 11-4
Taipei City, Nanyang Street, in 2013*

But, unlike water, which is categorically and empirically in one state or another, semantic information adds the contextual slipperiness of language to the distinction. No matter the perceiver's *umwelt* (uniquely perceived environment), steam will have the properties of steam. But the word "tripe" in reference to some Chinese cuisines, where it is a staple protein, has a radically different meaning compared to a context in which "tripe" is an insult.

Physical and Semantic Confusion

Just because the modes intersect doesn't mean it always works well. Sometimes, the semantic information we encounter is actually *contradictory* to the physical information at hand. In *The Image of the City*,

---

* Wikimedia Commons: *http://bit.ly/1xazYaH*

author Kevin Lynch explains that, even when a city street keeps going in a physically continuous direction, if its name changes along the way, it is still experienced as multiple, fragmented places.[*]

We tend to lean on language as a supplement to the otherwise confusing parts of our physical environment. Sometimes the language we add can be helpful, but often it goes unnoticed or only adds confusion.

In a legendary example from his work, Don Norman explains some of the problems with doors, and why the semantic information we often add to them is a crutch we use to correct for poor physical design. This portion is from the revised 2013 edition of *The Design of Everyday Things*:

> How can such a simple thing as a door be so confusing? A door would seem to be about as simple a device as possible. There is not much you can do to a door: you can open it or shut it. Suppose you are in an office building, walking down a corridor. You come to a door. How does it open? Should you push or pull, on the left or the right? Maybe the door slides. If so, in which direction? I have seen doors that slide to the left, to the right, and even up into the ceiling. The design of the door should indicate how to work it without any need for signs, certainly without any need for trial and error.[†]

The shape of door handles and how they indicate the proper operation of the door has been a touchstone of Norman's influential ideas since the first edition of *The Design of Everyday Things* in the 1980s. The example is a great one for teaching designers that the affordances of a designed object should be intrinsically coherent as to how they should be used, especially basic objects such as hammers, kitchen sinks, and doors.

Yet, there's more to a door than we might assume. Physically, there is a *doorway*—the opening itself—which is intrinsically meaningful to our bodies. It is directly perceived as an opening in a wall, providing a

---

[*] Lynch, Kevin. *The Image of the City*. Cambridge, MA: The MIT Press, 1960:53.

[†] Norman, Don. *The Design of Everyday Things: Revised and Expanded Edition*. New York: Basic Books, 2013:1–2, Kindle edition.

medium through which we can walk, in the middle of a solid *surface* of a wall. No signification—in the sense of something that means something else—is required.

That's where the simple affording information stops, because as soon as we add a *door* to the doorway, things get a lot more complex. Even though the door is physical, there are many mitigating factors involved in how we perceive its function. As Norman points out, we have to know whether the door opens inward or outward, sideways, up or down, and if we need to pull or twist something to open it, or if it's automatic, and what behavior will trip its sensors.

In Gibson's terms, a door is a *compound* invariant—a collection of invariants that present a combined, learned function of "opening" and "closing" doors. A specific door is a solid cluster of objects that works the same way each time, following its own physical laws. Even if it doesn't work like any other door, it persistently stays true to its own behavior.

Similar to how language means what it does because of conventional patterns of meaning, most doors fit conventional patterns or genres of door function. That is, even simple doors require learning and convention. We learn after a while that certain form factors in doors indicate that they work in one way versus another, not unlike the mailbox discussed in Chapter 7. Even if everything about the door is visible—its hinges, its latch mechanism—it still requires our having learned how those things function for us to put together the clues into the higher-order, mechanical affordance of door use. All of this speaks to whether we understand we are in a context in which we can go through an opening or not, and what physical actions will cause the events we need in that context.

Then, there is the nested context of the door: is it in a building where people are conditioned to avoid walking through unknown doors, such as in a highly secure office complex? Is it in a school where students learn a pattern of where to go from class to class each year? I still remember how it felt to start a new grade in school and be granted access to new rooms in new classes: the entire school felt as if it shifted under my feet, and old doors became clutter, whereas new doors became the new shape of places for what "school" meant to me...at least until the next summer.

No door is an island, so to speak. It's part of a larger construct of symbols, social meaning, and cultural expectation.

I had a recent experience with a door that reminded me of Norman's examples. In this instance, I nearly smacked my face into the glass entrance of an office supply store, because I didn't pick up on the "Pull" label next to the door handle. Here's a picture of the door in question.

FIGURE 11-5
A door leading into a retail store[*]

There were a lot of contextual elements that contributed to my embarrassing encounter:

- As in Norman's examples, the handles were not shaped in a conventionally distinctive way to indicate whether they better afforded pulling than pushing. In fact, they look a lot like the handles that one normally pushes.

---

* Photo by author.

- The doors are transparent glass, so I was already looking inside the store, trying to spot the department I was there to visit, barely paying attention to the door itself.

- The glass also allowed me to see the handle on the other side; and since most doors with the same shape handle on both sides open both ways, my perceptual system didn't bother looping more explicitly to cause me to consider any other possibility. As always, my body *satisficed*.

- The sign wasn't *invisible* to me—but my perception picked it up as *clutter* rather than its intended, semantic meaning. It was just an object between me and where I was going; an aberrant protrusion of gray into the glass. One, simpler set of information rode along on my "loops of least resistance" to override another, more complex set of information.

- Also note how there is little difference between the capital letters spelling "PUSH" and "PULL." So, in terms of raw physical information, this situation was relying on the narrow difference between "SH" and "LL"—on a label that was the same color as the door's aluminum.

- I was having a conversation with my wife and daughter, who were with me, so I was verbally preoccupied. Even though our cognitive abilities can take in lots of intrinsic, physical information at once, we have a difficult time picking up clear information from more than one semantic interaction at the same time.

- I was the first to reach the door, and by the time I did so, the sign was actually below my field of vision. So when the door didn't budge, the sign was of no help to me. Of course, my daughter's barely stifled laughter and exclamation, "The sign says 'Pull,' Dad!" helped to clue me in.

Beyond rationalizing my clumsiness, this detailed look shows how we can take a simple situation and do a rigorous analysis of environmental information to think through the cognitive scenario. We should always bring such a "close reading" approach to answering the central question we're exploring in this book: *will this environment be perceived and understood, in a real situation, with real people?* The reluctance and lack of patience in design work to do this kind of analysis is precisely why so many designs still have contextual confusion.

This door isn't an object on its own, but a system of invariants, nested in an environment of other invariants, from simple intrinsically physical information to higher-order, complex, and *signified* semantic function. And, it's nested within events involving people, some of whom are in an embodied state to comprehend "PULL" and some who aren't. Context isn't just one thing for everyone; it is shaped in part by the actions and perceptual state of the agent. From my perspective in this scenario, there was no clear line where affordance ended and signification began.

We see similar issues in the simulated objects and surfaces of digital places. For example, all of us have experienced receiving marketing content via email and deciding we want to unsubscribe from it. Most of these emails provide an easy way to turn off the subscription with only a click or two. Like most doors we encounter, we approach it with expectations driven by the invariants of convention and prior experience.

So, when my wife tried to unsubscribe from the deluge of emails she was receiving from Fab.com, she assumed it would work like the others. Tap or click "unsubscribe" in the email, then possibly verify the request at a web page. But she kept getting the emails. Take a look at Figure 11-6 and see if you can spot the problem. Notice the big, red button that would normally signify the invariant for "Yes, let me out of this!"—but here, it actually means "No, I decided to stay!"

The interaction presents a series of steps that conventionally end with unsubscribing. A big red button at the end of most transactions means: Yes, complete this irreversible action. But in this case, it does the opposite, confounding what the user has learned from invariants in the past. This interaction was also nested within a smartphone's display, rendering the view with tiny text that's almost unreadable. So, not unlike the door into the retail shop, the text wasn't doing much good here, and was easily trumped for a typical, satisficing user, relying on their cognitive "loop of least resistance."

Is this the end? Is it over? Ugh. That's so not Fab!

Okay, now to opt back in to all communications click the button below...

Opt Back in for Fab.com Communications

FIGURE 11-6

The "dark pattern" of accidentally resubscribing to Fab.com takes advantage of learned invariants

It's similar to a technique used in so-called *phishing* scams, which trick users into providing information they would not otherwise offer. Phishing is named that way—after "fishing"—because, like a hungry fish biting a baited hook, a user often acts based on learned invariants without explicitly considering all the environmental factors at hand.

When an interface takes advantage of our cognitive shortcuts, against our wishes, we tend to call that a "dark pattern"—a sort of "dark side of the force" usage of a design pattern. Whether the designers at Fab.com did this consciously or not, the effect is the same. It uses our forward motion through the environment against us rather than meeting the embodied expectations we bring to the invariants of our context.

Ducks, Rabbits, and Calendars

Semantic information gives us the remarkable superpowers of symbols, but at the cost of disconnecting language from the physical environment. The less contextual information we have, the more complicated signification becomes, whether with visual or textual semantic information. In *Philosophical Investigations*, Ludwig Wittgenstein famously regards a line drawing that could look like either a duck or a rabbit, and uses it as an example for how language works.[*] He refers to the figure

---

[*] Wittgenstein got the idea from an 1899 article by the early experimental psychologist Joseph Jastrow, who borrowed the figure from *Harper's Weekly* (which had republished it from a German humor magazine). The example here is from Jastrow (Wittgenstein's is a simpler line drawing) (*http://socrates.berkeley.edu/~kihlstrm/JastrowDuck.htm*).

in numerous places throughout *Investigations*. In one instance, he discuss how, if we place the picture among other duck pictures, it looks more like a duck, and more like a rabbit among rabbit pictures.*

FIGURE 11-7
From Jastrow's "The Mind's Eye," 1899†

Wittgenstein also explains that when we see such a figure, we don't usually say, "I see it *as a* duck," or "I see it *as a* rabbit." Instead, we say, "I see *a* duck," or "I see *a* rabbit." That is, in our natural manner interacting with language, we don't step back and distinguish between seeing something or seeing a representation *as* that something.

An optical illusion or visual trick such as the duck-rabbit works because it's an incomplete representation, constrained by its medium. In nature, we wouldn't confuse a duck for a rabbit; there would be enough physical information that we could pick up through active perception to tell one from the other.

But an optical illusion like this is not the physical world: it is a representation—a *display*—that leaves out the information we evolved to pick up when perceiving actual surfaces and objects. This is a quality that semantic information has generally; whether words, pictures, or gestures, it introduces ambiguities into our environment much more easily

---

* Ludwig Wittgenstein *Philosophical Investigations* Copyright © Basil Blackwell Ltd 1958. First published 1953. Second edition 1958. Reprint of English text alone 1963. Third edition of English and German text with index 1967 Reprint of English text with index 1968, 1972, 1974, 1976, 1978, 1981, 1986. Basil Blackwell Ltd. 108 Cowley Road, Oxford, OX4 1JF, UK

† Jastrow, J. "The mind's eye." *Popular Science Monthly*, 1899, 54:299–312.

than physical information. Of course, this picture could be expanded to finish the drawing of the animal, and that would make it more clear what sort of animal it is. Like Groucho's elephant in pajamas, though, this would spoil the "trick." Most information environments aren't jokes or optical tricks, however; they're meant to be understood.

Because semantic information is part of our environment, our cognition tries to use it in the same satisficing way we use floors or walls or stones lying on the ground. We try working with it and making our way through it as if it were physical. When we see a link in a website that says "Poetry," in the moment of action, we don't typically think to ourselves, "I am going to click a link that means poetry and it will take me to things that represent publications containing poems." We take the action expecting to then see and interact with objects containing poems. We "go there" to "look at the books." We reify and conflate, as if it were a passageway into a place. When we look at a particular book on a bookstore's website, we treat it as if it were a book we were looking at on a physical shelf at a local bookshop, if the website's design affords us the convenience to do so.

But the same sort of ambiguity that we see with the duck-rabbit can creep into our software structures. Recall in my airport scenario how I had assumed that my coworker could see my travel information in my calendar? This has to do, in part, with how Google Calendar uses the word "calendar" ambiguously, but it also has to do with how a calendar isn't just one display object anymore, but an abstraction that is instantiated in many different contexts.

Figure 11-8 displays some of these instantiations:

A. The object that iconically represents a calendar as represented in the Google Apps navigation menu.

B. Within the Web view, a calendar-like interface that takes up most of the screen, from the left column to the right edge.

C. Also in the Web view, the lists of "My calendars" and "Other calendars." These are actually calendar feeds but are *named* here as "calendars."

D. In TripIt's web interface, the "Calendar Feed" I use to create the published calendar-API version of my TripIt itineraries.

E. In its "Home Screen" interface, my iPhone also has a "Calendar" app icon, which also represents the idea of a singular calendar-object.

F. My calendar as shown when opened on my iPhone. It shows some of the same information as the Google Web view, but not all the same. Some is color-coded differently as well. It doesn't explicitly differentiate the "feeds" other than by color and by displaying the source of an event in its event-detail view.

FIGURE 11-8

The various instances of "calendar" from the airport scenario in Chapter 1

Example B shows that I have a Project Status Meeting scheduled in the middle of my flight to San Diego. That's because the scheduler didn't know I was on the flight: the flight's "calendar" is a feed generated by TripIt, and isn't visible to those who share my Google Apps calendar.

Did I understand how all this worked? Yes, when I thought about it explicitly. But it had been many months since I had set up the TripIt feed, so I had forgotten the rules for access permissions and was in too much of a hurry to think about them. In the satisficing actions we take in an everyday environment, we don't always take the conscious, explicit effort required to disambiguate all the different meanings of something. This is especially true if the environment's language conflates many functions into one semantic object—in this case, the word "Calendar."

There are many examples in Google's applications suite, and in their other products, where they go to great lengths to provide these contextual cues. However, the more complex the contextual angles and facets of an environment become, the more the design has to strike a balance between context clarity and cluttering an interface. Users look at a calendar to see dates and reference or create events; comprehending the entire rule-based environment is peripheral to the main purpose, even though it is at times a crucial aspect of the application.

In this case, I can hardly fault the design decisions behind Google Calendar; they've provided at least some cues: they use a differently textured background color (faint stripes) to indicate a subscribed feed versus an item that is actually part of my Google calendar data (a convention not necessarily followed in a calendar client application, however). Additionally, when I click on the flight event, it's clear that it is something that is part of the "AHTripit" calendar (see Figure 11-9), and that I could "copy to my calendar" if I wanted.

From an engineering perspective, everything works as it should; the system has a coherent logic that allows it to function with consistent rules. Even the interactive moment-by-moment mechanisms that I tap, click, or manipulate in these bits of software are fairly understandable. Where we find ourselves most muddled is in the information *architecture* of how the objects and places—and the rules that govern them—are represented with semantic information.

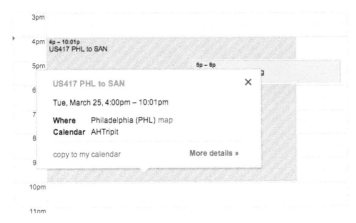

FIGURE 11-9

Google Calendar on the Web allows me to see what "Calendar" the event is part of, and gives a one-click method to add it to my present "calendar"

When I look at a predigital calendar, like the sort that hangs on a wall in the family kitchen, I know what I am seeing exists only in that place and time. But digital technology gives us the flexibility to create calendars that exist in many different forms. In a sense, there is no single calendar, no canonical object. It's an aggregate, a reification; when we ask, "Will the real calendar stand up?" either they all stand, or none of them do.

Semantic information is so second nature to humans that we simply overlook how deeply it forms and informs our experience. We can't expect end users, consumers, customers, and travelers to ponder the nature of signs, or spend time giving a close-reading analysis to all the stuff they have to work with every day. Design has to attend to this hard, detailed work so that users don't have to.

Design has traditionally been centered on objects and physical environments. There is no "language design" discipline—it's instead called "writing." There's nothing wrong with that, but we have to come to grips with the reality that language is a more important material for design than ever, especially with the arrival of pervasive, ambient digital systems. This distributed, decentered experience of "calendar" wouldn't be possible without it, so our next focus will be on what it is about digital information that disrupts and destabilizes the physical and semantic modes.

[*Part IV*]

Digital Information

The Pervasive Influence of Code

PHYSICAL AND SEMANTIC MODES SHAPED OUR CONTEXTUAL EXPERI-
ENCE ALL ALONE, up until the last century. All that time, the invariant structural principles of natural and built environments changed
very slowly, if at all. It's a third ingredient—*digital* information—whose
influence has so quickly disrupted how we experience the other two
modes. It's what has made so many user experience–related fields necessary to begin with.

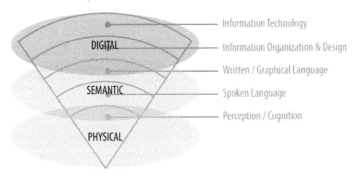

FIGURE IV-1
Digital information

Part IV explains the origins of digital technology, and why it is different
from the other modes. It then explores how digital information influences the way we understand the world, the way we make software, and
the properties of digital agents and simulated affordances.

[12]

Digital Cognition and Agency

The electric things have their life, too.
—PHILIP K. DICK

Shannon's Logic

For the realm of information technology, the word *information* has a specific history. Just as ecological psychologist James J. Gibson chose the
word for his work in psychology, Claude Shannon (1916–2001) appro-
priated it for his own, separate purposes. An American mathemati-
cian, electronic engineer, and cryptographer—often called the "Father
of Information Theory"—Shannon was the prime mover behind a way
of understanding and using information that has led to the digital revolution we're experiencing today.[*] His work during World War II, and
later at Bell Labs and MIT, is foundational to anything that relies on
packaging up information into bits (the word "bit" being a conflation of
"binary digit") and transmitting it over any distance.

One important part of Shannon's work is how he applied mathematical
logic to the problem of transmission, using an encoded (or encrypted)
form. Previously, engineers had tried improving the signal of electronic transmission by boosting the power. But that approach could
help to only a certain point, at which physics got in the way. Pushing
electrons through wires or air over a long-enough distance eventually
generates noise, corrupting the signal.

Shannon's revolutionary discovery: accuracy is improved by encoding
the information in a way that works best for machines, not for humans.
This turn goes beyond the sort of encoding seen with the telegraph,

---

[*] The amazing, fascinating history of information theory and figures like Shannon is beyond
our scope, alas. For a delightful telling of these stories, read James Gleick's *The Information:
A History, a Theory, a Flood.*

where codes were simple patterns of signals corresponding to words, common phrases, or (even more abstractly) just letters. Shannon's idea had origins in his cryptography work during World War II, when he saw that deciphering a message could be handled by analyzing language rather than semantically.

Author and historian James Gleick explains how Shannon proposed this approach in a secret paper written during the war, and in so doing, borrowed and recoined the word "information":

> Shannon had to eradicate "meaning." The germicidal quotation marks were his. "The 'meaning' of a message is generally irrelevant," he proposed cheerfully. He offered this provocation in order to make his purpose utterly clear. Shannon needed, if he were to create a theory, to hijack the word information. "'Information' here," he wrote, "although related to the everyday meaning of the word, should not be confused with it."[*]

By framing the signal of a transmission as a series of discrete (abstract) symbols, it became possible to enhance the accuracy of the transmission by *adding* symbols that help correct errors; this was extra information against which the receiver can check for breaks in transmitted patterns, or clarify the context of such an abstracted, semantics-free signal stream.[†] This approach is similar to how radio operators will use words like Alpha, Bravo, and Charlie for A, B, and C: in a noisy radio signal, it's hard to tell letters apart, especially given that many of them sound so much alike. Additional information contextualizes the bits of signal, helping ensure accurate reception.

So, Shannon's approach took human meaning out of the enterprise altogether. He took a scalpel to the connection between meaning and transmission, saying in his landmark 1948 Bell Labs paper, "These semantic aspects of communication are irrelevant to the engineering

---

[*] Gleick, James. *The Information: A History, a Theory, a Flood.* New York: Random House, Inc., 2011, Kindle locations: pp. 3848–53.

[†] Gleick, James. *The Information: A History, a Theory, a Flood.* New York: Random House, Inc., 2011, Kindle location: 3922.

problem."* Shannon redefined "information" much more narrowly as a stochastic construct, built from the most basic logical entity, the Boolean binary unit: yes or no, on or off, one or zero.

In formulating his *ecological* view of information, Gibson didn't discount Shannon's theories so much as set them aside: "Shannon's concept of information applies to telephone hookups and radio broadcasting in elegant ways but not, I think, to the firsthand perception of being in-the-world, to what the baby gets when first it opens its eyes. The information for perception, unhappily, cannot be defined and measured as Claude Shannon's information can be."† Shannon's approach to information can be "defined and measured" in part because it's the opposite of human language; it doesn't emerge through messy, cultural usage. It *begins* with definition and measurement, from abstract, logical principles, with mathematically clear boundaries.

From the human user's point of view, the native tongue of digital things is, by necessity, decontextualized. It doesn't afford anything for our perception, either physically or semantically, without translating it back into a form that we can not only perceive but understand.

That significant work of translation has a strong digital influence over the way we think about the world, the way we design and build environments with software, and the way the world around us now behaves. The idea that human meaning is "irrelevant to the engineering problem" is, in a sense, now part of digital technology's DNA and has a pervasive ripple effect in everything we digitize (Figure 12-1).

This is why I'm using the word "digital" so broadly, beyond the confines of machine languages and binary code. The more of our world we encode for machines, the more of it is opaque to us, out of our reach, detached from the laws that govern the non-digital parts of our world. We understand our experience by *coupling* with the information the environment provides us; but digital technology, by its nature, *decouples* its information from our context. It has forever complicated and changed the way we need to think about design's communication and craft.

---

* Shannon, C. E. "A Mathematical Theory of Communication." Reprinted with corrections from *The Bell System Technical Journal* July, October, 1948;Volume 27:379–423, 623–56.
† Gibson, 1979, p. 24

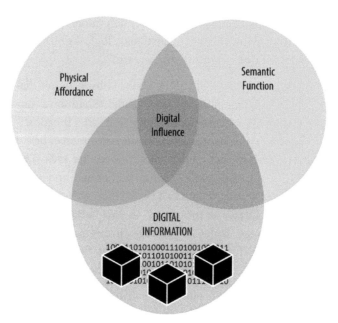

FIGURE 12-1

The Digital mode has a strong and growing influence over the other modes of information

Digital Learning and Agency

After Shannon's initial discoveries, information theory didn't stop at mere transmission and storage. There was another, somewhat more esoteric, area of inquiry going on for several generations: the theory of how machines—using symbolic logic—might do the job of *computing*. A "computer" had always been a human person, performing the professional role of computing mathematical operations; but human effort often results in human error, and humans can also keep up with only so much computational scale and complexity. So, by the mid-twentieth century, there had been a long-standing interest in ways to automate this activity.

In addition to Shannon, the work of people such as Alan Turing and Norbert Wiener—prefigured by similar efforts a century earlier by Ada Lovelace and Charles Babbage—led to the creation of machines essentially made of logic itself. Turing, in particular, championed the idea that computing is noncorporeal, not dependent on a particular medium or energy system. He invented the idea of an automated computing machine that functions entirely based on symbols—the *Turing machine*—that (in theory) could function based on rules built of Boolean, binary fundamentals, from the ground up. Anything that could be *represented* in mathematical symbols and logic could be computed. Not just mathematical problems, but all sorts of human ideas, questions, and communications—as long as they could be represented in the machine.* As a result of this line of inquiry, we now have technology that has *agency*; the ability to make decisions and take actions on its own.

This sort of agency has powerful, disruptive effects. Kitchin and Dodge put it this way in their book *Code/Space: Software and Everyday Life*:

> The phenomenal growth in software creation and use stems from its emergent and executable properties; that is, how it codifies the world into rules, routines, algorithms...Although software is not sentient and conscious, it can exhibit some of the characteristics of being alive... This property of being alive is significant because it means code can make things do work in the world in an autonomous fashion.†

But how does the digital system know anything about that world, which isn't made of abstractions, but actual concrete *stuff*? As Paul Dourish explains, we have to create representations of the world with which computers can work:

> Computation is fundamentally about representation. The elements from which we construct software systems are representational; they are abstractions over a world of continuous voltages and electronic phenomena that refer to a parallel world of cars, people, conversational topics, books, packages, and so forth. Each element in a software system has this dual nature; on the one hand, it is an abstraction created out of the electronic phenomena from which computers are

---

* For an excellent overview of how Turing's ideas intersect with Gibsonian ecological theory, see the section called "When is a Turing Machine Not a Turing Machine" in Louise Barrett's *Beyond the Brain* (2011). Also, see the following writings by Andrew Wells: Wells, A. "Gibson's affordances and Turing's theory of computation." *Ecological Psychology* 2002; Volume 14: 140–80, and ———. *Rethinking Cognitive Computation: Turing and the Science of the Mind*. London: Palgrave, 2006.

† Kitchen and Dodge, 2011:5.

built, and on the other, it represents some entity, be it physical, social, or conceptual, in the world which the software developer has chosen to model.*

Human memory is embodied and only occasionally somewhat literal (when we explicitly memorize something). But computer memory works by making exact copies of abstract representations. Computers don't find their way to abstraction from the roots of physical perception-and-action; they *begin* with abstraction.

Every representation has to be intentionally created for the system. This can be done by the people who made the system, or it can be done by some algorithmic process in which the system defines representations for itself. As depicted in Figure 12-2, whereas human cognition emerged from bodily perception and eventually developed the ability to think in terms of abstractions and symbols, digital computing works the other way around. People can go through their entire lives not *explicitly defining* the entities they encounter. But computers can do little to nothing without these descriptions.

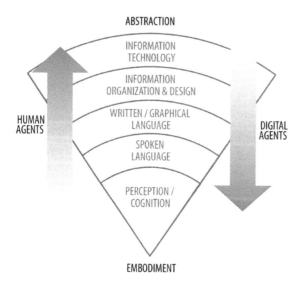

FIGURE 12-2
Humans and digital agents learn in different directions

---

* Dourish, Paul. *Where the Action Is: The Foundations of Embodied Interaction*. Cambridge, MA: MIT Press, 2004:137, Kindle edition.

Writing is already a form of code, with roughly standardized syntax, spelling, and letter forms. So, computers find writing to be a much easier starting point than spoken language. That is, it's easier to teach a computer a semantic definition of the *written* word "berry" than it is to teach the computer how to recognize the word when spoken aloud. Speech introduces all sorts of environmental variation, such as tone of voice or regional inflection.

Although teaching a computer to recognize the spoken word "berry" in some contexts is pretty challenging, teaching it to recognize a *picture* of a berry is even harder. Sure, we can program it to recognize a specific berry picture, but it really struggles to see any picture of any sort of berry and connect it to "berryness," which humans tacitly pick up thanks to our embodied experiences with them.

Computers, however, don't have bodies unless we add them onto the computing "brain." Teaching a computer to use a robotic body to find and pick berries is even more complex than visual recognition. It requires definitions not just about the visual qualities of berries, but how to gently harvest something so fragile in the first place, not to mention how to negotiate its body through everything else in the environment.* This insight about computers is called *Moravec's paradox*, named after AI researcher Hans Moravec, who was one of a group of scientists who articulated it in the 1980s. In Moravec's words, "It is comparatively easy to make computers exhibit adult level performance on intelligence tests or playing checkers, and difficult or impossible to give them the skills of a one-year-old when it comes to perception and mobility."†

Of course, since the time of Shannon and Turing, and even Moravec, computers have become much more adept at processing *fuzzy* ecological and semantic information inputs. Face and voice recognition, street navigation, and other complex pattern-matching capabilities are

---

* In fact, new embodied paradigms in robotics have resulted in robots that gracefully navigate all sorts of terrain, such as the naturally limbed but small-brained "Big Dog" robot designed by Boston Dynamics, a company recently acquired by Google (*http://www. bostondynamics.com/robot_bigdog.html*).

† Moravec, Hans. *Mind Children*. Cambridge: Harvard University Press, 1988:15.

more possible now with powerful, cheap processors and advanced algorithms. Still, these are extremely limited capabilities, with narrow contextual accuracy.

This isn't to say computers will never have embodied learning. There has been some cutting-edge research in *biocomputing*, which grows computers with organic cells, or even with bodies of a sort, in order to learn more environmentally. For most of us, however, our design work will not involve these exotic creatures. We need to make do with the silicon and bits that are available to us. That means we have to understand the layers of semantic substrate required to make our gadgets do the wonderful things we take for granted.

We can see this in action when Apple's Siri attempts (with often hilarious missteps) to understand "where's the closest gas station?" Here, Siri must rely on the *structure* of the vocalized vibrations and match them with semantic frameworks that are defined and generated as encoded language. Someone, somewhere, had to use writing to even start teaching Siri how to learn what we mean when we talk to it. Context had to be artificially generated, from already-abstracted inputs.

And when we use Shazam to recognize a song, the song is not meaningful to the device as it is to us. Shazam is matching the structure of the song with the structures indexed in vast databases. The emotional or cultural context of the song isn't a factor, unless it's defined by people in some way. For video content, Netflix has become a market leader in defining these subtle, oblique permutations, which they internally call *altgenres*, such as "Critically Acclaimed Emotional Underdog Movies" or "Spy Action & Adventure from the 1930s."* The Netflix categories exist only because of enormous work behind the scenes, translating between the nested variety of human life and the binary structures of digital information.

Everyday Digital Agents

We're increasingly giving our environment over to digital agents, programming them as best we can and then setting them loose to do their work. An example of simple digital agency is how my car (a Kia Forte

---

* Madrigal, Alexis C. "How Netflix Reverse Engineered Hollywood" The Atlantic (theatlantic. com) January, 2015 (*http://theatln.tc/1sKXxHF*).

coup) won't let me perform certain actions in its digital interface if the car is in motion. I was trying to Bluetooth-pair my phone from the passenger seat when I saw this screen. My wife, Erin, was driving. But the system didn't know that, so it followed the rules it was taught, making the function "Not Available" (Figure 12-3).

This is similar to the mechanical limitation that keeps me from turning off the engine while the car is still in gear. In both cases, it's a hidden rule in the system of my car, made manifest by limiting my action. But mechanical limitations can be only as complex as the limits of physical objects will allow. Digital information itself has no such mechanical restriction; it can enact as many thousands of complex rules as will fit on device's microchips.

FIGURE 12-3
"I'm sorry, Andrew, I'm afraid I can't do that." My Kia Forte, channeling HAL 9000*

That is, digital information has almost no inertia, compared to physical information. If we add to that lack of friction a huge number of more complex, algorithm-based agents, massively disproportionate effects can result. In 2010, the financial world got a bit of a scare when the markets took a momentary plunge of over 9 percent—nearly 1,000 points within minutes, equating to many millions of lost dollars—before recovering most of the drop by the end of the hour (see Figure 12-4). What happened? It turns out that it was due to automated

---

* Photo by author.

"high-frequency trading," conducted by computer algorithm. These trades happen much faster than humans could ever conduct business. At the time of the blip, this rapid automated trading accounted for somewhere between 50 and 75 percent of daily trading volume.*

FIGURE 12-4

The sudden, algorithm-generated dip that shocked the market in 2010 (graph from finance.yahoo.com)

It came to be called the *Flash Crash,* and it scared everyone enough to spur investigations and Congressional hearings. Eventually so-called "circuit breakers" were added to systems, but some critics are still wary of high-frequency trading software.† And maybe for good reason, since as early as 2012, a "single mysterious computer program" made high-frequency orders and then cancelled them—enough to account for 4 percent of US trading activity in that week. According to one news report, "the motive of the algorithm is still unclear."‡

This is the world we live in now, where we have to guess at the motivations not of Olympian gods, but of computer-process *daemons* whirring away in the nervous system of our global economy. Digital agents

---

* "Surge of Computer Selling After Apparent Glitch Sends Stocks Plunging." *New York Times* May 6, 2010 (*http://nyti.ms/1uzHTNF*).

† *http://en.wikipedia.org/wiki/2010_Flash_Crash*

‡ "Mysterious Algorithm Was 4% of Trading Activity Last Week." CNBC.com, Monday Oct 8, 2012 (*http://www.cnbc.com/id/49333454*).

208 | UNDERSTANDING CONTEXT

are natively mathematical creatures, unconcerned with slowing down enough for us to keep up, or being transparent about their inner dynamics, unless we design them to be otherwise.

Although it takes specialized knowledge to create a market-trading algorithm, laypeople increasingly have access to tools for making their own decision-making agents. For example, IFTTT—If This Then That—is a cloud-based service with which users can create "recipes" for simple procedural connections between other online services (see Figure 12-5). For example, "If I post a picture to Instagram, store a copy in my Dropbox archive." IFTTT is like a virtual Lego set made of semantic functions with which we can create our own digital helpers. It provides active digital *objects* we can use to conditionally invoke *events*, interwoven with defined *places*—and increasingly with *physical objects*.

IFTTT has started adding new triggers for physical devices, such as wearables and smart home products.*

Popular UP by Jawbone Recipes

Log my meals and their nutritional content into a Google spreadsheet
by stonq on Apr 29, 2013
used 695 times

Share Foursquare gym check-ins to your Jawbone UP feed
by kev on Apr 29, 2013
used 800 times

Automatically log lunch at X time everyday as a reminder fill in later.
by matth on Apr 25, 2013
used 191 times

Popular WeMo Motion Recipes

Post a Facebook status message anytime someone reaches for the cookie jar
by wemo on Jun 20, 2012
used 13 times

Tell me when it's time to clean up the litter box
by wemo on Jun 20, 2012
used 206 times

Text me if the door opens!
by wemo on Jun 20, 2012
used 535 times

FIGURE 12-5
Recipes from *IFTTT.com*

---

* *https://ifttt.com/jawbone_up* and *https://ifttt.com/wemo_motion*

These new tools change the nature of the places they're connected to, whether an online place such as Instagram, or a physical place like the home, or an object such as one's own body.

IFTTT has made a nicely understandable system that enables a lot of complexity with simple rules. Still, these invisible agents can scale only so far until an average person will have trouble keeping up with them all. Memory typically requires repeated exposure to a perceivable pattern, but the purpose of most such agents is to "set it and forget it." There are already many common set-and-forget services, like online subscriptions to medicine and groceries, or automated bill-pay withdrawals—and these will seem primitive and few in another 5 to 10 years. It leads us to question what will help us manage all this personal automation. Will we need agents for keeping track of our agents?

Ontologies

Computers are machines that do not need human-understandable context to function within and among themselves. Sure, we created them, but there is no intrinsic requirement that once made, they ever have to provide an output that we can comprehend. Early computers required their users to interpret hole-punched cards and patterns of blinking lights to read their computed results. For example, the 1970s Altair hobbyist computer (Figure 12-6) had only switches and red LEDs on its front panel as input and output mechanisms for entering and reading the results of simple programs.

As computers became more powerful, they could be used to store and process more-complex concepts. But those concepts have to be described and modeled for the machine to work with them. To accomplish this task, information science makes use of an old concept in a new way: something called *ontology*.

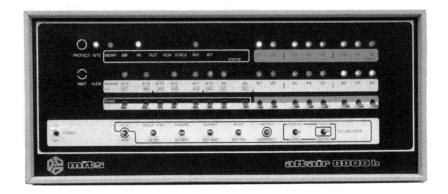

FIGURE 12-6
The Altair 8800b user interface*

For centuries, ontology has referred to the philosophical study of being, existence, or reality. It also has to do with the *categories* of things that exist, and the *relationships* between those categories. This *conceptual* sort of ontology is part of an ancient branch of philosophy called *metaphysics*. Language's role in ontological questions has increased in significance over the centuries, as philosophers (and anyone else concerned with language) have come to realize that language and "being" are fundamentally connected. What does it mean to say, "There is a calendar hanging on the wall, and I know it is there, and I know it has information on it that means X or Y"; and what does it mean to say, "We both exist in the same place and are experiencing the same calendar?" To consider the question fully requires talking or writing about it; ontological questions are, after all, questions.

Ontology is also a term used in information science for a related, but different meaning: the *formal* representation of a set of concepts within a domain, and the specification of the relationships between those concepts. That's a mouthful, but all it really means is the way we teach digital machines how to understand the inputs we expect them to process. A business software platform such as Microsoft Outlook has data objects that must be defined so that the system knows what its calendar is and what functions are expected of it. Google's search algorithms and

---

* Wikimedia Commons: *http://bit.ly/1xaAIws*

massive semantic databases have to know what people mean when they search for things related to calendars—all the synonyms and related products, conversations, or anything else that has to do with how we use the word "calendar" in English-speaking culture.

Sophisticated information systems require these sorts of definitions in order to make sense of the work we give them to do. Ontologies stand as a digital system's version of invariant structure for its nested semantic environment—the lens a computer uses to process human ideas and entities. For example, the BBC has a publicly available set of ontologies (see Figure 12-7) it uses for structuring its information, including what it means when it refers to a television "series" versus an "episode," or what it means to publish a "story" and its various related components.

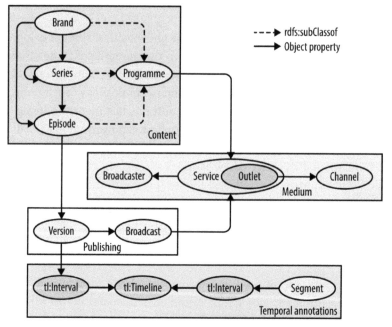

FIGURE 12-7
The "programme" ontology from the BBC*

In short, this is a foundation for how we teach digital systems about human context. There's plenty of digital information that computers share that is only about computing, so it doesn't require semantic

---

* *http://www.bbc.co.uk/ontologies/*

context. Yet, we made computers to be part of the human environment, so most of what they do eventually needs to be translated into signifiers that people can comprehend.

When designing systems for people to use, we should consider both the conceptual and formal definitions of ontology, because much of our work is about creating a bridge between those poles. Looking at the Google Calendar example in Chapter 11, we can see how ontology is at the center of the problem. What is "Calendar" in the Google ecosystem? In some places, the word is used to indicate the simulated physical calendar we see on a screen. In other instances, however, it indicates the subscribed calendar-feeds that are only subsets of the entire calendar environment. The digital layer has clear definitions for what these calendars are, because each construct has a machine-friendly name and description. But to the end user, they're all just "calendar."

Google had a related ontological problem in 2010 with the service it called Buzz, which attempted to integrate social networking into the successful Gmail platform. When Buzz rolled out, it created a prepopulated list of "friends" for every user, based on measurements gathered from users' Gmail history, such as frequency of contact.

Upon launch, many Gmail users were surprised to discover this new set of rules and structures that changed the meaning of their Gmail environment, which went from being about email to being about email-plus-something-else that wasn't entirely clear to them. The biggest problem was this: Buzz automatically decided for users just who those friends were versus people they didn't want in such a list, such as bosses, coworkers, or hostile ex-spouses. The system also, by default, publicly showed your list of friends—letting everyone know the people with whom you communicate most.* These missteps cost Google, among other penalties, 20 years of auditing by the United States Federal Trade Commission.†

---

* Carlson, Nicholas. "WARNING: Google Buzz Has A Huge Privacy Flaw" *Business Insider* (*businessinsider.com*) February 20, 2010 (*http://read.bi/1rpOyrE*).

† Wouters, Jorgen. "Google Settles With FTC Over Privacy Violations on Buzz" *DailyFinance. com*, March 31, 2011 (*http://aol.it/1vHPCgF*).

Buzz was working from an ontology that defined "friend" too simplistically, walking into the same trap that Facebook's Beacon had tripped only a few years earlier. "Friend" is *nested* in our lives, not a rigidly hierarchical entity. We might refer to someone as a friend in one circle of people but in another circle say that person is an acquaintance or partner. However, Buzz created a digital agent (based on an algorithm) that saw the world through a narrow spectrum that was efficient for the machine's perspective but disastrously wrong from the human point of view.

This happened even though Buzz was tested extensively within the huge corporate social context of Google before it was launched.* That prelaunch context was misleading, though, because a corporate environment has tacit cultural norms that make it a very different place compared to nonwork life. Add to this problem the fact that users had already become used to Gmail as an environment with predictable, invariant qualities. Buzz introduced new rules and structures, changing the architecture of how Gmail worked. It didn't just add features— it changed the nature of the environment fundamentally.

There are information-science specialists who can create ontologies that work well for machines, and there are philosophers who continue to explore what it means to "be." But, for those of us making user-facing environments, ontology is about establishing understandable *semantic function* that solves for the contextual gap between person and machine.

---

* Krazit, Tom. "What Google needs to learn from Buzz backlash" *CNet.com*, February 16, 2010 (*http://news.cnet.com/8301-30684_3-10454683-265.html*).

[13]

Digital Interaction

I don't design stuff for myself. I'm a toolmaker. I design things that other people want to use.
—ROBERT MOOG

Interfaces and Humans

WHEN WE INTERFACE WITH DIGITAL SYSTEMS, we're doing so through many layers of abstraction, so it's necessary to provide environmental elements that we can recognize and understand. That's essentially what computer interfaces are: artificial environments that bridge the gap between digital information's total symbolic abstraction and our perceptual systems' need for affordance, whether physical or simulated.

It's easy to forget that the word "interface" isn't necessarily about people. For many years, the word mainly had to do with how one machine interoperates with another. For example, an *API* is an *application programming interface* with which software engineers can make two applications share functions and data; and the acronym *SCSI* means *Small Computer System Interface*—a hardware standard for connecting devices and peripherals such as hard drives and personal computers (see Figure 13-1, left). Like most things related to digital systems, software and hardware interfaces work best when they are rigorously defined and kept to an efficient minimum, such as with a keyboard (Figure 13-1, right) or mouse. Overlapping, extraneous, or ambiguously defined interfaces are anathema to efficient, reliable digital system design.

FIGURE 13-1

Left: A "terminator" for a Small Computer System Interface, or SCSI (pronounced "scuzzy"), device chain;* right: a keyboard for the structured-language input from human fingers†

Both of these are hardware interfaces for sharing data between two systems. But in the keyboard's case, one of the systems is human. As we've seen, humans perceive and act in ways that are abundantly ambiguous and overlapping; we *satisfice* our way through our activities, and only tacitly and passively comprehend most of what we encounter. That is, humans are horribly inefficient, irrational systems. In spite of this fact, it's perhaps ironic that software-making organizations expend so much time on digital-to-digital interfaces, and so little on the interface between the digital system and the human, who is by far the most challenging, complicated system in the mix.

At their best, digital systems accommodate our physical and semantic informational needs quite nicely; at their worst, they require us to think and behave like computers, which is hard work for us squishy-brained animals. It's in this translation between digital and physical/semantic modes where we find the seemingly infinite varieties of architectural and design challenges that sparked the need for new fields of practice, like human-computer interaction, usability engineering, interaction design, information architecture, and others.

---

* Wikimedia Commons *http://bit.ly/1rpOXdA*

† Photo by author.

In only about 50 years, digital interfaces have gone through a rapid evolution, from an age of punch-card-driven mainframes to our current plethora of input methods that use high-resolution graphics, virtual keyboards, voice recognition, and motion-tracking sensors. There are other resources beyond this book for exploring all the varieties of human-computer interfaces and models of interaction with digital systems. Although we will touch on some specific interaction examples, our purpose here is a bit broader: to establish that interfaces are part of the environment we inhabit and are themselves smaller environments nested within the larger ecological context.

For a generation, software was made mainly for trained specialists in rarified environments, performing highly structured tasks. Now that most software is being made for regular people doing everyday stuff, software has to be reframed as *everyday environment* that laypeople expect to use as they do everything else around them—mailboxes, toasters, elevators, and bridges. This is the place of most software now—devices in the world that need to just work, without a lot of fuss.

Moreover, when we create digital *agents*, we have to do the extra work of translating between their black-box nature and the cognition of regular people. Most of this translation is done by using language.

Sometimes we get pretty close to success, but not close enough—as is demonstrated in the example of a common gas pump. Gas pumps use digital information to handle transactions between the pump, the store, and credit-card processing services. They're simple digital agents, but they are agents nonetheless—making decisions based on established rules in their software. When I tried pumping gas recently, I'm embarrassed to admit it took me a full minute to realize there was a sticker above the digital display (Figure 13-2) translating the passive-aggressive computer's demand that I "ENTER DATA." In such mundane examples, pervasively spread across our environment, every detail matters in shaping contextual clarity.

It bears repeating—especially for digital technology—that there is no such thing as a purely *natural interface*. Any digital system requires learning (or relying on learned convention) for an artificial user interface of some kind, because there will always be the need to translate the abstraction of digital information into invariants that users can comprehend, whether simple buttons, voice commands, mere labels, or sensor-triggered gestures.

FIGURE 13-2

A common workaround for talking with the digital agents among us[*]

Semantic Function of Simulated Objects

For most of human existence, an object was either an object or it wasn't. A picture of an object only represented something; it afforded seeing light of varying shades of color but not taking action with the object depicted.

In a famous example of this distinction, René Magritte's painting *The Treachery of Images* shows a tobacco pipe. Its caption says: "Ceci n'est pas une pipe." Or, in English, "This is not a pipe." It's a popular example for talking about signs, symbols, language, and all manner of fascinating semiotics issues. In our case, it helps make a point about representation in digital systems.

Magritte's picture of a pipe is, indeed, not actually a pipe. But how do we know? In part, because our perception-action loop can tell that it's just a picture: it's contained on a flat surface; it's a realistic depiction, but not nearly enough to be construed as a photograph; and it has a caption written underneath it, on the same surface plane.

The final test: the viewer's body can't actually pick it up, put tobacco in it, and smoke from it. That is, what makes it *not a pipe* is largely its lack of pipe-related affordances.

---

[*] Photo by author.

FIGURE 13-3

Magritte's The Treachery of Images (© Herscovici, Brussels/Artists Rights Society [ARS], New York)

And yet, the caption strikes the new viewer as strange. "Well, of course it's a pipe, what does he mean?" The conceit of Magritte's painting works because we don't go around separating semantic and physical information every day. We often use them as if they were interchangeable. As in the duck-rabbit example in Chapter 12, this pipe is something about which we normally say, "That's a pipe," rather than "That's a painting that depicts the physical aspects of an object with affordances that are related to a category of objects we call 'pipe'." We'd get very little done in the human world if we had to talk that way.

Digital technology has the ability to take this natural tendency toward conflation and use it to simulate physical objects and their behaviors. I can't smoke this pipe, but on a digital device's screen, I can "press" a pixel-rendered picture of a "button" to make the system do something. It's not a physical button, but within the rules of a digitally enabled interface, *it might as well be*. It's a picture of a pipe, but one I can smoke. It presents semantic information on a display in such as way as to behave as if it were a physical object. In other words, this is *semantic function, simulating physical affordance*.

An example of a big button lots of people use is in the Shazam mobile app; the app's main purpose is to help users figure out what songs are playing, wherever they happen to be. To do that, it presents a simulated-affording structure—a picture that looks like a button, as depicted in Figure 13-4. The drop-shadow and slight gradient make it appear like a raised, convex object, similar to many other physical buttons we encounter in our surroundings. Of course, Shazam also adds a bit of text helping to nudge the user toward understanding that this is not merely a decorative picture, but an interactive object. Interestingly, if you touch anywhere on the screen other than the button, nothing happens. The button is only a picture, but it presents itself as a physical object that demands we aim specifically for it—a way for this digital agent to make an educated guess that we want it to listen to a song.

FIGURE 13-4
The Shazam mobile app's primary control is a big simulated button that, when touched, scans the environment for musical patterns

An on-screen button is just one way semantic information can simulate physical affordances, making them "interactive"—a word that wasn't in prevalent use until the 1970s and 80s, when technology enabled previously inert parts of our environment to become things that, when we poked them, starting poking us back.

Interaction, and the design of interactions, largely originated with the emergence of electronic devices. And digital technology enabled those devices to richly simulate interfaces in ways that physical buttons on electrical gadgets couldn't achieve.

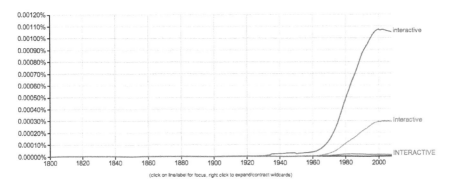

FIGURE 13-5

Google's Ngram Viewer shows usage of "interactive" climbing fast along with the rise of computing interfaces

Now, we have very complex interfaces full of many nested layers of objects. There are debates as to how closely to their physical counterparts these objects and their controls should be rendered. On one side of the spectrum, there's the *skeuomorphic* approach, which presents a literal translation of the physical surfaces and objects we encounter in the physical world. Sometimes, that copying can be gratuitous and unnecessary. Other times, it's important to re-create the physicality of analog objects, to provide familiar clues into learning the system's simulated affordances.

For example, with the Animoog app, users can play with an interface simulating an old Moog synthesizer—a culturally significant device whose form is a big part of the experience of using it. Abstracting those wonderfully retro controls (see Figure 13-6) into something less literal would disrupt the entire purpose of playing a simulated Moog. And yet, because the knobs are not physical, there is no "twist" gesture that feels like using real knobs. Instead, the interface relies on an up/down finger "scrub" gesture to make the setting go higher or lower. Simulation on glass digital screens can go only so far.

FIGURE 13-6

Animoog simulates the controls of a small Moog synthesizer

In recent years, there's been a raging debate in the design community about skeuomorphic versus *flat* design. The watershed moment was Apple's release of iOS 7, which went far into the direction of these so-called flat interface surfaces and objects.

Unfortunately, this polarity is misleading, because these are not a binary choice; the design approaches are on more of a spectrum. In Figure 13-7, which compares iOS 6 to iOS 7, notice the big difference between the Cancel and Send signifiers. Both versions simulate the same action, but iOS 7 has eschewed the faux-convex-recessed-button treatment. The reason why Apple is able to remove the button simulation is because most users have learned, through repeated exposure and growing convention, that the words "Cancel" and "Send," in this situated context, are action verbs that signify their respective functions. Outside of this context, these words could convey many other messages, but in software this sort of placement has an established, near-invariant meaning.

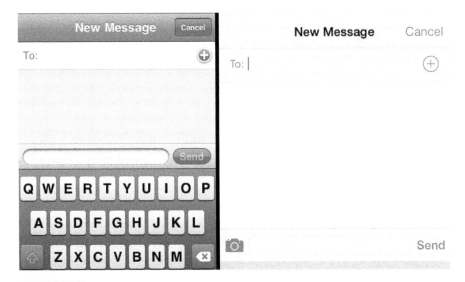

FIGURE 13-7
The Apple iOS 6 interface (left) compared to iOS 7 (right)

But notice that the Add button with the "+" symbol has a circle around it, giving a clear boundary that makes it more a button than the "+" character alone would do. Evidently, designers at Apple realized that the "+" wasn't enough by itself. Also note how iOS 7 adds a camera icon, making it possible for users to more quickly send a picture when messaging. It doesn't have three-dimensional gradients, but it's definitely an iconic signifier, mimicking the shape of a physical object, which is probably a better, more compact signifier than "Add Picture." Of course, given the changing form of photography devices, the conventional camera icon might soon become an anachronism, the way the floppy-disc icon (for "Save") has become today. Culture and language infuse all interfaces, where ingredients mix into semiotic stews of semantic interaction.

Interestingly, many users were having trouble with the new label-only controls, so Apple added an "Accessibility" option to turn on "Button Shapes," like the gray button-like shape shown in Figure 13-8. It clarifies the simulated affordance by subtly mimicking the physical information we associate with mechanical buttons.

New Message Cancel

To: | ⊕

FIGURE 13-8
An option in iOS 7 adds button shapes

Part of what this illustrates is that the context of what a simulated control does and how our bodies should interact with it, is fundamentally a linguistic question. Why? Because the information on the screen is all semantic in one way or another; it's either simulating objects, or presenting text for reading. It's using signifiers that are "drawn" on a surface. Whether a label or shape does enough work to signify its function is a matter of learned environmental convention, just like the meaning of words and sentences. Digital information is behind this transformation of our environment, and therefore the transformation of our users' contextual experience.

In the examples presented in Figure 13-9, we see a sort of spectrum of how objects use invariants to inform our behavior, from physical to semantic.

FIGURE 13-9
A range of physical to semantic invariant cues[*]

Here are the significant characteristics of each object (from left to right):

- The stairs are directly perceived by our bodies as affording upward motion. Their affordance is intrinsic to their invariant structure, nested within a building, nested within a city. And in keeping with

---

[*] All photos and screenshots by author.

the multifaceted way we perceive nestedness, the stairs' "meaning" to our bodies changes when we want to go down them or sit on one to look at a book for a moment.

- The Engine Start button also has intrinsic structure that, with experience, we've learned means it's an object that can be pressed into its surrounding surface. But that's as far as the intrinsic, physical affordance goes here. Without pressing it, we don't know what pressing this button ultimately does, unless we read the label—a signifier with semantic function, supplementing the object, informing us how this object is actually nested within a broader system that is otherwise invisible to us.

- The old version of the Windows Start button is similar to the Engine Start button in every way, except that it isn't a physical button (and in this case, not one we touch with our fingers). It's using graphical information to simulate the contours of conventional, physical buttons. It's also connected to a vastly more complex environment than what we find in even the newest automotive ignition systems.

- Last, we have a hyperlink on a bookstore's website. Just as we would use for the Windows Start button, there's a cartoon hand icon that functions as an avatar for the user's own hand (that is, linguistically, it's behaving as an actual *iconic* signifier), indicating (that is, acting also as an *indexical* signifier) where a click of a mouse will engage the digital surface. That surface has other signifiers on it—the words in the menu. These words equate to buttons because of learned conventions, such as the fact that a web layout with a list of words placed around the edges of the interface is most often a menu meant for navigating that environment. It may also use a convention of color-change when the user's hand-avatar (cursor) hovers over the label, as it does here. The same words elsewhere— outside a context that aligns with the menu layout convention— might not be recognized as hyperlinks. Labels used as links put a lot of pressure on the semantic context of the label, to signify not only its interactive nature, but also where it will take us or what it will do when we tap or click it.

This isn't a comprehensive spectrum; it just shows how information can range from the simply intrinsic physical to the highly abstract semantic. Designing such objects based mainly on concerns of aesthetics and style runs the risk of ignoring the most important challenges of simulating affordance through semantic function.

Unlike our interactions with physical objects, such as opening a kitchen drawer or swinging a hammer, we never directly control what software does; it's always mediated through layers of abstraction. The illusion of touching a thing in software and seeing it respond to our touch is a construct of semantic function, not a direct physical affordance. So, the cause-and-effect rules of software aren't perceivable the way we can see the action-and-reaction of physical objects and events, and they're not readable the way semantic rules are expressed in documents. We tap a button labeled X and hope the system will do X; what happens behind the scenes—how is X is defined, and does X also mean Y and Z—is up to the system.

Email serves as a good example of how semantic function can approach but not quite touch the physical affordances of actual objects and surfaces. As James J. Gibson argued, a mailbox is really a complex, compound invariant. Its function provides for more than just putting an object into another object—we perceive it as part of a cultural system of postal mail, so its function is to send a letter to an addressee. But perceiving that function depends on having learned a great deal about one's cultural environment and what one can expect of it.

Digital technology takes the physical affordances of how mailboxes and mail work and fully abstracts them into something made entirely of language—rule-based functions presented as metaphorical labels and iconography. Email has an "inbox" and "outbox," but there are no physical boxes. Not unlike the way digital clocks have virtually replaced the intricacies of clockwork-driven timepieces, email dissolves formerly complex physical systems into the abstractions of software.

Email gives us valuable abilities that we didn't have before, but it also loses some of the qualities we enjoy by working with physical mail objects. Especially now that we're so overwhelmed with the stuff, some innovators are trying to reintroduce a bit of physicality to the work of managing our email.

In 2012, America Online (AOL) started rolling out Alto, a new email platform (Figure 13-10). One of the principles behind its design is something called *stacks* that design lead Bill Wetherell says were inspired by noticing how his wife sorted physical mail from the post office:

- She would separate it into piles based on the type of mail it was, such as catalogues, correspondence, coupons, and bills.

- She'd place each pile in a part of the home where it was most relevant and likely to be used for its main purpose (coupons in the kitchen, for example).

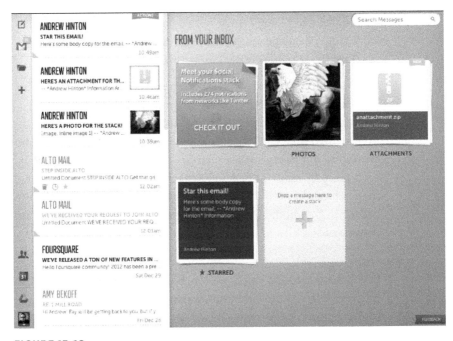

FIGURE 13-10

A sample of the simulated physical-stack approach for the Alto email platform

This is a textbook example of extended cognition: making use of the environment not just for sorting the mail, but arranging those objects within the home environment in such a way that they afford further action for managing their contents.

Wetherell says, "We started to wonder if we could re-create that same physical process but in the digital world." So, Alto presents—as one of the main interaction modes—graphically simulated stacks of mail. It also tries to sniff out what stack incoming email should go to so that the application can handle a lot of that piling for the user.[*]

There are some interesting challenges in trying to replicate these physical behaviors within an email application.

Recognizing the difference between real mail and junk mail

We're pretty good at quickly sizing up what sort of postal-service-delivered mail we're holding in our hands, because the physical qualities of the objects provide a lot of physical information to work from. Catalogs are heftier than personal letters or retail flyers. Envelopes are obviously handwritten versus bulk-printed.

In email, all those physical cues disappear, and we're left with the representational semantic information deliverable by SMTP servers and readable by email software. This not only makes it harder to recognize what each incoming item really is by just seeing it in our inbox, but also provides even fewer cues for quickly sizing up each piece of mail. This is one reason why Alto tries to sort the mail behind the scenes: a software algorithm can actually be more literate in the digital-information-based cues of digital mail than people can.

Stacking is cognition

In stacking physical mail, we touch each piece and think about it just enough to do some prework with it—a crucial part of the cognitive work we do with physical objects, especially when organizing them for later action. I know that when I've done this, it helps me to remember what's in each stack even days later, without having to go through each item in the stack again. By having the system automatically sort the stacks behind the scenes, the user misses this opportunity.

---

[*] Carr, Austin. "AOL May Have Invented Email's Next UI Paradigm," *Fast Company* (*fastcodesign.com*) October 18, 2012 (*http://bit.ly/1yV8zPD*).

Stacks in physical places

As mentioned earlier, Wetherell observed that his wife would place the mail in various parts of the house, where they were more likely to be processed later, related to their larger corresponding physical tasks. That is, these stacks are *nested* within other environmental structures and physical activities. A digital interface interrupts this house-as-categorizer function. Of course, it's possible our homes could eventually be pervasively digitized—with bedside tables and countertops where we can "put" stacks of our sorted, simulated mail. But that's probably more complicated than it's worth.

These are certainly not criticisms of Alto, which is to be applauded for tackling the challenges of improving how we use email. Alto is just a useful example of how a digital interface can go only so far in replicating the cognition-extending affordances of the physical environment. Allowing the user to work with simulated stacks is a worthwhile experiment. Think of how useful this capability would be in any search interface, for example, where you could pile and mark items the way college students can do in a library's carrels and stacks.

Modes and Meaning

For interface design, a "mode" is a condition that changes the result that the same action would have under a different condition. Complex machines and digital devices often have modes so that users can accomplish more things with the same number of controls. Modes are important to context because they establish rules of cause and effect for user action. They literally change the context of an object, or even a place.

A simple example of this is the Caps Lock key on a typewriter or computer keyboard, similar to the one depicted in Figure 13-11. When it's engaged, it remains in a mode that makes all the keys create capital versions of their corresponding letters; when it's disengaged, it goes back to lowercase letter typing. We make mistakes with this mode all the time, so much so that software password fields often remind us after a few tries that we have our caps lock engaged, which might be causing password failure.

FIGURE 13-11
A MacBook Caps Lock key, with its "mode on" indicator lit

Mode is a big challenge when designing understandable contexts. As technology becomes more complex, we ask a limited number of affording objects (keys, buttons, and so on) to do more kinds of work. In early word processors, pressing a particular key would cause the keyboard to change from a text input device to a text formatting or file management device. It worked like the Caps Lock key but affected a more radical shift of function. This sort of mode is known as *sticky*—it persists after you engage it.

Non-sticky-mode keys require being held down while using their mode, like the Alt or Control keys on personal computers. So, pressing only an S key while editing a document types the letter "s," but pressing and holding Control while typing S (in Windows) saves the document.

Sometimes, the application you're running changes what your keyboard's keys do entirely. Many computer games use the A, S, D, and W keys for moving a character through a game environment, corresponding to left, back, right, and forward, respectively—until a "chat" mode is activated, in which case typing displays letters and numbers, as usual.

When users are aware of modes and motivated to learn them, the negative effects can be minimal. However, when users are not aware of the mode, or their "muscle memory" causes them to take an action for effect A because, in the moment, they forgot the system's control was engaged for effect B, the results can range from annoying to disastrous.

I was recently using a rental car that had a new, interactive dashboard system. It was a horrible mess of confused signifiers and functions, in which controls that are usually physical knobs or buttons were subsumed by multilevel, menu-driven interfaces. That's not such a big deal if you're doing something infrequent and complicated such as syncing your phone to the car's Bluetooth system. But in this case, the car required me to interact with several layers of buttons just to switch between ventilation modes.

I've been driving for many years, so I'm used to controlling heat output with a quick twist of a knob or tap of an obvious button. Because auto temperature can change quickly on a trip, depending on the sun and other factors, it's one of those things I prefer to have "ready-to-hand" (as discussed in Chapter 6). In this rental car, however, the controls were more "unready-to-hand." It took at least four different interactions—all while staring at the system and not the road—to not only switch the screen into the Climate mode, but then select the mode of climate control I wished to use. And after all that, as Figure 13-12 shows, I then had to confirm my selection by pressing Done. Modes nested within modes within modes—something that could be truly dangerous while in motion.

FIGURE 13-12
Poking at a confusing modal interface (photo by author)

Design leaders have argued against using poorly implemented modes almost since consumer software was invented. Donald Norman was writing about them as early as 1981.[*] And interaction design pioneer Jef Raskin infamously railed against using any sort of mode-based inputs, because they almost always result in problems.[†] (He actually preferred the Control-key sort of mode that required a continuous action, calling them "quasimodes.") Even Raskin's son, designer Aza Raskin, has continued the mission against their misuse. He writes, "If a system contains modes, people will make mode errors; if we design systems that are not humane—responsive to human needs and considerate of human frailties, we can be guaranteed that people will make mistakes with sometimes cataclysmic consequences."[‡] For example, between 1988 and 1996, at least five fatal airplane crashes were directly attributable to mode errors; the pilots used systems in the cockpit in ways that were incorrect for the current mode setting.[§] The affordance of "pulling a switch" actually meant something entirely different depending on the setting of some other overall mode.

What modes do is change the fundamental meaning of action, and this is not something our perceptual systems intuitively know how to handle. In the natural world, a physical action has the same invariant effect, as long as you're nested in the same environmental layout—that is, physically situated in the same spot, with the same objects and surfaces. When we learn that doing X in layout Y has effect Z, we don't have to keep learning it. And our bodies evolved with that assumption nicely tucked away.

It took advanced technology to change the way the world worked. Wireless microphones, left in the "on" mode, can unwittingly broadcast private conversations. Opening your home's door with the alarm enabled can prompt the police to show up at your doorstep. These are

---

[*] Norman, D. A. "Categorization of action slips." *Psychological review*, 1981, 1(88):1–15.

[†] Raskin, Jef. *The Humane Interface: New Directions for Designing Interactive Systems.* Boston: Addison-Wesley Professional, 2000.

[‡] *http://www.azarask.in/blog/post/is_visual_feedback_enough_why_modes_kill/*

[§] Degani, Asaf et al. "MODE USAGE IN AUTOMATED COCKPITS: SOME INITIAL OBSERVATIONS." Proceedings of International Federation of Automatic Control (IFAC). Boston, MA. June 27–29, 1995.

very simple mechanisms, though, compared to the complexly and sometimes incoherently nested rulesets that digital technology now adds to our environment.

The poster child for digital modes is the post-iPhone smartphone. Before the iPhone, even the smartest of smartphones was essentially a cell phone with a physical keyboard, such as the Palm Treo or the once-dominant RIM Blackberry. The iPhone fundamentally changed the nature of what a phone is. Now, a phone is a "phone" like Doctor Who's Sonic Screwdriver is a "screwdriver"—the label is a quaint, vestigial nickname.

The iPhone turned the phone into an almost entirely modal device: a slab of glass that can be just about anything, depending on what application it is running. It can be a pedometer, a walkie-talkie, a synthesizer, a video-game console, a musical keyboard, and on and on. It transforms into anything that can be simulated on its surface. Apple's more recent Watch product continues this mode-device tradition, using its "crown" as a mode-based control that has totally different functions depending on the currently active software.

And unlike a physical device—such as an analog wristwatch—digital software allows a small object like a smartphone or smartwatch to contain an overwhelming legion of modal rules, all nested many layers deep.

For example, most smartphones now have geolocation technology that can provide your latitude and longitude at any given time, based on GPS satellites and other network location information, including WiFi access points. The capability is always present, but it's a mode that is only "on" when certain apps need to access it. Usually there is some visual clue that the mode is active, but it's easy to overlook whether your phone is in "object that tracks my location" mode or not.

Imagine the surprise of someone like software magnate John McAfee who, while hiding in Belize from serious criminal charges, found his location was disclosed by people on the Internet. How? Because reporters he'd invited to his confidential location took his picture with a smartphone, with his permission, and posted it as part of their story on their publication's website. Normally, that wouldn't be a big deal, but someone downloaded the picture and discovered that it still held the geolocation metadata added to it by the phone's camera application.[*] The folks who committed this gaffe were not techno-neophytes—they were net-savvy reporters and a guy who made his millions from designing and selling computer security software. It just didn't occur to them that a hidden mode in a smartphone was adding obscure location data to what looked, to the eye, like a harmless photo with no location-specific information.

The photo metadata issue is only one of thousands of mode-based complexities in a garden-variety smartphone. Celebrities whose personal pictures are hacked and shared can attest to this problem, as well: most were likely not even aware their phones were in an "object that puts all my pictures on a distant computer" mode.

Modes are not going away. In spite of their challenges or the thought-leaders who complain about them, there's an insatiable market demand for more capabilities, but a limited amount of space for visible settings controls. It's likely that mode complexity will only increase. So, our systems will need even more complex and multilayered mode-control settings that will make our current situation seem primitive in just a few years. We comprehend context most easily at a human scale, not at vast microscopic or macroscopic levels that we can't see or easily learn through exploration. This is another reason why digital agency is becoming more necessary: we need digital agents to help manage our digital agents.

---

[*] Honan, Mat. "Oops! Did Vice Just Give Away John McAfee's Location With Photo
    Metadata?" *Wired* magazine (*wired.com*) December 3, 2012 (*http://wrd.cm/1s34PCT*).

[14]

Digital Environment

No metaphor is more misleading than "smart."
—MARK WEISER

Variant Modes and Digital Places

THE RULE-DRIVEN MODES AND simulated affordances of interfaces are also the objects, events, and layouts that function as *places*, whether on a screen alone or in the ambient digital activity in our surroundings. So, changing the mode of objects can affect the mode of places as well, especially when objects work as parts of interdependent systems.

For example, let's take a look at a software-based place: Google's search site. Suppose that we want to research what qualities to look for in a new kitchen knife. When we run a query using Google's regular mobile Web search, we see the sort of general results to which we've become accustomed: supposedly neutral results prioritized by Google's famed algorithm, which prioritizes based on the general "rank" of authority, determined by analyzing links across the Web. Google also defines "quality" for sites in general. On the desktop Google site, there are paid ad-word links that are clearly labeled as sponsored results, but the main results are easy to distinguish from the paid ones.

But Google's Shopping site is a different story: when searching for products there, all of the results are affected by paid promotion, as illustrated in Figure 14-1. I actually wasn't aware of this until a colleague pointed it out to me at lunch one day.*

---

* Thanks to Richard Dalton (*http://mauvyrusset.com*) for this tidbit.

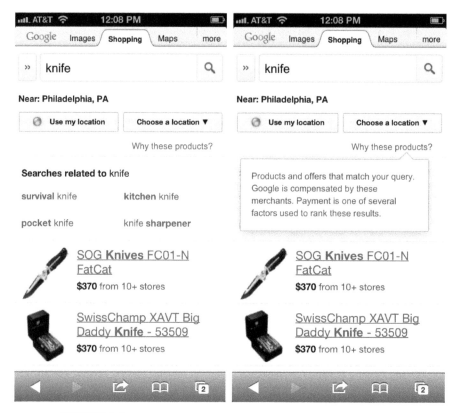

FIGURE 14-1

When in the Shopping tab, search results are driven by different rules, which you can see by clicking the "Why these products?" link

At least several factors are in play here:

- Google's long-standing web-search function has established cultural expectations in its user base: Google is providing the most relevant results based on the search terms entered. Although it's arguable as to whether these results are effective—or if they've been corrupted by site owners' search-engine manipulation—we still tend to equate Google with no-nonsense, just-the-facts search results, as a cultural invariant.

- Google's Shopping tab is listed right next to the Images, Maps, and "more" tabs—which, when expanded, show other Google services. The way these are displayed together implies that the rules behind how they give us results are equivalent. Objects that look the same are perceived as having similar properties. So, we aren't expecting results for Images to be prioritized by advertising dollar, just as we don't assume searching for a town in Maps will take us to a different-but-similar town because of someone's marketing plan.

- In the object layout of the search results view, Google Shopping provides no clear indication of this tab's different mode. The "Near: Philadelphia, PA" label indicates location is at work in some way, but the only way to know about paid-priority results is to tap the vaguely named "Why these products?" link at the upper right. It's nice of Google to provide this explanation, but users might not engage it because they assume they already know the answer, based on learned experience within Google's other environments.

There's nothing inherently wrong with making a shopping application function differently from a search application. But the invariant features of the environment need to make the difference more clear by using semantic function to better establish context.*

Foraging for Information

When we use these information environments, we're not paying explicit attention to a lot of these factors. In fact, we're generally feeling our way through with little conscious effort. So, the finer points of logical difference between one mode of an environment and another are easily lost on us. According to a number of related theories on information-seeking, humans look for information by using behavior patterns similar to those used by other terrestrial animals when foraging for food. Research has shown that people don't formulate fully logical queries and then go about looking in a rationally efficient manner; instead, they tend to move in a direction that feels right based on various semantic or visual cues, wandering through the environment in a nonlinear, somewhat unconsciously driven path, "sniffing out" whatever seems related to whatever it is for which they're searching.

We take action in digital-semantic environments using the same bodies that we evolved to use in physical environments. Instead of using a finger to poke a mango to see if it's ripe, or cocking an ear to listen

---

* An informative take on the filtered-place problem is in the book, *The Filter Bubble: How the New Personalized Web Is Changing What We Read and How We Think*, by Eli Pariser. Penguin Books, 2011.

for the sound of water, we poke at the environment with words, either by tapping or clicking words and pictures, or giving our own words to the environment through search queries, to see what it says back to us.

Marcia Bates' influential article from 1989, "The Design of Browsing and Berrypicking Techniques for the Online Search Interface," argues that people look for information by using behaviors that are repurposed from early human evolution. Bates points out that the classic information retrieval model, which assumes a linear, logical approach to matching a query with the representation of a document, was becoming inadequate as technology was presenting users with information environments of even greater scale and complexity.[*]

Bates has gone on to further develop her theoretical framework by folding "berrypicking" into a more comprehensive approach (see Figure 14-2), such as her 2002 article, "Toward an Integrated Model of Information Seeking and Searching." In that article, Bates argues that an "enormous part of all we know and learn...comes to us through passive undirected behavior."[†] That is, most search activity is really tacit, nondeliberate environmental action, not unlike the way we find our way through a city. Bates also points out that people tend to arrange their physical and social surroundings in ways to help them find information, essentially extending their cognition into the structures of their environment.

Bates' work often references another, related theoretical strand called *information foraging theory*. Introduced in a 1999 article by Stuart Card and Peter Pirolli, information foraging makes use of anthropological research on food-foraging strategies. It also borrows from theories developed in ecological psychology. Card and Pirolli propose several mathematical models for describing these behaviors, including *information scent models*. These models "address the identification of

---

[*] Bates, Marcia J. "The design of browsing and berrypicking techniques for the online search interface." *Online Review*. October, 1989;13(5):407–24.

[†] Bates, Marcia J. "Toward an Integrated Model of Information Seeking and Searching." (Keynote Address, Fourth international Conference on Information Needs, Seeking and Use in Different Contexts, Lisbon, Portugal, September 11, 2002.) *New Review of Information Behaviour Research*. 2002; Volume 3:1-15.

information value from proximal cues."* Card, Pirolli, and others have continued developing information foraging theory and have been influential in information science and human-computer interaction fields.

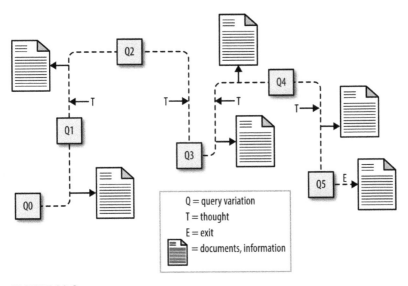

FIGURE 14-2
Bates' "berrypicking" model

I should point out that information foraging theory originated from a traditional cognitive-science perspective, assuming the brain works like a computer to sort out all the mathematics of how much energy might be conserved by using one path over another. However, even though Bates, Card, and Pirolli come from that tradition, it's arguable their work ends up being more in line with embodiment than not. The essential issue these theories address is that environments made mostly of semantic information lack most of the physical cues our perceptual systems evolved within; so our perception does what it can with what information *is* available, still using the same old mechanisms our cognition relied on long before writing existed.

---

* Pirolli, Peter, and Stuart Card. "Information Foraging" Xerox Palo Alto Research Center. *Psychological Review.* 1999; 106(4):643–75.

Inhabiting Two Worlds at Once

There are also on-screen capabilities that change the meaning of physical places, without doing anything physical to those places. Here's a relatively harmless example: in the podcast manager and player app called Downcast, you can instruct the software to update podcast feeds based on various modality settings, including geolocation, as illustrated in Figure 14-3.

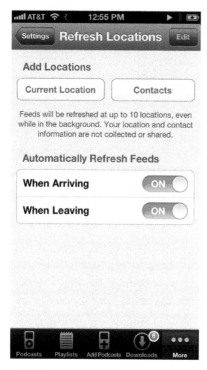

FIGURE 14-3

Refresh podcasts by geolocation in the Downcast podcast app

This feature allows Downcast to save on cellular data usage by updating only at preselected locations that have WiFi. It's a wonderful convenience. But, we should keep in mind that it adds a layer of digital behavior that changes, if only slightly, the functional meaning of one physical context versus another. Even without a legion of intelligent objects, our smartphones make every place we inhabit potentially "smart."

Another way digital has changed how we experience "place" is by replicating on the Web much of the semantic information we'd find in a physical store, and allowing us to shop online instead of in a building.

These on-screen places for shopping are expected more and more to be integrated with physical store locations. For big-box retailers that want to grow business across all channels, this means interesting challenges for integrating those dimensions.

Large traditional retailers are in the midst of major transition. Most of them were already big corporations long before the advent of the Web, so they have deeply entrenched, legacy infrastructures, supply chains, and organizational silos. These structures evolved in an environment in which everything about the business was based on terrestrially bound, local stores. Since the rise of e-commerce, most have struggled with how to exist in both dimensions at once. For example, if a customer wants to order something to be delivered or picked up in the store, it means the system must know where that user is and what store is involved to provide accurate price and availability information, as illustrated in Figure 14-4.

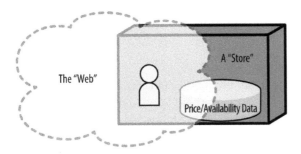

FIGURE 14-4
The user begins shopping on the Web—a place without location—but must be placed in a "store" to see necessary information about products

Conventions are starting to emerge for disambiguating the context of product availability. The approach adopted by Home Depot, shown in Figure 14-5, is becoming more common: for the product-listing view, the interface presents options to view All Products as well as Online Only and In My Store. This strategy seems pretty straightforward, but it turns out there are numerous complications when we unpack what these contextual labels really mean.

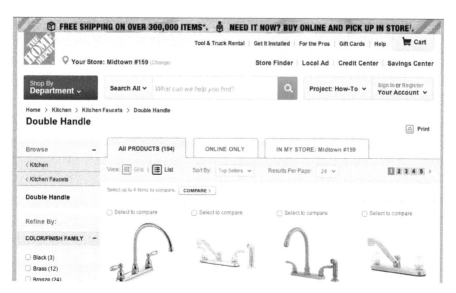

FIGURE 14-5

Home Depot's attempts to give semantic structure to the overlap of online and in-store shopping

All Products

In many online stores, "all products" can actually mean "all products we list online, but not everything you could buy in the store." This issue is improving, but lots of big retailers are still working to get their services infrastructure to handle the same inventory across stores and online. For stores that sell regionally sourced products such as lumber, this can be a special challenge.

Online Only

At first glance, this is a clear label that indicates products displayed on that tab are available only by ordering from the website. However, on some retail sites, what it really means is "these aren't available in 'Your Store,' so you need to order them from the site instead," even though they might be available in a store only a few miles away from "Your Store."

In My Store

I never selected a store and agreed to make it "mine." The website chose a store for me, using a third-party service that guesses my location based on the IP address the system thinks is assigned to my device's net connection. I know this only because I've learned it in my consulting work. However, many regular customers don't have that insider knowledge; they might not notice the choice was made for them at all. Sometimes, when systems make these choices for us, it's convenient. But it works only when it's accurate. Unfortunately, these geolocation-by-IP services are notoriously flakey, because there's no guarantee my IP address reflects my real location. For example, many customers do shopping from their workplace or via a coffee shop's WiFi connection. Corporate computers often use proxy connections for security reasons, and the proxy can be located many miles away. You can easily buy something thinking it will be ready for pickup at the store on the way home, only to find that it's actually waiting for you in another city.

The language is trying to create stability where systems are unable to promise it. There's always a point at which simplifying the environment obscures too much important information. The best way to handle a situation like this is not to fake simplicity but to embrace the complexity and clarify it by making it more understandable. For example, Lowe's Home Improvement has been experimenting with how to make the complex rules more clear, without obscuring important information that the customer really should understand, as depicted in Figure 14-6.

When the customer gets to a point on the site at which accurate location is relevant to action—such as in product lists with prices and availability displayed, or in the shopping cart—the site gently but unmistakably provides a message panel that urges the customer to take a moment to confirm the store choice. It's not a pop-up window that interrupts and obscures—the customer can keep shopping whether dismissing the embedded message or not, but it will continue to show up at important moments to ensure that the customer has confirmed the store before buying anything.

This is a digitally encoded business rule that the user needs to understand in order to use the environment. Like the ontology of "calendar" that we looked at earlier, here the ontologies of "store" and "shopping" and "purchase," and even "product," are still being sorted out for retailers who need customers to shop both in the cloud and in a store. Until systems can magically not only read your mind but know the exact location you want to get a product from, some version of this translation will be needed.

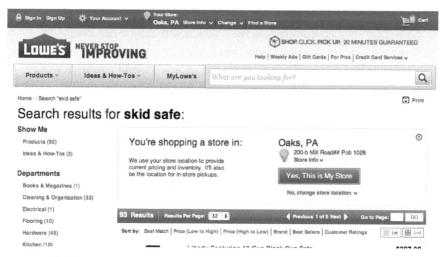

FIGURE 14-6

Lowes goes to some trouble to explain the complexity and avoid costly confusion about location

Location, Location, Location

We see digital influence at work even in subtle ways in our various online platforms. For example, as demonstrated in Figure 14-7, there are many ways to describe the location of a person.

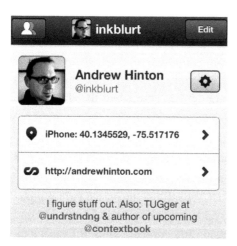

FIGURE 14-7

My Twitter profile, temporarily sporting an iPhone coordinate location

Physically

If I can see the friend, the friend is an object in the environment, exhibiting surface patterns that I recognize as that friend's face and body, and event-specifying information in the way the friend moves. The friend could be out of sight—occluded by another environmental surface—but I might still be able to hear the friend speak or make some other recognizable sound. Either way, the friend is within a relatively close distance to where I am.

Semantically

Semantic information gives us the ability to extend our *sensemaking* of location far beyond our human-scale perception. Because of the cultural system I'm part of, I understand that if my friend is "in Detroit," Detroit is a city in Michigan, which is situated on a map that I've seen thousands of times in my life. I probably couldn't tell you exactly where, but I know it's in the Midwest and close to the Canadian border. It's not precise, but it's a good-enough, *satisficing* concept that gets the job done.

Digitally

Suppose that I've met this person only online, over Twitter. At some point I wonder where he lives, so I check his Twitter profile only to find that it lists the person's location as iPhone: 37.404922,-5.992203, as in Figure 14-8. This is coordinate information that doesn't correspond with any semantic or physical reference point for me. Technically, this is semantic information, but in the context in which I'm seeing it, it's bound up with digital influence—it requires that I tap something to ask the software to translate it into a city name or a simple map.

Ambient Agents

There are physical objects and events in our surroundings that are digitally enabled; and these physical-digital agents are proliferating at a wild rate. Digital agent-objects are already more prevalent than most people realize, because they've been introduced into our lives in mostly mundane ways. For years we've been getting comfortable with on-screen digital agents such as an email client that decides on its own which messages are spam and which aren't. Thus, it's a small step to having a clothes dryer that stops when it senses the moisture is gone, or a thermostat that learns our habits and makes best-guess adjustments to home temperature. The consumer space is already awash in these gadgets, and many are networked so that we can control them from a kitchen console or personal smartphone.

These are all seemingly benign agents on their own, but as they add up, they become a layer of digital sentience pervading our surroundings. This can have a downside, as consumers discovered when refrigerators and other smart devices were hijacked by spam bots in late 2013,[*] or when electronics manufacturer LG had to admit it was collecting private viewing-habits data without customer knowledge.[†] These digital-information undercurrents transform our very dwellings from private enclaves to porous nodes on global networks—they change what "home" means. Generally, these technologies are created with the best of intentions. Yet, like all technologies, we have to learn their limits and consequences, and improve along the way.

Likewise, the networked objects of the urban landscape transform what cities are to us. In William Mitchell's ever-prescient words, "Rooms and buildings will henceforth be seen as sites where bits meet the body— where digital information is translated into visual, auditory, tactile, or otherwise perceptible form, and, conversely, where bodily actions are sensed and converted into digital information."[‡] Since those words were published in 1996, much of the world has found itself in exactly the situation Mitchell describes: our inhabited places are fundamentally different, whether online or offline, through the emergence of networked consumer technology and government infrastructures. We treat them like the invariant processes of nature, even though digital influence means these processes don't have to stay true to any natural laws at all.

Our cities and towns are becoming sensor-studded, agent-suffused environments that can improve our lives immensely, such as the cityscape of systems depicted in Figure 14-8. But they also require careful design and translation into people's everyday, tacitly aware understanding.

---

[*] "Fridge sends spam emails as attack hits smart gadgets." *BBC News Technology* January 17, 2014 (*http://www.bbc.com/news/technology-25780908*).

[†] Wakefiled, Jane. "LG promises update for 'spying' smart TV." *BBC News Technology* November 21, 2013 (*http://www.bbc.com/news/technology-25042563*).

[‡] Mitchell, William J. *City of Bits: Space, Place, and the Infobahn (On Architecture)*. Cambridge, MA: MIT Press, 1996:913–14, Kindle locations.

As inhabitants of these places satisfice their way through each day, they need the environment to let them know when objects aren't going to behave the way natural objects do. Retail store shelves can track body movements, age, and gender.[*] Safety-aware, cooperatively smart chemical drums can track how well their handlers are following safe-handling policies.[†] These are creatures of a sort that are not especially legible to us.

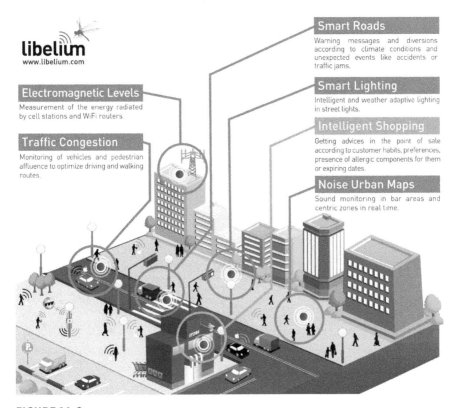

FIGURE 14-8

Detail portion of an infographic about smart cities, from Internet-of-Things platform provider, Libelium[‡]

---

[*] Ungerleider, Neal. "The Future of Shopping: Shelves That Track the Age and Gender of Passing Customers," *Fast Company* (*fastcompany.com*) October 15, 2013 (*http://bit.ly/1r8RsSw*).

[†] Kortuem, Gerd et al. "Smart objects as building blocks for the Internet of things," *Internet Computing, IEEE.* 2010;14(1):44–51 (*http://usir.salford.ac.uk/2735/1/w1iot.pdf*).

[‡] Courtesy, Libelium (*libelium.com*)

These are known challenges in computing fields. In a 2010 IEEE paper titled "Smart Objects as Building Blocks for the Internet of Things," the authors raise important questions about digital-agent objects:

> The vision of an Internet of Things built from smart objects raises several important research questions in terms of system architecture, design and development, and human involvement. For example, what is the right balance for the distribution of functionality between smart objects and the supporting infrastructure? How do we model and represent smart objects' intelligence? What are appropriate programming models? And how can people make sense of and interact with smart physical objects?*

The model, presented in Figure 14-9, describes smart objects across several dimensions, one of which the authors describe as "fundamental design and architectural principles: activity-aware objects, policy-aware objects, and process-aware objects."

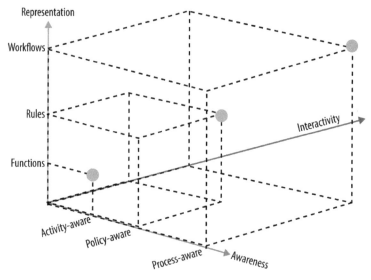

FIGURE 14-9

A model describing smart objects across several dimensions†

---

* Kortuem, Gerd et al. "Smart objects as building blocks for the Internet of things." *Internet Computing*, IEEE. 2010;14(1):44–51.

† ———. "Smart objects as building blocks for the Internet of things." *Internet Computing*, IEEE. 2010;14(1):44–51.

This and other models like it will be important for breaking down the types of agency these objects have, informing the design approaches we should take in creating and including them in designed environments.

In their book *Code/Space: Software and Everyday Life*, a particularly important idea explored by Kitchin and Dodge is that, not only do hardware and software *objects* have this kind of agency, but the "space" (in our terms, the *places*) we inhabit can have agency, as well—a quasi-sentience that's woven into the surfaces and layouts around us. Robots aren't only in the form of objects that behave like people or animals; entire buildings and cities can be "robots" of a sort.

This might sound ominous, and for good reason. Without diligent attention and foresight of its creators and users, the agency of pervasive digital infrastructures can erode human agency, independence, and privacy. In *Everyware: The Dawning Age of Ubiquitous Computing*, Adam Greenfield offers a thorough analysis of the implications of pervasively digital environments. One of Greenfield's theses states: "Everyware produces a wide belt of circumstances where human agency, judgment, and will are progressively supplanted by compliance with external, frequently algorithmically-applied, standards and norms."[*] We are used to living in environments in which, other than nature, everything around us happens based on the present or planned choices of human beings, but that arrangement is rapidly changing. We've created systems that use light-speed decision logic based on rules that are increasingly written by the systems themselves. Greenfield has dedicated himself to ongoing efforts at bridging the "black box" dimension of digital agency with the human-scale world that people can actually perceive and understand. The socio-political implications of "everyware" are deeply important. Although that's not our focus for this discussion, Greenfield's work is a good starting place for considering these issues.

When designing a system that depends on the perception of a human agent, the system should present invariant information that meets the expectations that human perception brings to the experience—the human *umwelt* (one's perceived environment). It's difficult enough to understand what all the "levers" in our lives actually do. Now, though,

---

* Greenfield, Adam. *Everyware: The Dawning Age of Ubiquitous Computing*. Berkeley, CA: New Riders; 2004:148.

we are faced with a world bristling with levers that do not look like levers; they are hidden from view or look and behave like something else entirely. These levers can create events too fast for our slow, embodied perception to pick up, much less understand.

Likewise, when designing a system that needs to perceive human context in helpful and accurate ways, the system itself should clearly signal *its own umwelt*—how it perceives and understands the human trying to interact with it. People tend to assume a digital agent is going to know more than it actually is capable of knowing; users of these agents risk making too many assumptions about the agents' intelligence. That's partly because intelligence is, itself, a reification. There is no actual thing we can point to that is "intelligence." But reification means we see intelligence where there often isn't any, perhaps to our great disappointment or risk. Digital agents need to be transparent about their limitations rather than present a simplified front that inaccurately promises human-like coherence.

This is why it's so important to understand how humans experience context. The parts of our environment that have been given digital agency should have an ontology that the human agent can comprehend, so users can understand what sort of creature the agent is, how to interact with it, and what can be expected of it.

[Part V]

The Maps We Live In

Information Architectures for Places and People

FOR THE REMAINDER OF THE BOOK, the main focus will be about how we use information to create architectures—environmental structures that shape the experience of "place." Prior chapters provided many examples of close-focus structures at the level of interaction; now, we will adjust our "zoom level" to be from a higher altitude, as we see how all those objects participate in systems of meaning. Like the natural environment, there are no places without objects, and objects ultimately define the moment-to-moment experience of place. But the overall coherence of the system brings *architectural* challenges to our work.

FIGURE V-1
A map, with people inside it. In this case, on the side of a favorite pizza joint in; Phoenixville, PA[*]

---

[*] Photo by author.

Information architecture is a discipline and practice well suited for attending to these challenges. It has been working with them in one way or another for decades. Early on, information architecture started as a way to make complex information *about* the world and its places understandable. Over the years, it has grown to also be a way to use information for creating places *in* the world itself. The framing device for understanding how semantic information forms environments will be "maps." But these are not just representational maps—they are maps we inhabit together.

Part V provides background about the discipline and practice of information architecture; it then explores what information architecture means for making the semantic systems—the "maps"—that we experience as places. It looks at how language functions in making the dimensions of those places across all information modes, both for individuals and organizations, and finally how these maps affect our social systems, and even our identities.

[15]

Information as Architecture

Every exit is an entry somewhere.
—TOM STOPPARD

Contemplating "Cyberspace"

INFORMATION HAS BEEN THOUGHT OF AS ARCHITECTURAL IN ONE WAY
OR ANOTHER FOR A LONG TIME. But, the extreme scale and complexity
of it that we now face is a fairly modern preoccupation. Mechanized
production certainly enabled a massive rise in information material,
but it was digital technology that truly allowed information to come
untethered from the surfaces of the world and replicate with seemingly
no limits. Information architecture is in many ways a response to this
digital unmooring and subsequent explosion, and it started even before
the Web.

Ideas and efforts have been around for many years that treat computer-
based information environments in physical, spatial ways, even though
they haven't necessarily used a combination of the words "information"
and "architecture" to describe them.

For quite a while, a popular term of art was *cyberspace*. Back in the early
1990s, Bruce Sterling explained how cyberspace isn't really some futuristic virtual-reality dimension; rather, it is something more mundane
and already here:

> Cyberspace is the "place" where a telephone conversation appears to
> occur. Not inside your actual phone, the plastic device on your desk.
> Not inside the other person's phone, in some other city. The place
> between the phones. The indefinite place out there, where the two of
> you, two human beings, actually meet and communicate. Although it
> is not exactly "real," "cyberspace" is a genuine place. Things happen

there that have very genuine consequences. This "place" is not "real," but it is serious, it is earnest....It makes good sense today to talk of cyberspace as a place all its own."[*]

Since its earliest days (Figure 15-1), the telephone has created a real-time conduit made of electricity—a sort of time-space wormhole, as path and place.

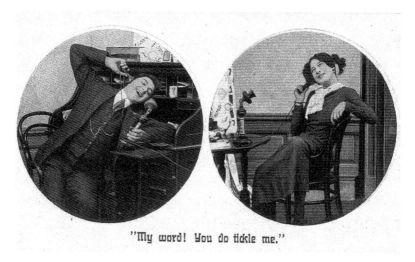

"My word! You do tickle me."

FIGURE 15-1
A couple enjoying the pleasures of cyberspace, in a 1910 postcard[†]

But as it turns out, even after the Internet arrived, cyberspace didn't last long as a place "all its own." It's become so interwoven into our environment that there's hardly a dividing line between one dimension and another. It is many places, all at once, all of them more or less woven into the physical dimension—what cyberpunk characters dismissively called "meatspace."

The writer William Gibson—who coined the term "cyberspace" in the 1980s—has himself had an evolving perspective on what it means to unleash digital information into the atoms that surround us. He's long

---

* Bruce Sterling, *The Hacker Crackdown*, Introduction. 1992. Retrieved from the HTML edition (*http://www.mit.edu/hacker/hacker.html*).

† Wikimedia Commons: *http://commons.wikimedia.org/wiki/File:CandlestickTelephones.jpg*

said that cyberspace hasn't turned out to be the virtual-reality construct he described in his early stories. He now sees cyberspace as everywhere. It has turned inside out and "colonized the world."[*]

> When I wrote Neuromancer, cyberspace was there, and we were here. [Now], what we no longer bother to call cyberspace is here, and those increasingly rare moments of nonconnectivity are there. And that's the difference. There's no scarlet-tinged dawn on which we rise and look out the window and go, "Oh my God, it's all cyberspace now."[†]

Cyberspace always sounded a bit exotic, but it isn't really all that mysterious. It's just a way of talking about how information has become disconnected from physical objects.

The more practical aspects of such an environment, as well as what it means to make that environment and navigate through it, have been a preoccupation throughout the twentieth century—from Vannevar Bush's "memex" in 1945, to Doug Engelbart's work in the 1960s. Both Bush and Engelbart were less technologists than humanists, using technology to augment and enhance human life. That is, the sort of thinking that grapples with cyberspace isn't ultimately about just the gadgets and networks. It's about the sort of world that humans create for themselves.

Since the Internet's arrival, there have been other milestone works about the human experience of information environments and what sort of places we are making with information technology:

- Information scientist Marcia Bates' work (see Chapter 14) brought a paradigm-shifting evolutionary perspective to how people experience and take action with information through exaptation of early-hominid strategies for exploration and survival.

- Howard Rheingold, inspired by the compelling and intimate community he'd experienced in the "WELL" (Whole Earth 'Lectronic Link), wrote a great deal especially in the 1990s about the future of social software, such as in his 1993 book *The Virtual Community: Homesteading on the Electronic Frontier* (MIT Press).

---

[*] Interview. *Paris Review* Summer 2011; Number 211.

[†] Garreau, Joel. "Through the Looking Glass." *Washington Post* Thursday, September 6, 2007.

- William J. Mitchell, a professor of architecture and media arts at MIT, and former director of the Smart Cities research group at its famed Media Lab, in his 1996 book *City of Bits: Space, Place, and the Infobahn* (MIT Press) and other works.

- Sherry Turkle's ethnographic research into MUDs, and her resulting 1997 book, *Life on the Screen* (Simon & Schuster).

- Brenda Laurel's influential *Computers as Theatre* (Addison-Wesley Professional), exploring the existential nature of information environments, in 1991.

- Janet H. Murray's 1998 book, *Hamlet on the Holodeck: The Future of Narrative in Cyberspace* (MIT Press), discussing, in part, how digital technology might enable literature to be something we physically inhabit.

These are all landmarks, but they're only a small sample, part of a large body of work making sense of how information establishes a sort of architecture that we are still coming to understand. These conversations began well before the advent of the Web or the commercial, public Internet. I mention this because, for many who went on to practice information architecture, this was the discourse that made "architectures of information" important and fascinating from the outset.

Architecture + Information

As for the label, "information architecture," several threads, especially since around 1970, spawned different usages and versions of the phrase for technologists, design and architecture practitioners, and, later, web professionals. They are all complementary in various ways, but have been somewhat separate domains, at least until recent years.[*]

In the early 1970s, there were already discussions at places such as IBM and Xerox's Palo Alto Research Center (PARC) about the broader challenges for structuring semantic information within digital systems into environments that would make sense to humans. Xerox PARC, in particular, included as part of its charter in 1970 to support "the

---

[*] A source for much of this background: Resmini, A., and Rosati, L. "A Brief History of Information Architecture." *Journal of Information Architecture* 2012;3(2).

architecture of information."[*] And in 1976, Richard Saul Wurman introduced the phrase "information architects" as part of the theme for the annual meeting of The American Institute of Architects in Philadelphia.

Wurman continued to develop his ideas on what he meant by "information architects," and went on to publish more books on the subject, including *Information Anxiety* (Doubleday), in 1989, and *Information Architects* (Graphis, Inc.), in 1997, in which he clarifies that his idea of information architecture isn't just about information graphics. He writes, "I mean architect as used in the words *architect of foreign policy*, I mean architect as in the creating of systemic, structural, and orderly principles to make something work—the thoughtful making of either artifact, or idea, or policy that informs because it is clear."[†] Note that Wurman does not say "make it *simple*." Complexity is to be made more *clear* to be *understandable*, even when it cannot be made more simple.

Prior to Wurman's 1997 treatise, Louis Rosenfeld and Peter Morville were noticing that the newly emerging World Wide Web was spawning information environments, and these "websites" were getting out of control. They saw that the anything-goes hyperlinking of the Web was undermining the needs of organizations, even as they were coming to depend on the Web as a crucial part of business. Morville and Rosenfeld saw an opportunity to use the ideas and methods from their expertise in library science in the service of making sense of the Web for those organizations.

They used the phrase "information architecture" because it seemed to them that the practice was less about designing the visual "pages" of the Web than what was "between" those pages—the paths and nodal structures that made up entire Web environments.[‡] This is why they called their early column in *Web Review* magazine "Web Architect." And it's why they used the term "architecture" for the methods and ideas collected in their groundbreaking book, *Information Architecture for the World Wide Web* (O'Reilly). When the concept of architecture for

---

[*] Hearst, M. "Research in Support of Digital Libraries at Xerox PARC." *D-Lib Mazagine* 1996.

[†] Wurman, R. S. *Information Architects*. Graphis Inc., 1997:16.

[‡] Champeon, Steven. "Interview: Lou Rosenfeld, Web Architect." ajaundicedeye.com. May 8, 1997 (*http://ajaundicedeye.com/stuck/archive/050897/article.html (retrieved 2014-04-18*)

a more understandable and navigable Web was unleashed, more books, methods, and ideas followed from others in the growing community. Those of us trying to figure out the big questions around what it means to create understandable, coherent, useful places on the Web—where people can understand what they're doing, where they are, and how to discover what they need—started gathering under the information architecture umbrella.*

Expansive IA

For many who identify as information architects—or at least as practitioners who do their work from an architectural point of view—the pre-Web, big-idea threads about society, complexity, placemaking, and systems have always been part of the discussion. But, some still see information architecture as a limited, specialty practice—really a set of methods—for organizing information inventories and static website hierarchies. Although these practices are still a critically important subset of what information architecture has become, there is a recent resurgence in a more expansive perspective.

Early, Web-centric information architecture practice was mainly about solving the problem of information disorganization and overwhelm, as a result of which users felt they were "drinking from the firehose" (as the saying goes). Even that metaphor is too limited now. Information has changed the hose, the hydrant, the firehouse, and the city itself. As a community of practice, information architecture is at a watershed moment, at which it has to re-embrace some of its early, expansive perspective to address the ambient-technology challenges we now face.

This expansiveness is not a "land-grab" from other practices. Complex problem domains have many dimensions and facets. Information architecture attends to only some of those, regardless of the work at hand. Rather, an expansive view means looking beyond the myopic focus of neatly contained systems of organization and arrangement. It means embracing the more complex challenge that Wurman first articulated

---

* It bears mentioning that other work that influenced the early information architecture community included academic papers and talks from Andrew Dillon, Gary Marchionini, and others, as well as practitioner-focused books such as Eric Reiss's *Practical Information Architecture* (Addison-Wesley Professional), Christina Wodtke's *Information Architecture: Blueprints for the Web* (New Riders), and Jesse James Garrett's *The Elements of User Experience* (New Riders).

in the 1970s: a way of seeing the problems we face with information, embracing their complexity while architecting what is needed to make that complexity "clear."

Most of this movement has grown in recent years, although less through books than through conversations, presentations, and papers. However, there have been books such as Peter Morville's ahead-of-its-time *Ambient Findability* (2005, O'Reilly) and Resmini and Rosati's *Pervasive Information Architecture: Designing Cross-Channel User Experiences* (2011, Morgan Kaufmann), which have helped establish a more expansive point of view. Most recently, Morville's *Intertwingled* (2014, Semantic Studios) presents information architecture as a way of dealing with big, systemic human challenges that go well beyond websites; Resmini's edited volume, *Reframing Information Architecture* (2014, Springer) is an explicit attempt to change the way we think about information architecture as practitioners and scholars.

These are just a few officially identified works about information architecture, but there are many others that frame it in other ways, in other facets of this vast discourse. Most of the innovation and discovery happening in the world of software design—and environmental design, generally—is being done by people who don't call their work "information architecture" to begin with. That's how the culture of practice works—all practices take time to coalesce under common language. We're in the midst of just such a long transition for information architecture.

About Definitions

While information architecture has many voices and many faces, for our current focus I want to establish a baseline for how I frame it going forward. For over a decade the generally accepted definition of information architecture has started with the phrase *the structural design of shared information environments*. The full definition includes specifics about websites, findability, and the community of practice (see Figure 15-2). But, as intended at its introduction, that first phrase acknowledges that the landscape is changing in its details, yet there will always be a need for making sense of environments. I have found it a valuable way to frame the work, and it has been a touchstone for everything we've covered in the book so far, so let's unpack it a bit.

Defining Information Architecture

We define information architecture as:

1. The structural design of shared information environments.
2. The art and science of organizing and labeling web sites, intranets, online communities and software to support usability and findability.
3. An emerging community of practice focused on bringing principles of design and architecture to the digital landscape.

Are these definitions definitive? Absolutely not. Our craft is new and still taking shape. We're clear on the center but fuzzy at the boundaries. This inherent ambiguity challenges us to think deeply and seek diverse perspectives.

FIGURE 15-2

The definition of information architecture, as presented (and, really, proposed) on AIFIA.org in 2002*

First, the key words *structure* and *design*. Here are their primary definitions, according to the *Oxford English Dictionary:*†

Structure

> The arrangement of and relations between the parts or elements of something complex.

Design

> A plan or drawing produced to show the look and function or workings of a building, garment, or other object before it is built or made.

Structure is implicitly about something complex, and how its parts are arranged in relation to one another to create and/or accommodate that complexity. All complex things have structure, but that structure isn't necessarily clear or understandable. This is why structures we rely on to handle complex, human-made systems require design.

Design, when brought to the problems of structure, is much less about "look" than "function." It's the explicit attention to the function of structural arrangement rather than the happenstance, tacit

---

* AIFIA was the Asilomar Institute for Information Architecture, later renamed the Information Architecture Institute. Archive.org link: *http://bit.ly/rwm8xMb*

† Structure: *http://www.oxforddictionaries.com/definition/english/structure*
 Design: *http://www.oxforddictionaries.com/us/definition/american_english/design*

aggregation of parts that occurs when structure is not deliberately considered. Form and function are inseparable; everything with form functions at least at the level of perception, and everything with function requires form to exist.

Next, the remaining parts of the phrase:

Shared

Adding the word "shared" was an effort to highlight how information architecture is mainly concerned with multiuser environments,[*] but I think we can safely set that qualification aside, now that being connected to an electronic communications network—all the time, everywhere—is more common than not.[†]

Information environments

This last phrase is what this book has been mainly about—establishing what we mean by these words. The prior chapters have explained that, in a sense, all environments are information environments; however, they involve several modes of information in various combinations, with different effects.

To my mind, information architecture as a practice is *centered* on the semantic information mode, but not *bound* by it. The practice also has to do with how the functions of the semantic mode inform the affordances of the physical mode, and how both are influenced by the digital mode. In my airport scenario from Chapter 1, information architecture would be a relevant practice for improving not only the digital software but the brand loyalty-program categories, the airport wayfinding, the way WiFi access is presented to users, and the structural design of how all these services conjoin to function as an environment.

Information architecture uses language as the primary material for stitching together the environmental invariants that language informs, and that inform language in turn.

In a branch of anthropology that concerns itself with how we form professional identities and learn from our peers, there is the idea that a "community of practice" has a "domain" around which it orbits and

---

* Author's recollection and community correspondence.
† Even relatively undeveloped societies now have pervasive access to cell phones and SMS.

coalesces—a sort of central concern.* For our purposes here, then, *the central concern of information architecture is how information creates environmental structure and supports environmental understanding.* One reason I've waited until this chapter to discuss information architecture explicitly is that, hopefully by now, those words have a lot more meaning for you than they would have had otherwise.

I suppose it doesn't have to say "environmental"—isn't all structure and understanding related to some environment? But I want to be sure we're always remembering we're working with situated, embodied structure and understanding, not just abstractions.

Also notice that I didn't limit the central concern to "semantic" information alone. That's because, at least for the purposes of this book, information architecture's semantic toolset needs to account for physical and digital information, as well—using semantic function in the service of helping *physical* bodies comprehend all manner of environments disrupted and changed by *digital* technology.

As for our focus on context, information architecture isn't only about context, and context isn't only about information architecture. However, context is certainly an important concern for information architecture practice, and context can certainly be made better by designing coherent, humane architectures of information.

---

* Wenger, Etienne. *Communities of Practice: Learning, Meaning, and Identity.* Cambridge, England: Cambridge University Press, 1998.

Mapping and Placemaking

There is no logic that can be superimposed on the city; people make it, and it is to them, not buildings, that we must fit our plans.
—JANE JACOBS

Maps and Territory

INFORMATION ARCHITECTURE IS LARGELY CONCERNED WITH BOTH DESCRIBING AND INSTANTIATING NEW PLACES, but these places are made largely of semantic information. Mapping is a method that people have invented to establish context, using semantic information for the task. Sometimes, maps describe something that isn't made yet. Often they describe something that already exists but is too big or complicated on its own. A map is a semantic-information artifact that helps us understand something about what it describes, even when it is describing itself.

This puts an interesting twist on how we normally think of maps and their relation to places. From one position, we can say that maps and the places they describe are not the same things, but from another position, maps are hard to separate from the places they are about, and they change what those places mean to us.

So, let's begin with the first position: "The map is not the territory." Those are the words of Alfred Korzybski, the philosopher and scientist who developed the theory of *general semantics*. Korzybski wasn't especially writing about cartography; his main point was that the concepts—and language—we use for the world aren't the same as the world itself; we need to realize that the way we describe the world can become reified so that it colors and constrains our factual understanding of it. Cultivating this perspective requires an explicit, deliberate effort that is necessary especially in the sciences, where empirical fact can sometimes be obscured or warped by our cognitive biases.

Of course, it's important to cultivate this perspective in design, as well. One reason why user experience design relies so heavily on research is that the approach acknowledges we have to get out of our own assumptions—our own "maps"—to better understand the "territory" of actual user behavior.

Then, there's the second position: in some ways, the map and territory are the same. Sure, a map is not literally the same as the dirt, concrete, and steel that make up the actual, physical territory, but we don't experience the world only as physical territory—we experience it in terms of *places*, which are as much cultural and linguistic for humans as they are physical. People use the full environment, maps and all; they don't go about their day analyzing how the map and territory are separate. They *satisfice* and conflate; they take tacit action and concentrate only when necessary.

Writing about cartography and the cultural function of maps, Edward Rothstein explains:

> By suggesting that all understanding may be a form of mapping, it turns maps into an archetypal example of human knowledge. Indeed, in discussing thoughts or feelings, people often invoke a cartographic universe. Feeling bewildered, one talks about "terra incognita," about "being at a crossroads" or "losing our way." Gaining understanding, one speaks of "putting things in perspective" and "being on familiar terrain." People come to know the world the way they come to map it—through their perceptions of how its elements are connected and of how they should move among them.[*]

Mapping is action toward understanding. This natural tendency to merge map and territory is what prompted Korzybski to coin his aphorism in the first place; he intended it as corrective advice. Realistically, we can't expect the people who use the environments we design to analyze them like general semanticists or research scientists. In terms of real human perception and action, the map and the territory are inseparable.

---

[*] Rothstein, Edward. "Map Makers Explore The Contours Of Power; New Study Tries to Break the Eurocentric Mold." *New York Times*; May 29, 1999 (*http://nyti.ms/1sL4yZ7*).

What Makes Places

Maps are complex semantic artifacts we use to understand context and place, which means they participate in the activity of *placemaking*—a term with many related meanings, from many different disciplines. In this discussion, we're going to use the term as shorthand for two things at once:

- The ecological dynamic James J. Gibson describes between the environment and the perceiver—the organic, *emergent* sort of placemaking that happens even in nature.

- The *intentional* design of an environment to be perceived and used as one sort of place versus another; in the terms of information architecture, placemaking is a heuristic described as that which helps "users reduce disorientation, build a sense of place, and increase legibility and wayfinding across digital, physical, and cross-channel environments."[*]

Recall Gibson's elements: place is a function of the relationship between an agent and the layout of its environment, and a place is a place only because it affords meaningful action. Places don't necessarily have solid boundaries, though artificially built environments might establish those more explicitly. We can create structures that we intend to be perceived as places, but it's up to the perceiver to find meaning in those structures that resonate as "place." I walk by buildings every day that are just objects to me; but if one smells like it has barbeque inside, it's an interesting place to me, indeed.

It's through making sense of "space" that placemaking happens, which then informs sensemaking, and so on, in yet another loop of human understanding. The issue of *space* versus *place* plays a role in the work of Otto Friedrich Bollnow, who tackled the issue in 1963 in *Mensch und Raum* (*Man and Space*) (Verlag W. Kohlhammer). Bollnow introduces the idea of "anthropological space"—that space is not an objectively existing entity, but a human construct. This insight is behind Bollnow's concept of *hodological space*, from the Greek roots "hodos," meaning

---

* Resmini, Andrea, and Luca Rosati. *Pervasive Information Architecture: Designing Cross-Channel User Experiences*. Burlington, MA: Morgan Kaufmann, 2011:55.

"path," and "logos," meaning "word" or "discourse." Hodological space is "a space of paths, and experience, and it corresponds exactly to what we perceive if we move between two different locations."[*]

Bollnow's hodological space is nicely compatible with the ideas we've explored so far. Ecologically, paths afford locomotion between places; and "paths" are one of Kevin Lynch's "elements" that make up a city. The context of a path is determined by what it connects, and the places it connects are bound up in the semantic, cultural needs and shared stories of the people traveling them. The space we live in is really made of places. In fact, Bollnow argues that our contemporary idea of *universal space* is a relatively recent invention "connected to the age of discovery and cartography of the 15th and 16th centuries."[†] Space is a collective, tacit agreement based on generations of culturally accumulated discourse. I think this is part of what philosopher Andy Clark is getting at when he says labels are a sort of "augmented reality trick" we use for modifying our environment.[‡] When we use the structures of language to explain the world to ourselves, we add to that world new structures that change what it is and what it means to its inhabitants.

There has always been a contextual relationship between *place* and *object*. A building is an object, albeit a large one; however, because of how it is used, and because people can fit inside its boundaries, it is usually experienced as a place. Likewise, a book is an object, but we read a book as a series of pages, which are also objects nested in the book, and then we refer to a particular paragraph as being in a place within the book. In a digital example, a smartphone camera app is represented as an object on a phone's Home screen, but after the app is "opened" and we are "in" it, the app has nested structures of layouts, providing places that align with categories of action: taking a photo, editing a photo, browsing a collection of photos, and so on.

This all sounds wishy-washy, until we remember that we're working from an embodied point of view, which always focuses on the perspective of a particular perceiver. Just as a tool can go from "present-at-hand"

---

[*] ———. *Pervasive Information Architecture: Designing Cross-Channel User Experiences.* Burlington, MA: Morgan Kaufmann, 2011:68

[†] ———. *Pervasive Information Architecture: Designing Cross-Channel User Experiences.* Burlington, MA: Morgan Kaufmann, 2011:69

[‡] Referenced earlier, in Chapter 9.

to "ready-to-hand" without the tool itself changing what it physically is, places can shift in what they are to a perceiver, depending on what action is happening in the moment. Context is a mutual, coupled dance between environment and active perception.

Railroads, Chickens, and Captain Vancouver

The semantic information we add to our environment plays a powerful role in how we comprehend, experience, and inhabit places. We might be able to draw a technical distinction between the physical information and semantic information around us, but in everyday, practical life, humans perceive these dimensions as one blended environment. To help illustrate this idea, here are a few stories about language and place.

ATLANTA

Recently, I returned to live in my city of birth, Atlanta, Georgia. Although Atlanta has a defined city-limit boundary encompassing around a half million people, what people culturally mean by "Atlanta" is the huge metropolitan area that Atlanta has absorbed: towns, cities, and suburbs that were once outside Atlanta's borders are now part of "the Atlanta Metro Area" (see Figure 16-1). The region is home to more than five million souls, making it the ninth largest metropolitan area in the United States.

When we moved back, my wife and I bought a house in the city of East Point. Although East Point is a city of its own, it's actually part of the Atlanta Metro Area, only about seven miles from downtown. East Point sounds like it would be in the eastern part of the city, but it's actually situated southwest of downtown Atlanta. Why is it called East Point, then? Because it was founded in the 1800s as the *eastern terminus* of a railroad that terminated in the west at...you guessed it, a town called West Point. The railroad came first, and the names of the towns came later. Context is nested. It shifts and evolves, even as our labels remain.

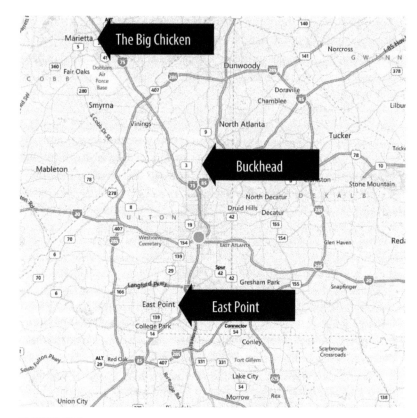

FIGURE 16-1
Atlanta, Georgia*

Atlanta also has a district known as Buckhead. The area was first settled in the 1830s, when Henry Irby started a general store and tavern
in this sparsely populated area of Georgia wilderness.[†] The community
that grew up around the store and tavern gradually became known as
Irbyville. According to a descendent, it was Irby himself who mounted
a large deer head and antlers in the area (possibly as a parody of aris-
tocratic folk who mounted such trophies on their walls); over time, the
name of the area changed from Irbyville to Buckhead. There are no
detailed accounts of how the name emerged as the official label. But if
it happens like a lot of similar language events, it probably started as
people telling each other directions, like, "Starting at the buck's head,

---

* via *Bing.com*, annotations by author.

† *http://www.buckhead.net/history/buckhead/index.html*

keep going north." The object Irby mounted inadvertently became part of the semiotic shape of the environment; it stood out enough that, through the organic activity of community wayfinding, it eventually became the most easily satisfied way of labeling the area.

Just up the road from Buckhead, in a subcity of Atlanta called Marietta, is the "Big Chicken"—a giant wooden chicken-shaped sign for a local restaurant (Figure 16-2). It's been a fixture at one of Marietta's major intersections since the 1950s. Marietta was never in danger of being renamed Big Chicken, Georgia, because it had been officially Marietta since long before the chicken appeared. Yet, the landmark is still central to the colloquial understanding of Marietta as a place; if you ever get directions from a local, there's a very good chance they'll begin with, "Well, do you know where the Big Chicken is?"

FIGURE 16-2
The Big Chicken in Marietta, GA[*]

In all of these cases, semantic information is central to the identity and use of a place, and semantic artifacts have become part of the de facto ecological landscape. Interestingly, all of them are also situations in which commerce—that prolific perception-action-loop of culture—initiated those landmarks and labels.

In the case of the Big Chicken, the artifact is still there, just as prominent a landmark as something more permanent might be, such as a uniquely shaped rock formation (like the one in, no kidding, Stone Mountain, GA).

---

[*] Wikimedia Commons: *http://commons.wikimedia.org/wiki/File:Thebigchicken.jpg*

VANCOUVER

Shared semantic narratives in a given culture are part of that culture's infrastructure of place. In the late eighteenth century, when Europeans under the command of Captain George Vancouver were mapping the coasts of the northwest Americas (Figure 16-3), they were providing their own names to what they saw, as they sketched out the contours of the landscape. Vancouver writes in his journal that the native people seemed to have a bizarre manner of navigating the sea.

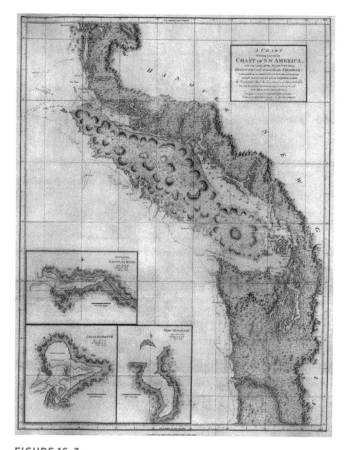

FIGURE 16-3

Map from the explorations of George Vancouver: "A chart shewing (sic) part of the coast of N.W. America: with the tracks of His Majesty's sloop Discovery and armed tender Chatham"*

---

* London : J. Edwards, Pall Mall & G. Robinson, Paternoster Row, May 1st, 1798 (*http://www.loc.gov/item/2003627084*).

For one thing, the natives didn't seem to understand the logic of going in a straight line, which seemed to the Europeans the most sensible way of moving over an undifferentiated expanse of water. However, the natives' winding routes were sensible from their perspective: they were navigating around places they believed to have powerful spirits or monstrous dangers, based on prior experience and shared lore. The natives didn't have a written map of these obstacles, but they were inhabiting a shared map, nonetheless.

For Vancouver and his crew, it was doubly bizarre that the natives were more concerned with the particularities of the sea and the shore, and were treating the areas inland as if they were mere nothingness. But for a native civilization that subsisted mainly on what the sea could give them—and much less interested in "taming the land" for agriculture or permanent fortifications—this reversal made sense.*

In essence, the Europeans and the natives inhabited separate *umwelts* ("perceived" environments; see Chapter 4), even as they inhabited the same ecological location. They were separated not only by language, but by their respective cultural assumptions about what is valuable and what is not. For one culture, the sea was full of meaningful places, and the land was mostly meaningless, mysterious space. For the other culture, the opposite was true: the land was full of potential for strategic settlements and agricultural production; the space was the sea— what they traveled through in order to get to the places that mattered to them. Vancouver and crew weren't an aberration. We all inhabit our own umwelts, in a sense. A family home is a different sort of place to the parent than to the child, and a city street is different for a police officer and a pedestrian, and these maps are reinforced by the cultures of parenting, childhood, policing, or civilian life.

Recall how we looked at the concept of *cognitive maps* in Chapter 7—it's a tricky metaphor because they aren't actually all that stable, and they rely a great deal on context. Not unlike those maps, the maps we share in culture are also dynamically in a state of "becoming" through our behaviors and beliefs. As anthropologist Charles O. Frake explains:

---

* Cresswell, Tim. *Place: A Short Introduction*. Oxford: Blackwell Publishing, 2004:9.

Culture is not simply a cognitive map that people acquire, in whole or in part, more or less accurately, and then learn to read. People are not just map-readers; they are map-makers. People are cast out into imperfectly charted, continually revised sketch maps. Culture does not provide a cognitive map, but rather a set of principles for map making and navigation. Different cultures are like different schools of navigation to cope with different terrains and seas.*

That is, we are all participants in the continual existence of these shared, cultural maps. Just as context is bound up in our action and perception, rather than a static, external property, these cultural structures we live in are reinforced, restitched, preserved, or disrupted by our participation in those cultures.

Captain Vancouver's European explorers might have been making literal, explicitly crafted maps of the terrain they were exploring, but they already had tacit "maps" that they inhabited before they ever left on their voyage. Not just the maps they carried in their hands, but a sort of map that emerges from collective cultural activity.

These tacitly inhabited maps are culturally bound information structures that we erect and reinforce through the narratives we share and the ways in which we communicate and behave. In some ways, these culturally determined semantic realities are even more important than the conventional maps we make, because the first sort sets the terms under which the second sort are created and understood. Culture creates invariant structures that determine how we understand our experience, and the interface for that cultural map is language—the very sort of information that makes the map in the first place.

Maps are not neutral information artifacts. Because they cannot contain every detail of the world, they can accommodate only certain, chosen aspects of our environment, our culture, and our own lives. As Rothstein's article on cartography explains, "maps are not just a progressive record of attempts to know the world; they are a record of

---

* Frake, Charles O. "Plying Frames Can Be Dangerous: Some Reflections on Methodology in Cognitive Anthropology" Quarterly Newsletter of the Institute for Comparative Human Development, 1977;(3):6–7.

attempts to construct and control it. Maps are not innocent. They select the data they wish to emphasize and ignore what is inconvenient. They are...instruments of power."[*]

Author and cartographer Denis Wood argues in *The Power of Maps* (The Guilford Press):

> The selection of a map projection is always to choose among competing interests; that is to embody those interests in the map...even if we confine ourselves to such superficially technical issues as the representation of angles and areas, distances and directions.[†]

Everything we make is full of decisions driven by someone's interests somewhere, whether we're conscious of it nor not. And maps are especially charged with political, social, and personal significance.

We have a great responsibility when creating information environments: even though contextual meaning ultimately depends on the perceiver, the environment has a lot of control over the perceiver's experience of that reality. Information architectures create maps we live in, and those maps reify choices, values, and agendas. They have always been a way for one party to define the world in categories that suit that party's own interests. What makes a place for humans has as much to do with these factors as what the physical affordances of a place provide.

Organizational Maps

Structure is always political because it always potentially implies something about how people are organized in relation to one another. Places are made of many things, not just the ecological surfaces of the physical environment. As anyone who has worked in a modern corporation can attest, there are many structures at work in business beyond the walls, ceilings, and floors of an office building.

---

[*] Rothstein, Edward. "Map Makers Explore The Contours Of Power; New Study Tries to Break the Eurocentric Mold." *New York Times*; May 29, 1999.

[†] Wood, Denis. *The Power of Maps*, 1st edition. New York: The Guilford Press, 1992:57. (emphasis in original)

In Figure 16-4, we see what some say is the first corporate organizational chart ever made—the diagram describing the structure of the New York and Erie Railroad in the mid-nineteenth century.* Railroads were a new species of human organization that required real-time coordination across vast distances and time zones. To function, railroads required semantic artifacts such as these as much as they required tracks and switches or headquarters buildings in major cities. To a large degree, the railroad *lived* in the system described by this chart.

Although it's common for the physical layout of an office structure to reflect the hierarchy of its inhabitants—big, corner offices for senior executives, smaller internal offices for middle management, open seas of cubicles for the rank-and-file—physical layout alone isn't enough for the complexities of large-scale business.

As David Weinberger explains in *Everything is Miscellaneous*: "Each company has one official org chart because the flow of authority needs to be simple and unambiguous for legal reasons, not just to create an efficient decision structure."† The environment—in this case the byzantine semantic architecture of legal regulatory rules—exerts controlling pressures on the shape of the corporate body, requiring it to make its own semantic structures to "couple" with those legal pressures.

Weinberger goes on to explain how this facet of information for the company describes only one official, enforced slice of the actual structures at work there. The rest tend to be more tacitly emergent: the networks of shared expertise, friendships, trusted partnerships, and other sorts of social connections.

Business uses semantic structures in other ways besides organizational command. For example, a company can recategorize workers from "employees" to "independent contractors" to avoid taxes and benefits costs—often with just a few clicks in a database.‡ Moving people semantically from one state of being to another can have a devastatingly real effect on those lives.

---

* The First Org Chart Ever Made Is a Masterpiece of Data Design Liz Stinson March 18 2014 *Wired.com* (http://wrd.cm/1t9Cnoe).

† Weinberger, David. *Everything is Miscellaneous: The Power of the New Digital Disorder.* New York: Times Books, 2007:182.

‡ Wood, Marjorie Elizabeth. "Victims of Misclassification," *New York Times*, December 15, 2013.

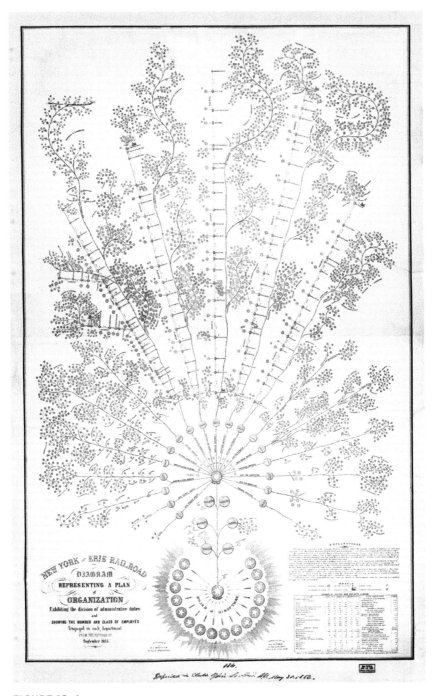

FIGURE 16-4

Organizational diagram of the New York and Erie Railroad, circa 1855

The organizational chart is just one example of how language creates structures that we inhabit. As humans, there's no escaping the places we make with information, whether we mean to make them or not. In information architecture practice, it's crucial to understand not only the official organizational structure, but the unofficial, tacit, cultural power structures, as well, both for the client or employer and the social structures that the organization serves—families, towns, and even other companies.

[17]

Virtual and Ambient Places

It's funny how the colors of the real world only seem really real when you viddy them on the screen.

—ALEX, IN *A CLOCKWORK ORANGE*, ANTHONY BURGESS

Of Dungeons and Quakes

SEMANTIC INFORMATION CAN BE TRULY IMMERSIVE. Whether it's an all-night dorm conversation or losing yourself in an engrossing novel, language can swallow our attention whole. When you add more layers to the semantic environment, meaningful experiences of place can emerge. Take a role-playing game such as Dungeons & Dragons (Figure 17-1). For the players, the physical surroundings—a friend's kitchen table or the back of a hobby shop—recede into mist as the shared story of the campaign becomes more palpable and compelling. Even as a teenager, when I was an active player, I marveled at how all it took was some scribbling on paper, some rules, and some dice to create a fully engaging environment that my friends and I could inhabit until dawn.

Digital technology is turning the sorts of rules and maps we find in a tabletop game into actively inhabited virtual places as well as radically transformed physical ones. We find one example in text-based Multi-User Dungeons (or Domains), more commonly known by their acronym "MUDs" (and variants MUSH, MOO, and so on). Invented almost as soon as computers with command-line interfaces could be networked, MUDs establish immersive environments in which players can interact as they find treasure and slay monsters, or in some cases just socialize and build new places and objects.

FIGURE 17-1
A game of Dungeons & Dragons, in progress*

In one such "social" MUD, called LambdaMOO (MOO standing for "MUD, Object Oriented"), writer Julian Dibbell witnessed the power of that immersive experience himself and wrote about it in his 1999 book, *My Tiny Life: Crime and Passion in a Virtual World* (Henry Holt and Company). At one point, he tried creating a map to help him fully comprehend the MOO, but found that it couldn't fully encompass all the wonders that had been created by LambdaMOO's denizens. He had an epiphany: "It occurred to me that there was in fact one map that represented the width, breadth, and depth of the MOO with absolute and unapologetic reliability—and that map was the MOO itself."[†]

LambdaMOO and other similar MUDs have a built-in scripting language that players use to create new parts of the environment; and the environment itself is often referred to as the game's *map*. The MOO has

---

* Photo by David Fiorito.

[†] Dibbell, Julian. *My Tiny Life: Crime and Passion in a Virtual World.* New York: Henry Holt and Company, 1999:50.

nested structures, all described strictly with written language, including the rules that govern the environment's programming. A typed command can create an object; when an entryway is added—an attribute that creates the ability to enter the object—it becomes a room. Rooms can be connected, and filled with other objects, which can be programmed to interact with players.

LambdaMOO in particular has a central gathering place—the Living Room, shown in Figure 17-2—where a loquacious cockatoo "object" is programmed to respond to actions such as being bathed, fed, or even gagged when it becomes too noisy. The player is represented as an avatar, which is essentially another object in the environment. The object-oriented approach to the environment works like a digitally reified, more strictly hierarchical version of James J. Gibson's elements: objects, places, layouts, and the rest.

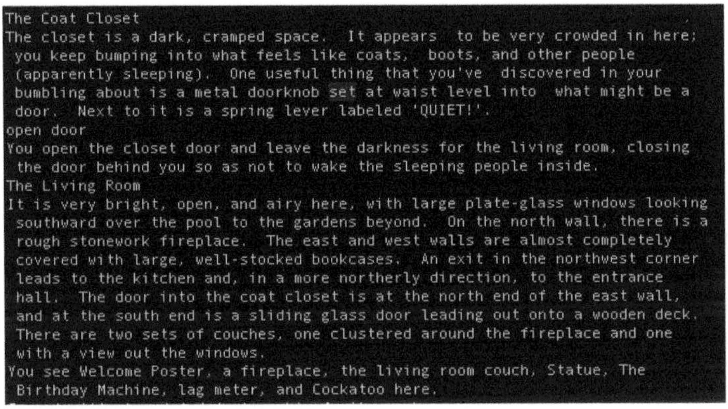

```
The Coat Closet
The closet is a dark, cramped space.  It appears  to be very crowded in here;
you keep bumping into what feels like coats,  boots, and other people
(apparently sleeping).  One useful thing that you've  discovered in your
bumbling about is a metal doorknob set at waist level into  what might be a
door.  Next to it is a spring lever labeled 'QUIET!'.
open door
You open the closet door and leave the darkness for the living room, closing
the door behind you so as not to wake the sleeping people inside.
The Living Room
It is very bright, open, and airy here, with large plate-glass windows looking
southward over the pool to the gardens beyond.  On the north wall, there is a
rough stonework fireplace.  The east and west walls are almost completely
covered with large, well-stocked bookcases.  An exit in the northwest corner
leads to the kitchen and, in a more northerly direction, to the entrance
hall.  The door into the coat closet is at the north end of the east wall,
and at the south end is a sliding glass door leading out onto a wooden deck.
There are two sets of couches, one clustered around the fireplace and one
with a view out the windows.
You see Welcome Poster, a fireplace, the living room couch, Statue, The
Birthday Machine, lag meter, and Cockatoo here.
```

FIGURE 17-2
The Coat Closet and Living Room in LambdaMOO

In his LambdaMOO adventures, Dibbell found that the MOO, populated mainly by grad-school academics and computer scientists, was an emotionally significant place for its users, where they were exploring sides of their identity and social life that might have been impossible otherwise. In a storyline that threads throughout the book, Dibbell shows how the brutal violation of an in-game character by one or more hackers (going by the name "Mr. Bungle") had an unsettling effect on the user whose in-game avatar was harmed. She was more surprised than anyone that the experience felt so traumatic that it brought her to tears; and the administrators who ran the MOO found themselves conducting a sort of Constitutional Congress to figure out how the MOO should be governed.* Reading the account now, one has to be struck by the questions the MOO leaders wrestled with, because they still sound so familiar and relevant for all our shared online environments, from intranets to social media platforms. The "cyber-bullying" and cruel "trolling" that have become epidemic in recent years all have early, awful seeds in the actions of Mr. Bungle.

Text-based MUDs and their ilk are still around and still have immersive power. But technology soon advanced to the point at which three-dimensional visual game spaces went mainstream. In the mid-to-late 1990s, I was obsessed with Quake, a genre-defining first-person-shooter video game. In particular, I was interested in the multiplayer variant that allowed players to compete in real time, in various versions of the game rules, from "Deathmatch" to "Capture the Flag." At the time, it was cutting-edge technology. The studio that created Quake, id Software, invented techniques for game design, decentralized networking, open APIs, 3D rendering, latency handling, and countless other infrastructure innovations that we take for granted today, and which are in use far outside game software.† It was also one of the first games to inspire a massive online community outside of the actual game itself.

I'll admit that I wasn't a very good player. I ended up spending more of my time setting up and "modding" game servers, and designing websites for teams (Quake "Clans"), complete with real-time scoreboards and sprawling, threaded discussions. Some of these experiences are what formed my own foundational ideas about what it means to make information environments.

Quake's action takes place in game levels referred to as "maps," of which you can see a later-version example in Figure 17-3. The open approach employed by id Software made it possible for creative people all over the Internet to create their own maps and game variants, some of which became much more popular than the ones that shipped with the game.

---

* Most of this story line is covered in a chapter that originally was an article in the December 23, 1993 edition of *Village Voice*, called "A Rape in Cyberspace."

† I cover some of the more relevant things about Quake for information architecture, in particular, in a 2006 article for the ASIS&T Bulletin. "We Live Here: Games, Third Places, and the Information Architecture of the Future," (*http://bit.ly/1wma8BC*).

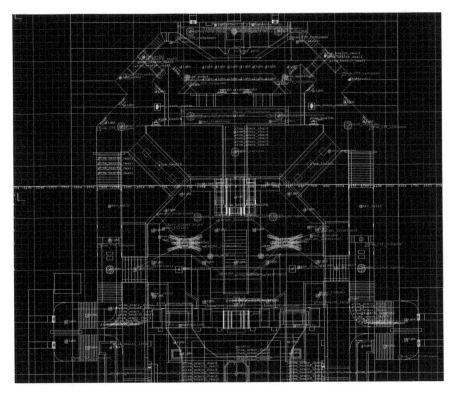

FIGURE 17-3
A Quake "map" as it looks as a wireframe view in a map editor

In the words of one pair of players I chatted with back then, while they were running practice sprints from flag to flag on a particularly challenging map, "We live here!" It was a self-deprecating jest about the amount of time they were spending perfecting their game, but it struck me then—and still does—as a fundamentally true statement. Whether it's the literally architectural simulation of a Quake map (see Figure 17-4), the word-based simulation of LambdaMOO, or the more subtly place-making qualities of a website or instant messenger platform, our lives meaningfully "take place" in these environments.

FIGURE 17-4

How one room of a Quake map looks as rendered in the game (map designed by Tom Boeckx for Quake 3 Arena, a more recent version of the game)*

The Porous Nature of Cyberplaces

Every retail website, social network, email platform, corporate intranet and smartphone app establishes structure that we come to understand as places—because that's how all terrestrial creatures self-organize their understanding of the environment. Even if we resist calling them cyber*space*, they are certainly cyber*places*; and there are more of them than ever. Each one is its own more-or-less contained contextual experience within the vast array of nested contexts in the environment. Although they seem to be contained within the screens of the devices we use to access them, that sense of containment is only an aspect of their interface. Most digital places are actually porous and connected.

Behind the scenes is an ocean of unfettered digital information, potentially connecting that site, app, or platform with anything else on the Internet. Even in the late 1990s, multiplayer Quake servers were not only generating the immersive experience of the game, but were also spewing real-time scores, player names, and network information to

---

* Found at *http://www.tomsdevshack.be*. Images borrowed under terms as seen here: *http://www.tomsdevshack.be/legal-information*

server-browsing platforms, which were then connected to all manner of game-finding applications, websites, scoreboards, and more. That was a novel concept in the mid-1990s, but not anymore. If I use my bank's smartphone app to transfer money from my account, my spouse can receive an immediate text message informing her about the transaction. If I post an update to Twitter, all sorts of third-party platforms can add it to their data stores or syndicate it into mash-ups.

There are offline interconnections, as well. Whereas online environments were once seen as a virtual escape from reality, they're now mostly a supplemental dimension we use to enhance and expand our physical, offline lives. So, digital placemaking is equally a way to close the distances of time and space between ourselves and our families, friends, and coworkers.

Outside of game platforms, we most often see structures that use built-environment tropes as *metaphors* rather than simulated buildings. Google Plus uses "circles," Facebook uses "groups," and Basecamp uses "projects"—all of these are labels standing for structures that instantiate places, defined by how they organize our online environment.

Figure 17-5 shows a feature in Microsoft's Windows Phone 8 operating system called "Rooms." The creators of the feature realized the phone could do a better job of helping users establish a sense of place for organizing their communication and tasks. In a post on the official Windows blog, Juliette Guilbert, a member of the design team, explains:

> It definitely takes a village, but our village needs all the help it can get. Now that my husband has his new [Windows phone], we've got it— in the form of Rooms, a new feature in Windows Phone 8. Instead of flinging frantic texts around, we can check the room calendar to see who's on deck. We can start a group chat so everyone's on the "What the heck is happening?" thread together. And when I add something to the grocery list or cancel a dentist appointment, the updates sync to my husband's phone. He's got the room pinned to Start, so its Live Tile even alerts him to the changes.[*]

---

* Guilbert, Juliette. "How I use Rooms on Windows Phone 8" Posted in Blogging Windows November 29, 2012 (*http://bit.ly/1yVcD2f*).

Although designers might think of Rooms as a metaphor, it's important to remember that users will likely take the label at face value. Because this is a relatively new feature, as of this writing, it remains to be seen just how successful it will be.

FIGURE 17-5
Three panels of the Windows Phone 8 Rooms feature*

These building-like metaphors have a long history online. LambdaMOO had "rooms" in which people could congregate, create objects, and collaborate. Since the beginnings of the Internet there have been applications with which people can visit digital places, such as IRC, Listservs, and UseNet. But in the mobile smartphone space, this attention to persistently shared, private placemaking is a more recent development.

Figure 17-6 presents another example of private placemaking called Avocado, a smartphone app that creates a special place for a couple to share messages, photos, lists, and a calendar.

The couple shares the same password for the app: even though it's just a string of characters, a password is a significant semantic object that represents intimacy, similar to sharing keys to one's home. (In fact, research shows that passwords are generally becoming tokens for

---

* Screenshots courtesy of Dan Klyn.

intimacy, especially among young people.)[*] There's a strong sense of connection that comes with that one bit of structural design. Other embodied architectural features of Avocado include the following:

- Interactions go beyond just pictures and words by directing users to perform bodily behaviors for some messages: kissing the screen for a kiss, or pressing the phone to one's chest to send a "hug."

- The "settings" and "profile info" of the app are about the couple, not just the one user; this further establishes the place as a shared one, equally owned by both users, even though it has instances appearing on separate devices.

- Even though you can log in to the service's website and use all the functions there, it's really optimized for the phone, which we treat more intimately as extensions of ourselves than desktop or laptop computers.

FIGURE 17-6
The architecture of the app has design choices that shape the nature of the place it instantiates[†]

---

[*] Richtel, Matt. "Young, in Love and Sharing Everything, Including a Password," *The New York Times*, January 17, 2012 (*http://nyti.ms/10iHFTy*).

[†] Images from *Avocado.io*.

According to its creators, "The move to more intimate applications is only natural, as maturing platforms like Facebook and Twitter lack functionality to provide real private sharing."* It's an interesting statement, given that both Facebook and Twitter provide mechanisms for making part or all of one's profile private; but the simplicity of having one app that equals one place, without any confusing privacy settings to configure your own structures, is part of the merit of the Avocado experience. Yet, even as privately constructed as Avocado is, it's still created to be a supplemental extension of a nondigital relationship. Shopping lists, calendars, and other shared tools are not about your "Avocado Life," but your "Real Life."

In addition to supplementing our friends-and-family life, digital places also augment our civic life. In the United States, controversy swirled over the launch of the website *Healthcare.gov*—the primary vehicle for connecting United States citizens with the services provided under the new healthcare legislation known as the *Affordable Care Act*. Upon launch, what many people discovered was a broken system that couldn't accommodate their needs, as illustrated in Figure 17-7. It was not just because of system overload, though; it was because the backend infrastructure and business rules driving it hadn't been sorted out yet.

We have a lot of visitors on the site right now.
Please stay on this page.

We're working to make the experience better, and we don't want you to lose your place in line. We'll send you to the login page as soon as we can. Thanks for your patience!

FIGURE 17-7

What millions of users saw when the ACA national website launched

---

* *http://techcrunch.com/2012/06/20/avocado-mobile-app-for-couples/*

Eventually, the problems were fixed, but the faulty launch highlighted a watershed moment in American civic life: it was the first time a government program of that massive scale relied almost exclusively on a digitally rendered place—the website—as the infrastructure for implementing sweeping legislative change. Even if citizens called by phone, representatives relied on the same site infrastructure. It wasn't an interstate system, made of concrete and steel; it wasn't hundreds of ACA offices established in federal buildings across the country; it was a website that the government required people to "go to" in order to access the service.

Digital places are part of our entire environment, including core civil infrastructures, such as healthcare, which accounts for almost a fifth of gross domestic product (GDP)* in the United States. They are nested among and within one another in ways both overt and hidden. The launch of the ACA site has to do with context at a national scale—defining the kind of place in which a country's citizens live.

When we look at these examples closely, we realize that they are all actually language in various forms—semantic information, enabled by digital technology, resulting in new objects and places in our environment. We need them to behave in ways that make sense—which means they need to "make place" in a sensible way.

Vacancy at the Luna Blue

The physical reality of a place is hard to separate from the language we use to talk about it; and when that language is turned into the machinery of software and networked systems, it can have a transformative effect on the "real" place. In a multiplayer game, a database error only interrupts the fun. However, when we depend on massively multiuser environments for real-life commerce, a bug can have more dire consequences. The Internet is, in essence, a massively multiuser environment, with many structures and rulesets establishing objects, places, and digital agents. Basically, we all live in a giant MUD together now.

---

* "Most Efficient Health Care 2014: Countries," Bloomberg.com, *http://bloom.bg/1yfGKON*.

Consider the Luna Blue Hotel: an 18-room facility on the Mexican coast, near the island of Cozumel. As a friendly, family-owned hotel with a great reputation, the proprietors of the Luna Blue were dismayed to discover that Expedia—a large gorilla in the travel-services jungle—was showing their hotel with "No Vacancy" even though they had plenty of rooms.[*]

Because Expedia is such a huge player in the travel space, the no-vacancy status spread all over the Web to other sites where people discuss or research where to stay when traveling to the area. These other sites included big travel services affiliated with Expedia, such as TripAdvisor (Figure 17-8) and Hotels.com—all of which eventually showed up as metadata in Google search results. A single error had a domino effect of erasing the hotel's availability from the layer of reality that mattered to it most. The ongoing saga went viral on Reddit and other sites, but Expedia's information about (and treatment of) the hotel only got worse over time, according to the hotel's owners.[†]

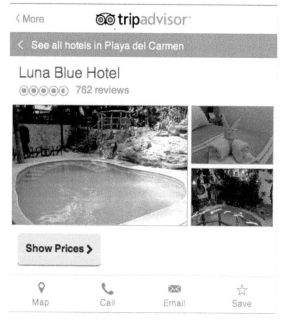

FIGURE 17-8

The Luna Blue, as shown via the TripAdvisor mobile website

---

* Jeffries, Adrianna. "One small hotel's long nightmare with Expedia (update)," The Verge (*theverge.com*) December 29, 2012 (*http://bit.ly/1oqphDg*).

† "Expedia: Bad for the Traveler, Bad for the Hotel" Posted in Luna Blue's PlayaZone (*playazone.wordpress.com*) December 4, 2012 (*http://bit.ly/1t9EBnF*).

Places are what they are due to all sorts of contextual information. In this case, an actual, physical place—with buildings, and tiki torches, and everything—was contextually compromised because the semantic map of the Web became distorted. This is just one example of how physical context can be usurped almost entirely by semantic context, when digital-information systems create such pervasive, global structures that make the semantic information the "reality of record."

The architectural issues here go far beyond the structure of a single website. They arise from the relationship between the backend systems and databases, the business rules instantiated in those systems, and how all that hidden, digital logic ends up being displayed in the language that's wrapped around a specific, physical place, like the Luna Blue. It calls into question the ontology of "Vacancy" as defined in who knows how many black boxes strung across the Web.

Information architecture can't concern itself with only the surface labeling within a particular context—it has to consider the cross-contextual meaning of such a label, and what rules behind the scenes might change what the label signifies. The word "vacancy" stands in for an immensely complex system of logistics and commercial logic. The business rules and technological underpinnings that drive the appearance of that label have to be part of an information architecture practitioner's consideration.

Augmented and Blended Places

Even though we experience them as immersive places, digital environments are still nested within our physical environment. Smart homes, RFID-tagged retail merchandise, mobile airport check-ins, GPS-enhanced cars, and even roadways bristling with digital signs and billboards mean that semantic information is now dynamically and actively engaged in our entire environment, not just static marks on surfaces.

Just as our smartphones are making us "cyborgs," any physical place is potentially also a "cyberplace," shaped by the maps of information we engage through the digital systems pervading our surroundings—the digital agency of the objects and surfaces that make up the Internet of Things.

Back in 2007, I took my daughter, Madeline, to the American Museum of Natural History in New York City (see Figures 17-9 and 17-10). One of the most fascinating exhibits was the Hall of Biodiversity, where a huge wall has thousands of species arranged in a sort of taxonomy of taxidermy. Oddly, though, they don't have labels. Instead, maps and digital interfaces supply the semantic scaffolding for understanding the exhibit.

FIGURE 17-9
The Hall of Biodiversity at the American Museum of Natural History in New York City*

The Hall has a row of kiosks with which visitors can navigate rich information about the creatures mounted above. Carefully designed displays of printed taxonomical hierarchies blend with digital displays of narrative content and the sensory flood of wildlife.

This carefully orchestrated information environment relies on the cognitive abilities of visitors—the perception-action looping and language interpretation that happens simultaneously among physical and semantic information modes. The "glue" that pulls it all together is enabled by the digital information that drives the interactive interfaces.

---

* Photo by Ryan Somma. *http://bit.ly/1Fx7LCg* CC license: *http://bit.ly/1vI2YJR*.

Keep in mind that the museum is a controlled environment, where the entire structure is created for a singular purpose. Architecture, interior design, and exhibit design can work together to establish a bubble-world in which everything integrates coherently. That's different from most of the world; the uncontrolled, uncurated one where we are expected to design and launch products and services.

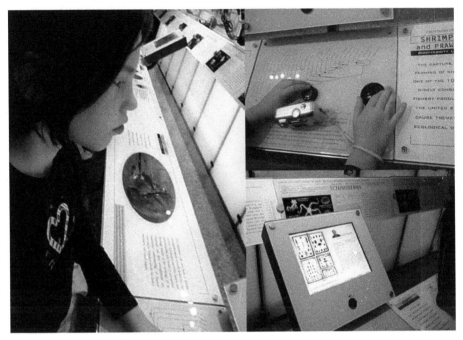

FIGURE 17-10
My daughter, Madeline, learning about natural history through cross-media interaction, on our trip in 2007

In the wild of noncurated places, there can still be fascinating transformations. Supermarket company Tesco created a similar wall-of-objects, which you can see in Figure 17-11, but in this case, the objects are two-dimensional simulations—wall-sized posters that look like store shelves full of products. Each product has a QR code customers can scan with their phones, purchase from an app, and then have delivered to their doors after they've arrived home.

This environmental innovation takes advantage of a real, contextual insight—subway passengers have to stand and wait for trains, and they are often in a hurry to get to or from home. In addition, they need to remember a list of things they should get at the store rattling around in their heads. Cleverly, these simulated store shelves take the context of customer behavior into account, bringing the store to the customer. This novel idea reportedly increased sales for Tesco's Home Plus brand by 130 percent.[*]

FIGURE 17-11
Shoppers scan simulated products for home delivery, while waiting for the subway[†]

Unlike the museum example, this is not a fully curated, choreographed environment. Yet it transforms one context into being another at the same time.

And the displays adroitly take advantage of the new objects now part of the environment: smartphones and persistently available mobile network access. It's the nesting of the posters within those other environmental invariants that make them what they are. Otherwise, they'd just be pictures of dish soap and soft drinks.

---

[*] "The next 10 years in mobile" techcentral.co.za November 25, 2011 (*http://bit.ly/1AoObqO*).

[†] Images from Flock promotional video for work done with Tesco/Home Plus (*http://vimeo. com/75586377*).

Both the Tesco and the museum examples offer places that immerse us in contextual layers, with physical and simulated-physical information. They use whatever manner of technology, language, and layout available to them, to more fully engage us in an experience, nudging us to act in ways that merely reading about sea life or grocery products would not.

In a sense, the smartphone potentially turns any environment into a richly interactive, semantically layered place. For example, take the relationship between restaurants and Yelp (Figure 17-12), the social reviewing platform that augments our understanding of the places of business in our environment.

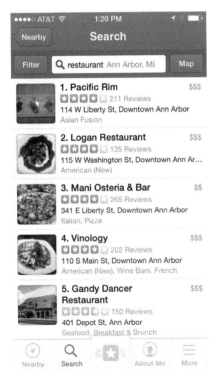

FIGURE 17-12

Yelp's search-results view, showing summary contextual information about restaurants in Ann Arbor, MI

Because Yelp provides ready contextual information for independent restaurants as well as chains, the reputation-information playing field is being leveled. Wherever Yelp is in heavy use, national-chain restaurant popularity has decreased, yielding ground to local, independent restaurants. Additionally, a one-star increase in an independent's rating affects its revenue positively up to 9 percent—a benefit that the chain restaurants don't experience.* Adding a digital-powered semantic-information dimension to the environment shifts the entire marketplace of restaurant-going.

Retail businesses are also taking advantage of the mobile viewport to the information dimension. Wegmans, a regional chain of upscale supermarkets, has a mobile application that shoppers can use to read Yelp-like reviews of products as well as assist in finding a product's aisle location in a specific store, as demonstrated in Figure 17-13.

This feature might not seem all that advanced, but it takes enormous coordination of a retailer's infrastructure to accomplish this trick. The Wegmans app also includes other capabilities, including an extensive recipe database and a shopping list feature. It's a great example of how a retailer is adapting to new expectations by providing tools that address the situational context of grocery shopping, not just the groceries alone.

There have been recent forays into literally merging the digital dimension with the physical. Yelp was also one of the first consumer mobile apps to add augmented reality (AR) to its platform in a feature it calls "Monacle." As Figure 17-14 illustrates, with Monacle, Yelp uses the phone's camera, GPS, and motion sensors to show a layer of review information over the screen's live, digital picture of the physical environment.

The AR capability certainly provides a captivating level of blended information. But, as is the case with the virtual-reality version of cyberspace, we find that this layering effect is more of an edge case. Simply reading the reviews in their regular, non-AR format is satisficing enough for most of our needs.

---

* Luca, 2011.

FIGURE 17-13

The Wegmans app shows the Aisle/Location of a specific product within your current store as well as product reviews

FIGURE 17-14

Yelp's Monacle feature, layering thumbnail review information over the surrounding street

Google Glass (see Figure 17-15), the search giant's well-hyped "wearable" device, is essentially a way to provide AR all the time, without having to hold a smartphone up to our faces.

Glass has been controversial for a number of reasons, one of which has to do with privacy. Because it can record pictures, video, and audio, it raises questions about whether the device too easily breaches the walls that we assume exist in social life. It's not the ability to record that sparks the concern, but the fact that Glass is meant to be worn continually like regular glasses and can be activated without the physical cues we're used to seeing when someone is about to take a photo or make a video with a conventional device or smartphone. The invariant events we count on to signify the act of recording are dissolving into the hidden subtleties of digital agency.

FIGURE 17-15
One feature of Google Glass is an AR function, layering the view with supplemental information*

The capability of Glass to "read" everyday gestures as triggers highlights how context can be several things at once—a coy one-eyed blink at someone across a room can also be a shutter-button press. In linguistics terms, a signifier intended to signify X is interpreted by another interpreter to signify Y instead. A speck of dust in the wearer's eye can trigger the digital agent without the unwitting wearer's consent—physical affordances interpreted as semantic function by digitally influenced devices.

---

* Promotional image from Google's Glass website: *http://bit.ly/1pxlcry* (retrieved 2014-09-07)

This is not unlike the hidden rules that caused controversy with Facebook Beacon, whereby a common action (a purchase on a separate website) could be recorded and turned into information of another sort, and unwittingly broadcast to one's "friends." Except, when it comes to Glass and other trigger-sensing objects, the boundary crossed isn't just between websites, but between the dimensions of our physical surroundings.

What this means for information architecture: the semantic functions we use to design information environments are no longer just hyperlinks contained in screens. They can now involve any action that users might take in any place they inhabit. It's an important overlap between interaction design and information architecture—where object-level interaction has potentially massive ripple effects across oceans of semantically stitched systems. Like Peter Morville tells us in *Ambient Findability* (O'Reilly), "(T)he proving grounds have shifted from natural and built environments to the noosphere, a world defined by symbols and semantics."[*] Language is the material for building what we need to make sense of our new environs.

The implications of how those interactions are nested in the environment—how they create cross-contextual systems of places, objects, and events—is an architectural concern. That is, it's akin to Wurman's mission for information architecture: "the creating of systemic, structural, and orderly principles to make something work."[†] Whether it's a pair of science-fiction eyeglasses, a living room gaming system's gesture-sensing interface, or a grocery store's geolocation feature, all these technologies are changing what it means to use information to make places, and the systems that make up our shared environment. In aggregate, they fundamentally reshape how our environment works.

The Map That Makes Itself

Rules and digital agency impart the ability of the map/territory to make more of itself. One way this happens is through something called *procedural generation*, which refers to the algorithmic creation of structure and content. Procedural generation is especially popular in video games,

---

* Morville, Peter. *Ambient Findability*. Sebastopol, CA: O'Reilly, 2005:41.
† Wurman, R. S. *Information Architects*. Graphis Inc., 1997:16.

in which it can make a unique map for each played instance. Unlike older video games, where each level was the same each time and part of mastering the game was about remembering the patterns of each level, procedurally generated games make players rely on perceptual-reactive skills more like those needed for new territories in the real world. Sim City and The Sims creator, Will Wright, made use of procedural generation in the game Spore, and it's also behind the chunky-but-weirdly-natural environments found in the poignantly immersive Minecraft, shown in Figure 17-16.* Entire unique continents can grow with little or no user input. Minecraft can randomly generate terrain, or the user can specify parameters that the game uses as a "seed" to create maps with preferred features, such as a snowy mountain range or jungle biome.

FIGURE 17-16
Minecraft world generation is procedural, but can be "seeded" to create essentially the same structures from one world to the next, with slight variations in surface detail

Most "maps that make themselves" aren't so literally self-generating, but more dependent on user activity. Algorithms can provide structures and functions that tap into the collective work of the user base to grow rich semantic topologies.

For example, some websites have contexts that are defined entirely by algorithm, such as Flickr's photo-browsing context based on *Interestingness* (Figure 17-17). Here's how Flickr's describes Interestingness:

---

* At least I find Minecraft to be this way. Played in survival mode, without assistance of plugins or cheats, it's one of the most meaningfully engaging video game experiences I've ever had.

There are lots of elements that make something 'interesting' (or not) on Flickr. Where the click-throughs are coming from; who comments on it and when; who marks it as a favorite; its tags and many more things which are constantly changing. Interestingness changes over time, as more and more fantastic content and stories are added to Flickr.[*]

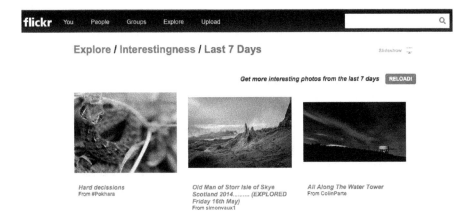

FIGURE 17-17
Flickr's Interestingness facet, in the current version of the platform[†]

Even though they have some procedurally generated features, environments such as Flickr, Craigslist, and Wikipedia are more rule-frameworks than static web structures. Such frameworks can channel user content creation into rapidly generated cyber-landscapes. In 2006 alone, Wikipedia grew by over 6,000 articles per day—each one a new page adding to its vast corpus.[‡]

This organic perspective reminds us of the question: where does the system end and the user begin? Ecologically, we are part of our environment; this principle doesn't stop being true just because an environment is made largely of language and bits. In a sense, these environments are morphing and evolving through the efforts of several resources at once: digital algorithm-agents scouring and crunching raw information into new content; armies of product development teams updating their functionality and architecture; and millions of

---

[*] *http://www.flickr.com/explore/interesting/*

[†] *https://www.flickr.com/explore/interesting/7days/*

[‡] Wikimedia Commons: *http://bit.ly/1AoOnXh*

inhabitants creating new content, tagging it, linking and commenting, adding layer upon layer of semantic material that feeds the system's appetite for new information.

Whether the software is making more of itself, or users are generating more territory through publishing, commenting, discussing, and uploading, the effect on user perception is pretty much the same: the environment grows and grows, expanding, reshaping, and shifting under our feet. As Resmini and Rosati put it, pervasive information architectures are "evolving, unfinished, unpredictable systems."* The map is also territory, complete with its own ecosystem of species migration, stormy weather, continental drifts, and the occasional exploding volcano.

Metamaps and Compasses

These ever-expanding, unpredictably evolving maps become territories in their own right at such scale that we need "metamaps" for understanding them. We also need the equivalent of compasses for finding our way through their more uncharted wildernesses.

Although it is well past its day at the top of the hype curve, Second Life (see Figure 17-18) is an interesting object lesson in how navigation of our surroundings might become more about the semantic information landscape than the physical one.

Even though Second Life does its best to mimic the ecological nature of the physical structures we have in our "first life," in actuality these structures can change at any moment. Giant buildings can be moved, deleted, or just "put away" into an owner's personal inventory. Whole islands can shift or disappear from day to day.

---

* Resmini, Andrea, and Luca Rosati. *Pervasive Information Architecture: Designing Cross-Channel User Experiences.* Burlington, MA: Morgan Kaufmann, 2011:60.

FIGURE 17-18
A now-decommissioned virtual home of the IA Institute, in Second Life

The information we rely on in the physical world to be invariant can actually be quite *variant* in Second Life. So, the information its dwellers come to rely on most is the meta-information: the dynamic, semantic information that informs players where activities are happening or where friends are located, all on the Cartesian grid of Second Life's highly variant, digital topology. On a trivia group's regular Tuesday gathering, it might be meeting in a cloud city, a jungle, or a skyscraper. The members don't rely on the faux-physical landmarks, but the semantic ones, because they can be searched and found even more quickly than a user can "fly" or "teleport" to the location to check it out in person.

Perhaps the most prescient part of Second Life isn't its virtual-reality landscape, but its navigation interface, the Viewer, whose menu bar is shown in Figure 17-19. Its residents use this tool to basically "fly by instruments" the way a real-life pilot must use only the cockpit's instrument panel to fly in a fog.

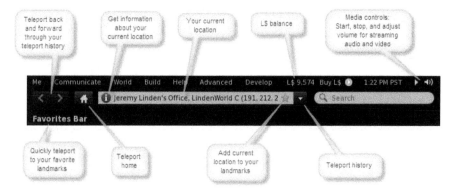

FIGURE 17-19

From a tutorial on how to use Viewer version 2, on the official Second Life Wiki[*]

More and more, we are now navigating our world by the language we put into the stratosphere with digital technology rather than by physical landmarks, even though physical objects are much more stable in nonvirtual life. We want to know which store has something in stock, which theater has the movie we want to see at our preferred time, or which bar has more of our friends hanging out in it on a Friday night. It's this dimension of ever-shifting semantic information that we want to track and navigate. In that sense, our smartphones are now acting as "Viewer" devices for navigating the "First Life" world around us.

Yelp (Figure 17-20)acts as a sort of compass in the sense that you can use it to filter your environment by various factors—choosing your "true north" by facets such as average review, distance, or price.

Increasingly, our tools for navigating our environment are becoming more personalized, as well, keeping track of our preferences so as to create new "true norths" that are unique to us. The Google Now service is one of a number of newer technologies that aim to tell us what we need to know before we have to ask. Before it was acquired, a similar service called Donna (see Figure 17-21) explained that it "pays attention for you so you can focus your time on the people you're with."

---

[*] *http://wiki.secondlife.com/wiki/Viewer_2_Quick_Start_Guide/Interface_overview*

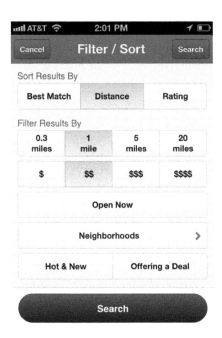

FIGURE 17-20

Yelp's Filter and Sort interface is a sort of sextant for navigating local resources

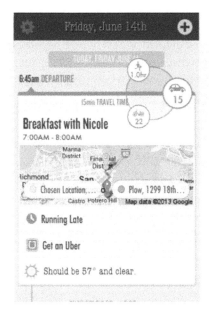

FIGURE 17-21

Donna, now acquired and discontinued by Yahoo, was a pioneer in the personal-compass app category

By knowing what's in our calendars and address books and tracking our email activity as well as (increasingly) our general activity patterns, these services aim to be digital agents that do some of the heavy lifting for us, narrowing and distilling the essentials of the information in our environments—creating bite-size maps-of-the-map and the equivalent of arrows pointing us in a direction, saying "wear warm clothes today" or "leave early due to traffic." They do their best to understand our context, and in turn to improve our experience of that context.

These wonderful metamaps and compasses don't work effectively all on their own, though. They need to use information from somewhere, and that information has to have the right qualities to be trusted and comprehended.

Let's recall that these navigational aids and digital agents are only as smart as the structures provided to them in the environment to begin with. Google's search ranks sites higher when they're well-structured and effectively made places. Donna can tell us to leave early because someone created an API with which the service can know about traffic, weather, and geolocation—all of which required effective labeling and metadata. A pricing service can send a text message alerting us that there's a sale in a store we're visiting because someone took the time to define and structure the frameworks that make those connections possible. The rules these agents use for behavior have to be defined as part of their architectural infrastructure. Digital agents need structural cues, too. No matter how smart they get, there's work to be done in the environment for bridging between physical, semantic, and digital information.

And we shouldn't forget: no matter how enabled by artificial intelligence, such metamaps and compasses tend to become less accurate as they try to be smarter and more richly relevant to context. The bigger the gap we're trying to bridge, the more it's subject to the fog of ambiguity; this is especially the case when the environment's information involves tacit familiarity versus explicit definition.

We should also remember what we learned about maps: that they're always interpretations of the environment, and they serve some set of interests. The same is true of mediating, augmenting tools. What they choose to show us is always driven by an agenda, intentionally or not. As users, we should always be wary of what that agenda might be. As designers of these entities, we should provide enough transparency to let users in on the priorities and interests being served by the way the elements and rules are assembled.

[18]

The Social Map

Talk is essential to the human spirit. It is the human spirit. Speech.
Not silence.

—WILLIAM GASS

Conversation

IMAGINE A BUSY DINER ON A SATURDAY MORNING AND ALL THE CON-
VERSATIONS GOING ON THERE: a family at a table where parent and
child negotiate about eating the eggs before the waffle; a couple making plans for the rest of the weekend; a man on a cell phone recon-
necting with whomever he met on a date the previous night. There
are also visible gestures, facial expressions, and body language woven
into the activity of talk. Not to mention the newspapers and magazines
being perused over coffee—conversations mediated by publishers and
writers. There are also people texting via SMS, reading news and sharing stories via email, checking their "feeds" of friends and family on
Facebook and Twitter, or gazing at pictures on Instagram and Flickr.
They're using these threads of information in their table talk, showing friends at the table what is on their phones as part of the topic at
hand, and using it the other way around—taking pictures of food and
friends, and posting them to the cloud. Conversation is still about people talking with people, but it's now an everyday thing to not just be in
one place at a time, but in two or more simultaneously.

We tend to think of conversation as something that fills the gaps
between actually doing things. By now, though, it's hopefully clear
that talking is actually a quite tangible form of "doing," and that we
wouldn't be doing much at all without language, which exists because
of the need to converse.

Conversation is made manifest all around us. All human-made environments are conversations in action. Cities and their structures exist because people had conversations, and they instantiate the meanings of those conversations in stone, concrete, glass, and steel. Before print and literacy became widespread, buildings such as cathedrals were the primary medium for telling stories and broadcasting messages. Later, libraries became the meta structures that house the published artifacts of the slow-moving print-based conversations of our culture.

Structures are conversations, but of course, conversations also have structures. Watch two people talking, and you'll pick up on tacitly informal patterns of tonality, inflection, facial expression, posture, and gesture that add up to a sort of punctuation, signaling whose turn it is to speak and the structural relationships between statements. There are formal structures for conversations as well, such as Robert's Rules of Order, a system invented in the nineteenth century for better organizing discussions by deliberative bodies such as parliamentary gatherings or board meetings.

There used to be a fairly clear distinction between real-time, spoken conversation and a written or published one via postal mail or other printed media such as books and newspapers. But now, that distinction is dissolving under our button-pushing fingers, as we publish our communiques without need of paper, printing presses, or supply-chain distribution.

Conversation doesn't exist in a vacuum; it is inextricable from the properties of its media. Just as the joints in a creature's limbs evolved to suit the invariant structures of the environment, the way we converse also evolves within—and is shaped by—our environment. To paraphrase Marshall McLuhan, the medium really is an intrinsic property of the message.* So, when digitally enabled environmental properties are added to our environment, those shape the message, too.

One thing the emergence of persistent, pervasive digital networks has done is remove a lot of the environmental context that conversation evolved in, changing the nature of how conversation works. We need

---

* Marshall McLuhan famously posited that "the medium is the message" in his 1964 book *Understanding Media: The Extensions of Man* (MIT Press).

to learn new properties of the environments we use to communicate; as we've seen, many of those properties don't necessarily work like the world used to.

Social Architectures

Those of us who use Twitter a great deal have become accustomed to occasionally committing a faux pas known as a "DM Fail." This is when a user means to send a direct message (DM) but instead posts a tweet publicly. For example, Figure 18-1 shows one in which two information-architecture community members had an exchange they allowed me to capture. Austin Govella accidentally tweeted "Love you": a message he meant to be a private communication to a family member. Of course, part of the now-familiar tradition of the DM Fail is to gently poke a bit of fun at the mishap, as Tanya Rabourn happily did in this example, with a delightful "#win" hashtag celebrating the moment.[*]

FIGURE 18-1
A garden variety "mistweet" and a gently snarky response

This is not an error we would normally commit in the nondigital environment, where so much ecological information is available to let us know both for whom a message is intended and who else might be able to hear it. Even in a phone conversation, there's an assumed context of privacy that's specified in the environment: a phone receiver pressed

---

[*] Thanks to Tanya Rabourn and Austin Govella for permission to bring this exchange into the book.

to your ear whereby you hear only one other person's voice, close to the microphone of his own receiver. What is it, then, about the Twitter environment that confuses the context enough for people to make this error?

When Twitter was first launched in 2006, it was mainly as a supplemental service for cell phone "texting" via Short Message Service (SMS),* allowing friends to subscribe to one another's messages when sent to the Twitter SMS address of 40404. For example, rather than my having to text something like "Heading to the bar on my corner to watch the game" to a bunch of different people individually (some of whom might not be interested in my status), I could just send it to 40404. Then, Twitter would forward it to friends who have subscribed to (or "followed") my Twitter messages. The SMS origin is why tweets are limited to 140 characters: SMS protocol has a limit of 160 characters per message, and 140 leaves room for adding contextual information such as the username of the "tweeter."

As part of the protocol for Twitter, users can use commands of a sort to follow or unfollow people, change other preferences, and even make a specific message be a direct message instead of a public tweet, with the syntax "d username message"—"d" being the command for "make the rest of this a direct message."

So, even when Twitter was mainly SMS based, there were plenty of opportunities for misdirected private messages. If you receive a message from a friend or loved one on your cell phone, the natural, learned reaction is to just text her a response. It's a conversation: we're so used to having them without thinking about using special commands, it's hard to learn the new habit of checking what sort of message it is you've received and then remembering to add "d username" before your response. Adding to the problem, the phone's environment doesn't provide enough information to differentiate the context. In the physical environment, we have to make a major change in our bodily position (or the volume of our voice) to go from a private conversation to a public proclamation. But, in a digitally generated environment, it takes only the difference of a typed character or two.

---

* SMS is actually the most widely used data channel on the planet; for much of the developing world, SMS is their equivalent of the Internet.

Even when using a more recent smartphone and a Twitter client, it can be easy to make the mistake of responding in the wrong way. On an iPhone, for example, my Twitter client's direct-message interface is almost identical to my phone's native SMS interface (Figure 18-2). Recall that a digital user interface is basically graphical semantic information role-playing as physical information—a simulated structural environment.

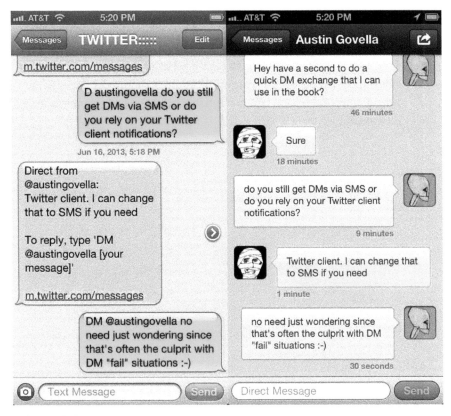

FIGURE 18-2
A direct-message exchange, on Twitter (via Tweetbot) and SMS

If you're explicitly attending to the details of these views *as interfaces*, it's not hard to spot their differences. In Heidegger's terms from Chapter 6, that would be the much less natural and efficient "unreadiness-to-hand." However, when we're having a conversation, we're not paying much attention to the interface; we're treating it as "ready-to-hand" by default by *attending to the communication, not its container*. This is another example of the tacit way in which we engage our environment, *satisficing* in the moment. For the act of replying to someone, my perceptual system concerns itself with only a few bits of information—the words written by the other person, the field where I can put words to answer him, and the Send button. These are the invariant elements of the environment that matter to me in the midst of the conversation. The rest of it becomes *clutter*, unless I've worked to train myself to think twice and look at the other clues. In this case, I have to check if Twitter sent me the message, which makes the difference between a public conveyance or private communication.

The way the *object* is designed for interaction can have a disproportionate effect on how the *place* is experienced as architecture. Twitter provides an environment for communication, structured by its architecture of labels and rules, and instantiated by various client interfaces, as illustrated in Figure 18-3.

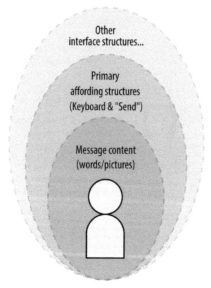

FIGURE 18-3
The layers involved in a Twitter direct-message exchange

The client application is actually an important factor; rules embodied in the client can change the context of what Twitter is to a particular user. Twitter has historically been more of a service that informs disparate objects and places rather than a place itself. It has its own website and app, but even then, many people never use the official Twitter interfaces. Back when Twitter would show up to only a hundred or so posts in a feed, I recall how confused I would be when people I followed would tweet so much it kept me from seeing what others were saying. I later discovered that they were using client applications that cached thousands of tweets from their feed—removing this environmental limitation. Spamming Twitter didn't look like a problem from their point of view.

The client also changes what our actions mean for one another. Twitter's API provides the ability to mark tweets as "favorites." Early in my own Twitter usage, I didn't use this feature much, other than to mark tweets that contained links I wanted to read later. (Unfortunately, this ended up being a dustbin I never managed to revisit.)

But, after I began using a smartphone app as my Twitter client, I could set the app to give me immediate notification when one of my tweets was "favorited" by someone else. I then realized that I began using favorites differently, as if everyone else also had their client set like mine. Tapping the little "favorite" star became a way to give a sort of "nod" to the tweet's writer. I set a mode that created a new invariant, and it sets my expectation that everyone else is in the same *umwelt*, or environmental perspective, that I've created for myself. I might be having a half-imagined moment of conversation with the other person and never know it.

The rules-architecture of a social platform has a huge impact on determining what kind of places it instantiates and what sorts of conversations and actions happen there. The rules we make manifest in social software require our explicit, careful attention. Even a simple Listserv mailing list has rule structures that have been shown to encourage and allow trolling and "flame wars" because they lack the social environmental feedback mechanisms available to us in nondigital conversation.[*]

In his book *Here Comes Everybody: The Power of Organizing Without Organizations* (Penguin), Clay Shirky uses an ecological analogy that nicely speaks to the environmental perspective we've been exploring:

---

[*] Clay Shirky makes this and other surprisingly still-relevant points in his 2004 essay, "Group as User: Flaming and the Design of Social Software," (*http://bit.ly/1uzVZOZ*).

When we change the way we communicate, we change society. The tools that a society uses to create and maintain itself are as central to human life as a hive is to a bee. Though the hive is not part of any individual bee, it is part of the colony, both shaped by and shaping the lives of its inhabitants. The hive is a social device, a piece of bee information technology that provides a platform, literally, for the communication and coordination that keeps the colony viable. Individual bees can't be understood separately from the colony or from their shared, cocreated environment. So it is with human networks; bees make hives, we make mobile phones.*

Mobile phones certainly are a factor. Just as the invention of elevators helped make skyscrapers a possibility, a whole new networked-device category enables new structures and rules that accommodate new sorts of activity.

Regardless of device, though, place structures can still result in different sorts of conversations. An often-mentioned difference between Facebook and Twitter is that Facebook requires symmetrical friending—mutual agreement to be "friends." But Twitter employs the looser asymmetrical following: I can follow someone, but that someone doesn't have to follow me in return.

That doesn't keep many people from obsessing about who is following them or not, but it does create a contextual expectation that differs from Facebook or other symmetrical connection platforms. Of course, on Facebook, this anxiety is only increased after users catch onto the fact that even its "Most Recent" mode for its News Feed is being filtered by a hidden, undisclosed algorithm; nobody really knows who is seeing their posts, or if they're seeing all of them from their friends. When a label that sounds so solidly invariant turns out to be procedurally generated, it tends to make us question every other supposedly solid element.

Extending Shirky's analogy, we do not inhabit just one hive with one set of structures and rules. Although we've always, in a sense, lived in multiple "hives," each with their own sets of rules (home, work, school,

---

* Shirky, Clay. *Here Comes Everybody: The Power of Organizing Without Organizations*. New York: Penguin Press, 2008:17.

club, and so on), we now need to be *simultaneously present* in them all. It's like trying to play baseball, football, and tennis, at the same time while making breakfast, while having intelligent conversations about each activity.

Throughout any given day, a regular person might be "present" and attending to conversations in any number of places:

- A conversation about a project in a workplace email thread
- A management discussion on an employer's intranet
- Keeping up with the news feed from friends and family on Facebook
- Discussing professional topics with other practitioners on LinkedIn
- Bantering with other fans of a sports team, under a Twitter hashtag
- Engaging in photo-sharing on Instagram
- Texting with family via phone SMS

This isn't an extreme example; the chances are that if you're reading this book, you're simultaneously plugged into roughly this many places. Each has its own interaction design conventions, and each has its own architectural "rules of order" and structural constraints as well as its own cultural norms and nuances of expression. For example, you can't assume a "favorite" in Twitter will be interpreted the same way as a "like" on Facebook, and your sense of humor on Instagram might come across as unprofessional on LinkedIn.

It's important to remember, though: conversation isn't only about "social software" or "social media." Conversation has been the main activity of social context since long before the invention of cities, much less the arrival of the Internet. Software and its capabilities are new arrivals, but they affect the *nature* of the conversations we have as well as their content.*

---

* It means we talk about "content" more than we used to, because it's semantic material that's so easily detached from the origin. This means that we must explicitly plan and manage how that content is governed and published, as in the practice of Content Strategy.

"Proxemics" as a Structural Model

Architectures are generally social environments, so they build on the behavior patterns humans embody in social life. These are tacitly constructed, but identifiable, and they can inform how we should design all sorts of places. In the 1960s, the cultural anthropologist Edward T. Hall described how physical distance affects social communication and coined the term *proxemics*. Hall believed that by studying the way people interact spatially, we can learn things not only about social activity but about how to create environments that better accommodate or even encourage different sorts of sociality, such as "the organization of space in...houses and buildings, and ultimately the layout of...towns."[*]

Hall developed a model for distinguishing different levels of intimacy based on physical space. He stressed that the distances are not necessarily the same in all cultures, only that the emotional and social engagement between people can be correlated with physical distance, as illustrated in Figure 18-4.[†]

Hall's model works nicely with an embodiment perspective because the distinctions emerge from what sorts of communication are physically afforded by various proximities. Additionally, the structure is spatially nested, which fits with how we perceive the environment. Here are the communication "levels" by layer:

Intimate
> Allows whispering, embracing

Personal
> Face-to-face and high-touch conversations with close friends and family

Social
> Interactions with acquaintances or friends-of-friends, such as a handshake, and the ability to hear one another clearly at a conversational volume

Public
> Performing or speaking in public, which requires a louder voice and larger gestures

---

[*] Hall, Edward T. "A System for the Notation of Proxemic Behavior." *American Anthropologist* October, 1963; 65(5):1003–26.

[†] Some details gathered from the Wikipedia article on Proxemics (*http://bit.ly/1t9Hl4c*).

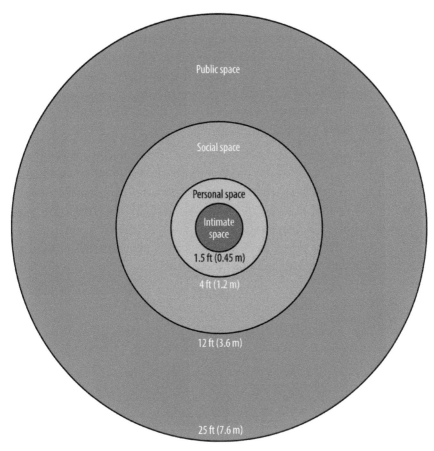

FIGURE 18-4
Proxemics model of personal distance*

Because none of these interactions happen without motion and activity, Hall also broke each of these into "close" and "far" phases to indicate the transitional stages we move through as we socialize through our day.

This model isn't all there is to proxemics, but it provides us a helpful structure for thinking through the way we create architectures online, both for social media and for other interactions, such as the overtures of a retail website to gather personal information, or make product recommendations.

---

* Wikimedia Commons: *http://commons.wikimedia.org/wiki/File:Personal_Space.svg*

We might learn from this that we should make structures that let users gradually build trust and intimacy with one another and the environment. For example, don't expose personal information to social-platform "friends" by default; instead, let users establish distinctions over time. Or, don't allow a digital agent to be too helpful too soon, because it can feel like presumptuous overfamiliarity (and the assumptions can often be flat-out wrong).

The way we define categories of for social relationships determines fundamental structures of social architecture. Flickr has always had a simple, three-tier construct that roughly aligns with proxemic distance: Contact, Friend, Family (Figure 18-5). I assume others, like me, use these with some interpretive flexibility—for example, keeping some family members as contacts and some close lifelong friends as family. But Flickr lets us interpret this for ourselves.

FIGURE 18-5

Flickr's dialog box for choosing among contact categories

When creating a Flickr account and becoming a new user of the platform, it's pretty clear that these three simple tiers are nested: Family sees everything; Friends see a subset of that; Contacts see a subset of what Friends see. But, it would be even better if that were reflected here as a reminder.

LinkedIn doesn't have an especially clear proxemic progression (Figure 18-6) represented in its relationship categories.

The interface says, "Only invite people you know well and who know you," but we know LinkedIn is a professional-profile-based site—so what does "know well" really mean in this context? And what if categories overlap? For example, what if we are both friends and colleagues? There are multiple dimensions at work here and not much context for why we'd choose one over another.

FIGURE 18-6

LinkedIn's dialog box for categorizing a new contact

Hall also developed a model that explained two different ways that cultures tend to communicate and understand information: "high context" and "low context." High-context cultures rely more on the surrounding signifiers and tacit information that informs a communication. These cultures count on consistent, invariant meanings that they assume everyone will "get" even if not spelled out explicitly. By contrast, low-context cultures need much more explicit communication; they can't rely as much on tacit information to clarify meaning.*

Any social environment's architecture can constrain its users to being more on the high- or low-context scale, in terms of how well they understand one another. Architectures that demand all communication and context-setting be only through highly structured, predefined limits can, perhaps ironically, manage to strain out all the "noise" that would otherwise add meaningful nuance to communication. The limits of these structures can stifle social connection in the name of engineered purity. At the same time, allowing a lot of high-context communication can open up room for chaos and cruft, making it difficult to

---

* Hall, Edward T. *Beyond Culture*. New York: Anchor Books, 1976.

monetize or manage a social software platform. These are tough challenges, either way, but the dynamics should be understood and worked through purposefully, not ignored.

Identity

Each digital place has environmental elements that nudge or outright constrain us into being different sides of ourselves—our personalities, interests, and modes of expression. Not unlike the Luna Blue Hotel example in Chapter 17—in which vacancy disappeared on the Web even while it had empty rooms—our identities are also partially constructed from the databases across the Internet. For everyone who knows us only by that information, we are what it says we are.

There are arguments and evidence from many disciplines, from philosophy to psychology, contending that a person's individual identity is not a singular, stable thing. Whether one believes there is some immutable core to the human self, it is clear that such a core—if it exists—is not all that matters for defining who we are. Indeed, we don't exist in a vacuum. We're part of an environment, including many other people who experience us and have an impression of who we are. And at the same time, they influence us and our actions, beliefs, and preferences in ways we're only recently fully coming to understand.

Back in the early days of the public Internet, researcher and theorist Sherry Turkle described how living online, in digital information structures, has made the facets of our identities explicitly delineated. This is in contrast to our offline selves, which have historically been defined more tacitly and subtly. In her 1997 book *Life on the Screen: Identity in the Age of the Internet* (Simon & Schuster), she explains how the Internet has brought us to a literal culmination of what postmodern theorists had been saying about identity for the prior several decades: the self is a "multiple, distributed system...a decentered self that exists in many worlds and plays many roles at the same time." Turkle then goes on to show how these "worlds" and "roles" have gone from being tacitly emergent entities that don't necessarily have clear boundaries, to being things we can enact in an explicitly defined way in specific, clearly bounded contexts. Using Multi-User Domains (MUDs) for her ethnographic field work, she shows how people explore different sides of themselves, acting out facets of their personalities in separate, clearly defined places—in one, a hyper-masculine and demanding warrior, while in another a fey, androgynous elf. She makes the point that this provides many options for habitation and life experience, leaving "real life" as just "one more window."*

There are still places where role-players get to put on various personalities and digital bodies. But in one sense, this ability has become mainstreamed into the many social platforms people inhabit. We have online profiles at many different sites, each of which is engineered around a specific set of information about us. We're often finding ourselves choosing which platform is best for a particular picture or personal moment, or choosing which of our identities to use for making a comment somewhere, as shown in Figure 18-7.

And these choices matter. For example, LinkedIn doesn't ask what my favorite bands are or what five things I would take to a desert island, or what sort of people I want to date. It asks for business-related information such as work and education history—its context as a career-oriented place is largely defined by the semantic categories it gathers from us.

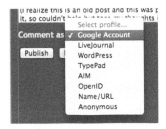

FIGURE 18-7
Blogspot gives users the ability to log in using one of a number of net-defined "identities" to comment on a post

So, LinkedIn defines the role one plays on LinkedIn, and in turn, that's the identity one has when visiting there. The same goes for a dating site, or a personal journaling platform. Even an e-commerce site provides constraints for our role and identity; for example, Amazon, where the information categories constrain my role to being a consumer among other consumers, is a place where I can engage in conversations and self-expression, but always about products that I and others might consume.

---

* Turkle, Sherry. *Life on the Screen: Identity in the Age of the Internet.* New York: Touchstone, 1995:14.

What has changed since Turkle's writing in 1995: there's no longer a neat division between "real life" and life "on the screen." Screens are now everywhere, as apertures into the pervasive, networked information dimension. There is no stepping away from the computer to live in "meatspace" versus "cyberspace" anymore.* These other contexts are always-on and invariantly available. It's hard to think of any networked experience that is still a fully walled garden; they all have tendrils working their way into syndicated feeds, email alerts, live chats, and other channels.

Sometimes, a service is polite enough to ask if we want to connect one context to another, which is good. But these connections still come with complications.

For example, lately, Google has been nudging users to consolidate their profiles, sweetening the encouragement by showing you how much "better" your identity will look and sound if you combine them, as is shown in Figure 18-8. Sounds fine on the face of it, but notice the disclaimer in the figure: "Links to your channel will still use [*your YouTube username*]."

FIGURE 18-8

Google suggests I merge my personal Google account and the Google Plus account I have from my employer's Google Apps platform

---

* Turkle, in fact, came to see this, as well, and the point is part of her argument in her later book, *Alone Together: Why We Expect More from Technology and Less from Each Other.* She sees it as part of an unhealthy corrosion of human communication. Personally, I see it not as necessarily corrosive, but a sort of phase transition from one mode of community to another.

One problem with an environment made of names is that you can't easily just shirk one and move on to another. Then how will my identity be nested if I say yes to this? In which ways will it be merged and in which ways will it not? It's not clear.

I've wrestled with a similar issue just within Google's Gmail platform. As Google grew its services portfolio, I created a new "Google Apps" identity so that I could use Gmail with my own *andrewhinton.com* domain; however, when I did, I already had years of email archives and history with my existing email address at gmail.com. Then, I joined a consultancy that was using Google's Apps for Business service. Google has integrated all three of these into its Plus social platform, but I've found no useful way to merge or coordinate the three identities. Even in the Google ecosystem, I am represented by at least several different profiles. On the Internet, it's a challenge to be represented as a single object, with a single label, even when you want to.

My Facebook identity is another version of me online; and around the time of the Beacon experiment, I realized my Facebook identity was being recognized on other sites, far beyond Facebook. That's because Facebook recognizes me through embedded code in websites—such as online retailers or magazines—that have nothing explicitly to do with Facebook. So many places I go, I see my face or the faces of Facebook friends embedded out of context.

When I first encountered this pattern, it was disconcerting because it wasn't clear if my face was something other people were seeing or if it was just showing up for me (see Figure 18-9). It's one of those things that took explicit, reflective attention—and repeated exposure—to accept this new pseudo-presence of my "self" in all these other places. Even now, though, if it's embedded in some way new to me, it can still take me off guard.

This contextual cloning and splintering of my online self is happening far beyond Facebook's many connections. For example, my American Express account is embedded in the digital context of my accounts at Amazon and Delta Airlines. These digitally formed places are not merely supplemental to our identities, because we rely on them as primary infrastructure for our social contexts.

FIGURE 18-9

How is it that my Facebook profile is integrated into Microsoft's Bing? The rules make sense to the network, but not to me

In one interview, a teenager explains the consequences for a friend of hers, not for a "social network" site, but a phone texting channel:

> Not having an iPhone can be social suicide, notes Casey. One of her friends found herself effectively exiled from their circle for six months because her parents dawdled in upgrading her to an iPhone. Without it, she had no access to the iMessage group chat, where it seemed all their shared plans were being made.
>
> "She wasn't in the group chat, so we stopped being friends with her," Casey says. "Not because we didn't like her, but we just weren't in contact with her.[*]

At one time, having a listing in the phone book was an essential bit of semantic information, providing an interface between a person or business and civic life. If you weren't in the phone book, you were disconnected from a huge dimension of social infrastructure. But now we need an account in every digital place where our friends, family, or customers expect us to be. If we aren't *represented* in those places, we don't *exist* in them.

---

[*] "What Really Happens On A Teen Girl's iPhone." Huffington Post, June 5, 2013 (*http://huff.to/1wiaBWx*).

These places can become so necessary in our lives that they can actually go from being pleasant to oppressive. As the currently reigning Übernetwork, Facebook serves again as a good example. Although Facebook's user numbers have continued to increase, many people are finding that if they keep an account at all, it's only out of necessity. They are afraid of disappearing entirely from the place where so much of what defines them and their community happens, but they consider it more of a chore than a delight.

One recent study found many factors in play for why Facebook has become a contextually complicated place. The report finds that teens can't freely express their identities with their peers the way they might otherwise, because so many parents, teachers, and other adult community figures have joined Facebook, as well.* But even among peers, "looking good, both physically and in reputation, is a big deal." There's pressure to uphold a positive image, in part because there's pressure for one's shared information to be "liked" in order to know if it's valued or appreciated by peers. Everything can be "watched and judged."

Many teens are finding respite by creating accounts in other platforms, such as Twitter, Tumblr, Instagram, or Reddit. For many, there's a clear awareness that it's because those places have different architectures through which they can express themselves with less restriction and oversight, and with less pressure to comprehensively define so much of themselves for consumption by every "role" they play in their lives.

For example, Tumblr has exploded recently as a teen social platform. One teen in the study said he uses it more because, "I don't have to present a specific or false image of myself and I don't have to interact with people I don't necessarily want to talk to." That is, Tumblr is a different kind of place whose structures are less demanding about defining oneself or compelling a user to take so many actions to be part of the system.

Like Twitter, Reddit, and other less-demanding platforms, one benefit is you're not compelled to identify your real name to viewers. You can experiment with what you're interested in culturally and socially, and only tell trusted friends your username. A common usage pattern

---

* Madden, et.al. "Teens, Social Media, and Privacy," Pew Research Internet Project, May 21, 2013 (http://pewrsr.ch/1w3flBK).

on Reddit is the "throwaway" username: users will create a temporary login just to ask a single embarrassing or private question, often actually putting some version of "throwaway" in the name itself. Reddit makes it easy to do this, or it wouldn't be so common. The rules of the environment shape the behavior of its inhabitants.

A principle we keep returning to is that we're part of a nested, evolutionary ecology. We are the way we are largely because of the structures and affordances of our environment. So, if that's the case, all the stuff that makes up our identities—personalities, social connections, personal history, and so on—work the way they do with the assumption that the world around us works in a particular way, as well. Facebook has grown, in part, by providing mechanisms for every facet of our social lives. It sounds like a fine goal, until we realize that Facebook—in trying to be so many different places at once—disrupts our cognitive ability to distinguish what sort of place we are in, which in turn disrupts our ability to know which side of ourselves we should be presenting to others.

As other social platforms continue to innovate and expand their scope in order to grow their user base, they create similar disruptions. This social dissonance is not just in our heads but is directly coupled with the dissonance of structure in these environments. Our identities are coupled, for good or ill, with the structure of place. Unstable or collapsed context architectures result in unstable or collapsed identities.

Collisions and Fronts

The way social structures can collapse or be unstable isn't a sign that we're disingenuous or duplicitous; having these sides of ourselves is just how we are. Erving Goffman, one of the most influential sociologists of the twentieth century, argued that we naturally put on "fronts" that we use to control the way others perceive us in various facets of our lives. He framed these personas in theatrical terms: we have a "backstage" self that is more relaxed and personally open, a "front-stage" self that is more controlled and cultivated for public or professional interaction, as well as a "core" self that is mostly internal, the way we relate to ourselves. And, of course, there can be various facets of each, depending on the situation one is in.

I suspect these fronts are natural adaptations to the complexity of human relationships. We're usually not conscious we're doing it, because it's not something we plan to do; it's just how we behave. This dynamic works just fine as long as our fronts align with the environment we're in—acting in one way when among our best friends, in another way when at work, and in another when visiting elderly relatives. When in each of those contexts, there is unambiguous information specified in the environment informing us who we're with, and where.

When Facebook's Beacon was causing waves, sociologist and ethnographic researcher Sam Ladner explained that what was going wrong with Beacon (referencing Goffman's concept) was what she calls a "collision of fronts."

> Facebook's Beacon didn't work because it forces people to use multiple fronts AT THE SAME TIME. If I tag a recipe from Epicurious.com, but I broadcast that fact to friends that perceive me to be a party girl, I have a collision of fronts. If my boss demands to be my friend, I have a collision of fronts. If I rent The Notebook on Netflix, and my friends think I am a Goth, I have a collision of fronts.[*]

Imagine if all the places you thought of as important places in your city or town were somehow merged into one place: at a smaller scale, it might be your bedroom, kitchen, and front porch; simultaneously, at a larger scale, it could be your workplace, your home, your gym, and—in a weirdly timeless way—your high school reunion, one that doesn't last only a weekend, but goes on and on as you try conducting the rest of your life. In its need to grow without boundaries, Facebook collapses contexts by creating many doorways that feel as though they will take us to separate places, but they all drop us into the same big place at the same time.[†]

Soon after Beacon, Facebook added tools for creating and managing "groups," but they weren't especially good for privacy. A few years later, they overhauled what the platform meant by "groups" entirely, to allow

---

[*] Ladner, Sam. "What Designers Can Learn From Facebook's Beacon: the collision of 'fronts'," Posted at *copernicusconsulting.net* November 30, 2007 (*http://bit.ly/10iKhAW*).

[†] "Facebook & your privacy," *Consumer Reports* magazine June 2012. (*http://bit.ly/ZELYHC*).

more private management between smaller clusters of friends, but the settings for them (as well as for all the privacy controls) are hard to find and understand, in spite of Facebook's almost-annual attempts to improve their usability. As late as 2012, *Consumer Reports* was calling Facebook's privacy controls "labyrinthian." Changing the rules so often only further confounded users.

For Mark Zuckerberg, Facebook's creator, the labyrinth hit close to home in 2012 when his sister Randi discovered that a photo from her personal Facebook status feed was shared with an audience not only outside her own Facebook page, but on Twitter—outside of Facebook entirely.

Ms. Zuckerberg complained to the Twitter user (named Callie Schweitzer), saying that sharing her photo in such a way was "way uncool," to which Callie responded as depicted in Figure 18-10.

FIGURE 18-10
A Zuckerberg brouhaha*

But according to the Buzzfeed article about this brouhaha, Ms. Schweitzer more likely saw it not because she was subscribed to Randi's feed, but because she's friends with Randi's sister, who was tagged by name in the photo, which made the picture show up in the sister's news feed, as well.†

---

* Screenshot by author.

† *http://www.buzzfeed.com/jpmoore/mark-zuckerbergs-sister-complains-of-facebook-pri*

There was a hearty round of schadenfreude among web dwellers when this occurred; people frustrated with the platform's convoluted privacy controls were more than happy to see a member of Facebook aristocracy suffer from the same contextual collision that had vexed the common folk for years.

The problem arose in part because Facebook's environment uses names in ways we don't use them in regular conversation. When typing a name into a status or photo post, Facebook automatically looks for names in your friends list that match, and provides an auto-suggest-and-complete interaction. Facebook also makes it a default setting for users to allow being tagged in such a way, and for items tagged thusly to show up in the news feeds of friends of the tagged person—and it's hard to tell that the tagged person didn't post it herself.

A similar issue occurs on Flickr: the system publishes any pictures tagged with your name as a primary place in your profile. In the mobile app (Figure 18-11), tapping the Photos Of button reveals a gallery of such pictures; in my case, because I never get around to tagging pictures of me with my own name, these are nearly all pictures made by other people.

FIGURE 18-11
Flickr's mobile profile presentation

Someone new to Flickr could easily assume the Photos Of area is actually curated by me—after all, I'm the curator of the other structures: Sets, Groups, Favorites, and Contacts. The convention in most social networks has been that the user controls what represents him in his profile. Adding to the confusion, these icons are all presented as if they are similar in kind—apples with apples—even though one is not like the others.

So, even though social platforms claim to be giving users ways to manage context, the walls and windows keep shifting; the rules are so slippery, we environmentally learn that we can't trust key structures to be invariant. Like some of the teens studied by Pew, one way users have combatted this confusion is to just create multiple accounts, one for their "front-stage" self, and another for their "back-stage" persona—a practice Facebook actively condemns. According to Facebook's official policies, multiple profiles can cause you to be exiled from Facebook:

> On Facebook, people connect using their real names and identities. We ask that you refrain from publishing the personal information of others without their consent. Claiming to be another person, creating a false presence for an organization, or creating multiple accounts undermines community and violates Facebook's terms.[*]

What this policy misses is the fact that people are not just one thing in all places and all times, among all people. Real "community" leaves room for the multiple fronts of one's identity. It's only because Facebook has created such a muddle within the shell structure of a singular profile that people have given up on making sense of it, and decided instead to create their own separately defined contexts for their social fronts.

The Ontology of Self

What we're witnessing in social software platforms is a clash between different definitions of the self and what an identity actually is, not to mention what a "friend" is. Recall that the word ontology can be used in two different ways: first, it means the conceptual, human question of being, and what something "is"; and, second, it means formal, technological definition of an entity (what attributes does it have that define what it is in the system?).

---

[*] *https://www.facebook.com/communitystandards/*

Digital logic leaves little or no room for the tacit nuances of organic, nondigital life. To achieve anything even close to the rich complexity of natural human meaning is one of the most challenging things computer science can attempt—hence the still-awkward interactions we have with voice-controlled computers, or the erratic usefulness of "natural language search." Those capabilities require many expensive layers of artificial intelligence, which is still far from being consistently reliable outside of narrowly defined use-cases.

Facebook puts a lot of the work on users' shoulders to figure out how to make the many dimensions of one's identity fit the very few "slots" provided by its data models and controlled vocabularies.

For example, Figure 18-12 shows the top portion of Facebook's form for gathering one's "Basic" profile information, as it stood circa 2012. I've exposed the selections in two of the drop-down menus to illustrate how Facebook was using a limiting ontology of identity.

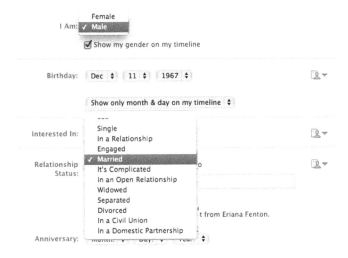

FIGURE 18-12
Facebook's previous gender and relationship choice lists

First, note gender. In the twenty-first century, much of the world has come to realize that we are gendered in ways that are far more complex than the binary setting of male or female, and that gender is (like identity itself) largely constructed by cultural and social context. It's good to know that a few months after I first drafted this section, Facebook changed to a more inclusive approach for gender specification: the menu choices are Male, Female, and Custom; selecting Custom reveals additional fields, as demonstrated in Figure 18-13, with even the lovely nuance of pronoun choice.

FIGURE 18-13
Facebook's updated Gender selection interface

Also note the drop-down selection for Relationship Status in Figure 18-12. The choices present a list of mutually exclusive categories that don't accommodate the complexity of actual relationships. For example, what marriage isn't "complicated" in one way or another? The list also infers that there is a sort of linear progression to a romantic relationship: from Single to "In a relationship" to Engaged and then to Married. (Let's set aside the unsettling feeling we get if we extend that implied line through "It's Complicated" and the rest.) But the truth is, a real romantic relationship doesn't move in a linear fashion through these clearly defined states. Not to mention the more legally specific constructions, many of which are defined differently from one municipality to another.

And yet, for anyone who has dated and had even a semi-serious relationship in the age of Facebook, this drop-down list can be vexing. Why? Because Facebook has become an official part of how couples define their relationships. The changing of one's relationship status has become part of the prevailing cultural environment, as much as wearing a partner's varsity-letter jacket in high school or offering an engagement ring in a marriage proposal. Because there are already culturally conventional markers for engagement and marriage, those selections are somewhat less problematic than others. But the really difficult one is Single versus "In a relationship"—at what point in one's dating life does an individual (or a couple) switch from one to the other?

In analog, semantic life, this is a tacit inflection point that emerges uniquely for everyone. But here, it has to be a clearly defined signal—a flipped switch.

This issue seems trivial at first, but Facebook is such a major factor in how others in the world understand who we are that this choice has a great deal of pressure on it. I personally know people who have stopped dating because of arguments over this tiny semantic choice.

There's an obvious question underlying this entire issue: Why does the platform require answering this question with a selection from a defined list? Why can't there just be a free-text field, with perhaps a list of suggested phrases, the way Facebook added the Custom field for gender?

The answer is probably because the information isn't only for regular users. The collected data needs to be structured as attributes for data-mining advertisers. Facebook is asking us to identify ourselves within the definitions of a map that is partly not intended for us. In doing so—as we rely more and more heavily on infrastructures such as Facebook to mediate our identities—they structure *what and who we are to one another.*

So, on Facebook, filling out your personal profile isn't just about telling other people about yourself on Facebook. It's also connecting you with semantic information categories that can be structurally searched and analyzed in ways that would not occur to you. And why would it? It's happening in an abstracted process outside of your perception.

Now that Facebook has introduced what it calls Graph Search, all those public factors are fodder for analysis to identify you in whatever ways searchers wish to interpret the data. People can use that information to profile users based on religion, gender, age, and even sexual orientation.[*] And because "Big Data" can be used to find patterns we would never dream of, these factors are discoverable through triangulation, even if users haven't made those fields in their profile explicitly public.[†]

---

[*] van Ess, Henk. "The Creepy Side of Facebook Graph Search." PBS.org Mediashift January 24, 2013 (*http://to.pbs.org/1AoOYYV*).

[†] Green, Jon. "Facebook knows you're gay before you do," Americablog, March 20, 2013 (*http://americablog.com/2013/03/facebook-might-know-youre-gay-before-you-do.html*).

It's not just Facebook that's using this sort of shadow-of-yourself analysis to target messages. The Barack Obama election campaign used these techniques with such skill that they had a better sense of how individuals would vote than the individuals had themselves.* And big-box retailer Target can accurately market baby products to people who don't even know they're pregnant yet.† Keep in mind, these last two examples aren't driven only by web behaviors, but by data gathered from many other now-publicly-available sources. The information modes we're familiar with—our everyday semantic utterances and bodily activities—are increasingly tethered to digital-information data stores, ready to be harvested.

Digital theorist, futurist, and philosopher Jaron Lanier has railed against such misappropriations of personal information. In *You Are Not a Gadget: A Manifesto* (Vintage Books), Lanier reminds us that the Shannon construction of information (as discussed in Chapter 12), by its nature, creates limitations in how we describe ourselves and our environment:

> Recall that the motivation of the invention of the bit was to hide and contain the thermal, chaotic aspect of physical reality for a time in order to have a circumscribed, temporary, programmable nook within the larger theater. Outside of the conceit of the computer, reality cannot be fully known or programmed.
>
> Poorly conceived digital systems can erase the numinous nuances that make us individuals. The all-or-nothing nature of the bit is reflected at all layers in a digital information system, just like the quantum nature of elementary particles is reflected in the uncertainty of complex systems in macro physical reality, like the weather. If we associate human identity with the digital reduction instead of reality at large, we will reduce ourselves.

---

* Issenberg, Sasha. "A More Perfect Union: How President Obama's campaign used big data to rally individual voters, Part 1." *MIT Technology Review* December 16, 2012 (*http://bit.ly/1wwD6AN*).

† Duhigg, Charles. "How Companies Learn Your Secrets," *The New York Times*, February 16, 2012 (*http://nyti.ms/1CQFQsQ*).

The all-or-nothing conceit of the bit should not be amplified to become the social principle of the human world, even though that's the lazy thing to do from an engineering point of view. It's equally mistaken to build digital culture, which is gradually becoming all culture, on a foundation of anonymity or single-persona antiprivacy. Both are similar affronts to personhood."[*]

Lanier is pointing out the ways in which the digital mode of information can influence and ultimately warp the way we identify ourselves. Of course, a business is a business, and advertising is what drives revenue for Facebook and many other social platforms, which wouldn't exist but for that revenue. So, the answer isn't to vilify the business as a business. A good start would be doing a better job of providing transparency around user information, ideally giving users some level of agency in how their information is being used, other than having to leave the platform altogether.[†]

As designers of these inhabited, living maps, we need to realize how deeply we are affecting the lives of people who use what we make. The defined attributes we wrap around people (as well as objects, events, and places) that we might assume are only supplementary can easily become fundamental in their effects. Facebook is only one obvious example of these issues; they're just as important when designing a corporate intranet or a patient database for a healthcare system.

Networked Publics

Digital places, structured by systems of labels and rules, are not just something we visit as an optional distraction anymore. And, when an environment becomes more of a requirement, it's more about civics than mere socializing. Author and professor Clay Shirky states in clear terms how the structures and rules we create in these places affect our lives:

---

[*] Lanier, Jaron. *You Are Not a Gadget: A Manifesto*. New York: Vintage Books, 2011:201.

[†] The question of whether people must agree to give up their personal data in order to participate in the platform is related to a bigger question: at what point does something like Facebook become a kind of monopoly utility, to which people have a right to access?

> Social software is the experimental wing of political philosophy, a discipline that doesn't realize it has an experimental wing. We are literally encoding the principles of freedom of speech and freedom of expression in our tools. We need to have conversations about the explicit goals of what it is that we're supporting and what we are trying to do, because that conversation matters.[*]

We are co-inhabiting digital governance structures legislated by software engineers, counseled by marketers, advertisers, and corporate board members.

In her dissertation on social software, *Taken Out of Context: American Teen Sociality in Networked Publics,* social media scholar danah boyd (her capitalization) explains that there is not really just one "public." Rather than saying "*the* public" it's more accurate to refer to "*a* public" among many. She states, "Using the indefinite article allows us to recognize that there are different collections of people depending on the situation and context. This leaves room for multiple 'publics.'" She explains that publics are not necessarily separate from one another: they overlap, and are nested with smaller publics inside larger ones. (From a Gibsonian perspective, this might suggest that people group together in an overlapping, nested way similar to how we perceive the environment; this would make sense, given that people are part of the environment, as well.) In addition, boyd mentions that there are also emergent collectives working against the grain of the status quo, referred to as "counterpublics."[†]

Publics are shaped in part by how they are mediated, and boyd argues that "networked" publics are different from the "broadcast" and "unmediated" publics that came before; she says the proper frame for the structures and rules we put into the networked environment is *architecture*: "Physical structures are a collection of atoms, while digital structures are built out of bits. The underlying properties of bits and atoms fundamentally distinguish these two types of environments, define

---

[*] As reported by Nat Torkington in his notes of Shirky's talk (*http://oreil.ly/1t9HBA9*).

[†] boyd, danah. *Taken Out of Context: American Teen Sociality in Networked Publics Dissertation;* University of California, Berkeley. 2008, p. 18

what types of interactions are possible, and shape how people engage in these spaces."* In fact, citing William J. Mitchell's *City of Bits: Space, Place, and the Infobahn*, boyd explains:

> Mitchell (1995) argued that bits do not simply change the flow of information, but they alter the very architecture of everyday life. Through networked technology, people are no longer shaped just by their dwellings but by their networks (Mitchell 1995: 49). The city of bits that Mitchell lays out is not configured just by the properties of bits but by the connections between them.†

The way we use semantic function to make environments adds up to a sort of urban planning and architectural practice, and not merely in a metaphorical sense. This is architecture that we literally live in together.

To elaborate, boyd lays out four "Properties of Networked Publics" that make them different from the other sorts of mediated publics:‡

- Persistence: Online expressions are automatically recorded and archived.
- Replicability: Content made out of bits can be duplicated.
- Scalability: The potential visibility of content in networked publics is great.
- Searchability: Content in networked publics can be accessed through search.

Additionally, "the properties of networked publics lead to a dynamic in which people are forced to contend with a loss of context."§

In ecological terms, these are new invariant properties of our environment that don't behave in the way in which our embodied perceptual system expects. As anthropologist Michael Wesch explained in Chapter 2 about the experience of looking at a webcam and trying to understand

---

* boyd, p. 24
† boyd, p. 25
‡ boyd, p. 27
§ boyd, p. 36

what sort of social interaction one is experiencing, we don't have any gut-level grasp of what expression means in such a disembodied, wide-scaled context.

For an online environment like Facebook or Google's Buzz and Plus, there are no intrinsic physical structures for us to rely upon for knowing where we are, or where the objects we create are (such as photos or status updates), and who can see them. The system has to simulate those structures for us, not only with graphical simulation of surface structures, but semantic relationships of labels.

It also has to build in structures for giving us a sense of others' behavior, or attempts to meet or learn more about us; but such structures struggle to behave like physical social life. On LinkedIn, for example, there are mechanisms for knowing who looked at your profile (Figure 18-14), if you allow others to know you looked at theirs; it's something that wouldn't really exist outside of digital information.

WHO'S VIEWED YOUR PROFILE

Your profile view settings must be changed to see who is viewing your profile.Change Settings

FIGURE 18-14
Checking who viewed your profile in LinkedIn

Just because anything can be linked to anything doesn't mean it's the right thing to do. The environment might make perfect sense in its requirements and its engineered execution, but it isn't truly habitable until, in the words of information architect Jorge Arango, it "preserves the integrity of meaning across contexts."* It must make sense not just to the map itself, but to the people who live in it.

---

* Arango, Jorge. "Links, Nodes & Order: A Unified Theory of Information Architecture," (*http://www.jarango.com/blog/2013/04/07/links-nodes-order/*).

Composing Context

Making Room for Making Meaning

If semantic environments are the maps we live in, and they help us make sense of the other modes of information we encounter, how do we go about creating them? Is it different from the way we're used to making applications and websites, services and strategies?

The good news is this: context isn't made of mysterious ether; it's a result of bodily engagement with the language and objects of an environment. In other words, context depends on stuff we can touch, create, shape, and arrange—elements that we can *compose*.

Part VI takes a few steps toward perspectives, principles, and techniques that can help us consider context in our design work. It discusses what composition is, and the materials we use for composing context. It also covers how users make sense of their world through narrative, and offers some considerations for how we do research, analysis, and modeling that can build on the understanding we've explored in prior chapters.

FIGURE VI-1

A modern subway map provides a composition of semantic information—an abstracted model, disconnected from the literal shape of streets above-ground; it's an early example of infrastructure that allows people to navigate by label more than physical structures*

---

* Wikimedia Commons: *http://commons.wikimedia.org/wiki/File:Milano_Subway_map.svg*

[19]

Arrangement and Substance

A poem is a little machine of words.
—WILLIAM CARLOS WILLIAMS

Composition in Other Disciplines

WHY COMPOSITION? To COMPOSE something is to arrange it, to relate all its parts, and to determine its substance. It's a great way of thinking about how we handle context, because context is all about how we understand relationships between elements. Composition is an important concept in just about every field of human creation, which makes it a useful way to think about cross-channel, ambient environments that can involve so many different kinds of media and information. Let's take a look at some of them:

Writing

The combination of elements such as tone, theme, setting, and voice within a structure, such as the classical essay framework of "Introduction—Body—Conclusion," or the way the narrative arc of a plot gives structure to a novel. At a more granular level, composition has to do with sentence structure and parts of speech. Poems, too, have compositional elements—from the established forms of sonnets and sestinas to the smaller formal techniques of free-verse line-breaking and semantic improvisation.

Music

For music, composition is its "musical form." It's the structure or plan of a piece of music: its arrangement of repetitions and differences and structural patterns. What makes a Rondo different from a Sonata, and what makes them both different from a live improvised jazz performance, is the structural decisions made manifest in their compositions. Composition is such a central idea in music that we colloquially refer to the piece of music itself as a "composition."

Graphic arts and photography

In any sort of picture, composition has to do with the artist's structural choices of perspective and framing as well as the formal arrangement of the picture's subject or subjects. It determines what is put in the frame and what is left out, and how the things pictured relate to one another within the frame of what the viewer can see.

Film

For movie-making, composition inherits everything from photography and writing and (usually) music, but adds the complexities that come with stringing many pictures together quickly over time. The way one shot makes sense (or not) when juxtaposed with another shot is a composition issue. For example, in a filmed conversation between two people, each should be facing a consistently distinct direction toward the other party; otherwise, it's hard to track who is talking with whom. Films also use *establishing shots* to situate the action—a brief view of a cityscape or the outside of a restaurant, before focusing on a conversation. Beyond specific shots, composition also has to do with how the film is edited together, scene to scene, and how one scene sets context for the action in the next as well as how all the scenes come together to create a narrative whole. Film is the twentieth century's most advanced medium for tackling the challenges of placemaking and sensemaking that come from de-contextualized information: in film, there's no longer a single stage in a theater to hold context together. The film must artificially establish the invariant container of each scene. (Software can still learn much from the way the "grammar" of film constructs context.)

Architecture

For the built environment, composition refers to the arrangement of essential architectural elements, starting fundamentally as a single surface and on through various combinations, into meaningful components: rooms, corridors, windows, stairways, vestibules, courtyards, and so on. The way these are chosen, arranged, and connected are what determine the nature of the environment; they make the difference between an apartment building and a corporate campus, a parliamentary chamber and a nightclub. Architect Louis Kahn famously remarked that an architectural plan is a "society of rooms" and explained how that society is "knit together with the elements of connection."[*] The connections are what define the relationships between the rooms and what give them much of their meaning and utility, and vice versa.

Qualities of Composition

There are common qualities and issues that we see across all the aforementioned sorts of the composition:

Composition is about relationships that make up the whole
One can't consider the composition of a thing without considering its totality and how the whole is greater than the sum of its particulars. Context is about how elements relate to one another, which puts composition right at its center.

Composition is nested
In all the examples from other disciplines, the arrangement of elements creates nested relationships. A picture begins with its boundaries as its outer shell. It contains representations or formal abstractions, some of which might continue to contain one another, and so on. One approach to built-environment architecture is to start with the primitive foundation of a mere surface and then add complexity outward, while simultaneously starting with the outer shell of the surveyed building site and designing structure inward from that setting. Film has a nested grammar for orienting the viewer, such as providing establishing shots before close-ups, situating details within the larger story arc or *mise-en-scène*. It makes sense that these fields would compose their artifacts in this nested manner—it's how we, as terrestrial creatures, comprehend everything.

Composition requires (and creates) structure
Without structure, nothing has composition; putting elements in relation to one another creates structures in the environment, and vice versa, since creating structure is always composition of one sort or another. It's important to point this out because otherwise, we tend to forget the next point...

---

[*] Kahn, Louis. (Twombly, Robert, Editor) *Essential Texts*. W.W. Norton & Company: 2003:254.

Composition is not neutral

There's no way to abdicate responsibility when composing something, because saying yes to a structural choice means saying no to the alternatives. Inclusion is also exclusion. You can't have a door in every spot of a wall, or else there's no longer a wall. You can't show everything in a painting; you can show only what the frame will contain. And, you can't label something with every possible bit of relevant language, because it eventually ceases to mean anything in particular. For something to have any affordance or semantic function, it needs invariant structural qualities.

Composition makes an argument

Because structure isn't neutral, to compose something is to make an argument about what something should be and how it should work. As information architect Andy Fitzgerald has wonderfully put it, in a talk about digital design, built architecture is "rhetoric for spaces."[*] As with maps, every composition has an agenda, whether it's intentional or not. A Rothko color-field painting makes an argument that it can be made of shades of color and nothing else; Quentin Tarantino's *Pulp Fiction* makes an argument that it can disrupt linear time but still have a coherent narrative; and Facebook's policy against multiple accounts makes an argument that having a single profile with one's real name is "good" and the alternative is not. Composition, done well, makes manifest an opinion of what relationships should exist, and which should be primary, secondary, and so on. And that argument is what creates the conditions under which an agent is trying to understand context.

Composition means we have to make decisions about what things are, what they mean, and how they relate to one another, all coming from an understanding of how people will perceive the environment.

---

[*] Fitzgerald, Andy. "Taxonomy for App Makers IA Summit 2013, Baltimore, MD," (*http://www.slideshare.net/andybywire/taxonomy-for-app-makers*).

As Film Does to Stage Plays...

In semantically dominant environments, in which so much of the structure is created with language, the meaning of a given structure can shift radically based on the context of the perceiver. In one of the classic examples of how context works, early twentieth-century Russian filmmaker Lev Kuleshov created a short film showing the face of a famous Russian actor of the time, intercut with unrelated scenes: a bowl of soup, the body of a child displayed at its funeral, a beautiful woman sitting on a divan.

In the motion-picture version, it appears the actor is reacting uniquely to each scene: hunger, grief, lust. The still-image representation presented in Figure 19-1 doesn't provide the full effect; in the film itself, the actor is in motion—sitting still for the camera, but breathing (to the point of sighing) and showing subtle facial reactions to whatever he is witnessing.

Of course, the trick here is that the clip is showing exactly the same few seconds of facial expression across all three contexts.

Kuleshov created this strip out of unrelated found footage to illustrate how the cinematic composition technique called "montage" can evoke narrative for an audience, even if there isn't any actual intended narrative in the individual pieces. Composition can bring implicit meaning to information that the pieces of information themselves do not necessarily contain. Although film displays images captured from the interaction of light and physical information, its physical information is only that captured light, frozen in two-dimensional frames. It lacks the intrinsic perceptual information we have in nonmediated life. If we were in the room with this actor, watching a scene on stage, we would see the entire situation. And that's what very early dramatic films were: captures of stage plays. Film came into its own as an art form by breaking ties with the "real" situation, and cutting that reality up into slices, rearranging it to make new possibilities of meaning.

FIGURE 19-1
Frames from each section of the Kuleshov film*

As for places in our environment: semantic information has always given us the capability to change the meaning of a place. From cave paintings to murals and political broadsides, we've transformed surfaces into radiators of meaning that alter our experience of a physical place.

Digital technology does to that semantic-information ability what film did to staged narrative: it makes it possible for us to edit, intercut, and splice what *place* is to its inhabitants.

---

* Captured with screenshots from YouTube: *http://bit.ly/1z2CSQV*

Something to Walk On

The more heavily an environment relies on semantic information for its structure and meaning, the more it requires us as designers to pay explicit attention to careful definitions in its composition, which requires stable points of reference. In *Digital Ground: Architecture, Pervasive Computing, and Environmental Knowing* (MIT Press), Malcolm McCullough argues for what the book's title names—a *grounded* experience in the digital age: "Not all is flux. Much as a river needs banks unless it is to spread aimlessly like a swamp, the flow of information needs meaningful contexts. Even in an age in which distance has been annihilated, location still matters."*

---

* McCullough, Malcolm. *Digital Ground: Architecture, Pervasive Computing, and Environmental Knowing.* Cambridge, MA: MIT Press, 2004:47, Kindle edition.

McCullough attends to the challenges of "digital ground" from an interaction-design perspective, but because of the ambient and social qualities of how "technology accumulates locally," he positions this work "more closely into alignment with the concerns of architecture."[*] Later, he builds on that point: "The role of computing has changed. Information technology has become ambient social infrastructure. This allies it with architecture. No longer just made of objects, computing now consists of situations."[†] Those situations are dynamic, perceived-and-acted, and contextual. For people to interact effectively, the architectural composition that grounds those interactions must be situationally sound—it must make sense as an environment.

Even when considering plain old written text, it turns out that the physical context of an actual book has an effect on how understandable and learnable the semantic "content" might be. People using paper begin to really learn the material more quickly, over time, than those who are trying to fully understand it through an e-book interface.[‡] One study showed that recall of a novel's plot was significantly poorer on a Kindle device than on paper.[§] Just like walking from one room to another loses the tacit connective tissue of the physical surroundings that helped form a "memory," not having actual pages in a physically navigable book can take valuable information out of the equation.

What is true of objects can be true of places. When digital environments such as Twitter or Facebook continually innovate, grow, and change their "feature set" to please the marketplace, they often change fundamental rules in their architectures that alter the invariant qualities that attracted and kept users to begin with. What felt like a comfortable home-away-from-home can suddenly become more exclusive and cold, or noisy and fragmented.

---

[*] ———. *Digital Ground: Architecture, Pervasive Computing, and Environmental Knowing.* Cambridge, MA: MIT Press, 2004:19.

[†] ———. *Digital Ground: Architecture, Pervasive Computing, and Environmental Knowing.* Cambridge, MA: MIT Press, 2004:21.

[‡] Szalavits, Maia. "Do E-Books Make It Harder to Remember What You Just Read?" *Time* (*time.com*) March 14, 2012.

[§] Flood, Alison. "Readers absorb less on Kindles than on paper, study finds" *The Guardian* (*guardian.com*) August 19, 2014 (*http://bit.ly/11z8CCn*).

Or, it can become something else entirely—a confusing panopticon of swirling signifiers, where the language one uses in the environment—such as "liking" a tweet or post—morphs into a more complicated lever with invisible connections and rules. Even at Harry Potter's Hogwarts School of Witchcraft and Wizardry, where the staircases would move around to connect different entrances in the school's towers, the patterns were at least learnable, and the towers didn't change into city parks. But when Twitter announced that it might change to an algorithm-driven feed—rather than the "everything" feed that has grounded the experience for seven years—many of its citizens were dismayed, because that move would fundamentally change what Twitter is to them.*

The foundational concern for shaping context is determining what McCullough calls the "banks of the river" as the stable, invariant structures of our environment. The individual objects of interaction certainly contribute to the overall situational context. But they're given much of their meaning by how they are nested within the broad, invariant structures of a whole architecture.

Consider the challenges of Google's latest social infrastructure. After the privacy debacles of Google Buzz (Chapter 12), Google rallied by creating Google Plus—an even more ambitious, comprehensive social platform, which has been slowly integrated into all of Google's platforms over time. Having learned a tough lesson with Buzz, Google has tried to go above and beyond the call of duty in making sure users understand the labels and rules of the new environment.

For example, Google Plus launched with a "Circles" metaphor used to organize contacts. In some ways, it's a brilliant use of the label: it borrows from the idea of "social circle" and shares *some of* our natural social-circle behaviors—we can create connections with people by multiple facets such as shared interests or family connections.

But in other ways, Circles are not like the social circles of non-Plus life. Our real relationships emerge "bottom up" through social activity, and only sometimes have any "top-down" definition. Natural social

---

* Ingram, Mathew. "Twitter CFO says a Facebook-style filtered feed is coming, whether you like it or not" (*gigaom.com*), September 4, 2014 (*http://bit.ly/1zvQrcl*).

connections also usually lack hard boundaries, and our proxemics tend to be fluid over time, closer to one group for a while, but drifting into more closeness with a different group later.

Although it's possible to create circles that we name based on "close friends" versus "acquaintances," Plus doesn't know when someone in one of those circles goes from "close" to "not very close at all"—we'd have to consciously move them from one circle to another. Plus, the circles are presented to us as equally sized, separate structures, until we select one, as in Figure 19-2.

FIGURE 19-2
A slice of the Google Plus Circles interface

Still, Google has worked hard to teach the users of Plus about how the invariant structures and rules of Plus work.

There is one challenge that Plus faces: the more complex the environment, the harder it is to keep coherent and invariant structures across so many different contexts, such as the channels, services, and devices connected to Plus. For example, in desktop browsers, the Plus site makes it clear when I'm reading within the *place* of a specific Circle. So, when I'm catching up with family in my Family Circle (which I defined), any post I create is limited to that Circle. It makes intuitively physical sense—just as if I were in a room with my family and listening to them, I'd expect what I said to be in that room, with those people.

Contrast the desktop with the architecture of the Mobile iOS version of Plus (Figure 19-3), for which the rules change. A post I make while reading inside a Circle defaults to Your Circles—something easy to miss, especially if I've learned the environment from the desktop. Instead, I must go through multiple steps to change my post to be in the Circle that I already think I am "in."

The composition of Google Plus—the arrangement and relationships between its parts—does a much better job of making sense than Buzz did, but just this one wayward structure disrupts its coherence. This breaks one of Resmini and Rosati's heuristics for information architecture: consistency, the capability of an information architecture model "to suit the purposes, the contexts, and the people it is designed for (internal consistency) and to maintain the same logic along different media, environments, and times in which it acts (external consistency)."[*] Consistency isn't about just the details, but really about the coherence of meaning from one context to the next. It's another way of attending to invariance for environmental design.

For environments that depend on semantics, information architecture determines the invariant, nested structures that act as the river's banks, the valley, the surrounding hillocks, and which way is north. The continual, ever-shifting challenge for information architecture involves finding a balance between order and resilience: establishing invariance necessary for understanding to happen, while providing flexible room for being human.

---

[*] Resmini, Andrea, and Luca Rosati. *Pervasive Information Architecture: Designing Cross-Channel User Experiences.* Burlington, MA: Morgan Kaufmann, 2011:55.

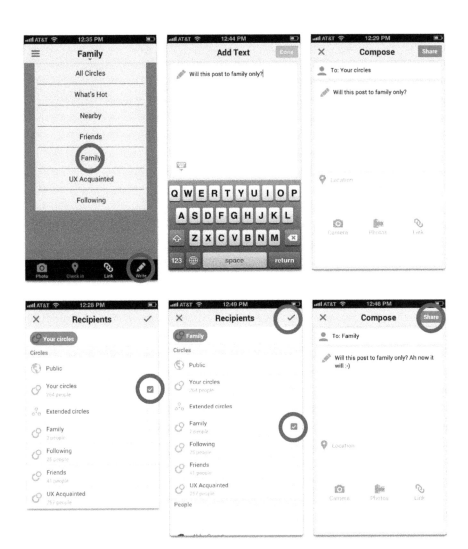

FIGURE 19-3

The steps required on Google Plus mobile to post in the circle you're already "in". The test message I'm writing is "Will this post to Family only?"

[20]

The Materials of Semantic Function

"When I use a word," Humpty Dumpty said in rather a scornful tone,
"it means just what I choose it to mean—neither more nor less."
"The question is," said Alice, "whether you can make words mean so
many different things."
"The question is," said Humpty Dumpty, "which is to be master—
that's all."
—LEWIS CARROLL, THROUGH THE LOOKING-GLASS

My cow is not pretty, but it's pretty to me.
—DAVID LYNCH

Elements

To address how information architecture composes context, we need to look at what materials the practice requires for designing environments. What are the elements that it uses—the bricks and mortar, studs and joists—that create the joinery of coherently nested places?

The material for information architecture is mainly the semantic function of language. Names, categories, links, and conditional actions are not just for organizing objects but for also establishing place and shaping systemic relationships for entire environments. We can distill these elements into three categories (Figure 20-1): Labels, Relationships, and Rules.

 **Labels**

Relationships

Rules

FIGURE 20-1
My own take on the materials of information architecture: Labels,
Relationships, and Rules*

I've mentioned these in various forms in previous chapters, but bringing them together into a three-part list helps solidify them as a model.

These three items loosely correlate with the three levels in a model developed by information architect (and colleague) Dan Klyn: Ontology, Taxonomy, and Choreography (Figure 20-2).

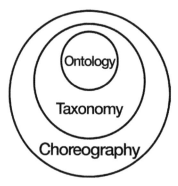

FIGURE 20-2
Dan Klyn's model for information architecture: Ontology, Taxonomy, and
Choreography†

I should note a few things about these models:

---

* Icons by *webalys.com*.

† Interpreted from a version by Abby Covert.

- These are general framing devices for helping us think through what we are making, and with what elements. However, I still recommend learning about the details—topics such as controlled vocabularies, synonym rings, metadata standards, and thesauri—from methods-based resources on information architecture and information science.

- I'm explaining the parts of these models in tandem, one pair at a time, because they resonate nicely with each other, but I don't mean to fully equate them. Labels have a lot to do with ontology, and vice versa, but they're lenses on how we locate specific meaning, not synonyms.

- There are other models for these ideas that I'm not including here.[*] They are all wonderful in their own ways. I encourage everyone to investigate them all and find the perspectives that help you most.

Labels and Ontology

Label: The word sounds deceptively trivial, like something we spit out of a grocery-store pricing gun. But, as Chapter 9 points out, labels are powerful, flexible devices that make it possible for us to have language at all, allowing us to create what philosopher Andy Clark calls the "new realm of perceptible objects."[†]

We could just as easily say "names" or "categories" or "classes" but these would be subsets of all the things we can mean by "labels." A label can be something we add to a physical object, or it can be the mechanism we use to talk about something that isn't specific or physical at all; for example a category, such as "jazz." It can be the name of a person, a code for a concept, or a class in a CSS file.

---

[*] I should mention that Jorge Arango also has a three-part model: Links, Nodes, and Order, that I really like as well. There is no single, right model for all this. I see all models as provisional, contextual, and nested among one another. Jorge's model is available at *http://www.jarango.com/blog/2013/04/07/links-nodes-order/*.

[†] Clark, Andy. *Supersizing the Mind: Embodiment, Action, and Cognitive Extension (Philosophy of Mind)*. London: Oxford University Press, 2010:1145–6, Kindle locations.

Clark further explains that "the simple act of labeling the world opens up a variety of new computational opportunities and supports the discovery of increasingly abstract patterns in nature."[*] Labeling the world structures it beyond what the structures of physical information alone can support. Ontology is a way of constructing a fully defined label; taxonomy is a way of associating labels with one another in a system of meaning.

Labels can be graphical or textual, or even gestures, but whichever way they appear, they function as language. We tend to think of labels as "extra," because a thing is the same thing whether it has a label or not. Hopefully, though, our foray into context, cognition, and language has made it clear that labels are anything but merely extra. Labels change the experienced nature of the things they name and otherwise signify.

For information architecture, labels are central. They're the ingredients we use for categories and classification schemes. They're the signifiers we use to represent the function and behavior of relationships and rules as well as the effects of digital agency. Even when we add longer text as instructional information, the instructions are finally just definitions for labels.

In semantic interfaces, labels are also the environmental objects that get the attention of agent perception; users seek them out to pick up information about where they can go, how the environment is nested, and what objects and events are available there. Users look for structural cues from the graphical user interface, as well, but words are always eventually necessary for context.[†] Far beyond interfaces, the purposeful definition of every component and connection within a service, system, or organization requires the use of labels.

---

[*]   ———. *Supersizing the Mind: Embodiment, Action, and Cognitive Extension (Philosophy of Mind)*. London: Oxford University Press, 2010:1128–32

[†] It is telling that, in the current move toward "flat" design, it's the simulated objects such as buttons that are being removed, putting even more weight on labels for establishing invariant structure.

Ontology is the way we establish the meaning of labels in semantic systems. As I've mentioned before, I'm not using the word in precisely the formal, technical manner or the conceptual, philosophical manner, but in a way that involves both. As Dan Klyn puts it succinctly, ontology is about "what we mean when we say what we say."[*]

Whether a formalized, technical ontology is necessary, there should be clarity about the semantic cornerstones that will set the alignment for everything else. Most organizations run on inherited assumptions and arbitrarily accumulated convention. They can stay in business for years, selling "product" to "customers" but never settle on what those words actually mean to the company. But, when their market is disrupted and complicates what their product is and who their customers are, the explicit definition of those terms becomes critical to survival.

When companies invoke a metaphor such as "the funnel" for marketing and retail, or "cloud"—as in *cloud computing*—the term eventually influences the way those companies think about and design their services.

"Cloud" has become a particularly pernicious rubric in the last few years. What's wrong with "cloud"? It obscures complexity rather than making it understandable.

Consider Apple's iCloud service. I'm often frustrated trying to understand how the places of iCloud work. For example, Figure 20-3 depicts a dialog box warning me if I turn off iCloud syncing for "Documents & Data, all documents stored in iCloud will be removed from this Mac." I've encountered similar warnings when changing iCloud settings, and each time I'm struck with anxiety, trying to sort out the difference between "there" and "here," and which documents on my laptop's drive are "in iCloud" and which are on my hard drive. This message box does nothing to help me remember the specific location of my files. What if none of them are on other devices? Does it delete them entirely? If they're on my laptop, why wouldn't they just be left there, but disconnected from syncing with the cloud service?

---

[*] Klyn, Dan. "Understanding Information Architecture." January 13, 2014 (*http://bit. ly/1x5o8Ql*).

FIGURE 20-3

An ambiguous and not very helpful iCloud message box: iConfused

According to one study, many Americans think cloud computing has something to do with actual clouds. Of the 54 percent of those surveyed who claimed never to use cloud computing, 95 percent actually do use cloud services without realizing it. When asked to explain what the cloud is, people tend to fake their way through the explanation.[*]

Ontology is at the root of this problem. There's no coherent invariant structure implied by the metaphor. In fact, cloud is an abdication of that architectural responsibility. It avoids the question of "where is my stuff, and what is happening to it?" by pretending as if no hard edges have to be understood—instead, the magic vapor in the sky will take care of it all for you. A cloud is, by definition, disconnected from the ground—it's a nonplace. But the fact is, your information is definitely in one or more places, on storage media in server farms that take up acres of land and gigawatts of electricity. It has rules and boundaries

---

[*] Citrix. "Most Americans Confused By Cloud Computing According to National Survey" August 28, 2012 (*http://bit.ly/125vdXZ*).

associated with it, structures that most users do not see or understand. We can use buildings because we can see the joinery in them and the complexity of their structure. A cloud has no clear structure. Though it can be pretty from the outside, from within it's just fog.

One of the more troublesome terms to define online is "account." Every place seems to need us to have an account, but an account is not something we can really point to or put our hands on. It's another reified idea, because an account is really just language. We can use the term for just about any sort of business relationship, which is why we end up with something like Figure 20-4, which shows an example at Kohls department store's website.

FIGURE 20-4
Kohl's disambiguation of "account"

The word "groups" can also be a bedeviling bit of semantic architecture. In physical life, your body can only cluster with one group of bodies at a time, and there's lots of tacit information about each group's context. But online, there are only labels, links, and conditional rulesets that form the architecture of these groups. You can be logged in to many at once, and the only way to differentiate between them is through their display-based signifiers. Also, the structures and rules that make it a group can differ widely from one group to another.

Google's use of the *groups* label is widespread, as is amply demonstrated in Figure 20-5. There are groups that you can create in your Contacts for use in Gmail; there are Google Groups (based on the long-acquired Deja News, which was a UseNet mirror); the Groups in the Google Apps for Business email platform, like personal Gmail groups but for businesses and custom domains; and others. You can convert a Business Apps Email Group to a Google Groups for Business Group, but doing so is daunting and requires comprehending both administrative paradigms. All this is not to mention the new Google Plus dimension of Circles that now intersects most of the Google ecosystem.

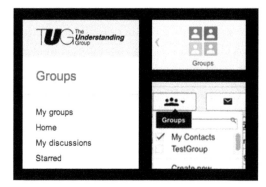

FIGURE 20-5
Just a few examples of groups among the many in the Google ecosystem

Undoubtedly, Google has defined formal ontologies for all these species of group in their backend systems. Yet, Google's environment struggles to establish coherent semantic function on the frontend, for human users. Data architecture does not equal information architecture, though each certainly depends on the other for user success.

Making multicontextual structures understandable is a difficult architectural problem to solve, especially when adding multiuser access. What users need is for those problems to be *solved*, not ignored. Rather than pretending everything is "seamless," we instead need well-crafted seams that we can see and understand how to use. In the words of Mark Weiser, one of the early pioneers of ubiquitous computing, we should make "beautiful seams" that transparently reveal the inner workings of these clockworks we now inhabit.* Our bodies can perceive how stairs work because of the structure implicit in the seams joining their surfaces. Likewise, semantic environments need seams that clearly indicate where and how one context joins to another. Seams demand the work of ontology, because seams are possible only if the edges of elements are defined in the first place.

---

* Greenfield, Adam. "On the ground running: Lessons from experience design." June 22, 2007 (*http://bit.ly/1oqMMvQ*).

Relationships and Taxonomy

Relationships are the associations between elements in an environment. A relationship is really an abstraction. Even with physical information, we don't perceive relationships, per se; we perceive surfaces and objects, which are nested as layouts. But the context of one thing's relation to another brings additional meaning for those elements.[*]

Sometimes, it's the nested relationships of superordinal to subordinal places and objects, as in a smartphone where an app is contained in a home screen, contained in the mobile device itself, all aggregating into the compound object we call "smartphone."

Moreover, sometimes these relationships are about the *connections* between separate objects or places. Ecologically, we evolved to depend upon these connections as stable paths. Thus, we tend to expect even our digital connections—from hyperlinks to API calls—to be invariant, even when we perceive only the outer effects of their digital inner workings.

Just as a river can connect various cities with trade, digital connections can make relationships that entire markets depend on. Consider when Twitter changed its API in 2012, removing support for RSS and limiting the API's usage by certain third-party clients: app developers who had depended on the old API as an invariant part of the environment found themselves without a product anymore.[†]

To work with semantic relationships, we use signifiers that indicate what is related. These signifiers are also labels, with all the qualities of labels, as previously outlined. In user interfaces, we pay a lot of attention to these semantic signifiers because they have to do all the heavy lifting for expressing relationships. A bakery on the street can be called "Jane's" on the sign, but the smell of bread and the baked goods in the window can do the rest of the work. Online, though, we need semantic equivalents of the smell of bread and the shop window, from the company name to the metadata for Yelp, Google, and the rest.

---

[*] In previous work, I've used "connections" here, but I now think "relationships" is a better way to frame the idea.

[†] Warren, Christina. "New Twitter API Drops Support for RSS, Puts Limits on Third-Party Clients." Mashable.com Sept 5, 2012 (*http://mashable.com/2012/09/05/twitter-api-rss/*).

In fact, with digital information, we can make relationships between things that we can't even see but whose well-defined relationships are crucial for infrastructure. The relationships defined in database schemas are arguably now the majority of important semantic-information relationships in our world.

Web-centered information architecture has long been concerned with hyperlinks and their relationships; but hyperlinks—though revolutionary in their own way—are only one way we establish relationships online or off. Here's a question I find myself asking often in projects: in what way can information architecture use semantic information to shape and clarify the relationships between physical life and digital function? Starting with that frame of mind can open up many opportunities for great work, beyond hyperlinks.

A general term we use for making relationships with language is *taxonomy*. There's a common assumption that a taxonomy is always a hierarchical classification scheme—a "tree-shaped" structure, with the broadest category at the top, and subsequently narrower categories on the way down. That's a common *type* of taxonomy, but not the only one.

Taxonomies are always semantic in nature, and they always have to do with the relationships between elements. But, they can take many forms, such as lists, hierarchies, matrices, facets, and even continuums or systemic maps.* Many of the models in this book are actually taxonomies, expressed as diagrams.

The term comes from two Greek roots: "taxis," which means the ordering or arrangement of things; and "nomos," which is "anything assigned, usage or custom, law or ordinance." In *Organising Knowledge: Taxonomies, Knowledge, and Organisational Effectiveness* (Chandos Publishing), Patrick Lambe defines taxonomy as "the rules or conventions of order or arrangement."† Taxonomy creates relationships that arrange and order units of meaning. And, it can do so using an explicitly defined rule, or through tacitly emergent convention, or through some means between those extremes.

---

* Lambe, Patrick. *Organising Knowledge: Taxonomies, Knowledge and Organisational Effectiveness.* Oxford, England: Chandos Publishing, 2007:10.

† ———. *Organising Knowledge: Taxonomies, Knowledge and Organisational Effectiveness.* Oxford, England: Chandos Publishing, 2007:4.

Hence, taxonomies are *the ways we arrange the world with language.* They're what we use to represent the physical and semantic information of our environment, creating structures and relationships, classifications and nested places. They're the way we put joinery between semantic surfaces into the environment.

Ontologies and taxonomies have a symbiotic relationship; arguably you can't truly create one without the other. Ontologies require defining, and definitions are (by definition!) about relationships that give context to the thing defined; taxonomies have a hard time being very solid until at least some of the key terms in them have been well delineated, or else they can become too porous, absorbing generalities until they lose specific utility.

Taxonomies follow some physical, ecological principles, even though they're semantic. In an insight that echoes J. J. Gibson, Lambe explains how people usually start with "basic-level categories" that are not "the most granular, atomistic elements in our world. They tend to be whole objects we can identify and act upon in a direct way. Linguistically, we have shorter and simpler names for them compared to other objects, and they tend to be accessible things that populate our everyday world."[*]

We begin with things such as "apple" and "clock." We then work our way out and up to larger, broader categories (fruit, orchard, harvest, timepiece, engineering) or inward and down to smaller bits (tyrosinase enzyme, fructose, molecule, pinion, spring, atomic structure of brass). This pattern we have with language correlates with the way we perceive physical information: at the body-relevant level first, and then working our way beyond that level to the broadest canopy around us and down to tiny objects—attention that we augment with telescopes and microscopes.

When we navigate an environment, we pay attention first to the objects that are most relevant to our needs as well as our bodies, even when considering semantic information. When I visit a hospital or other building with medical offices, I need to figure out which office has the doctor I want to see. Hopefully, I find a directory of some sort in the lobby, where I can find my doctor's name and office number. I'm not

---

[*] ———. *Organising Knowledge: Taxonomies, Knowledge and Organisational Effectiveness.* Oxford, England: Chandos Publishing, 2007:16.

interested in learning the entire building, and I'm not interested in how my doctor is related to all the others. Likewise, I don't care just yet what rooms are inside my doctor's suite—I won't worry about that until I'm in the waiting room. We treat all sorts of environments this way, from websites and cable TV guides to subways and cities.

Taxonomies can help us translate between different perspectives—serving as a Rosetta stone between cultural *umwelts*. For example, in an effort to help scientists better explain climate change, some have been creating guides to improving the way scientists translate the language of theory to the language of laypeople, as shown in Figure 20-6.

Terms that have different meanings for scientists and the public		
Scientific term	**Public meaning**	**Better choice**
enhance	improve	intensify, increase
aerosol	spray can	tiny atmospheric particle
positive trend	good trend	upward trend
positive feedback	good response, praise	vicious cycle, self-reinforcing cycle
theory	hunch, speculation	scientific understanding
uncertainty	ignorance	range
error	mistake, wrong, incorrect	difference from exact true number
bias	distortion, political motive	offset from an observation
sign	indication, astrological sign	plus or minus sign
values	ethics, monetary value	numbers, quantity
manipulation	illicit tampering	scientific data processing
scheme	devious plot	systematic plan
anomaly	abnormal occurrence	change from long-term average

FIGURE 20-6

A table of terms and their public meanings, with recommendations for more accurate communication of the intended meanings*

This table reminds us that there is often no one way to label something that has the same information scent or explicit definition to everyone—it can even mean opposite things in different contexts.

---

* Somerville, Richard C. J., and Susan Joy Hassol. "Communicating the science of climate change." *Physics Today*, October, 2011:51.

When we design environments in which different perspectives are in play, we can use taxonomies to create thesauri to do these translations. We can also use *faceted classification*, an especially powerful taxonomical form. Developed in 1932 by Indian librarian S.R. Ranganathan, this "colon classification" approach gives us a technique to create highly scalable, adaptive classes based on combinations of mutually exclusive category lists. For example, we could use three simple categories to string together the classes for an online document repository: Author :: Date/Time :: File Type. There is no superordinal or subordinal structure; there is only a string of attributes, in unique combinations (ensured here by the fact that no one author will have created more than one file at exactly the same time). If more metadata were needed, we could add more facets.

Faceted classification is an excellent invention for accommodating the nested, nonlinear ways we experience context. It can expand and recombine to take on new perspectives and permutations, and provides us with the means to come at the world from multiple angles of entry. It's essentially categorization as *collage* rather than a single lens.

But be prepared: it can be surprising how resistant business and technology partners can be to a non-single-hierarchy worldview. The Cartesian habits that make us want a single hierarchy are deeply ingrained.

Rules and Choreography

By rules, I mean prescribed principles, guidelines, or conditional procedures for action. Like relationships, rules themselves are not perceived directly. We instead perceive the information we use to make them, or we perceive their effects, but the logic that makes a rule work is abstract. The etymology of the word "rule" tells us that it's always been about language: pronouncements, directives, orders, stipulations, and so on.

Although rules are language-based, they can be embodied in the environment. The simple wall in the field shown in Chapter 1 instantiates a rule about what can move from one side to the other, or perhaps the ownership of the land. A complex rule, with conditional logic, can determine that cars can cross a drawbridge until a boat needs to be let through. The bridge's action makes the rule manifest, but the semantic expression of the rule came first.

We also use semantic information to put rules into our environment all the time. The line painted down the middle of the road is a semantic expression that we treat as if it were physical. Likewise, the law stating we should not cross over that line is another semantically expressed rule. When we make a contractual agreement, we are agreeing to abide by semantic environmental structures—many of which are signified by defined labels, or "terms" of the agreement.* And, as we've seen, software is made of rules, and its conditional logic works as a sort of legislation for software-dependent environments.

It is important that we expand the concept of information architecture as sharing responsibility for rule definition. The early focus on the *arrangement of content* for browsing, searching, and retrieving is only a microcosm of the larger concern: planning and structuring *environments for habitation*.

One way of thinking about the rules is as a set of instructions for how environments should behave—a sort of *choreography* for the coupled dance between agents, the elements we design, and the elements of the environment that are already there.

We can think of choreography as a predefined set of instructions, as in traditional ballet. But, we can also think of it as a set of patterns to be recombined and improvised, as in tap and swing dancing. As Klyn puts it, "The essence of choreography is the placement of meaning and structure into a flow with a specific context."† The flow is the continual action of the agent's embodied engagement with the elements of the environment; the context is ultimately how the agent understands those elements and how they relate.

Consider a quintessential, traditional information architecture project such as designing the taxonomy and search for a retailer. Even though this sort of design problem has had known solutions for many years now, we're still evolving the way websites handle the nonlinear, idiosyncratic actions of "shoppers." For one thing, retailers must learn that not everyone is actually a shopper. Site visitors are often using

---

* The use of the word "terms" as part of a contractual agreement is one of the lovely examples of synecdoche (essentially conflating a signifier with the whole of what it represents) we rely on to both communicate and create our environment.

† Klyn, Dan. "Understanding Information Architecture," January 13, 2014 (*http://bit. ly/1x5o8Ql*).

products as proxies for learning, dreaming, or solving a problem. And they come at the task of looking at products from many different situational contexts.

People *satisfice* when they browse and search—they engage whatever most immediately triggers the "scent" related to their present situation. In fact, "browse" and "search" are reified ideas that have more to do with the way the system constrains choice of action than the sorts of actions a user might take without such constraints. Everything a user does boils down to taking action in the environment, seeing what happens, and calibrating further action based on that feedback loop. Putting words in a search field or tapping on a label are both just different forms of tossing language at the world and seeing what the world gives you back. We can't choreograph those activities in a linear, predefined manner. All we can do is have the right patterns to gracefully dance along with whatever moves the user might make.

Information architecture must accommodate the way people actually find and create their own meaning. So, for example, if we define "navigation" as the reified menus of lists found in sites and apps, we miss the point entirely. As Resmini and Rosati memorably say, "We say navigate, but really mean understand."[*] Navigation isn't really about the "chrome"—the fly-outs, mega-menus, and sidebar lists. It's about taking action in the *whole* environment toward discovering the next needed action and the next after that. People look for the right "scent" of semantic function, and resort to the machinery of navigation menus mainly when other actions aren't improving the scent.

So, architectures can't always engineer people's actions; they have to accommodate and assist them, instead. Resmini and Rosati refer to this capability as *resilience*, an information architecture heuristic they define as "the capability of a pervasive information architecture model to shape and adapt itself to specific users, needs, and seeking strategies."[†] It doesn't require space-age intelligent systems. Often, resilience is just a matter of creating simple structures that have facets and options that catch users where they are, from their particular points

---

* Resmini, Andrea, and Luca Rosati. *Pervasive Information Architecture: Designing Cross-Channel User Experiences.* Burlington, MA: Morgan Kaufmann, 2011:66.

† ———. *Pervasive Information Architecture: Designing Cross-Channel User Experiences.* Burlington, MA: Morgan Kaufmann, 2011:113.

of view. A website might not need some advanced algorithm to get a user to the right input form if the site's structure simply uses better information scent and instructional content. Likewise, a cross-channel service can accommodate great complexity just by providing the right hubs of service interaction, clearly orchestrated, to allow customers to move among them in their own idiosyncratic ways. Resilient conditional frameworks can make the difference between a dead, static museum of information and a living, breathing environment that the user experiences as an embodied conversation through action.

Sometimes, a linear path is necessary—for trained workers doing rote data entry, perhaps. But most software isn't being made for those situations anymore. Some amount of wandering is often the most valuable part of the experience. Information architectures are constructs that help people understand their own actions, situations, and needs; good information architecture helps people discover their ultimate narrative along their own, uniquely wandering path.

We've mainly learned these lessons on websites for the last 20-odd years. Now we need to use these lessons in how we use information to ground, inform, scaffold, and nudge people's understanding beyond the confines of individual computer screens, or within just one piece of software.

IFTTT (If This Then That) is accessed by users through a website or an app, but it's actually a cross-channel service framework that has the potential to let users create architectures of their own for any networked device. For users to understand how to use IFTTT (see Figure 20-7), the service has to articulate itself in a way that provides clear instruction. Consequently, it crafted a clear taxonomy for the building blocks and functions available: Channels, Triggers, Actions, and so on. A "channel" is one of the cloud-based services; a "trigger" is the "this" object in "if this then that." "On/Off" is binary mode setting for whether the recipe is active or inactive. These work almost like facets do—mutually exclusive sorts of elements that, like noun, verb, and adjective, perform specific roles in a grammar of digital-agent assembly.

The choreography here is twofold: the rules packaged into a kit of digital objects, and the dance the user can create by playing with the parts to make new, soft machines.

Service design brings a comprehensive approach to choreography, where designers consider every context in a service ecosystem. Service designs don't necessarily involve digital information, but it is telling that the discipline has grown so much in the post-Internet age, when services can involve so many channels and information layers not previously available. With smartphones and ambient devices, services can be choreographed intimately with individual user action, on the fly.

FIGURE 20-7

Taxonomy of functions on IFTTT, from the service's website at *IFTTT.com*

The Uber car service is a recent favorite example of service design. Uber uses a smartphone app as a customer's interface to a service that helps find a ride from a group of Uber cab drivers near the customer's location, as shown in Figure 20-8, left.

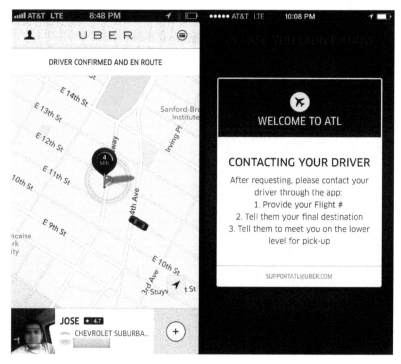

FIGURE 20-8
After requesting a car, I can watch my driver (identity obscured here) on the way to pick me up, live on a New York City map

Even though I'm standing in the midst of the unplanned, open environment of a busy cityscape, as soon as I engage the Uber service, I'm gently lifted into a service experience in which nearly everything is automated and requires very little of my effort. The driver arrives where I am—I don't have to chase and hail cabs. I have contextual information about the driver's identity, vehicle, and arrival. And when I get to my destination, I don't have to fuss with a tip—the service is set up to pay its drivers without bothering the customer. The "tip" comes in the form of a quick one- to five-star review I can choose to complete in the app.

Speaking of context, when I finish my New York trip and arrive in Atlanta, the Uber app is ready with a helpful instructional message (Figure 20-8, right) specifically designed for the Atlanta airport context—complete with which level of the airport I should use for pickup.

Although any service has opportunities for improvement, there is much to appreciate in the Uber experience, at least based on my interactions as a customer. It turns a regular car into a digital object, along with the driver and the passenger, but without *making the customer feel like an object*. It doesn't hide seams that users need to see but does hide the ones they don't.

There are well-considered interactions at the level of interface here, and a great deal of technical prowess enabling the service. But there's an architecture at work, as well: the labels, relationships, and rules that choreograph the coordination between physical location, semantic sensemaking, and digital systems. Whether anyone on Uber's design team *calls* these aspects information architecture or not, this is information in the service of environmental structure and understanding. It requires an architecturally coherent system for placemaking and sensemaking, through and through.

The Organization as Medium

The level of choreography we see with services such as Uber is very difficult to achieve, even for a start-up that has no "legacy" baggage to corrupt its mission. But, like it or not, most of our work tends to be with existing companies that have longer histories—full of barnacles, cluttered basements, and skeletons in the closet.

Because organizations are essentially made of information—they are what they are because they're "organized" after all—there's no reason why they can't be used as raw material for creating great contextual experiences, contextually aware capabilities, and clear, beautifully "seamful" architectures. However, doing it requires facing some truths about the nature of organizations.

There's an adage called Conway's law, named after Melvin Conway, who introduced the idea in 1968. It states that organizations that design systems "are constrained to produce designs which are copies of the communication structures of these organizations."[*] The nested structures of the organizational environment become a collectively binding map of the way that organization sees the world, nudging it into creating all environments in its image.

The organizational map is often bound up with its existing machinery—the dysfunctional plumbing of its infrastructure. The map is in turn further etched into the organization by those stubbornly influential systems. Kohls can't magically make a single, consolidated place where a customer can manage both the credit card account and the web-shopping account, because they're fundamentally separate businesses—a bank and a retailer—merely portraying themselves under one brand. Delta has millions of customers and deep legacy data structures that already understand "Silver, Gold, Platinum"; it's beyond nontrivial to blow it all up and start over with a more scalable loyalty structure, so they resort to bolting on new dimensions that don't nest coherently.

Google can't easily change what it means by "groups," partly because some of the features are acquired systems that had to be grafted onto decade-old infrastructure. Apple, as disciplined as it might be in its design aesthetic, is only mortal, and struggles to create a coherent layout between its many deep silos and existing services infrastructures. Organizations are organisms of a sort, with their own perceptions, learned habits, and joints that bend only one way or another.

Technology departments tend not to concern themselves with how everything relates to everything else, but to focus mainly on the mechanics of engineering for defined requirements. Rather than *composition*, computer science—and IT engineering—is often more focused on what it calls *decomposition*, whereby a complex system is broken down into parts in order to better organize its work and maintain it. This is certainly a necessary effort, but it often becomes an end in itself, losing the original holistic context of the system. As Paul Dourish notes, "The typical conception of context in technical systems is of information of a middling relevance."[†] When the environment is "decomposed" into tiny objects, they become the most relevant elements in the work, losing the composed context for why the parts should exist.

---

[*] Conway, Melvin E. "How do Committees Invent?" *Datamation* April, 1968; 14(5):28–31. (Retrieved 2009-04-05)

[†] Dourish, Paul. *What We Talk About When We Talk About Context.* 2004.

In built-environment architecture, this effort of establishing the full purpose and context of a building before designing it is called *programming*. (Alas, this word has other uses in IT departments.) Different from something like a project charter—which is normally used only until resources are assigned and a project has kicked off—an architectural program (or "brief") is a constant touchstone throughout the process. It's the first articulation of *why* a building is to exist and what its functional value should be, and it's the continually updated standard by which the specifics of design are evaluated.

The way we document and articulate our work shapes the way the work is done. No matter how much more advanced our technology becomes, our failure to grasp the importance of "language as infrastructure" will undermine our ability to solve contextual problems.

And, when companies define their business rules, they are using language to establish how the world will work, long before anyone is explicitly "designing" anything. In my experience, however, more often than not I've seen the business side of the organization abdicate much of the responsibility for the rigor of business rules, opting instead to just generally state vague wishes and leave the hard details to IT.

Making complex, pervasive systems work well contextually will require more and better effort from business and design stakeholders in collaboratively composing business rules. That's because business rules are *architecture*. They are blueprints—maps—that describe the natural laws of the to-be-made territory. They use language to create molds, which will then be used to cast the gears and armatures of the machinery upon which the business depends.

So, one challenge for information architecture practitioners is to not only understand the end user, but to understand the organization that is making something for the user to begin with. Large organizations especially have trouble with semantic confusion because there are so many different political factions and cultural silos involved. Departments of engineers, marketing professionals, and executive management all tend to understand language from different perspectives. Any user-experience designer who has tried to explain why "research" is necessary, even though the Marketing/Communications department has done lots of "research" already, has experienced the pain of these disconnects.

As information architect Abby Covert says in her book *How to Make Sense of Any Mess*:

> I once had a project where the word "asset" was defined three different ways across five teams.
>
> I once spent three days defining the word "customer."
>
> I once defined and documented over a hundred acronyms in the first week of a project for a large company, only to find 30 more the next week.
>
> I wish I could say that I'm exaggerating or that any of this effort was unnecessary. Nope. Needed.
>
> Language is complex. But language is also fundamental to understanding our direction.*

Meaning is a participatory sport, in which the game can seem completely different depending on the perspective of any given player. But, we can minimize risks if we work to understand the collage of perspectives and learned meanings that will be perceiving the structures we introduce to the world. Semantic information is *also* the territory. There's already a map driving the creation of new environment, whether we acknowledge it or not. *Semantics are never "just semantics."*

I like the thought of the organization as a medium for understanding—a material we can reframe, recalibrate, refine. This is basically what we're doing when we introduce new language into organizations; powerful semantic function can get into the body politic and change its shape, like stem cells that grow new bones over time. No joke; I've seen it happen!

But even if we don't change the organization as a whole, we still need to change parts of it enough to accommodate and support the new architectures it needs; otherwise, the new organs are easily rejected, abandoned, or neutralized through assimilation.

---

* Covert, Abby. How to Make Sense of Any Mess. (Author) 2014.

[21]

Narratives and Situations

The Universe is made of stories, not of atoms.
—MURIEL RUKEYSER

People Make Sense Through Stories

BEFORE COMPOSING SOMETHING *new* WE SHOULD UNDERSTAND WHAT IS ALREADY THERE. But we've already established that there is no stable, persistent "context" to begin with—that it emerges through action. So, how do we understand the current state if it won't sit still? The key is in studying the experience from the points of view of the agents involved and how they think and behave. Those points of view provide the dynamic landscape—and the principles we derive from it—that puts everything else into perspective. These agents can be individual users, groups of them, organizations, and even digital actors. Let's begin with how humans work—and how they understand their experience as *narrative*. Recall our working definition: *context is an agent's understanding of the relationships between the elements of the agent's environment.*

The environment exerts more control over that understanding and action than we often realize, but that influence over the experience has its limits. Ultimately, the final interpretation and recollection of any experience is up to the individual who has it.

As we learned earlier, a stone lying along a path can be clutter, a tool, or a piece of a wall—it all depends on the context the agent brings to the perception of the stone. People find meaning in the environment even when there is no semantic information there at all: clouds can look like trains and elephants; the burn marks in toast can look like a religious icon; tree branches can look like human arms. The way we perceive our environment in the moment is through information pickup, but the way we understand our experience is through narrative.

Humans make sense of the world through stories. Unlike our nearest primate cousins, we have the ability to follow a substantial narrative such as in a conventional-length movie. Our brains don't only react to each moment of action; we can also integrate complex threads of story over a significant period of time.* We bring this ability to our own lives and how we find meaning in our actions and experiences. What we do in a given day might or might not have linear causality or rationale. But, we can't help seeing a narrative (Figure 21-1) when looking back on those disparate events. Our personal stories are what we construct for ourselves in hindsight.

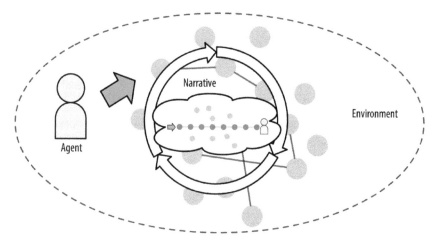

FIGURE 21-1

Narrative is a function of the agent's action and perception in the environment

Consciousness is not a single entity; it involves many processes and specialized systems across the entire organism, many of which aren't obviously connected.† Remember, we perceive-and-act by using *soft assembly* (Chapter 4): our bodies are full of tiny sensemaking systems and feedback loops for which there is no empirically identifiable "boss" in charge. It's the coalescence of all those disparate systems that makes

---

* Hughes, Virginia. "How Monkeys Watch Movies and People Tell Stories," *National Geographic* November 7, 2013 (*http://bit.ly/1rpQC33*).

† Gazzaniga, Michael S. "The Storyteller In Your Head," *Discover*. Spring, 2012 (*http://bit. ly/125yRBa*).

it possible for us to perceive ourselves as discrete, coherent selves with personal histories. Consciousness emerges because we have the ability to interpret our experience, reconstituting it into a narrative whole.

A lot of this story-weaving happens in what we colloquially call "daydreaming." It turns out daydreaming is a complex family of psychological activities that take up much more of our lives than we realize, and could even be the mind's default state.[*] Stories, and their indirect lessons, have even been shown to be a superior way of teaching children new behaviors than just-the-facts instruction.[†]

Although it's true that most of our actions in a given moment aren't explicitly conscious, our later recall of those actions tends to be a conscious, narrative-weaving act, even if it's a split second afterward. In fact, the effect left on us from the pain or pleasure of an experience is largely reconstructed from only parts of what we actually experienced, according to what's been called the *Peak and End Rule*: "Global evaluations are predicted with high accuracy by a weighted combination of the most extreme affect recorded during the episode and the affect recorded during the terminal moments of the episode."[‡] For example, if asked to rate our enjoyment of a movie every few minutes as we're watching it, the average of our ratings during the movie doesn't necessarily correspond to how we rate the movie after it's over. So, we might see a film that's actually quite mediocre, but rate it highly if it has a great middle and ending. This effect can work the other way, as well—a really crummy ending can drastically harm our remembered experience of an otherwise excellent film.

Other research has qualified this finding: even though the emotional effect is strong, it doesn't mean we remember the *facts* of the peak and end any better than the rest of the experience—and, the memory is more affected by the end than the peak.[§] Those strong emotional points, and strong emotion in general, can shape and distort our nar-

---

[*] Gottschall, Jonathan. *The Storytelling Animal: How Stories Make Us Human.* Boston: Houghton Mifflin Harcourt, 2012:11.

[†] *Dev Sci.* September, 2011;14(5):944–8. doi: 10.1111/j.1467-7687.2011.01043.x. Epub 2011 Apr 28 (*http://www.ncbi.nlm.nih.gov/pubmed/21884310*).

[‡] Kahneman, Daniel, and Amos Tversky. *Choices, Values, and Frames.* First edition. Cambridge, England: Cambridge University Press, 2000:769.

[§] Kemp, Simon, Christopher D. B. Burt, Laura Furneaux. "A test of the peak-end rule with extended autobiographical events." *Memory & Cognition* January, 2008;36(1):132–8.

ratives in relation to actual facts. According to one neuroscientist, "We all have narratives....We're all creating stories. Our lives are stories in that sense."[*] Initial, direct perception occurs outside this narrative construct, but it generates and feeds the narrative; by the time we are *aware* of and reflecting upon any perception, it's part of our narrative.

Context emerges out of action and sensemaking. But that doesn't mean the environmental elements we design don't have any structural, narrative influence. Even though we can't literally reach into a person's consciousness and meticulously create an experience, we can definitely shape the environment in a way that all but guarantees one sort of an experience over another. People don't visit Disney World and mistake it for Las Vegas; and they don't visit Amazon and mistake it for the Library of Congress. The structures of those environments, the combinations of what actions they enable, make them places that nudge people into particular sorts of experiences that meet specific needs.

Still, ultimately, information architectures invite agents into a dance with the environment, in which the outcome is always unique, no matter how immersive or carefully sculpted the structures and rules we create.

Intentions and Intersections

I remember going to Disney World with my parents when I was around seven years old. At the time, I was crazy for space stuff—astronauts, moon landings, everything. I'd heard of Disney World's Space Mountain and couldn't wait to see it in person. This was the 1970s, so there was no website to read about the attractions; our only knowledge was based on a few scraps gathered from pictures on TV. My parents and I assumed it was going to be like an indoor museum of space-themed exhibits. After all, what else would be in a big futuristic dome-like structure (see Figure 21-2) like that?

---

[*] Hayasaki, Erika. "How Many of Your Memories Are Fake?" *The Atlantic*, November 18, 2013 (*http://theatln.tc/1wmrcrg*).

FIGURE 21-2

Space Mountain: an enclosed environment, with few external cues about its internal structures. Photo by author

My dad was the one who took me inside. After waiting in line for a while and getting strapped into a rocket-shaped rail car, imagine our surprise when we took off at high speed through a twisting, jarring, and nearly dark roller coaster—my dad gripping my waist, afraid I'd slip out into the void. It was thrilling, but not what we were expecting. When we finally disembarked, stunned and bewildered, we wondered how we hadn't realized what we were getting ourselves into.

I tell this story to illustrate the slippery relationship between experience and design. Space Mountain is an exceedingly immersive environment, purposefully designed, and structurally linear. If anything could exert complete control over an experience, it would be something like that ride. And yet, my dad and I didn't experience it in quite the way Disney's Imagineers intended. We misunderstood the context of place, and misread signifiers—semantic functions and physical affordances—until it was too late to back out. (Of course, when I was older, I couldn't wait to go back and ride it again!)

What we design is environmental (Figure 21-3), and the environment exerts control over what is possible to perceive and act upon. We didn't emerge from Space Mountain recollecting it as a water ride, or a rock concert—that would've been nonsense. But, we did manage to slip through an unintentional loophole, because our expectations remained unchanged until we were zooming through the dark.

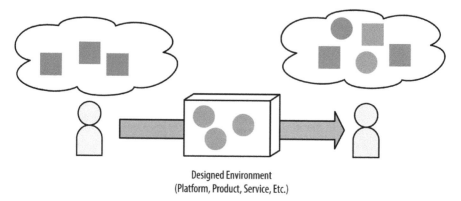

Designed Environment
(Platform, Product, Service, Etc.)

FIGURE 21-3

Designed environments should meet people where they are, and supplement their narrative with what they to take away from the experience

Context involves the stories people bring along with them. Their recollections of prior experience, combined with their "feel" for where they're headed (whether an explicit goal or a tacitly meandering direction), are part of the context for which we design. As much as we'd like to think that we can completely control the experience and reset the users' expectations, we can't fully control their narrative. We can only influence it, nudge it, with environmental conditions—sometimes significantly, and sometimes only marginally, but never completely. For my dad and me, roller coasters were always outdoors, and enclosed attractions were always more subdued, based on our learned experience.

Of course, I love Space Mountain and I hope Disney never retires it. It's a thrill ride, and it did its job. However, when people need an environment to meet the expectations of invariance that it signals, only to find out it's not what it seems, the result is real damage—to people's trust, or worse.

The Tales Organizations Tell

Users aren't the only ones with a narrative perspective, or who work their way through an environment in an embodied, tacit manner. Organizations are made of people, so when all those different individual perspectives are added together, an aggregate narrative emerges. Or, many narratives emerge from subcultures in the organization, which frequently conflict with one another. Often, you can see the narratives rubbing against one another in the structural distortions and fissures of the environments the organization creates.

Take, for example, the global navigation structure for the Starbucks website shown in Figure 21-4.*

FIGURE 21-4
The Starbucks website global navigation menu

Even before opening each top-level mega-menu, it is clear that there are several cultures within the company that are trying to express themselves within the "top" structure of the site. Why is there Coffee but also Coffeehouse? Because *Coffeehouse* is actually a label for Starbucks' foray into entertainment media, part of its attempt to make itself a lifestyle brand that goes beyond coffee and snacks. It borrows from cultural affectation more than from clearly signified indication of its contents. What is Menu? It's about the food and drink available at the physical Starbucks shops, which some might think of as more related to the Coffeehouse menu item, but the relationship is muddled.

Card is about the ways in which customers can use the object of "card" to have a "rewards" account with Starbucks, but it's also about gift cards, which are not the same as "rewards membership" cards. This distinction is not easy to discern, even after reading the site's content. One part of the company is pushing a rewards program; another part is pushing the ability to transact within the nested structure of a long-term "account" relationship with Starbucks, and another is managing the product/service of gift cards. It turns out, however, that gift cards and rewards cards are not well connected in this service ecosystem. We haven't even touched on the public-relations-driven priorities of the Responsibility area, or the confusing relationship between Shop and Menu (am I in a Starbucks store of sorts while I'm on the site?).

---

* Hat tip to Dan Klyn for making me aware of this example.

These are elements that do not nest; they are parts that are not well composed. It's not a "society of rooms" as much as a "jumble of objectives." They reflect silos in which specific sets of requirements were met, but then thrust into the pile of "brand" like one might jam a juicer into an overstuffed attic.

What I hope is, after the preceding chapters, this no longer seems a hopeless mish-mash, but a sort of X-ray film with which you can begin to diagnose the structural problems of labels, relationships, and rules. It's the first step toward considering how it might be improved with a clear ontology, a well-formed taxonomy, and a resilient choreography across the service life cycle. Information architecture can address the contextual dissonance here by identifying the joints in the Starbucks semantic universe and prescribing how they should be mended and reshaped.

The card, the physical store, the smartphone app, and the website all seem to have different perspectives on how the entire ecosystem should operate. The language facing the user is part of the problem, but the deeper problems come from how the organization uses language to define what it's putting into the world in the first place.

Semantic information behaves as organizational infrastructure, as depicted in Figure 21-5, explicitly and tacitly, in at least two dimensions—in a vertical stack from the user-facing language of interfaces all the way to the entities in a data architecture, and in a horizontal dimension across all the channels the organization uses for interfacing with customers and partners.*

Layers like these are what make manifest the organizational narrative. The stories it tells itself are etched into its infrastructure, its departmental org charts, and its communication channels. Understanding the organization is an essential part of information architecture. No matter what user research discovers, it is often overshadowed by the hidden narratives and maps that such research could bring into visibility when used on the organization itself.

---

* You can find a related concept involving two axes in *Pervasive Information Architecture: Designing Cross-Channel User Experiences*, p. 183.

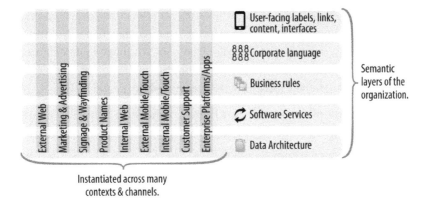

FIGURE 21-5
Semantic layers of an organization, across a sampling of channels

If the organization is trying to develop its own product and service spectrum but is also acquiring products and services by purchasing third-party platforms and companies, these two narratives will clash without careful architectural attention. Or, if the organization is driven by silo-generated narratives, even its internally created structures will scrape against one another and distort coherence by the time they reach the user.

Recall the Google Groups example: acquired or newly developed layers of the Google ecosystem, all created to be some kind of "group" capability, but without really defining what "group" means in the context of all the others. Or, consider Apple's iTunes, which has long ago lost any coherent sense of being a music application, contorting itself over the years into a surreal goulash of ingredients: a multimedia purchase channel, a media file-management platform, a software app purchase store (but only for some kinds of software), customer-account management portal, and driver of core operating system components.

In all these cases, ambitious new platforms were added to existing ones, rich feature-sets were integrated into the environment, and teams shipped working software that *technically* delivered on each project's requirements. And yet, it ended up rendering confusing, frustrating experiences.

More often than not, if we pay adequate attention to how language is acting as infrastructure, we have more success when we make new things. The answer to the question "What are we making" should attend to more than the roster of features on a wish list, whether the list comes from an executive or voice-of-the-customer data. It is fundamentally an *ontological* discussion that uses language to determine *what* the organization is doing to the existing environment, and *why*, before jumping to *how* features will be acquired or added.

Narratives and situations all contribute to the way context is composed through the ongoing engagement between agent and environment. The compositional elements aren't limited to what happens in a project room. When devising the information architectures for these omni-channel environments, we need to consider multiple points of view, based on real-life understanding of people, systems, *and* organizations.

Situations over Goals

Organizations have a vested interest in their stories. Regardless of what challenges they face in their current dysfunctions, their aspirations tend to be toward efficiency, linearity, and planned outcomes. The received wisdom of user experience can often be just as vested in those assumptions. For example, a sacred tenet is that we should understand the *goals* of users and design for those goals. That principle sounds fine on its face, but the truth is more complicated. Remember: our preconscious, tacitly comprehended encounters with the environment are what drive most of our actions in a typical day. And, the way we experience something is based more on our peak-and-end heightened recollection than the actual facts of the activity.

It turns out, there's no straightforward way to always know someone's goal. The goal is often a reification—part of a story that didn't exist before the activity. When watching how people actually think and behave outside of a usability lab—starting before they've engaged a product or service, and seeing how they behave all the way through—we find many of these goals emerge and take form *during* that engagement, rather than being fully formed plans ahead of time. And, they can be very different afterward than they were up until moments before the experience was completed.

People "confabulate" their experience to the point at which, according to neuroscientist Michael Gazzaniga, "listening to people's explanations is interesting...but often a waste of time."[*] For neuroscience research, it might be a "waste," but I still believe hearing people's stories is important work for designers, because we're not scientists trying to understand the brain; we're designers interested in how people understand their experience, even if the story is distorted in retrospect. We should definitely learn how users formulate and think about their goals. We just need to get underneath those stories and figure out what's contributing to them.

In one of my projects some years ago, a financial services company wanted to provide investors or their trusted partners with the capability to change power of attorney for their assets on the website rather than having to use a paper form. When we talked to users about how they had done this in the past, their recollections were about "getting a form, filling it out, and mailing it in." The main issues they remembered having were more about understanding the form, and the annoyances of printing, completing, and sending it.

So, what was missed in these interviews? Most of what was really important, it turns out. Because they knew we were working on a website, these users often unconsciously tried meeting us halfway by framing their answers in terms that they assumed we needed. Especially if we asked them, "What were your goals?"—they of course answered in the terms the questions established: framed as goals. Besides, who wants to believe they do anything without first having a goal? It would be embarrassing to tell your banker, "I didn't really have a plan; I was just feeling my way through."

But if we asked without priming the users with that context, their storytelling would be closer to the raw situation they were in—for example, "I just got remarried, and I want to be sure this time my spouse and I have ownership sorted out responsibly," and not "I guess I'd look for the right form to fill out."

---

[*] Gazzaniga, Michael S. "The 'Interpreter' in Your Head Spins Stories to Make Sense of the World," *Discover Magazine*, August 1, 2012 (*http://bit.ly/10jfDHF*).

When we studied click-path logs of people who eventually found and used the proper form, we found their paths wandered—like the information-scent berry-pickers we humans are—working through what they could find about their current contextual needs. Many of these visits reached a point at which they stopped for a while, only to return and mysteriously type a specific string of characters into the search field, leading them straight to the forms they needed to choose from. When we investigated further, we discovered customers were actually trying to use the site, then calling customer service in frustration, and learning how to search for the form directly. This *full-service journey* had to be analyzed to understand what users were doing—it couldn't be captured by looking at site analytics alone. The actions with the PDF form were nested within a longer arc of seeking, finding, learning, and conversing.

Meanwhile, the engineers in the company's IT department wanted to *determine the task* and create a *linear progression* to it. But, we could tell that few people would recognize that linear path to the task, because the goals that engineering assumed people had already decided on were, in most cases, yet to be discovered.[*]

The environment was missing the semantic functions needed to build the contextual bridges between the organization's systems and the real-life situations of customers. The choreography had huge gaps, if it could be called choreography at all. The rules started and stopped very close to the bureaucratic process—which the technology was merely going to replicate in digital form—rather than reaching outward to provide conditional frameworks for people to discover their next steps.

The site was missing environmental scaffolding that could catch users from whatever angle they entered. For example, two customers might be trying to change ownership for spouses, but one just got married, and another just got divorced. Those are vastly different situations that entail different considerations and advice, some of which should address needs beyond this specific task.

---

[*] There are rich resources on situation-based design, from HCI research done by people such as Lucy Suchman, Jean Lave, and Bonnie Nardi, who have adapted concepts from Situated Action Theory and Activity Theory. One place to start is Nardi's edited volume, *Context and Consciousness: Activity Theory and Human-Computer Interaction.*

Yet the site had no content or structure that addressed these life situations. Why not create these structures and explanations as a mediating layer in the environment? Then, search results could display information-scent for topics such as "divorce" or "marriage" or "death in the family." That became the strategy: creating the contextual middle layer that connected the user's current story with the form-based task—something that should've been there all along, even before converting the PDF form into a web application.

This was a complex problem to solve, even though it didn't involve advanced gadgetry or ambient digital agents. However, the principle in this project is the same for any environment: how does the environment meet people where they are? How does it couple with people's cognitive apparatus and give the right stepping-stones for discovering their needs? How is the arrangement of parts composed so that people have the right structures for learning and understanding?

[22]

Models and Making

I always prefer making frames: making context rather than content.
—BRIAN ENO

A Fresh Look at Our Methods

THE METHODS WE USE for information architecture—and for design practice generally—are mostly sound and valuable. Attending to context doesn't mean we throw everything out and start over. In fact, most of our tools and processes are suitable for figuring out context anyway, even if we haven't been thinking of it that way until now.

Personas, Scenarios, Site Maps, Card Sorts, Journeys, Service Maps, Content Inventories—most of these tend to be focused on the *elements* they represent—the objects and events—but not as much on the *relationships* between those elements. We might mention them, but they're often treated as the negative space between touch-points and interactions, not explicitly analyzed in the foreground.

Additionally, there are assumptions baked into a lot of our methods, models, and documentation. For example:

- The typical approach to mental-model task analysis—extracting tasks from interview transcripts—not only leaves a lot of the really important context in the transcript, but also doesn't account for ethnographic observational data and the distortions of user self-reporting.

- Card Sorts, if considered from an embodied perspective, are really about how people sort words on cards, not how they will find their way through an environment using those labels as infrastructure.

- Personas tend to identify goals, but as we've seen, goals are largely fictional—even if the people the personas represent tell us "these are my goals"—because they're actually not very good judges of what motivates them in the immediacy of perception-action.

- Journey Maps, although often impressive artifacts great for collaborative understanding, can often be linear happy-path descriptions that lull us into a comforting story.

These issues don't mean these techniques aren't useful. We just need to analyze them and be sure we aren't treating them like wizard spells, which, when we say the words and do the right motions, compel the right design solution to magically appear. Understanding and shaping context requires deeper and broader attention beyond the immediate face of a problem or project. Most design teams have little appetite for the rigor necessary to get it right. Still, as the world becomes more complex, our approach has to meet that complexity on its own terms.

Observing Context

In my own work, I've come to realize that understanding context requires immersing myself to some degree in the full context for which I am designing. Trying to understand that context through surveys, testing, or analytics is like trying to understand the Grand Canyon through postcards and satellite data. You don't really get it until you walk along its edge and experience its depths in person. As bebop inventor Charlie Parker once said, "If you don't live it, it won't come out of your horn."

There are many great research methods for doing design work, all of which have their particular strengths. However, for a rich understanding of user context, the gold standard is *applied ethnography*. Ethnography, generally speaking, is a method used in social sciences, wherein a researcher will immerse herself in the world of the subjects being studied, usually over long periods of time. That's a great approach for scientific purposes, but design projects don't have years or even months for research. So, we have to use techniques in a more specific, applied manner. It doesn't render the deep understanding that academic-grade ethnography gathers, but—if done well—it gets us much closer to understanding user context than any other approach.

A methodology called *contextual design* marries some of the best in human-computer-interaction science with applied-ethnography approaches.* Developed by Karen Holtzblatt and Hugh Beyer in the 1990s, it leads cross-disciplinary teams through stages of Inquiry, Interpretation, Consolidation, Visioning, Storyboarding, User Environment Design, and Prototyping. As you might guess from the method's name, it is obsessed with context; and it keeps the integrity of the contextual "chain of evidence" from beginning to end. The method is comprehensive (and even exhaustive), but it is flexible enough to be adapted to nearly any scope or design challenge, as long the work follows the method's principles.†

One of my favorite aspects of contextual design is how it requires collaborative analysis and ideation with designers, potential users, and other stakeholders. Different perspectives introduce differing opinions, but that "noise"—which might be considered merely inefficient and inaccurate in traditional process modeling—is actually a huge benefit. Just as we can't really "see an object" in a two-dimensional picture in a lab, but need to be able to move around it from different angles in the flesh, various team-member perspectives give us a richer perception and understanding of how people live and work in their real-life environments.

Contextual design is well suited to understanding multiple perspectives—creating the collage of maps and journeys we need—because it can generate multiple models for each user-session interpretation. These models can illustrate cultural context, workplace layout, and off-screen habits, as well as the traditionally recorded workflows and task sequences. By doing this for each person observed and then combining them into a wide-angle view during the consolidation phase, you get a more three-dimensional understanding of the current state.

Contextual design doesn't dwell on semantics as a major area of focus, but language plays an important role in the approach. Really watching and listening to users means paying attention to the language they

---

* Beyer, H., and K. Holtzblatt. *Contextual Design: Defining Customer-Centered Systems.* San Francisco: Morgan Kaufmann, 1998.

† Other great resources: *The Ethnographic Interview* (Spradley); *Observing the User Experience: A Practitioner's Guide to User Research* (Goodman, Kuniavsky, Moed); *Practical Ethnography: A Guide to Doing Ethnography in the Private Sector* (Ladner); *Interviewing Users: How to Uncover Compelling Insights* (Portigal).

use to learn how it informs, supports, and exerts pressures on how people do their work. For example, on one project in my past, we not only observed how customer service representatives did their jobs with the full environmental resources around them—from both the tools on-screen and the physical material in their cubes, such as folders and cork-boards—we also tracked the way they talked about the work: the keywords they used and the way they meant them. It allowed us to develop a new taxonomy for tagging calls that better matched the cultural map of how the workers understood the task. That taxonomy was the lynchpin connecting the quality of metrics, the clarity of customer communication, and even the information architecture of the call-center software. That's why I tend to track the language I hear, alongside the other contextual design artifacts; the language is the spine that enables the entire organism to function as a coherent whole.

Regardless of how you learn to do it, taking an ethnographic approach is essential. Everything else is supplemental at best or misleading guesswork at worst. Unfortunately, many clients and employers still do not understand and value this approach. Sometimes, they fear designers will learn the wrong things from regular workers and customers, or they value measurable data over observation-based insight. I've found myself resorting to "sneaking in" some bits of ethnographic interaction during usability testing, or asking friends "off the clock" to show me how they go about some related task. By hook or by crook, even a taste of applied ethnography can go a long way toward enlightening a project.

Some years ago, I worked with a nonprofit that provides content and community services for people affected by breast cancer: patients and their families, friends, and caregivers. It had launched a website in the mid-1990s as a place where users could read and learn from medically sound, layperson-friendly content about the disease and its treatment. It published both original content and doctor-approved summaries of breast-cancer research. A few years after its launch, its creators had decided to add a simple discussion forum to see if users would find it helpful. To their surprise, the forum soon grew to be as important a part of the website as the published content. In fact, it turned into the busiest breast-cancer-related community on the Web.

There were two macro-contexts in play: an area providing top-down, officially edited and published content, and another area where users were creating their own, bottom-up, informally written and shared content. The two areas weren't well-integrated, and didn't yet officially inform one another. Likewise, the curator-edited area had grown unwieldy in its structure, unable to handle the varieties of content that were now being published as it expanded to cover more topics.

Through contextual interviews, we learned how users' personal narratives had been violently disrupted by disease, changing the course of their personal stories. As an environment, the site had to provide a variety of paths and places for users to handle different emotional states, life-changing decisions, and mundane-yet-essential practicalities around the many facets of diagnosis and treatment.

One of the things we discovered was that people's needs shifted considerably from one moment to the next, depending on what phase they were experiencing. A patient who was recently diagnosed with cancer was often in a state of high emotional arousal—a near panic—and unable to comprehend complicated, multifaceted information layouts or technical content. Yet, within a short time, that same person would often become an expert researcher, throwing herself (or himself) into a voracious "flow state" in which volume and complexity were suddenly welcome. The site needed to embrace these shifts of perspective, not resist them with rigid consistency.

Also, when we started, we wondered if the seemingly bifurcated nature of the website was a problem. However, it turned out that having the community side and the officially edited side of the site was a boon. They each addressed different needs. Interestingly, for some users, the forum would become their main home on the site, where they'd often ask their questions first before consulting the edited content. A review of the forum content found that it was surprisingly accurate when the full thread of a conversation was taken into account: its inhabitants did a great job of policing the neighborhood. Most users said they found better answers more quickly by asking a question in the forum than from querying Google.

The forum was also treated as a meaningful, real place. Some users were far-flung and had no access to in-person group support, so they relied on this community for that vital aspect of their care experience. And, when someone would be preparing to go into the hospital for a longer stay, their friends would create "care packages" of thoughts, pictures, prayers, and other virtual objects that were as cherished as any real gift basket could ever be.

Like other websites I had helped design in the past, I approached this one as a system of activity hubs (see Figure 22-1), with contextual connective tissue stitching them together. In this case, though, the information architecture strategy had to avoid the trap of seeing it as a big article repository with a forum attached. We had more success by thinking of the website as a participant in existing narratives—a supplement to personal storymaking.

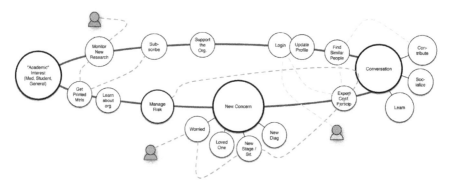

FIGURE 22-1

One of the architectural models used to think through the "hub" places users might visit, in whatever order necessary, to find their own way to sensemaking. The labels here were functional descriptors, not the final taxonomy. This was one of several artifacts used to work out the site's information architecture*

There are plenty of sorts of design that don't require research, and there are plenty of talented, experienced designers who can make an excellent phone app or consumer gadget without resorting to contextual inquiry. But, that's because more often than not they already have tacit contextual knowledge sufficient for creating that design. I would still argue that getting at least a small taste of observing someone else would provide validation and a reality check, but success can still happen without it.

---

* Credit where it is due: I borrowed this approach from work I once saw by user experience designer Wolf Noeding, circa 2006.

However, I can't imagine devising an architecture for this nonprofit organization and its constituents without immersing myself to some degree in their lived experience, and seeing how they work through it.

Perspectives and Journeys

One contextual conundrum we run into is how users often reify their goals and stories when self-reporting their experiences. When we add to that the tendency of organizations to assume that people have nothing else going on in their lives but the specific task put before them, we miss out on a lot of context.

During the financial services Power of Attorney project described in Chapter 21, I developed a Situation-Need-Task (SNT) model (Figure 22-2). I have continued using it because it challenges my own assumptions about what people are doing and why, and it helps to keep my perspective honest.* It reminds me that people don't just drop out of the sky to perform a task. They always begin in some situation that has emerged in their lives. They must then comprehend what they need— tacitly or explicitly or somewhere between—and only then, perhaps, locate and understand how to complete a task.

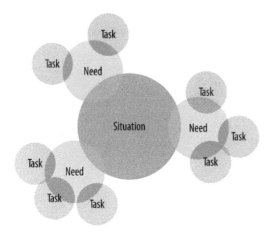

FIGURE 22-2
A Situation-Need-Task (SNT) model; situations spawn needs, which lead to tasks

---

* Hinton, Andrew. "Beyond Findability," Workshop for the IA Summit, presented by the Information Architecture Institute, 2009 (*http://bit.ly/1s3NBW9*).

Notice the model doesn't use the word "goal" anywhere. As in a competitive game, a goal is something that you already know is there, something for which you aim. But, on the financial-site users often had to first discover what game they were playing, and they had no idea at the outset what the goal was. Either they didn't know they needed to fill out a form, or they didn't know which form it was, why it needed to be done, or how to do it properly.

Returning to our retail example from Chapter 20, if one person has a broken kitchen faucet, but another is renovating an entire kitchen, they might both enact a "task" of "typing 'kitchen faucet' into a search field." The results of that search need to be shaped so that they accommodate the different perspectives that these two situations bring to the task, as illustrated in Figure 22-3. For a broken faucet, the customer might need parts or an instruction manual for the faucet bought at that store a year earlier. The renovator, however, might be wanting beautiful scenes of renovated kitchens, with showroom-designer faucets in the spotlight.

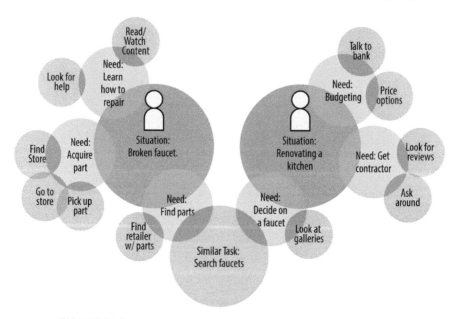

FIGURE 22-3
The same search phrase, generated by two different user needs

A digital system—object, service, site, application, or whatever—needs users to understand its workings in order to complete tasks. This next model (Figure 22-4) shows how, if we shift perspective just a bit, there's a sort of continuum that must be bridged. Ultimately, this continuum comes back to the question of ontology and what something means to the agent. When the environment can address the organic, analog context of the human agent's need, there can be adequate support for bridging between system and person.

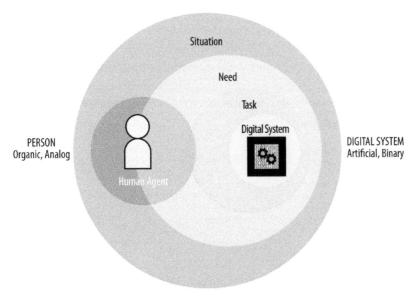

FIGURE 22-4
A different angle on situation-need-task

When we consider the cross-channel qualities of service design, or the growing complexity of objects, interfaces, and controls for interaction design, or the omni-platform challenges of content strategy, we have to map out entire systems and the contexts they influence. This includes the digital systems, but also the cultural and physical layers.

It's important to name and define the key attributes of each of these systems, along with their functions. Yet, it's also important to understand how they work as an integrated, distributed system, or "ecosystem"—what Resmini and Rosati call "ubiquitous ecologies."[*] Even if the parts are not intended to be connected, or are created by completely

---

* Resmini, Andrea, and Luca Rosati. *Pervasive Information Architecture: Designing Cross-Channel User Experiences.* Burlington, MA: Morgan Kaufmann, 2011:52.

different businesses, the user still experiences them all within *the same environmental context*. Just such a situation is described in the airport scenario from Chapter 1, and illustrated in Figure 22-5.

TripIt brought contextual information to the calendar; the Delta app brought contextual information to TripIt. The Delta app fed the boarding pass to the iPhone's Passbook app—which seemed to be alerting a "calendar" event because it varied from the phone's usual "invariant" event patterns. Plus the physical and semantic wayfinding within the airport itself contributed to the overlapping contextual information. For the person in the airport, it's all one environment, even if the originators of these different services weren't thinking that way when they created the software.

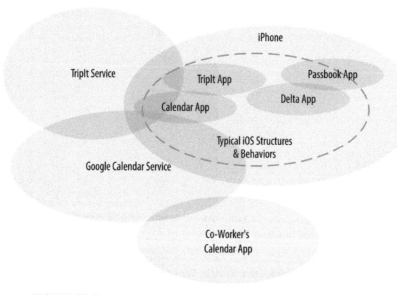

FIGURE 22-5
Contextual nesting, experienced as one ecology

I've mentioned collage several times already, but here is where the idea especially takes hold—in the way we accommodate so many contextual angles and perspectives. Real-life environments are collages of many parts, some of which are interconnected on purpose, some which are that way accidentally, and some of which clash when they should be complementary. Each element needs to do its best to be created with awareness and to complement the others.

For example, a typical *User Journey* map would be created for only one user at a time, normalizing user action across a linear timeline (Figure 22-6). A "journey" is typically a story, after all—but as we've seen, narrative can leave out a lot of contextual background.

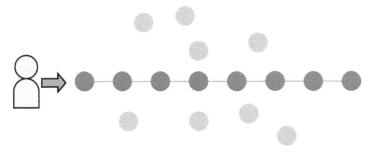

FIGURE 22-6
A typical user journey model reifies a linear story

In Figure 22-6, the gray circles represent aspects of the story that might have actually been important to the agent but were ignored in the retelling. Regardless of how many channels and touch-points a typical journey map captures, it creates a sort of fiction that—while an insightful illustration of one path—doesn't capture the points of view of other services, systems, and agents that are intermingled with the environment. These journey diagrams are useful, but we should always be asking if there are other contextual perspectives that should be added to the mix.

Again, the idea of collage comes into play here. What if we instead map the actual, messy, wandering paths of people, and capture their nested perspectives? It would allow us to see how the elements of a shared environment are understood from key points of view, based on the real behaviors of every agent involved.

In Figure 22-7, the gray circles are fewer, because it turned out people had behaviors that the linear journey overlooked, and some circles that were ignored by one perspective were important to another. It also helps us see which parts of these journeys have high shared importance and how the overall environment's nested structure is understood by each party. Even though we can never capture every single detail of every possible agent's perspective, just adding one or two other perspectives can bring valuable multidimensional insight.

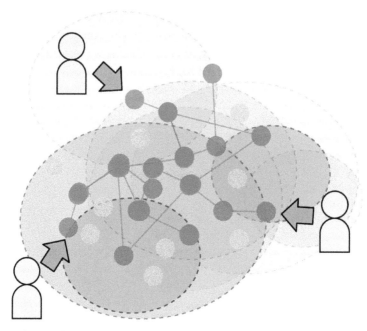

FIGURE 22-7
A collage approach can capture multiple perspectives

As architect and philosopher Christopher Alexander explains in his (essential reading) essay, "A City Is Not a Tree," each hierarchy or linear structure is just one perspective in a complex latticework of relationships.[*] It's important to understand those points of view, but just as important to see them in the full fabric of people's lives.

Now that humans are not the only thinking, acting objects in our environment, we have to include digital agents in our ethnographic work. Ethnography is traditionally about people, but what does it mean for us to also spend some time observing and understanding what digital agents do? Additionally, these agents are often just part of a broader system of technology and culture, much of which is beyond immediate view.

As we learned earlier, complex semantic systems are, in essence, maps, and maps have agendas. They select for some information over other information. They reinforce some assumptions and break others. The

---

[*] Alexander, C. "A city is not a tree." *Architectural Form*, April/May, 1965:172.

more sophisticated and rich the rules behind the environment, and the more digital agents it employs, the more the *environment* has agency *as a whole*.

We've not delved far into artificial intelligence and "smart systems" here. However, information architecture (like all areas of design) increasingly needs to understand what context is like from the perspective of the system, as presented in Figure 22-8. How does the system "perceive" the world, and the humans in it?

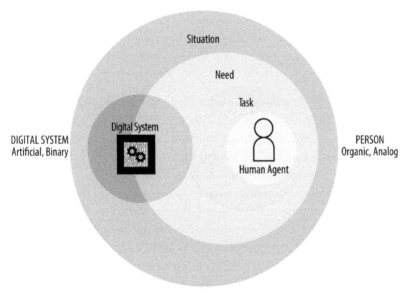

FIGURE 22-8

What happens when we reverse the players, and consider the situation, need, and task of the System, as it interacts and shapes context for the Person?

A useful exercise in any design involving digital agents is to work through how they see the world, and what situations and needs drive their discrete actions. What does the human agent look like to the digital agent? Try treating the user as an object in the environment that the system needs to find, interact with, keep an eye on, edit, or save, or whatever else we do with data. What is the ontology that describes and defines the human, its actions, and its context to the system?

These questions are ultimately part of defining what the system is to begin with, and how it categorizes the world we expect it to understand. Of course, we can't interview systems (at least, not yet?), but we can learn a great deal by looking at user research from this angle as well as partnering with the technologists who programmed and configured the systems, or the business analysts who've documented them.

Structures for Tacit Satisficing

In our super-rational age, we tend to want to create super-rational structures. And, as we've covered, organizations have a strong interest in planned efficiencies. But, as Richard Saul Wurman says pointedly, "Order doesn't equal understanding."[*] Our culture tends to fetishize order, even at the expense of meaning. If everything is lined up neatly in a spreadsheet, it seems to have a kind of authority. If information is contorted into a comfortably controlled hierarchy, we're glad somebody figured it out, and we take it as authoritative.

Western school systems are modeled on these tacit cultural maps, the same ones that ran railroads and factories. Yet, there are alternative options. Consider the Montessori classroom. In Montessori education, students can explore among various stations, or hubs, in the room. As is illustrated in Figure 22-9, typically, in an early-age setup, there are stations for activities such as drawing and painting, working with shapes, musical instruments, language arts, and simple math. Montessori teachers will give an introductory session with each type of station; the students are then allowed to explore them, mostly at their own pace and in their own order. It affords children the ability to construct their understanding of the objects and activities by interacting with the materials rather than in the abstract. Additionally, it doesn't prize consistency and efficiency over self-discovery, sensemaking, and personal narrative.

Note that the options in a Montessori class are selected carefully, as are the objects and materials that are on offer. This is intended to nudge students toward particular kinds of learning. It's a highly controlled environment but with a great deal of freedom compared to the more factory-like education approach in traditional schools. It instantiates decisions about what is important and what the students should be able to do without prescribing their every action or pace of learning.

---

[*] *Information Anxiety*, 1989, p. 48.

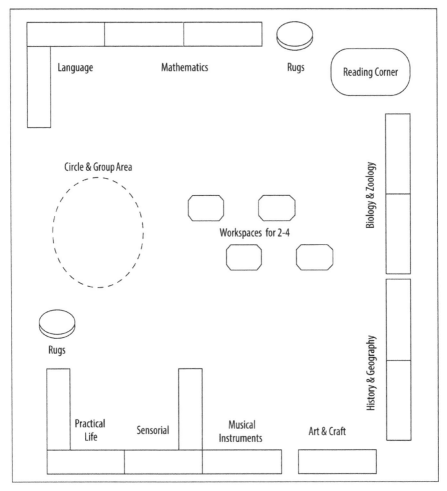

FIGURE 22-9

A Montessori classroom layout concept, showing stations for engaging and learning various activities and subject categories*

To some, this looks terribly inefficient and chaotic. But in fact, students are learning a great deal—discovering the world for themselves, in their own way. This is an architecture that depends as much on the theories that drive the pedagogy and the categories of learning styles aligned with subject matter as it does on the physical structures themselves.

---

* Drawing by author. Based loosely on concept posted at *http://csetjy.blogspot.com/2012/06/classroom-layout.html*.

In fact, it's these *language*-bound principles that provide the environmental invariants for the design of a successful Montessori classroom, whereas the *physical* layout varies from one school to the next.

This *constructivist* approach to allowing people to figure out the world in their own way is precisely how we can accommodate so many different people, with so many different needs and personal contexts.

Setting up structures for people to choose from based on their own path isn't a radical concept; it's something we use a lot, even if we haven't thought of it in this way. In one example (see Figure 22-10), financial services company Vanguard breaks down several possible ways to browse, understand, and choose investment funds.

The landing page offers a crossroads with signage explaining the environmental constraints to which each path will lead. Some people will want more constraints than others.

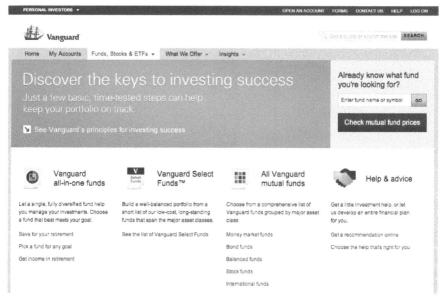

FIGURE 22-10
Vanguard's "hubs" for catching the users in several contexts of fund shopping

Google, which connects millions of people across nearly every digital context you can think of, has been sharing research on user behavior across channels and places. In one report, it explains that the multiplicity of information resources now available means that customers aren't following as much of a linear path as they once did. For example, in marketing there is a well-worn metaphor of the *sales funnel*: customers start out in the broad "mouth" of the funnel as being just aware of a product or brand, then show explicit, more-focused interest, then active consideration, and so on, until finally purchasing. This metaphor has been an implicitly accepted "map" of marketing and sales for many years. But in Google's research, it finds the metaphor isn't as relevant now:

> The sales funnel isn't really a funnel anymore....Today's shoppers bounce back and forth at their own speed in a multi-channel market-place. They switch devices to suit their needs at any given moment. They search; go off to look at reviews, ratings, styles, and prices; and then search again. They see ads on TV and in newspapers and online. They walk into local stores to look at products. They talk to friends, over the back fence and on social media. Then it's back to ZMOT for more information. In short, the shopper's journey looks less like a funnel and more like a flight map.*

Now that there are so many more information sources online, the digital environment becomes the "home base" for considering and triangulating what customers learn from the traditional information hubs. The brick-and-mortar stores become just another information source rather than the necessary end-point for final decision-making.

In essence, people use the environment as youngsters use a Montessori classroom, finding their own "flight path" between contexts. The most successful marketing approaches, therefore, are putting environmental structure into the world that enables rather than short-circuits this behavior. Rather than relying on broadcast information, brands are instead using broadcast as a supplement to the online conversations, then (when they behave themselves) politely and helpfully engaging in those conversations.

You might look at things like this and ask: but where's the context? Precisely. The structures aren't forcing context so much as accommodating its unique emergence in each agent's experience. Finding the right hubs and stations for people to *satisfice* through, calibrate within,

---

* ZMOT Handbook. Google, 2012, p. 11.

and narrate to themselves means that we don't have to plan out every possible use case—after all, it's impossible at today's levels of complexity anyway. Instead, we provide environments that are resilient, accommodating, similar to what game designer Will Wright, in reference to digital games, calls "possibility space":

> Players navigate this possibility space by their choices and actions; every player's path is unique. Games cultivate—and exploit—possibility space better than any other medium. In linear storytelling, we can only imagine the possibility space that surrounds the narrative: What if Luke had joined the Dark Side? What if Neo isn't the One? In interactive media, we can explore it.*

There is much that conventional digital design can learn from game design, especially in terms of structure that encourages and supports unstructured action and learning.

Blueprints, Floor Plans, Bubbles, and Blobs

We can do the research, do the analysis, and understand the many perspectives and paths involved in people's contextual narratives. But how do we go about making the plans for such indeterminate structures?

From early in my own experience as an information architect, I have understood the "architecture" part of the name to be not just a metaphor, but about a new form of actual architecture. So, it didn't take me long to lose patience with conventional site-map tree hierarchy diagrams. They treat a website's information environment like the directory structure of a file server. In fact, websites broke away from "one page per level" information structures long ago. Now that the Web is just one layer in a multidimensional environment of many channels, modes, and states, tree hierarchies are more unrealistic than ever; we're increasingly likely to work on projects that have no obvious web interface at all. As a result, I rarely make a tree hierarchy diagram as a deliverable anymore.

---

* Wright, Will. "Dream Machines," *Wired Magazine*, April 2006;14(04).

Whether using an application such as Visio or OmniGraffle, or a drawing on a whiteboard or paper, exploring the possible structures of information environments needs to allow for flexibility. We need to be careful to avoid locking ourselves out of contextual possibilities.

Knowing what we do now about embodiment, it's no surprise that the medium and technique we use for our working artifacts has a direct effect on our cognition. If we start in a medium that's time-consuming or tedious to change, we're more likely to settle for whatever expression we already have. Our first try at an intricately drawn and connected schematic starts to look pretty good when we consider the work it will take to reorient shapes and reconnect magnets. This isn't even to mention the paralysis that detailed interface wireframes can cause—the inertia against making changes convinces us they aren't necessary and tempts stakeholders to just run with what is pictured.

The more our first effort uses polished, squared-off, and perfectly aligned objects, the more their "order" can easily masquerade as understanding. Context controls conduct, and the contexts we manufacture with our design artifacts can have unexpected, limiting effects on our solutions.

Interestingly, Tim Berners-Lee, in his original proposal describing the World Wide Web, explains that, "When describing a complex system, many people resort to diagrams with circles and arrows. Circles and arrows leave one free to describe the interrelationships between things in a way that tables, for example, do not. The system we need is like a diagram of circles and arrows, where circles and arrows can stand for anything."* Expressing "web-natured" environments as societies of circle-shaped contexts has roots in the nature of the medium.

When I read Sir Berners-Lee's statement, I was relieved, because I've been working with circles and blobs for years but feeling a bit ashamed when I compared my work with my more graphically disciplined colleagues. That's because I tend to begin by throwing everything I can think of onto a page (digitally or otherwise), letting it scatter like mercury. Then, I wallow in it until patterns begin to emerge, and I begin

---

* *http://www.w3.org/History/1989/proposal.html*

stitching together relationships and functions, and nested overlaps. Usually this works much better if I've done some contextual observation and other research to get the problem space under my skin a bit.

On purpose, these circles and blobs, like those in Figure 22-11, involve the least possible intrinsic structure. The shape of the object can constrain us to seeing it only one way. A brick says, "I'm a brick; put me in a wall." But a smooth, circular river stone says, "I'm a circle—I could be anything."

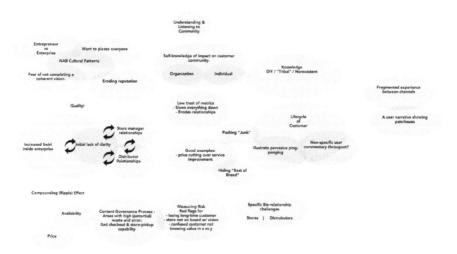

FIGURE 22-11

A typical bottom-up starting point when I'm working on an information architecture problem (blurred to protect confidentiality)

Imagine my delight when I learned that serious, built-environment architects do something similar. They call them *bubble diagrams* (see Figure 22-12).* There's a marvelous variety of them out there, which I find encouraging. Architects have to follow stringent guidelines for their official, deliverable documentation. But when working through the early stages of structure, they can play with it more freely—and look at the rich variety in how they make bubbles.

---

* Thanks to Jorge Arango, an architect by training, for introducing me to bubble diagrams.

These diagrams are how architects can play with contextual structure at varying levels of abstraction, cheaply and quickly, without binding their thoughts to the hardwired angles of drafting rulers or CAD software. Even if making them digitally with connectors between, they are easier to rearrange on a whim, rather than strict boxes that have to choose which sides are connected and which are not.

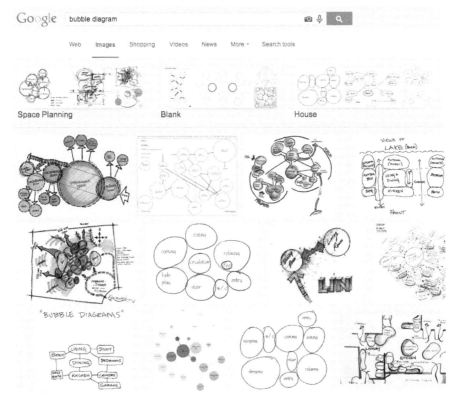

FIGURE 22-12
The marvelous variety one finds when querying "bubble diagram" using Google's Image search

Likewise, when exploring possible futures for any sort of information environment, such as a website, mobile app, or even a full-service ecosystem, using circles and blobs can be freeing.

I've used them for doing something I call *functional modeling* (a phrase I borrowed from systems engineering, for which it means something much more formal). Figure 22-13 shows a functional model about the online capabilities needed for a fictional art-supplies retailer.

A Simple (Pretend) Functional Model Example: Art Max Art Supplies

Quality Shopping

Art Max needs to support discerning art supplies shoppers:
- Clear that Art Max knows superior quality/brands
- Recommends higher quality, regardless of price
- Expert reviews + customer reviews heavily considered

Accessible Learning

Art Max emphasizes learning about art and how to use materials:
- Expert tutorials provided for a basic techniques and uses of most common materials and tools.

Available Anywhere

All digital information available in wifi-enabled stores, for personal devices & via kiosks; learning multimedia playable on all major platforms; customer profile & tools mobile-adaptive.

Enables easy, rich sharing of content by Art Max's dedicated, discerning customer following that shares often via sites like, Tumblr, Flickr, and Pinterest. Art max is then better able to become the source of choice for customers' ambitions and "leveling up" in materials quality.

Sharing

Art Max provides tools for cultivating preferences in art supplies and tools of the trade, helps customers remember context of their prior purchases and makes suggestions based on what similar artists have done.

Social Platform Presences

Tools & Resources

FIGURE 22-13

A functional model coalescing decisions about priorities and capabilities, without crossing into literal structure or interface design

Usually, I generate a functional model based on lots of raw material generated from contextual inquiry and stakeholder interviews. Sometimes I use that to do an affinity-clustering exercise on my own or with my team, but sometimes I take that raw material into a stakeholder workshop, where we explore affinities together. The exercise is often even more valuable for the discussions it prompts than the artifacts it produces.

The main point of the modeling, though, is to work through high-level definitions and decisions about what the nature of the environment should be—that is, what categories of function does it bring into the world?—without discussing actual, literal design and structure. This way, we work through some of the big questions without the distraction of "why isn't my department in the global navigation?" or "why doesn't the app have our promotions blinking at the top?" Trying as hard as possible to resist leaning into literal design is a useful discipline. It avoids using interface solutions as a poor proxy for making real decisions about business models, strategies, and brand definitions.

Even after this sort of modeling, it's still risky to introduce the distractions of interfaces. Architecture still hasn't found a direction. In *Contextual Design: Defining Customer-Centered Systems* (Morgan Kaufmann), Holtzblatt and Beyer argue that it is essential to "design the structure" first—getting the architectural framework right before rendering the object-level design of UI. Writing in the early 1990s, they call this *User Environment Design*, and unabashedly refer to it as architecture of "floor plans" before working through the object-level details of interaction.

> As a floor plan for the system, the User Environment Design shows the parts and how they relate to each other from the user's point of view. The User Environment Design shows each part of the system, how it supports the user's work, exactly what function is available in that part, and how it connects with the other parts of the system, without tying this structure to any particular UI. With an explicit User Environment Design, a team can ensure that the structure is right for the user, plan how to roll out new features in a series of releases, and manage the work of the project across engineering teams. Basing these aspects of running a project on a diagram that focuses on keeping the system coherent for the user counterbalances the other forces that would sacrifice coherence for ease of implementation or delivery.[*]

Even though *Contextual Design* predates the public-and-commercial Web, and so much else that has emerged in the past 20 years, it offers a way of thinking about environment that still deserves to be more understood and adopted in mainstream software design.

The floor-plan approach takes the architecture of a system seriously as architecture of places where people take action. It introduces an embodied understanding of the way the system can be inhabited, but it still does so at a level of abstraction that allows change and iteration. In Figure 22-14, you can see how a typical floor plan mainly displays the most important aspects of the arrangement of places, each established to support a particular set of functions for inhabitants. The shapes of rooms and what seem to be decorative details are actually ways of establishing the function of each place: the purpose of an eat-in kitchen is also to accommodate a circular table, with a nice view; the modern family room is about electronic entertainment through a television screen, so it doesn't need as many windows, and is tucked away in a corner of the structure.

---

* Beyer, H., and K. Holtzblatt. *Contextual Design: Defining Customer-Centered Systems.* San Francisco: Morgan Kaufmann, 1998:24.

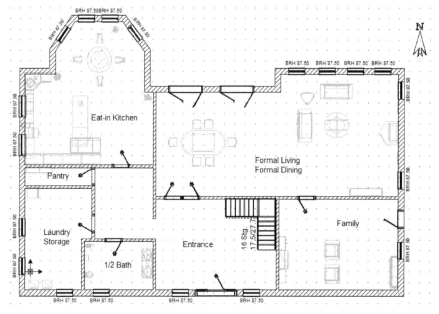

FIGURE 22-14
An example of a residential floor plan[*]

The object-design-level details come later, but the functional structural arrangement must be established first. Information architecture models can also use this level of abstraction to show how one context relates to another, how they cross over and inform one another, and their priorities in relation to the whole.

An example of a draft version of just such a diagram is shown in the right half of Figure 22-15. In this project, a functional modeling exercise that rendered the egg-shaped model on the left provided the defined priorities that informed an early version of actual site structure, in the map on the right.

I've found that if the diagram becomes too complicated and baroque, it raises a warning about how understandable the environment will be. A retail environment that is about "products" and "learning" and "managing projects" can accommodate a lot of complexity within those essential, high-level functional categories. Then, those categories can help define the essential nature of the outer structures of a nested website or other environment.

---

[*] Wikimedia Commons: *http://commons.wikimedia.org/wiki/File:Sample_Floorplan.jpg*

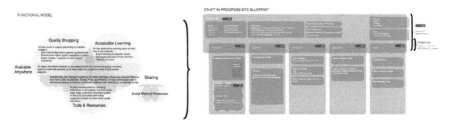

FIGURE 22-15

A functional model leads naturally to high-level structures in an early version of a basic floor-plan-like structural map

Note how the map on the right of Figure 22-15 isn't using interconnecting lines but overlaps to show structure. By using semitransparent shapes, the map can indicate where summary versions or borrowed functions of some areas might overlap within other nested structures.

This overlap of content and function is something that's possible in digital places that is less possible in physical ones. Structural definition is still needed to establish nested invariants, but software makes it possible for contexts to be replicated and connected in useful ways across the invariant barriers. The challenge is to ensure that they don't blend so much that the environment is trying to allow the user to do everything from everywhere. Even if the kitchen can borrow some of the entertainment function of the family room, it shouldn't be made to be both at once, which would obliterate the essential character of both places. A house with no walls or defining characteristics among rooms is just a big shed with furniture inside.

Likewise, a retail website's account section might cross over with the site's global header; and its authentication state might cross over with features at a store's kiosk or checkout counter. These are not separate boxes connected by arrows, but nested, overlapped contexts, ambiently intersected.

The most value I've found in this approach is how it seems to intuitively tell a story about places and contexts, and how they relate to one another. One of my first clients as a full-time information architect (a fairly new role and title back in 1999–2000) was a nonprofit organization that brought together research scientists and large technology companies to funnel money to graduate student programs. It did this to cultivate talent and make it possible for companies to share "precompetitive" research. Bringing together so many different players meant the organization existed as a sort of confederation of research scientists, universities, and technology corporations.[*]

Since its website launched in the mid-1990s, it evolved like so many do: starting as a few linked pages only to later metastasize into a tangle of confused categories, wandering click-paths, and ad hoc features.

Our research found mixed feelings with the organization and its community: scientists who'd become more entrenched in their own subcommunities, divisions between appointed managers and regular folk, and enmity between academics and business leads.

We realized that the site had become a visible instantiation of that discord: a messy tangle of priorities in tension. A new information architecture would mean more than just organizing all their content. It meant making an environment whose places encouraged mutual understanding. It was a chance to create a system of contexts that could help heal a professional community, and in turn be a sort of civic structure to support mutual habitation.

We tried expressing that strategy using a traditional tree-shaped site hierarchy diagram. The response was less than enthusiastic. The structure came across as a pecking-order pyramid, where the subcommunities were relegated to second-class status. We realized the traditional tree structure wasn't accurately portraying the strategy, which was actually to be more of a community building where a central atrium of important news and announcements tied everyone together.

The stakeholders needed something more than a schematic for information organization. So, as is demonstrated in Figure 22-16, we created a kind of floor plan, but one that showed how various contexts would overlap. It showed defined areas based on function, nested within the main container of the parent organization. Then, it showed how the subcommunities would have their own somewhat independent satellite areas—based on a common template but sharing a news-based context with the parent organization. It allowed the subcommunities to have

---

[*] A version of this story was first published in *UX Storytellers—Connecting the Dots*; Jan Jursa (September 1, 2010) *http://amzn.to/1x5rmDE*.

their own places, but it continually reinforced a friendly, overarching presence of the parent organization—the benevolent "house" that sustained the subcommunities' "rooms."

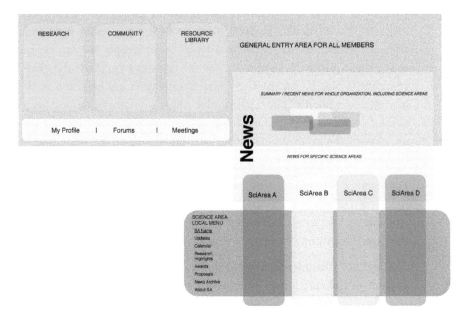

FIGURE 22-16
A version of the "floor plan"—which we called a "blueprint"—for a science organization, in a circa 2000 project (identifying specifics omitted)*

This new approach brought a great sigh of relief to the stakeholders: they could imagine themselves moving around in those places, collaborating in common areas, and focusing on specialized communities and functions in others.

Of course, this was a simple, almost cartoon-like, expression of structure. There was still much work to be done sorting out the navigation logic, roles, permissions, and many other issues. Nevertheless, this conceptual blueprint—composing the arrangement of defined contexts—was the model everyone needed to have a shared understanding of would be designed and built. I had no idea at the time why this worked out, but I now realize it likely has to do with how people understand

---

* A version of this diagram was first published in: Van Dijk, Peter *Information Architecture for Designers: Structuring Websites for Business Success.* Rotovision: September, 2003.

nesting better than hierarchy, and how semantic information needs to establish structure but with awareness of how people need information to be environment more than discretely defined, logical abstraction.

I've used a similar approach for figuring out the multiple simultaneous contexts in a particular physical place, or with a particular user over time. If we map all the contextual layers, even simply, we can begin to see them piling up. It helps us see the cognitive demands the environment is placing on the user: how many layers are expected to be attended to explicitly? How many quiet, hidden layers are making decisions the user might not know about or has forgotten about? How many are making demands, interrupting each other with no apparent awareness of the others?

For instance, let's examine the problem of a user's contextual experience in her own family room. With the proliferation of new, ambient technology and mobile access, what contexts are in play that might be part of the nested environment where we might introduce a new product?

Figure 22-17 illustrates how several elements might come together for analysis or information architecture direction, as described here:

- Overlapping shapes that roughly represent contextual layers, each identified and defined

- A scale for attention requirement, estimating between Explicit and Tacit

- A new scale for how noticeable and understandable the digital agents are, from Perceivable to Hidden

- A quick indicator showing what information modes are most in play for each contextual layer

Such a mapping technique could give us a sense of how a person might perceive and understand the information at work in this place, which is a sort of mash-up of many places at once. The blue contextual layer, for example, is about the digital "black box" sitting in the front of the room (such as a Microsoft Kinect device), which might have a sensor range for "reading" the human agent's bodily actions, even though the human is mostly unaware of it day to day. The other layers could be all sorts of things—thermostats, WiFi networks, and so on. And the same model could be adapted to see the world from the digital agent's point of view, as well.

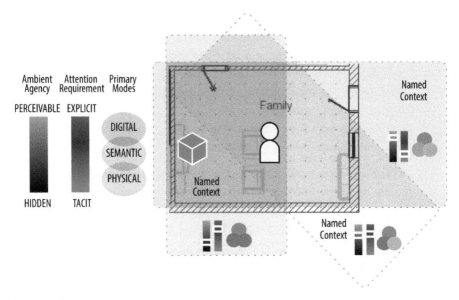

FIGURE 22-17

Adapting modeling approaches for analyzing how different context layers affect a place like a home's family room

Usually, designers and consumers both will focus on the objects in a room like this. Yet, the objects—whether software or hardware—are only part of the picture. There's also a contextual dynamic that's happening between these layers of the environment and the room's inhabitant. If we just let these layers be invisibly amorphous, we lose out on the ability to shape and improve them.

Naming these contexts is the first step toward designing them. By naming them, we bring them out of the ether, so we can define them and come to understand them. It makes us consider explicitly what these contexts are connected to outside of the immediate perception of the user; what other systems and agents, rules and relationships? We can be explicitly mindful of how we make this environment, rather than tacitly ignore its full effects on the user's life. As information architect Abby Covert says, "Intent is language."* What do we *intend* these contexts to be? What is their *nature*?

---

* Covert *How to Make Sense of Any Mess*, 2014.

As we track the layers involved in any situation, and we begin seeing them pile up, we then must ask ourselves: how can we make the environment's seams, joints, and activities more perceptible? How does it semantically represent its rules? Do those semantics provide invariant qualities in the environment, so the human agent can understand the digital influence over physical meaning? Is there just too much going on? Ultimately, we're getting to the bottom of how agents understand the relationships between elements in their environment.

These are idiosyncratic techniques that I've found useful; they're certainly not a methodology.* I share them only as pointers toward new approaches. Understanding context means revisiting and questioning how we plan, model, and make. It means inventing new ways of comprehending, analyzing, and architecting in this strange, new world we've made for ourselves.

---

* For readers who want more detailed tools and methods, an excellent, more exhaustive approach is available in the final chapters of Resmini and Rosati's *Pervasive Information Architecture*.

Coda

So HERE WE ARE, finishing with a *coda*. In musical terms, it's a final passage that brings a movement to an end. It gives the audience a chance to take a breath and reflect.

In musical scores, it has a signifier that looks like this: ☦

* * *

In ethics and psychology, a well-worn thought experiment concerns something called *The Trolley Problem*. There are various versions, but it goes something like this:

> There is a runaway trolley heading down the tracks. Ahead of it, you see five people tied up and unable to escape. You're standing far from the train yard, but you're next to a lever. You know if you pull the lever, the trolley will switch to a different track—but that track has one person tied to it, also unable to escape. You have only two options—leave well enough alone, while five people die, or pull the lever, so five may live while one will die. Which option is the right choice?

Depending on how the problem is phrased, people's answers can vary. But in many cases, around 90 percent of respondents say they would pull the lever—kill the one to save the five.

* * *

In a variant of the trolley problem, the survey results tend to change. This version says there is only the one track, with the five potential victims. And you are on a footbridge over the track. Although you are not near a lever, you *are* next to a very large person who, unlike you, would surely stop the trolley due to his size. He only needs a little shove.

In this case, the numbers nearly reverse: people have a harder time with the thought of physically pushing someone to his death, even to save more people. A recent study by "neuroethicists" put people in a functional MRI (fMRI) machine to study what their brains were doing during this conundrum. The different stories—just words, mind you—caused markedly different activity in the parts of the brain that wrestle over what we think of as "morality."

And not only were they just words that caused these people's bodies to have such varying responses; the words described situations. And those situations presented very different bodily contexts. It would seem the presence of a lever and the distance from what happens when it is pulled allows people to be more detached and utilitarian, whereas the thought of one's body pushing another body off a bridge is too close for comfort, no matter the moral calculus.

* * *

We are surrounded by levers. Levers that control things we see, and things we don't. Levers that control levers, which control even more levers. These levers are made of ones and zeros, and they can mean one thing a second ago and a different thing right now. They can even make new levers; they can learn to think. They multiply, ripple, and coalesce into the vast, invisible oceans of information around us...on us...through us.

* * *

For a while, when trying to explain to people what information architecture is, I'd joke that it was really "just getting paid for metaphysics." It rarely got more than a quizzical chuckle; it's not a very funny rejoinder, I suppose. My intended effect was self-deprecation—like saying "they pay me to blow hot air." But then I realized, I was just working out my anxieties about my professional identity. I'm still working them out.

* * *

Anyway, back to metaphysics. It's hard to define, even though it's one of the oldest branches of philosophy. Mostly it's about trying to answer big questions about *being* and understanding. Not just "what is in the world, and how does it work?" but "why does it work that way, and what does that mean?" Science eventually answered many of the questions of early metaphysics. But measurement can't answer everything. Even with all our scientific knowledge, when the empiricist says, "this is a brick," the metaphysician still has to ask, "but what *is brick*?"

* * *

It's funny, metaphysics started as merely an editorial label. "Meta" roughly means "beyond" or "after" in Greek. Early editions of Aristotle's writings usually placed his work on "physics" *first*, then appended the other work, "after" the physics content, and labeled it as *meta-physics*. Aristotle himself didn't call it that; he used a phrase meaning "first philosophy" for the subject matter that his posthumous editors placed (ah, irony) last.

So, even the name of this ancient conversation is tangled with the nature of objects, order, and labels. Of course, in later centuries scholars took this literally to mean "do not learn this other 'metaphysics' stuff until you've first learned the physics." Time and context have a complicated relationship.

* * *

There's really nothing that matters to us as humans that isn't somehow wrapped up in language. The ancients who first used the word "poet" were using a word that meant "maker"—because they understood that their poets made more than poems. They made worlds.

We've always been a linguistic sort of animal, immersed in symbol, suffused with story. But, we now have to call upon our uncanny ability to *make sense* with a degree of commitment and rigor we might never have summed before. The digital world we've made requires it. Where we are, who we are, what we are: these are big questions, not just for philosophers.

* * *

So much of our work is for mundane market needs, operational efficiencies, iterative improvements. Now and then, if we're lucky, we get to work on "meaningful" projects. At least, that's one way to look at it.

But from another perspective, we're always working with meaning. And people spend most of their time in these mundane, everyday places— office cubicles, grocery stores, highways, living rooms. Think of all the meaning, in aggregate, that can be a little more *good*, a little more *clear*.

Working on the answers to big, hard questions is worthwhile even when it leads to making things better in small, soft ways, where people really live. It seems to me that's the context where all of this stuff matters the most.

* * *

When I checked the definition for *coda*, I learned it comes from the Italian for "tail." It evoked an image I can't seem to shake: an elephant, wearing pajamas, who has been my companion for many months, nearly filling my rooms as it worked its way slowly through my house.

And now, I watch as my strange companion has found its way, finally, to my home's rear exit. It squeezes its bulk past the door's narrow affordance, and its dangling tail—this *coda*—is the last thing I see as the creature lumbers happily into the world.

I know that's not what the word really means. I suppose that's just what I bring to it.

[*Index*]

simulated wall-of-objects as, 291–292

smartphone turning environment into, 293–295

blobs, bottom-up starting point on information architecture problem using, 406–407

Blogspot, login, 319

blueprints, 412–414

Bollnow, Otto Friedrich, on anthropological space, 265

boyd, danah (her capitalization)
    properties of networked publics, 335
    Taken Out of Context, 334

brain
    as central processing unit, 40–41, 145–146
    generating experience, 77
    in wayfinding and environmental learning, 116
    schema of, 72–73

Broca's Area, 141

Brown, John Seely, 122–124

bubble diagrams, 406–407

built environment, 113–116, 371

Burgess, Anthony, 277

Bush, Vannevar, 255

Buzz (Google), roll out of, 213, 346

C

calibration of action, 51

card sorts, 387

Card, Stuart, 238–239

Carroll, Lewis, 351

categories
    as subsets of labels, 353
    as symbolic mode, 134
    purpose in information architecture of, 351

categorization, writing and, 163–164

checklists, 167–168

Chomsky, Noam, 146

choreography
    in model of information architecture, 352–353
    rules and, 364–370, 384

Circles interface (Google Plus), 346–349

circumstances, as element of context, 21, 23–24

City of Bits (Mitchell), 12

cityscape of systems, 246–247

Clark, Andy
    on labels as new realm of perceptible objects., 353
    on labels in language, 156–158, 163
    on labels modifying environment, 266
    on self-engineering, 159
    Supersizing the Mind, 61–62

classes, as subsets of labels, 353

Clay Shirky
    Here Comes Everybody, 311
    on communication changing society, 311–312

cloud computing, using term, 355–357

clutter, 106–107

Code/Space (Kitchin and Dodge), 15, 203, 249

cognition
    about, 35
    acting upon information, 60–61
    agency and digital
        every digital agents, 206–209
        learning and agency, 202–206
        ontologies, 210–214
        Shannon's logic, 199–202
    embodied, 42–48
    emergence of human, 204
    in built environment, 113–114
    mainstream view of, 39–41

cognitively-active vs. cognitively-passive way-finders, 115–116

cognitive map
    about, 116–117
    culture and, 271–272

company organizational charts, 274

compasses, metamaps and, 300

complexity of thought, writing and, 165

composition
    importance of, 339–341
    paying attention to definitions in, 344–348
    qualities of, 341–345

compound invariants, 91, 186

computer-like way of understanding cognition, 40–41

computers
    automating, 202–203

embodied learning of, 206–207
interfaces and humans, 215–219
memory of, 203–204
processing fuzzy ecological and
semantic information
inputs, 205
simulation interaction on
approaching physical
affordances, 226–229
design of interactions, 220–223
interfaces and, 220–223
range of information, 224–226
teaching inputs to process, 211
teaching use of robotic body, 205
writing vs. spoken word for, 204
Computers as Theatre (Laurel), 256
concepts, as symbolic mode, 135
conditional actions, purpose in
information architecture
of, 351
conscious attention, spectrum
of, 67–70
consciousness, 70, 374–375
conscious reflection, 43
consistency, internal and
external, 348
constructivist approach, 402
context
about, vii–viii, 3–4
definition of
conventional, 20–25
working, 25–27
information architecture and, 262
observing, 388–392
contextual design, 389–390
Contextual Design (Beyer and
Holtzblatt), 408–409
contextual, language as, 138–140
contextual nesting model, 396
contextual structures, challenges of
sorting through, 4–9
contractual agreements, use of word
term in, 364
controls
environmental, 70–73
privacy, 326–327
conversations, 305–307
Conway, Melvin, 369
Conway's Law, 369–370
counterpublics, 334

Covert, Abby, How to Make Sense of
Any Mess, 372, 415
creating infrastructure, 156–158
cultural meaning, sorting out
vagaries of, 9
culture
cognitive map and, 271–272
meaning and product, 120–124
cuneiform tablet, 167
cyber-bullying, 280
cyberspace
as place, 253–255
meatspace vs., 320
porous nature of
cyberplaces, 282–289

D

Damasio, Antonio, Descartes'
Error, 67
daydreaming, 375–376
decision fatigue, 69
definitions in composition, paying
attention to, 344–348
Delta Airlines website, accounts
embedded into, 321
Descartes' Error (Damasio), 67
design
affecting physical experience of
products, 179
definition of, 260–261
environment as, 377
relying on memory in, 82–83
The design of browsing and
berrypicking...(Online
Review), 238–239
The Design of Everyday Things
(Norman), 59, 86, 185
detached objects, 99–100
Dibbell, Julian, My Tiny Life,
278–280
Dickinson, Emily, 141
Dick, Philip K., 199
digital agents, 206–209
digital devices. *See* computers
digital environments
ambient agents, 245–250
changing meaning of physical
places, 240–241
foraging for information,
237–239
nesting and, 96–97

graphical parking sign, 151
graphic arts, composition in, 340
Graph Search, Facebook, 331
Greenfield, Adam, Everyware,
    249–250
groups, using term, 357–358, 369,
    381–382
Guilbert, Juliette, on using
    Rooms, 283

H

Hall, Edward T.
  high and low context model, 317
  on proxemics, 314–317
Hamlet on the Holodeck
    (Murray), 256
haptic interfaces, 154
HCI (Human-Computer
    Interaction), 41, 175
Healthcare.gov, launching of, 286
Heidegger, Martin, 65, 99–100
Here Comes Everybody (Shirky), 311
hierarchies vs. nesting, 94–95
hierarchy of categories, learning, 97
Highly Superior Autobiographical
    Memory, 75
Hinton, Erin, 206
Hinton, Madeline, 143, 289–291
Holtzblatt, Karen
  Contextual Design, 408–409
  contextual design
    development, 389
Home Depot, giving semantic
    structure to overlap
    of online and in-store
    shopping, 241–243
How to Make Sense of Any Mess
    (Covert), 372, 415
hubs, websites using, 402–403
Human-Computer Interaction
    (HCI), 41, 175
humans
  as symbol-laden, 156
  culture, meaning and
    product, 120–124
  emergence of cognition, 204
  environment
    built, 113–116
    cognitively-active vs.
      cognitively-passive way-
      finders, 115
    social, 117–120

experience of information
    environments, 255
  interfaces and
    about, 215–219
    approaching physical
      affordances, 226
    design of interactions,
      220–223
    modes and meaning, 229–234
    range of information, 224–226
    simulation interaction
      on, 220–223
  language and, 419
  making sense through
    stories, 373–376
  memory of, 203–204
hyperlinks, establishing relationships
    using, 360

I

iCloud service (Apple), 355
icons
  as graphical information,
    148–149
  as signifier, 130–131
ideas vs. information, in
    affordances, 55
identity, constructed, 318–324
If This Then That (IFTTT), cloud-
    based service, 209–210,
    366–367
The Image of the City (Lynch),
    113–114
implicit vs. explicit memory,
    environment and, 80–81
indexes, as signifier, 131–133
information. See also physical
    information
  cognition acting upon, 60–61
  digital. See digital information
  ecological psychology definition
    of, 36
  foraging for, 237–239
  language creating meaningful, 59
  pace layers of, 31–32
  proliferation of, writing and, 164
  recoining word, 200–201
  storage and retrieval of, 164
  transmission of, writing and, 165
  use of word, 27
Information Anxiety (Wurman), 28,
    257

as muddle, 76
design relying on, 82–83
embodied perspective on, 76–77
environment and explicit vs. implicit, 80–81
human vs. computer, 203–204
learning and remembering vs., 78–79
learning environment and, 74–81
relying on humans for, 118
types of, 75–76
wayfinding data and, 116
memory reconsolidation, 78–79
mental-model task analysis, 387
Merleau-Ponty, Maurice, 65
metamaps, compasses and, 300–304
metaphors
role of, 145–146
users taking at face value, 284–285
Metaphors We Live By (Lakoff and Johnson), 145–146
metaphysics, 418–419
methods, looking at, 387–388
Microsoft Bing, Facebook profile integrated with, 321
Microsoft Windows Phone 8, operating system, Rooms in, 283–284
The mind's eye (Popular Science Monthly), 191
Minecraft, as procedural generation example, 297–298
Mitchell, William J.
about, 256
bits and flow of information, 335
City of Bits, 12
on language and architecture, 159
on networked objects of urban landscape, 246
mobile phones. See also smartphones
as ready-at-hand objects, 103–104
models and making
blueprints, 412–414
bottom-up starting point on information architecture problem using blobs, 406–407
bringing several elements together for analysis or information architecture direction, 414–415

bubble diagrams, 406–407
contextual nesting model, 396
floor plans, 409–411
functional modeling, 407–408
looking at methods, 387–388
observing context, 388–392
situational search model, 394–395
situation-need-task model, 394
SNT (Situation-Need-Task) model, 393
structures for tacit satisficing, 400–405
systems perceiving world and humans in, 399–400
User Environment Design, 408–409
user journey model, 397
modes, meaning and, 229–234
Montessori classroom, 400–402
Moog, Robert, 215
Moravec, Hans, 205
Moravec's Paradox, 205
Morville, Peter
Ambient Findability, 259, 297–298
Information Architecture for the World Wide Web, 257
Intertwingled, 259
on hyperlinking of Web, 257–258
Three circles of information architecture, 150
MUDs (Multi-User Dungeons), 277–280, 319
Murray, Janet H., Hamlet on the Holodeck, 256
music, composition in, 339–340
My Tiny Life (Dibbell), 278–280

N

names
as subsets of labels, 353
purpose in information architecture of, 351
narratives and situations
intentions and intersections, 376–378
making sense through stories, 373–376
situations over goals, 382–385
tales of organizations, 378–381

digital displays of narrative
content as, 289–291
merging digital dimension
with physical., 294–297
metamaps and
compasses, 300–304
simulated wall-of-objects
as, 291–292
smartphone turning
environment into, 293–295
cyberspace as
about, 253–255
porous nature of
cyberplaces, 282–289
in organizational maps, 273–275
language creating, 267–274
making, 265–266
mapping and, 263–264
networked systems having
transformative effect on
real, 287–289
virtual
Dungeons & Dragons game
and, 277–280
porous nature of
cyberplaces, 282–289
Quake game and, 280–282
Playfair, William, time series of
exports and imports,
149–150
Plus (Google)
Circles interface, 346–349
social platform, 321
Polanski, Roman, 48–49
Polanyi, Michael, 69
PORT elevator system, 84–86
Power of Attorney project, 393
The Power of Maps (Wood), 273
pragmatics, in linguistic
structure, 129–130
preferences, keeping track of,
302–303
presence-to-hand, 100
privacy controls, 326–327
private sharing, 286
procedural generation, in map
making, 297–299
proliferation of information, writing
and, 164
proxemics
as structural model, 314–318

model of personal distance,
314–315
publics, definition of, 334
punctuation, in languages, 169–170

Andrew Hinton is an information architect at The Understanding Group (TUG). Since the early '90s, he's been helping organizations of various shapes and sizes make better, more habitable places with information. Andrew is co-founder and past board member of the IA Institute, and is a frequent speaker at UX and other industry conferences. From his pre-consultant life, he holds an MA in Literature and an MFA in Poetry. He presently lives with his wife in Atlanta, where his daughter often visits, and their dog, Sigmund, finally has a big yard of his own. You can find links to Andrew-related things, including this book, at *andrewhinton.com*.

Have it your way.

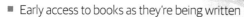

9 781449 323172